ISBN: 978129003509

Published by:
HardPress Publishing
8345 NW 66TH ST #2561
MIAMI FL 33166-2626

Email: info@hardpress.net
Web: http://www.hardpress.net

MODERN PLUMBING
ILLUSTRATED

Modern Plumbing Illustrated

A COMPREHENSIVE AND THOROUGHLY
PRACTICAL WORK ON THE MODERN
AND MOST APPROVED METHODS
OF PLUMBING CONSTRUCTION

THE STANDARD WORK FOR PLUMBERS, ARCHITECTS, BUILDERS,
PROPERTY OWNERS, BOARDS OF HEALTH AND PLUMBING
EXAMINERS, AND FOR TRADE CLASSES IN PLUMBING

By R. M. STARBUCK

AUTHOR OF "QUESTIONS AND ANSWERS ON THE PRACTICE AND THEORY OF
SANITARY PLUMBING" (2 VOLS.), "QUESTIONS AND ANSWERS ON THE
PRACTICE AND THEORY OF STEAM AND HOT WATER HEATING,"
"MECHANICAL DRAWING FOR PLUMBERS," ETC., ETC.

Third Edition Revised and Enlarged

FULLY ILLUSTRATED BY FIFTY-EIGHT DETAILED PLATES
MADE EXPRESSLY BY THE AUTHOR FOR THIS WORK

NEW YORK
THE NORMAN W. HENLEY PUBLISHING COMPANY
132 NASSAU STREET
1915

Copyright, 1915, by
THE NORMAN W. HENLEY PUBLISHING COMPANY
COPYRIGHT, 1906, BY R. M. STARBUCK

COMPOSITION, ELECTROTYPING, PRINTING, AND
BINDING BY TROW DIRECTORY, PRINTING AND
BOOKBINDING COMPANY, NEW YORK, U. S. A.

PREFACE

THERE is possibly no branch of construction work which has undergone within the same given time such great changes of a far-reaching nature as plumbing construction. These changes look to the betterment of sanitary conditions, and are going on continually. As a consequence of all this, any work relating to plumbing construction to be of real value to the reader must deal with modern methods and appliances, for the old-time construction called for such entirely different methods, materials, and appliances, that the trade of the younger plumber of to-day has little in common with the trade which the older school of plumbers learned in their younger days.

The practice of filling books on plumbing with instructions and historical data concerning old-time plumbing construction has no features to recommend it, and the author, believing in the truth of this statement, has avoided the employment of all such material. The ambitious plumber of to-day, if he is to keep abreast of the times in his chosen line of work, cannot afford to waste much time in gaining knowledge of an obsolete nature.

Many factors have taken part in the advancement of sanitary construction.

The good features that have arisen in plumbing construction are not to be credited to any one influence, but to many and varied influences. In the first place, the people of this country have been educated to demand and to expect the best possible living conditions, and the result is that the standard is constantly being raised. The public years ago began to demand more efficient regulation of plumbing construction in towns and cities, and the results arising from this demand and its fulfillment have been of the best. Municipal plumbing ordinances are constantly being revised or added to in the effort to provide the public with the most perfect sanitary conditions that are to be obtained. Competition is another factor which has brought results.

Manufacturers everywhere have striven to improve their goods, and the advancement which they have made in all lines in recent years is truly wonderful. The plumber whose duty it is to execute work of construction has been most influential in bringing about changed conditions. It is he who is better able than others to observe the good points of different methods and devices, and their deficiencies, and to him is due the credit of very many of the improvements in the construction of the plumbing system which the public now enjoys.

PREFACE

So far as it is within his power the author has endeavored to acquaint his readers with the improvements that have been effected in the many different directions.

The work is designed to cover the entire field of plumbing as far as possible. It takes up not only plumbing as practiced in towns and cities under strict plumbing regulations, but plumbing construction under conditions obtaining in country districts, where the problems which arise are often of an entirely different nature, and where there is not in existence any public regulation of sanitary work.

The subjects considered cover a variety of lines of work, including fixture work in detail, the construction of the drainage and vent systems in detail, and complete plumbing systems of buildings of various kinds.

The work is designed essentially to cover subjects pertaining to drainage alone, but it is clear that in many instances the subject of water supply is closely associated with the drainage problem, and the author has therefore deemed it advisable in several instances to go somewhat into the general subject of water supply. This is especially true of country plumbing systems and of the systems of large city buildings.

In conclusion, the author would say that to him the collection and arrangement of the information which "Modern Plumbing Illustrated" contains has been a matter not only of much labor, but of much pleasure as well. It is a subject which has held his interest for many years, and the interest which he has long had in all that pertains to the betterment of plumbing construction and to the betterment of the plumbing trade at large will always continue.

It is his sincere hope that the following pages may hold information of interest and of value to his readers, and that they may prove a source of help in time of need.

In bringing out a new edition of "Modern Plumbing Illustrated," the author becomes more fully aware that in the years which have passed since its first edition appeared, the science of plumbing has seen no great change in any of its essential principles, and whatever advance has been made has had largely to do with the developing and perfecting of detail. Such additions as have been made to this present edition will therefore be found to be along such lines.

August, 1915.

CONTENTS

	PAGE
PLATE I.—The Kitchen Sink — Laundry Tubs — Vegetable Wash Sink	15
PLATE II.—Lavatories—The Pantry Sink—Contents of Marble Slabs	21
PLATE III.—The Bath Tub—Foot Bath—Sitz Bath—Child's Bath—Shower Bath—Trimmings for Baths and Lavatories—Setting Marble Floor Slabs	29
PLATE IV.—Water Closet Connections—Venting of Water Closets	35
PLATE V.—The Low-down Water Closet—Operation of the Water Closet by Flush Valves—Water Closet Ranges	41
PLATE VI.—The Slop Sink—The Urinal—The Bidet	47
PLATE VII.—The Hotel or Restaurant Sink—The Use of Grease Traps	53
PLATE VIII.—Refrigerators—Safe Wastes—Tank Overflow—Floor Drains and Drips from Ice Houses, etc.—Laundry Waste—Creamery Waste	59
PLATE IX.—Refrigerator Lines—Bar Sinks—Soda Fountain Sinks—Exhausts, Drips, and Blow-offs of Steam Boilers, etc.	63
PLATE X.—The Stall Sink—The Horse Trough—Frost-Proof Water Closets	67
PLATE XI.—Connections for S-Traps—Venting	71
PLATE XII.—Connections for Drum Traps—Practical Requirements of Venting	79
PLATE XIII.—Soil Pipe and Soil Pipe Connections	85
PLATE XIV.—Supporting and Running of Soil Pipe	93

CONTENTS

	PAGE
PLATE XV.—The House or Main Trap and Fresh Air Inlet	99
PLATE XVI.—Floor and Yard Drains—Subsoil Drainage—The Cellar Drainer	107
PLATE XVII.—Water Closets—Water Closet Floor Connections	113
PLATE XVIII.—Local Venting	121
PLATE XIX.—Bath Rooms	129
PLATE XX.—Bath Rooms	135
PLATE XXI.—Bath Rooms	141
PLATE XXII.—Bath Rooms	147
PLATE XXIII.—Poor Practices in Plumbing Construction	153
PLATE XXIV.—"Roughing-in"—Use of Cleanouts	159
PLATE XXV.—Testing of the Plumbing System—The Water Test—The Air Test—The Smoke Test—The Peppermint Test	165
PLATE XXVI.—Continuous Venting	173
PLATE XXVII.—Continuous Venting for Two-Floor Work	177
PLATE XXVIII.—Continuous Venting for Two Lines of Fixtures on Three or More Floors—Practical Requirements of Venting	181
PLATE XXIX.—Continuous Venting of Water Closets—Circuit Vents—Loop Vents	185
PLATE XXX.—Plumbing for Cottage House—General Remarks	189
PLATE XXXI.—Construction of Cellar Piping—The House Drain, House Sewer, etc.	193
PLATE XXXII.—Plumbing for Residences—Use of Special Fittings—Brass Piping	199
PLATE XXXIII.—Plumbing for Two-Flat House—Rain Leaders—Regulation of Plumbing Construction in Tenement Houses, Lodging Houses, etc.	203
PLATE XXXIV.—Plumbing for Apartment Building—Systems of Hot-Water Supply—Range Boilers, etc.	209

CONTENTS

PAGE

PLATE XXXV.—Plumbing for Double Apartment Buildings—Filtered Water Supply 215

PLATE XXXVI.—Plumbing for Office Buildings 221

PLATE XXXVII.—Plumbing for Public Toilet Rooms—Causes of Siphonage in the Unvented Plumbing System 225

PLATE XXXVIII.—Plumbing for Public Toilet Rooms 231

PLATE XXXIX.—Plumbing for Bath Establishment—Tanks for Storage and Supply 235

PLATE XL.—Plumbing for Engine House and Stables—Factory Plumbing 239

PLATE XLI.—Automatic Flushing for Schools, Factories, etc. . . 243

PLATE XLII.—The Use of Flushing Valves 249

PLATE XLIII.—Urinals for Public Toilet Rooms 253

PLATE XLIV.—The Durham System—The Destruction of Pipes by Electrolysis 259

PLATE XLV.—Construction of Work without Use of Lead . . . 269

PLATE XLVI.—The Disposal of Sewage of Fixtures Located below Sewer Level—Automatic Sewage Lifts—Automatic Sump Tanks 275

PLATE XLVII.—Country Plumbing—Water Supply 283

PLATE XLVIII.—Construction and Use of Cesspools 291

PLATE XLIX.—Construction and Action of the Septic Tank—Underground Disposal of Partially Purified Sewage—Automatic Sewage Siphons 297

PLATE L.—Pneumatic Systems of Water Supply—Hydraulic Rams—Pumps—Water Supply by Siphonage—Pumping by Windmill—Capacity of Tanks—Protection of Supply Pipes against Freezing 307

PLATE LI.—Water Supply for Country House—Double-Acting Ram—Cistern Filters—Hot-Water Supply 323

CONTENTS

	PAGE
PLATE LII.—Thawing Underground Water Pipes by Electricity	329
PLATE LIII.—Double Boilers	335
PLATE LIV.—Hot-Water Supply for Large Buildings	341
PLATE LV.—Automatic Control of Hot-Water Tanks	347
PLATE LVI.—The Three-Pipe System of Supply	351
PLATE LVII.—The Softening of Hard Water for Domestic Purposes	355
PLATE LVIII.—Special Problems and Devices in Hot-Water Supply	359
Suggestions for Estimating Plumbing Construction	365

INTRODUCTION

MANY of the readers of "Modern Plumbing Illustrated" have long been acquainted with the same title applied to another work by the same author, which is now no longer published. A few remarks relating to the several steps through which this work has passed may be of interest.

In January, 1899, Mr. Starbuck published a novel work relating to plumbing construction, known as "The Starbuck Plumbing Charts."

This work consisted of fifty blue-print plates showing a variety of work relating to plumbing systems of various kinds, including both detail work and complete systems. The work filled a requirement which had never before been met, and was cordially received by the plumbing fraternity at large. After a short time, however, it was seen that the "Plumbing Charts" were deficient in many respects, and as a result this work was replaced in 1900 by a far more extensive publication, known as "Modern Plumbing Illustrated." This work was still in the form of blue-print plates, without text, but double the size of the original plates, and meeting practical requirements to a far greater extent than the original work. The work in the form of blue prints has had an immense sale during the past six years among all interested classes, including architects, master and journeyman plumbers, boards of health and plumbing examiners, contractors, etc. Meanwhile, however, vast improvements have been made in all branches of plumbing construction, with the result that much of the work shown in the 1900 publication has now been so far improved upon that it has seemed best to the author to again revise the work.

In the work of revision it has been found inadvisable to make use of any of the plates of the 1900 publication, and accordingly each illustration of the present publication has been drawn especially for this work. Whereas the fifty full-page cuts of the 1900 work represented some seventy separate illustrations, the present form shows more than twice this number.

INTRODUCTION

The greatest improvement in "Modern Plumbing Illustrated," however, is to be found in the addition of a large amount of text, and in carrying out this part of his work the author has endeavored at every point to convey the information imparted in as concise a manner as possible, while at the same time making it entirely clear and comprehensive.

As each successive revision of the work has been undertaken, it has been the aim of the author to purge it of all unnecessary and obsolete matter, and to keep it as far as possible entirely up to date.

PLATE 1

THE KITCHEN SINK—LAUNDRY TUBS

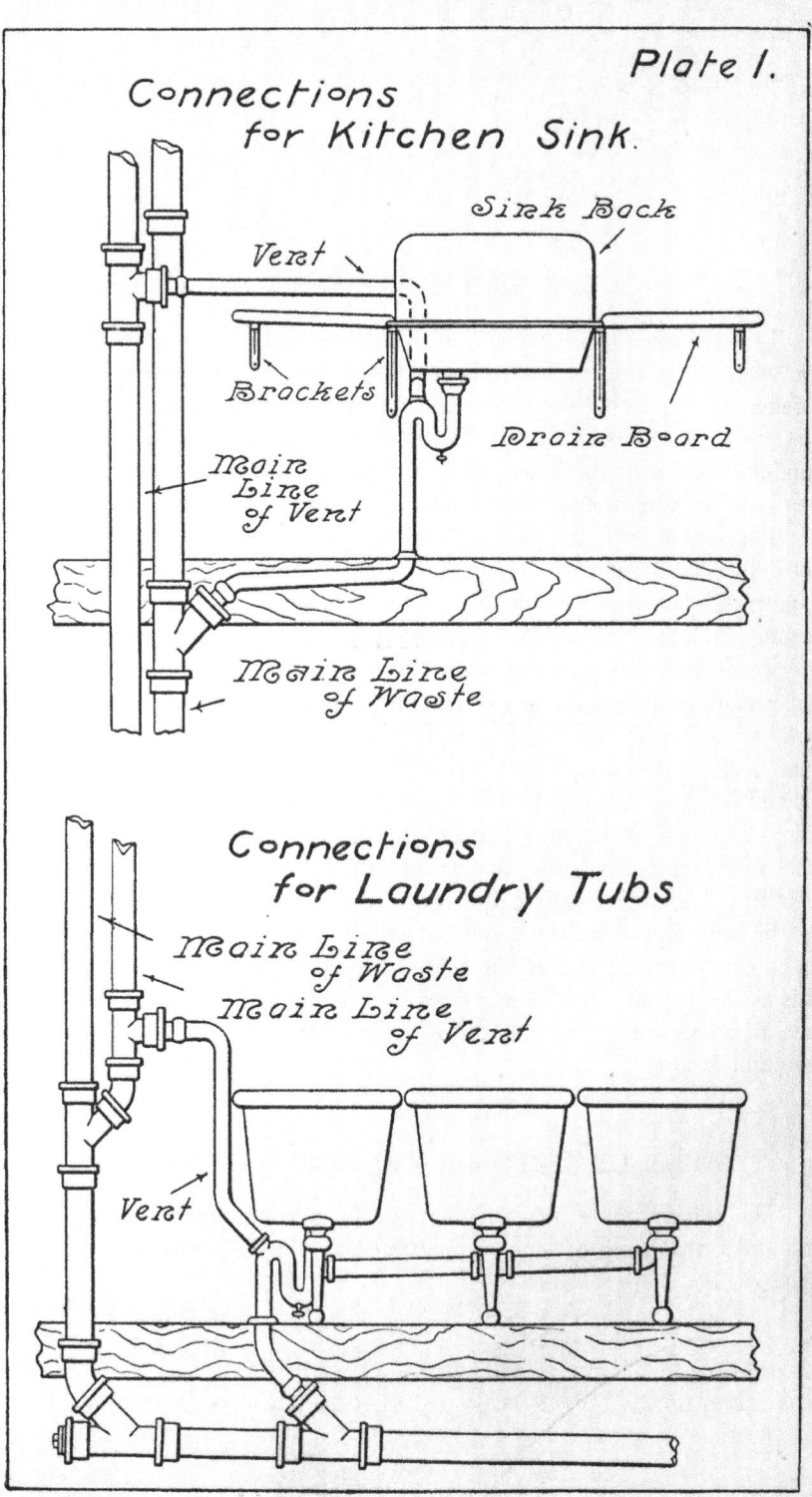

THE KITCHEN SINK

The kitchen sink is made of plain, galvanized or enameled cast iron, slate, soapstone, and porcelain. The waste for the kitchen sink is generally 1½ inch, though the tendency is toward the use of 2-inch pipe. As this fixture is usually subject to greater use than any other plumbing fixture of the house, and as much greasy matter enters it, even with the utmost care, 2-inch pipe is often preferable to 1½ inch.

The vent for the trap of the kitchen sink should be of 1½-inch pipe. In connection with this fixture, especially in large residences, restaurants, boarding houses, or wherever a large amount of dish-washing and cooking is done, a grease trap will often serve the fixture much more satisfactorily than the ordinary trap. An illustration and description of such a trap will be found under Plate 7. Sinks are generally set about 32 inches from the floor, this measurement being to the top of the sink. This height may be varied an inch either way, to suit the desires of the owner. As the kitchen sink is so much in use, and demands so much hot water, the preference in the matter of such supply should be given this fixture over all others. A quick supply of hot water may be secured by connecting the flow pipe from the range into the hot-water pipe at the top of the boiler instead of into the side of the boiler as generally done. This is of special value when hot water is required at the kitchen sink in the morning, the range fire having been allowed to go out the night before.

TABLE OF SIZES OF CAST-IRON SINKS

The following sizes are for plain, galvanized, and enameled cast-iron sinks, the depth of sink being 6 inches, and the dimensions in inches.

12 × 12	12 × 20	14 × 22	16 × 16
12 × 14	14 × 14	14 × 24	16 × 20
12 × 16	14 × 18	14 × 26	16 × 24
12 × 18	14 × 20	15 × 27	16 × 28

16 × 30	18 × 36	20 × 40	22 × 62
16 × 36	18 × 42	20 × 42	22 × 76
17 × 28	20 × 20	20 × 48	23 × 42
17 × 30	20 × 24	20 × 60	23 × 48
17 × 35	20 × 26	20 × 72	24 × 48
18 × 18	20 × 28	21 × 42	24 × 50
18 × 24	20 × 30	22 × 36	24 × 80
18 × 28	20 × 32	22 × 40	24 × 120
18 × 30	20 × 36	22 × 42	26 × 52
18 × 32	20 × 38	22 × 48	

The most satisfactory sizes of kitchen sinks for family use are, viz.: 18 × 36, 20 × 36, and 20 × 42. If space allows, 20 × 42 is the preferable size. Sinks 18 × 36 are largely used in the cheaper class of work.

All sinks are cast with the bottom pitching toward the outlet end. Therefore there is no necessity of setting the sink so that its top is other than level.

A valuable device for use in connection with the kitchen sink is the flexible wooden sink mat. This mat, being flexible, will fit into any sink, and in the case of enameled or porcelain sinks keeps the surface from being scratched by pots and kettles. It also prevents breakage in setting dishes, etc., into the bottom of the sink.

VEGETABLE WASH SINK

A fixture now much used in high-grade kitchen work of residences, hotels, restaurants, clubs, etc., is the vegetable wash sink.

This fixture is generally made of enameled cast iron or porcelain, and is provided with a standing overflow at one end, so that the water may fill the sink, which is of considerable depth, without flowing into the waste.

The waste and vent for the vegetable wash sink are of the same size as for the kitchen sink.

LAUNDRY TUBS

Laundry tubs, or wash trays, are made of porcelain, enameled cast iron, soapstone, slate, and artificial stone.

The connections for this fixture are shown in Plate I. The

LAUNDRY TUBS

waste outlet from each section of the laundry tubs should be 1½ inches in size. The main waste and trap for a two-part laundry tub may be 1½ inches, and for laundry tubs of three to six sections, the main waste and trap should not be less than 2 inches in size.

The vent from the trap of a set of laundry tubs should not be less than 1½ inches in size. Formerly this fixture was made of wood, the several sections sometimes being lined with sheet metal. The use of the wooden laundry tubs or wooden sink should be prohibited, as the wood readily absorbs moisture and filth, and the fixture soon becomes unsanitary.

For use in general work, such as for dwelling houses, and the less pretentious residences, laundry tubs either of slate or soapstone give excellent service.

Laundry tubs of artificial stone are much used in the cheaper grades of work, but often have the disadvantage of cracking and crumbling, especially if installed in cold places, where frost may work into the stone. A strong cement for mending artificial stone, slate, and soapstone tubs may be made of litharge and glycerine formed into a paste, which is very hard when it has set, and very durable.

In many instances, especially in flats and apartment houses, the laundry tubs are located in the kitchen, close to the sink. When so located, it is customary in some sections to allow one trap to serve both fixtures. This is considered poor practice in any case, and especially when applied to such fixtures as the kitchen sink and laundry tubs. Each fixture should be separately trapped. Although the use of the drum trap is not popular in certain sections, in connection with laundry tubs it may be used to great advantage many times, for it can usually be located more advantageously than the S trap, and is of sufficient diameter to easily receive any number of waste pipes that may be required to enter it. In its use, a less length of fouled waste connection to the trap is able to throw impure odors into the room than in such a connection as shown in Plate I.

When the kitchen sink and laundry tubs are each to be located in the kitchen, and especially when it is necessary to economize space, the combination kitchen sink and laundry tub may be used to advantage. This fixture combines the two fixtures in one.

Plate II

LAVATORIES

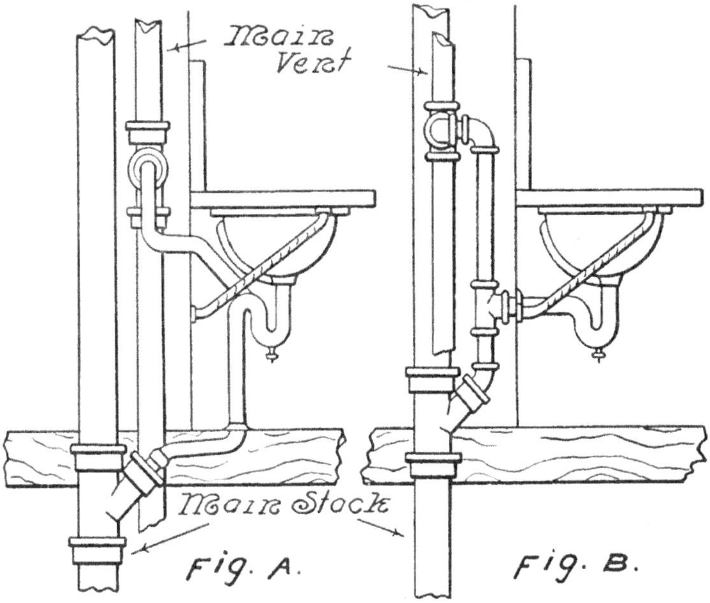

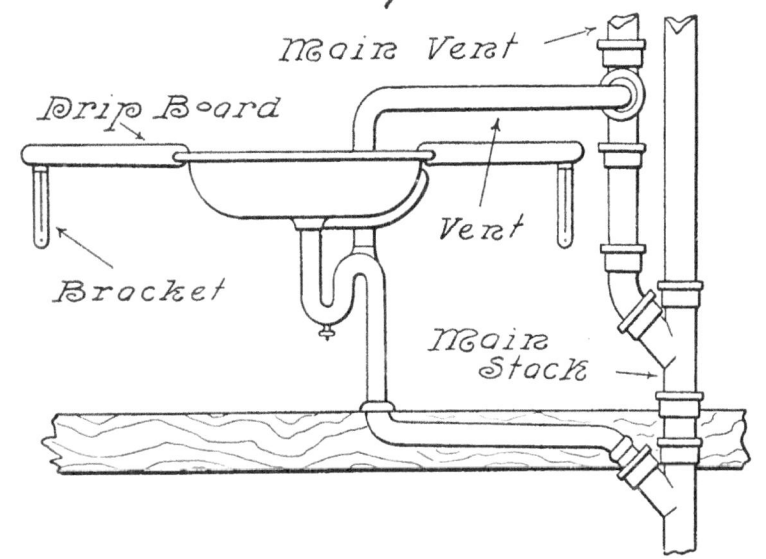

LAVATORIES

LAVATORIES are generally made of marble, enameled cast iron, or porcelain.

Marble is fast being superseded by enameled cast iron and porcelain. Marble lavatories present opportunity for the collection of filth in the joints and corners between the marble parts and between the bowl and the marble.

Enameled cast-iron and porcelain lavatories are cast in one piece, which includes both the back and the bowl, for which reason there is no necessity of setting the bowl, and therefore no possibility that it may become loose and need resetting, as often happens in the use of marble lavatories.

Being cast in one piece, there are no joints to fill up with filth. It is for these reasons that enameled cast-iron and porcelain lavatories are preferable to marble.

The waste from the lavatory is generally of $1\frac{1}{4}$-inch pipe, but should never be as small as 1 inch, a size which is sometimes used. The trap vent should also be $1\frac{1}{4}$ inches in size. The lavatory should be set so that its upper surface is about 31 inches from the floor. The height may, of course, be varied to suit the desires of the owner.

The trap of this fixture is very liable to stoppage, not from greasy matter as in the trap of the kitchen sink, but from soap, lint, and hair.

Two methods of making waste connections for the lavatory may be followed, shown in Plate 2 by Figs. A and B. The waste may be carried to the floor, as in Fig. A, or directly back to the wall, as in Fig. B. The latter method is preferable, as the waste connection so made is shorter, there is less of the work exposed to rough usage, and a separate entrance into the main soil or waste pipe may always be secured. The vent of the half S-trap may be taken off farther from the seal than in the case of the full S-trap, resulting in a lower rate of evaporation, and the half S-trap is less subject to siphonage than the full S-trap, owing to the long outlet arm of the latter. Usually when the half S-trap can be used for the lavatory, or, in fact, for any other fixture, the continuous method of venting may be applied, as shown in Fig. B. This method is of great advantage to any fixture, and is fully described under Plate 26.

An objection to the use of the patent overflow bowl, such as shown in Figs. A and B, is that the overflow soon becomes coated with filth, which often throws off foul odors into the room. The use of scented soaps increases this objectionable feature.

The same thing occurs in public toilet rooms when a line of several lavatories is served by a single trap at the end of the line. This long line of fouled waste pipe sends out its foul odors into the room through the outlet of each bowl.

Italian and Tennessee marble is the material mostly used for marble lavatories.

On good work, lavatory top slabs are countersunk, with moulded edges, and $1\frac{1}{4}$ inch thick. The backs and ends for lavatories may be 8, 10, 12, 14, 18, or 20 inches in height.

The standard sizes of marble slabs for lavatories are 19×24, 20×24, 20×26, 20×28, 20×30, 22×28, 22×30, and 22×36.

On the better grades of work the larger sizes of slabs, with high backs, are mostly used.

Lavatory bowls may be obtained either round or oval, with common overflow or patent overflow. Round bowls are made of 12, 13, 14, 15, and 16 inch diameter, the 14-inch bowl being largely used on general work.

The sizes of oval bowls are 14×17, 15×19, and 16×21.

The bowl is generally fastened to the marble slab before the latter is set in position. The bowl is attached by means of bowl clamps. Three or four bowl clamps may be used on round bowls, but not less than four on oval bowls.

The slab is drilled out to receive the clamp bolt, the hole being cut under at the bottom. The bolt is held firmly in the marble slab by means of lead poured in around it and caulked, the under cut at the bottom clinching the lead and preventing it pulling out. The joint between the bowl and the marble is made with plaster-of-paris.

In connection with the subject of marble work, the making of marble cements may be of interest. Portland cement withstands water, as also a cement made by soaking plaster-of-paris in a saturated solution of alum, the mixture being baked and ground into a powder and applied by mixing with water. A putty made of litharge and glycerine is also good.

THE PANTRY SINK

Pantry sinks commonly in use are made of sheet copper; the higher grades are of enameled cast iron and of porcelain.

A very satisfactory pantry sink may be constructed by lining a wooden box, of proper dimensions, with white metal. The back and drain boards should also be lined with the same material. This work requires the services of a skilled workman, for it is a difficult matter to lay the metal smoothly and to finish the joints and seams so that they may be as nearly invisible as possible.

Many of the more pretentious residences now have a breakfast room in addition to the dining room, each being provided with its own special pantry sink.

The size of waste for the pantry sink should be $1\frac{1}{2}$ inch; the size of trap vent should also be $1\frac{1}{2}$ inch.

The pantry sink should be set so that the top of the sink is about 32 inches from the floor.

CONTENTS OF MARBLE SLABS

In connection with the subject of marble lavatories the following table will be found of value. Marble slabs are sold by the foot, and from this table the contents of any slab from 6×12 inches to 47×62 inches may be quickly found. The figures in the top horizontal line show the widths of slabs, and the figures in the left-hand vertical column show lengths. In estimating on slabs with finished edges it is customary to add one inch in length or width, as the case may be, for each finished edge.

The following example will show the manner in which the table is to be used:

It is required to find the contents of a marble slab 20×24 in., having both ends and the front edge finished, with 10-inch back. Adding 1 inch for each finished edge, gives the slab dimensions as 21×26 in., and the dimensions of the back as 11×26 in.

Find in the side column the length, 26 inches, and in the upper line the width, 21 inches.

To the right of the 26, and under the 21, will be found the contents of a slab 21×26 in., 3 feet 10 inches, and in the same manner the contents of the back will be found to be 2 feet, giving a total of 5 feet 10 inches. End pieces will be found in the same way.

MODERN PLUMBING ILLUSTRATED

CONTENTS OF MARBLE SLABS

WIDTH IN INCHES.—(Continued.)

Length, Inches	27 ft. in.	28 ft. in.	29 ft. in.	30 ft. in.	31 ft. in.	32 ft. in.	33 ft. in.	34 ft. in.	35 ft. in.	36 ft. in.	37 ft. in.	38 ft. in.	39 ft. in.	40 ft. in.	41 ft. in.	42 ft. in.	43 ft. in.	44 ft. in.	45 ft. in.	46 ft. in.	47 ft. in.
27	5 1	5 5	5 10	6 3	6 8	7 1	7 7	8 0	8 6	9 3	9 6	10 0	10 7								
28	5 3	5 5	6 1	6 6	6 11	7 7	7 7	8 8	8 9	9 9	9 9	10 10	10 7								
29	5 5	5 8	6 3	6 6	7 1	7 7	7 11	8 5	8 9	9 9	9 10	10 4	10 11								
30	5 8	5 10	6 6	6 11	7 4	7 11	8 3	8 8	9 3	9 6	10 3	10 7	11 2	11 5	11 8	12 3	12 10	13 0			
31	5 10	6 3	6 6	7 1	7 6	8 0	8 5	8 11	9 6	10 0	10 6	10 11	11 5	11 11	12 6	13 0	13 5	13 11			
32	6 0	6 5	6 11	7 4	7 11	8 3	8 8	9 1	9 9	10 3	10 10	11 4	11 10	12 5	12 11	13 5	13 11	14 5			
33	6 3	6 8	7 1	7 7	8 0	8 5	9 0	9 5	10 0	10 6	11 1	11 7	12 2	12 8	13 2	13 8	14 2	14 8			
34	6 5	6 10	7 4	7 11	8 3	8 8	9 3	9 8	10 3	10 10	11 4	11 11	12 5	13 0	13 6	14 1	14 6	15 1			
35	6 7	7 0	7 7	8 1	8 6	9 1	9 6	9 11	10 6	11 1	11 7	12 2	12 9	13 4	13 11	14 5	15 0	15 5	14 0		
36	6 9	7 3	7 9	8 3	8 11	9 3	9 10	10 4	10 11	11 3	12 0	12 6	13 2	13 6	14 2	14 9	15 3	15 10	14 8		
37	6 11	7 5	7 11	8 6	9 1	9 6	10 1	10 8	11 2	11 9	12 4	12 11	13 7	14 1	14 8	15 3	15 10	16 5	15 3	14 4	
38	7 2	7 7	8 2	8 9	9 4	9 11	10 5	11 0	11 6	12 2	12 10	13 4	13 11	14 6	15 1	15 8	16 3	16 10	15 8	15 3	
39	7 4	7 9	8 4	8 11	9 6	10 0	10 7	11 2	11 9	12 5	13 0	13 7	14 3	14 10	15 5	16 1	16 7	17 3	16 2	15 8	15 4
40	7 6	7 11	8 6	9 2	9 9	10 4	10 11	11 6	12 2	12 9	13 4	13 11	14 7	15 3	15 10	16 5	17 0	17 7	16 8	16 1	15 10
41	7 8	8 2	8 9	9 4	9 11	10 6	11 2	11 9	12 5	13 0	13 7	14 3	14 11	15 7	16 3	16 10	17 5	18 0	17 1	16 6	16 3
42	7 11	8 4	8 11	9 7	10 2	10 9	11 5	12 0	12 8	13 3	13 11	14 7	15 3	15 11	16 6	17 3	17 10	18 6	17 6	16 11	16 8
43	8 1	8 6	9 1	9 9	10 4	10 11	11 8	12 3	12 11	13 6	14 2	14 11	15 7	16 3	16 11	17 6	18 2	18 11	18 0	17 4	17 1
44	8 3	8 8	9 4	9 11	10 7	11 2	11 11	12 7	13 2	13 10	14 5	15 2	15 11	16 7	17 4	18 0	18 7	19 4	18 6	17 10	17 6
45	8 5	8 10	9 5	10 2	10 10	11 5	12 2	12 10	13 5	14 1	14 9	15 5	16 3	16 11	17 7	18 4	18 11	19 8	18 11	18 3	17 11
46	8 7	9 0	9 8	10 4	11 0	11 7	12 4	13 1	13 8	14 4	15 0	15 8	16 6	17 3	17 11	18 8	19 3	20 0	19 4	18 9	18 4
47	8 10	9 2	9 11	10 7	11 2	11 11	12 7	13 3	14 0	14 7	15 5	16 0	16 10	17 6	18 3	19 0	19 7	20 5	19 9	19 2	18 9
48				11 0	11 5	12 1	13 0	13 6	14 3	15 0	15 8	16 4	17 2	17 10	18 8	19 4	20 0	20 10	20 3	19 7	19 2
49				11 2	11 9	12 4	13 2	13 9	14 6	15 3	15 11	16 8	17 6	18 3	19 0	19 8	20 5	21 2	20 8	19 11	19 7
50				11 4	11 11	12 7	13 5	14 0	14 9	15 5	16 4	16 11	17 10	18 7	19 5	20 1	20 10	21 7	21 0	20 5	20 0
51				11 6	12 2	12 9	13 7	14 3	15 0	15 9	16 7	17 4	18 2	18 11	19 9	20 6	21 3	22 0	21 6	20 10	20 5
52				11 8	12 4	13 0	13 10	14 6	15 4	16 0	16 11	17 8	18 6	19 4	20 2	20 11	21 8	22 5			
53				11 11	12 6	13 2	14 1	14 9	15 7	16 3	17 2	17 11	18 10	19 7	20 6	21 3	22 0	22 10			
54				12 2	12 9	13 5	14 3	14 11	15 10	16 6	17 5	18 4	19 2	20 0	20 10	21 8	22 5				
55				12 5	12 11	13 7	14 6	15 3	16 1	16 10	17 8	18 7	19 6	20 5	21 3	22 0					
56				12 7	13 1	13 10	14 9	15 5	16 4	17 1	18 0	18 11	19 10	20 9	21 7						
57				12 9	13 3	14 0	14 11	15 8	16 7	17 5	18 3	19 3									
58				12 11	13 6	14 3	15 2	15 11	16 10	17 8	18 7	19 6									
59				12 11	13 8	14 5	15 4	16 2	17 1	17 11											
60				12 11	13 10	14 7	15 7	16 4	17 4												
61				12 11	13 11	14 10	15 10														
62				12 11	13 11	15 0															

Plate III

BATHS

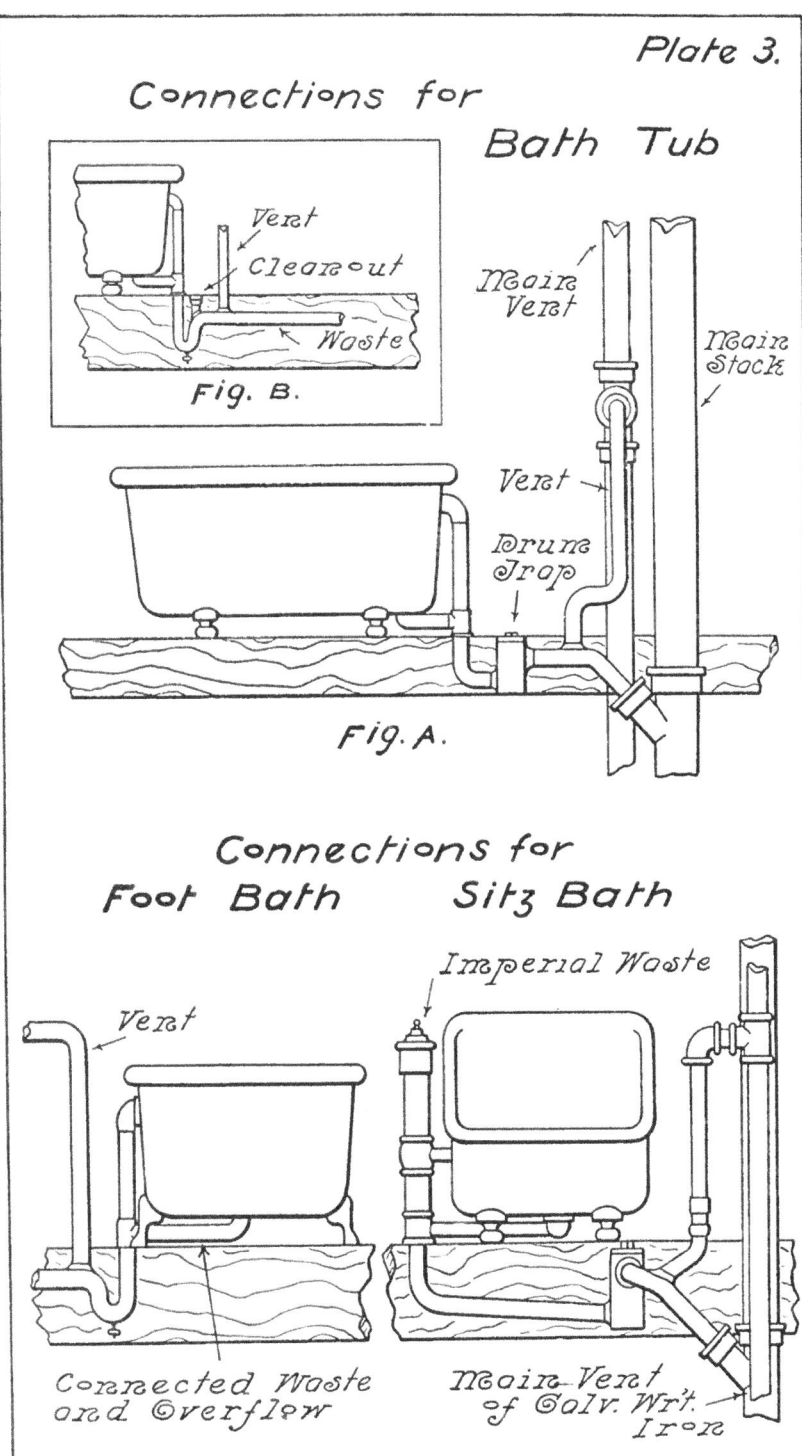

THE BATH TUB

Most of the higher grades of bath tubs are now made of porcelain or enameled cast iron, with a wide roll rim.

The less expensive styles of bath tubs are made of an inferior quality of enameled cast iron; of steel body with copper lining, known as "steel-clad" tubs, and of steel body, enamel painted.

Of the cheaper grades, the steel-clad bath tub gives good service, but the enamel-painted tub, although making a good appearance when new, in many instances soon takes on a very shabby appearance, owing to the wearing off or cracking off of the enamel paint.

The bath-tub waste should be $1\frac{1}{2}$ inches in size, and its trap vent also $1\frac{1}{2}$ inch.

The regular sizes of bath tubs are, viz.: 4 ft., 4 ft. 6 in., 5 ft., 5 ft. 6 in., and 6 ft. The 5 ft. and 5 ft. 6 in. sizes are generally the preferable sizes. The two smallest sizes are too short for the comfort of the bather, and should be used only when space will not allow the use of a larger size. The old-style sheathed-in tub is no longer installed on new work. This form of bath tub presented much opportunity for the collection of filth around its upper edges, and was not nearly so cleanly a fixture as the modern bath tubs, which are easily kept clean, especially in the case of the porcelain and enamel-lined bath tubs.

It is often required, in the use of enamel-painted baths, to put on a new coat of enamel. When this is to be done, the surface of the tub should first be made as clean and smooth as possible, following which a sufficient number of coats of white lead should be applied to prevent the dark color of the tub from showing through, after which the enamel may be applied. In connection with the bath tub, the use of traps of the drum pattern is good practice. A better grade on the outlet of this trap may often be secured than from the S-trap, and the cleanout of the former is much more accessible. When the S-trap is used under the floor, as in the case of the bath tub, an excellent method of providing a cleanout is the one shown in Fig. B, Plate 3.

This makes the cleanout accessible without the removal of flooring, a thing which is necessary ofttimes in order to operate the cleanout at the bottom of the S-trap.

Whenever the latter is used the floor above it should be screwed down, so that it may be taken up as easily as possible in the event of repairs to the trap.

FOOT BATH—SITZ BATH—CHILD'S BATH

The use of foot, sitz, and child's baths is not found to any extent except in bath rooms of the best residences. They do not represent a necessity as does the common bath tub, but are luxuries which add much to the comfort of the bath room.

The waste for each of these three baths should be 1½ inch in size, and the trap vent also 1½ inch. In general, the principles that apply to the ordinary bath tub apply also to the foot, sitz, and child's baths.

THE SHOWER BATH

The shower bath generally to be found in the private bath room consists of a cast-iron, enameled, or porcelain receptor set upon the floor, around which the piping is arranged, the whole being inclosed by rubber curtains. The waste is connected to the receptor, and should be 1½ inch in size, the vent being of the same size.

An excellent shower device is also made for use in connection with the lavatory. It consists of a swinging bracket with a shower at the end of it, the swinging part being connected with a supply pipe at the back of the lavatory, the spray being thrown down into the bowl.

TRIMMINGS FOR BATHS AND LAVATORIES

As plumbing is now constructed, even the cheaper grades of work include a large amount of nickel work, in which there is a great variety of material to select from.

Bi-transit wastes are extensively used on baths and lavatories of the better grades. This device allows the waste to flow out by the lifting of a plunger instead of the ordinary plug. It adds a certain finish to the fixture, but also adds a complication which provides additional surface, which may become foul and produce odor. In general the simpler plumbing devices are the more satisfactory. Nickel-plated supply pipes should be of iron-pipe size, rather than of tubing, as the former can be screwed into the concealed iron piping, while the tubing must be connected into it by soldered joints, which are not so substantial.

Combination cocks for baths and lavatories are very satisfactory. Both hot and cold water are led into the same cock in the combination devices, and by properly regulating the supply of each, the water may very easily be tempered as desired.

Fuller work is almost entirely used on high grade work, notwithstanding that the quick closing of this work is often accompanied by vibrations and disagreeable rumbling of the pipes, which is entirely absent in the slower closing compression work.

On much of the cheaper work cast-iron, nickel-plated lavatory brackets are used. These are not satisfactory, as in time the iron will rust through the nickel plating, and the bracket will present a very shabby appearance.

SETTING MARBLE FLOOR SLABS

Marble slabs are much used under all bath-room fixtures. In setting the marble slab the floor should be cut out and the floor slab set in to such a depth that the top of it comes about a quarter of an inch above the floor. The floor slab should never be set on top of the floor if the latter is of wood. In connecting a water closet to a floor slab, a brass floor flange and rubber gasket should be used, the former being secured to the slab by means of expansion bolts, and set in plaster-of-paris to give it a good bearing. The floor slab itself should properly be set in plaster-of-paris and leveled, where necessary, to give it a level surface. If not given a good level foundation the slab will be liable to rock.

Slate is another material used to considerable extent for floor slabs.

Plate IV

WATER CLOSET CONNECTIONS

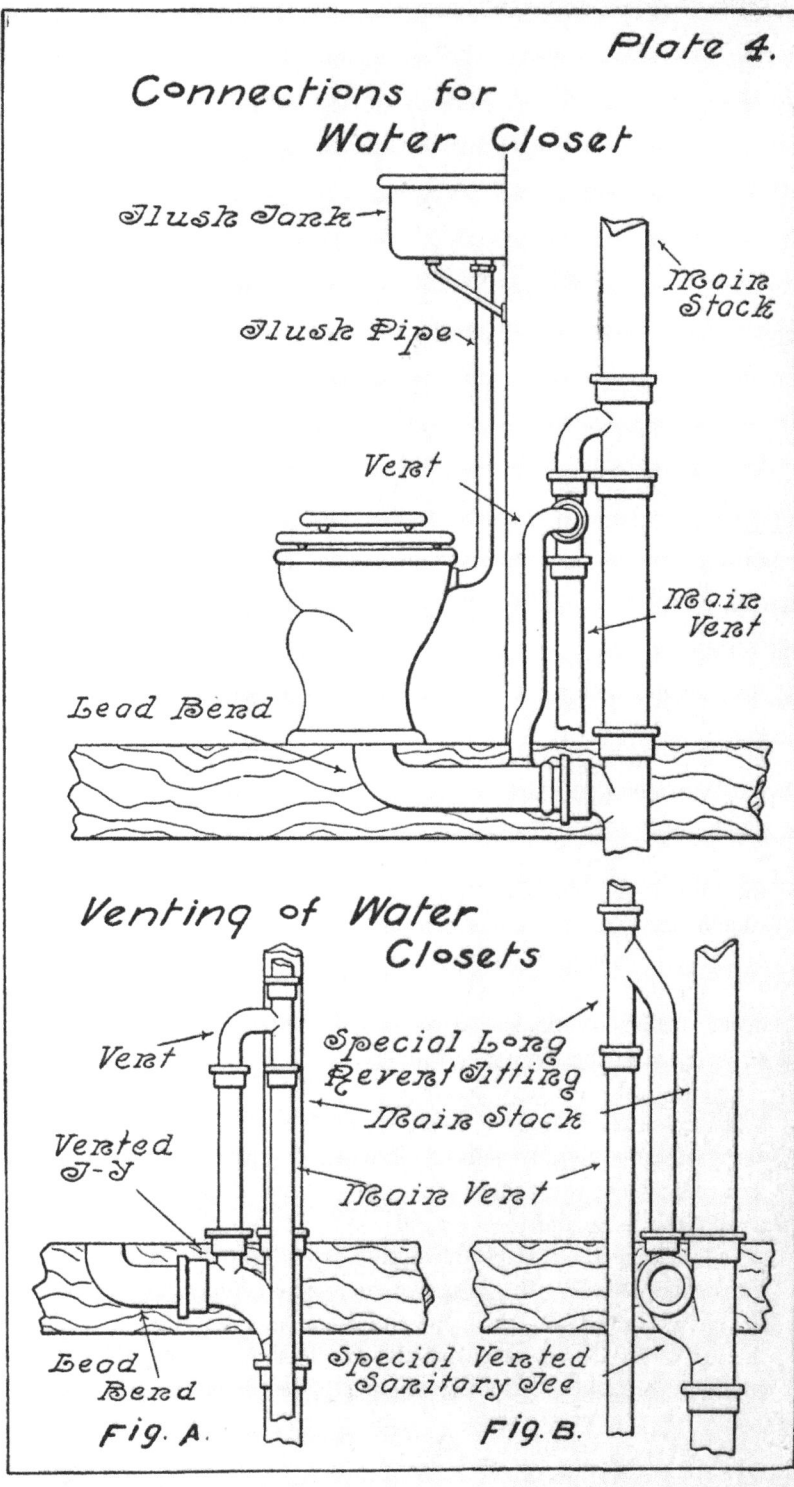

WATER CLOSET CONNECTIONS

The waste for the water closet should be 4 in. in size, but never less.

When cast-iron soil pipe is used, the connection is made by means of 4-in. lead pipe or a 4-in. lead bend, the pipe or bend being wiped to a brass ferrule which is caulked into the soil pipe, and the floor connection generally being made by means of floor flanges, the latter being considered under Plate 17. The connection of the water closet to wrought-iron soil pipe is shown under Plate 45.

The water closet should never discharge into a soil pipe of less than 4 in.

The lead bend is generally connected into a T-Y or modified form of this fitting. It is preferable to connect into a bend and Y-branch, as shown in Plate 40, Fig. D, or into the same combination of fittings arranged vertically. Such connection is often impossible, however, owing to lack of space, although in larger work, such as public toilet rooms, it may often be used without difficulty.

The water-closet flush tank should be set so that the bottom of the tank is as nearly 6 ft. from the floor as possible. This tank should be of seven gallons capacity, although on cheap work tanks of five gallons capacity are largely used.

The flush pipe from tank to closet should be $1\frac{1}{4}$ in. in size, but never smaller, as this size is required to deliver the required volume of water with the necessary rapidity.

The flush pipe may be connected rigidly to the water closet or by means of a slip joint or rubber elbow. The latter two connections are preferable, as any settling of floors or slight movement of the fixture does not result in breaking off the connection to the bowl, as often happens in the use of rigid connections.

The flush tank should always be provided with a flush valve of the siphon pattern. In the use of this valve, simply a slight pull on the chain is needed to flush the entire contents of the tank, while in the use of the ordinary flush valve the flushing of the water closet continues only so long as the chain is pulled down. The flush may be operated in many other ways than by a chain and pull—by the weight of the person using the fixture; by the opening or closing of the door; by means of a push button operating a crank or lever to which the chain is attached. The latter method allows the tank to be concealed behind walls or partitions. This method not only allows the unsightly high tank to be concealed, but also enables the working parts of the flush tank to be located in such a place that mischievous or ignorant people are unable to destroy or damage them in any way, an evil often encountered in public toilet rooms.

THE VENTING OF WATER CLOSETS

The vent from the water closet should be 2 in. in size, but never of smaller size.

The vent pipe is usually connected to the lead bend, but should never be connected to the crockery itself, as such a connection must necessarily be rigid, and the settling of floors, slight movement of the fixture, etc., will result in breaking off the vent horn.

When connected to the lead bend the vent should always be taken from the top of the horizontal part of the bend—never from the vertical part, as when so constructed it is much more liable to stoppage.

Fig. A shows an excellent method of venting from the vent hub of a vented T-Y, a common stock fitting, the vent pipe being of cast or wrought iron.

Fig. B shows the use of special waste and vent fittings, of which numerous styles are now on the market.

This waste fitting is so arranged that the branch to the fixture enters the side of the main body of the fitting, thus allowing the fixture to set closer to the wall than is possible with the waste fitting of Fig. A. Work such as shown in these two illustrations is growing in favor, and serves to show the decadence of lead work and the increase in the use of cast and wrought iron in plumbing construction.

Venting being employed chiefly to prevent the siphonage of fixture traps, it is unnecessary to vent a water closet which is located close to its stack and in a position secure from siphonic influences. A water closet set close to the stack, on the top floor, and without other fixtures on that floor wasting into the same stack, is an example

THE VENTING OF WATER CLOSETS

of this. A water closet located at a considerable distance from its stack, however, should always be vented, for through the long horizontal connection the waste would necessarily move slowly, particularly if the pipe were nearly level, and an obstruction, such as might be caused by paper, etc., might result in setting the water back sufficiently to fill the pipe, and this body of water in flowing out might create sufficient suction to partially or entirely destroy the seal of the water-closet trap.

In the case of fixtures located on floors above the water closet the influence of siphonic conditions may also be felt, for as waste from these fixtures descends in large volume past the entrance of the lead bend, the air becomes somewhat exhausted, and is not renewed quickly enough to prevent a part of the trap seal being siphoned or sucked out.

This loss may amount to but a few drops, but when continued indefinitely may result in the complete loss of seal, aided, as it often is, by additional loss due to evaporation in the case of fixtures seldom used.

As far as the siphonage of the water-closet trap is concerned, this danger is less to be feared than in connection with smaller traps, for the reason that to produce siphonage of a column of water 4 inches in diameter requires much stronger influences than to produce the same result on smaller traps.

Nevertheless, the water-closet trap is probably much more subject to siphonage than it is generally supposed to be, and if strict ordinances regarding its protection were not established and enforced, the trouble arising from this cause would be much more extensive than it now is.

There is probably no part of the plumbing system which occasions so much trouble as the ball cock which supplies the water-closet flush tank with water.

Two styles of ball cock are in use, the bottom supply and the top supply.

Bottom supply makes neater looking work, but in other respects the advantage seems to be with the top supply.

In the bottom supply the ball cock is located at the bottom of the tank, while in the top supply it is at the top, and therefore much more accessible in the event of repairs. This is especially true of tanks located close to ceilings.

Under these conditions, if provided with a bottom supply, the tank must be taken down to repair the ball cock, while in the case of top supply it can usually be repaired without such inconvenience. Ball cocks may be further divided into two classes, direct and indirect pressure. The indirect pressure ball cock, which is commonly used and least expensive, is generally provided with a 5 or 6 inch copper ball, which closes the valve by its buoyancy. The direct pressure ball cock works on another principle than the indirect, the water being conducted to the rear of the plunger, thereby adding the force of the water pressure to the buoyancy of the float in closing the valve. In the direct pressure ball cock, a heavy ball or float must be used, as a considerable weight is necessary to enable the ball cock to open against pressure. The light copper ball used on the indirect pressure ball cock would be inadequate to perform this duty.

Glass floats are now much in favor in connection with ball cocks, as they provide sufficient weight and are more durable than the copper floats which are now largely used.

As a result of keen competition, copper floats are now largely made of sheet copper that is so thin that it can withstand almost no rough usage.

Some of the necessary requirements in a ball cock is that it shall be as nearly noiseless as possible, quick closing, easy to repair, of simple construction, and made of a high grade of metal free from impurities, so that the water may not act chemically upon the valve seat and destroy it.

Plate V

THE LOW-DOWN WATER CLOSET—FLUSH VALVES—WATER CLOSET RANGES

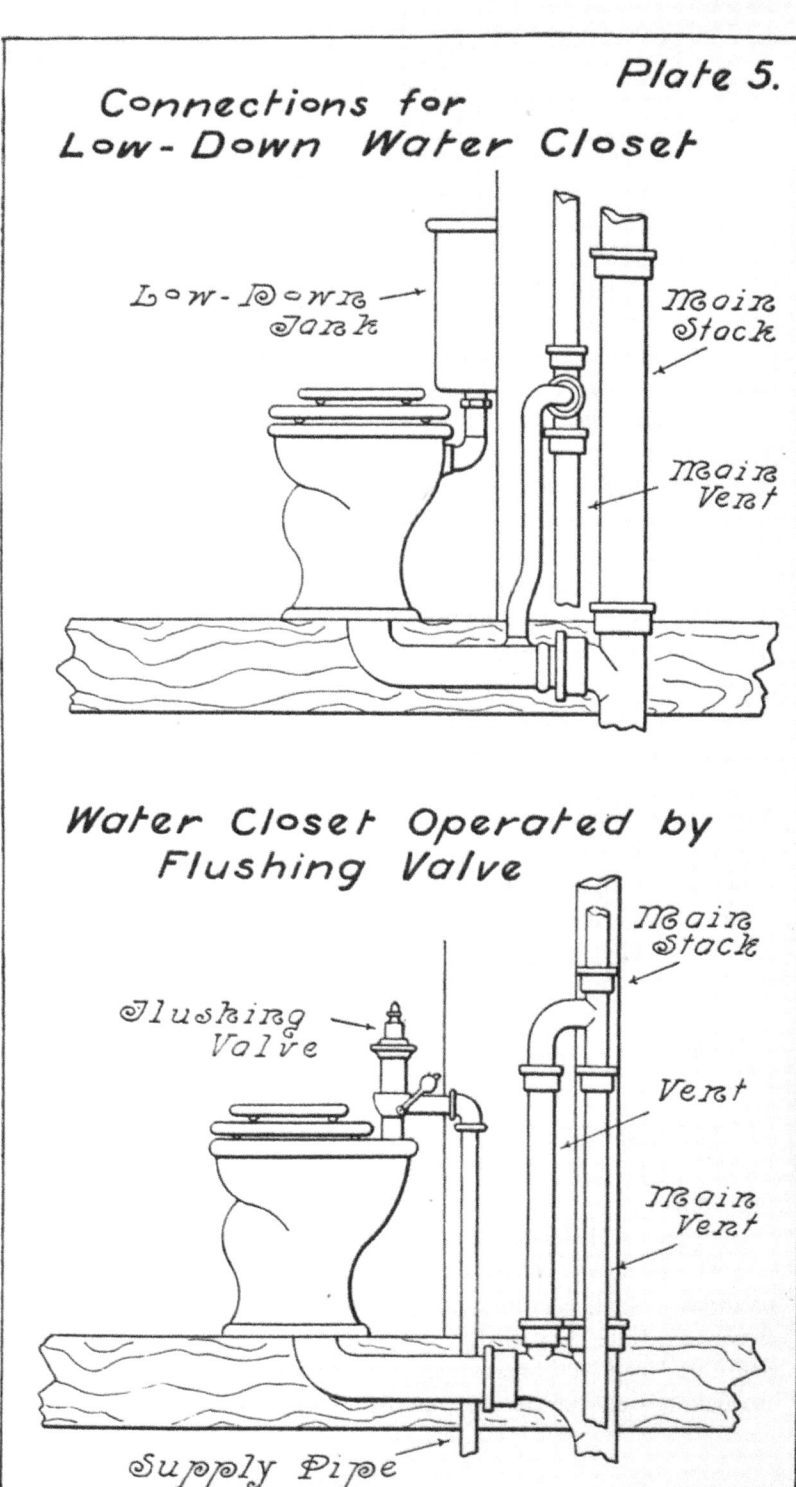

THE LOW-DOWN WATER CLOSET

The low-down water closet appears to be displacing the high-tank water closet to a large extent. Some of the advantages of this style of water closet are, viz.: the flush tank is more accessible, and, being covered, prevents dust, dirt, etc., from entering the tank and doing harm to the valves; and, because of the small elevation required, it may be used in many places where the high tank could not be used.

The low-down tank, however, requires the setting of the water closet further out into the room.

With the exception of the differences in the flushing arrangement, the principles that apply to the high-tank water closet also apply to the low-down style.

The flush of the low-down water closet as it enters the bowl has very little head, while in the case of the high tank it has a head due to an elevation of 6 ft. This lack is made up by providing a much larger flush pipe, in order that a large volume of water may enter the bowl with sufficient rapidity to produce siphonage. A water closet of the siphon pattern should be used in connection with the low-down tank, as enough water cannot enter to produce good results except by siphonage.

OPERATION OF THE WATER CLOSET BY FLUSH VALVE

The flush valve is a comparatively recent device, introduced for the purpose of flushing the water closet without the use of the flush tank.

Urinals and slop sinks may also be flushed by the same device.

The advantages of the flush valve are many. It may be operated on direct or tank pressure, on high and low pressure; it is noiseless; it may easily be concealed; it may be made to work automatically; and it may be used in many places and under many conditions where it would be very difficult and unsatisfactory to use a tank closet.

It is used very extensively in public buildings, in marine work, and in high-class residence work.

The subject of the application of the flush valve is considered further under Plate 42.

WATER CLOSET RANGE

While range closets are not to be compared with individual water closets as sanitary fixtures, the high-grade modern range closets represent a great step in advance of the old-style range. The great objection to the range water closet is that soil entering one of the compartments is not carried away at once, as soon as the use of it has ceased, but must remain until the flush for the entire range operates. During this interval it is throwing out into the room foul odors, and when this same thing is occurring in the case of a number of compartments it can plainly be seen that the range water closet is not so conducive to the maintaining of a clean, sanitary toilet room as is the individual water closet with its immediate flush. The flush of the individual water closet, moreover, is more effective than that of a range, and there is less liability of fouled surfaces in the former. The range water closet consists in general of a long trough, directly into which the several seats open. In the modern range this trough may be above the floor or below it. In the latter case, the bowl of each compartment has the appearance, to those not familiar with the subject, of being an ordinary individual water closet. A closer investigation, however, will show that it is not what it first appears to be.

The range closets now used are generally automatically flushed, the flush operating at stated intervals. This interval may be made longer or shorter by operating the valve on the supply pipe to the tank.

Most ranges are now provided with an automatic siphon which is started when the flush enters the range, and continues until the water in the flush tank drops to such a level that air is admitted to a pipe communicating with the crown of the siphon. This breaks the siphon, and the rest of the water that enters the range remains there until the next flush.

This water prevents the surface of the range trough from becoming fouled.

WATER CLOSET RANGE

The action of the automatic flush and siphon is strong, and very satisfactory.

The best feature of the modern range water closets, however, is the local vent which is provided with many of them. At the end of the range a 12 or 14-in. opening is provided with a collar to which the local vent pipe is attached, and the latter carried into a heated flue. Such a flue should not fail to be heated throughout the year.

The action of the local vent under a strong draught is very effective in the use of the range water closet. The draught draws impure air into the range through each seat opening, not only carrying it out of the toilet room, but preventing the odors occasioned by the use of the fixture from rising into the room.

The range water closet should not be used without a strong-acting local vent. Modern range water closets are generally of enamel-lined or porcelain ware, which is far more cleanly for the purpose than cast iron, such as was formerly much used. Of the modern styles of ranges, the type in which the seat opens into the range trough through a short bowl attached to the trough is preferable to the longer bowl, which presents greater opportunity for fouling. The latter is a serious matter in connection with the range water closet, as there is no flush around the bowl as in the individual water closet. Many cities prohibit the use of range closets, and this is a proper regulation, as the toilet rooms of schools, factories, etc., where the range is mostly used, are difficult to maintain in a cleanly condition at best, and the use of individual water closets reaches the desired end much more satisfactorily.

Plate VI

THE SLOP SINK—URINAL-BIDET

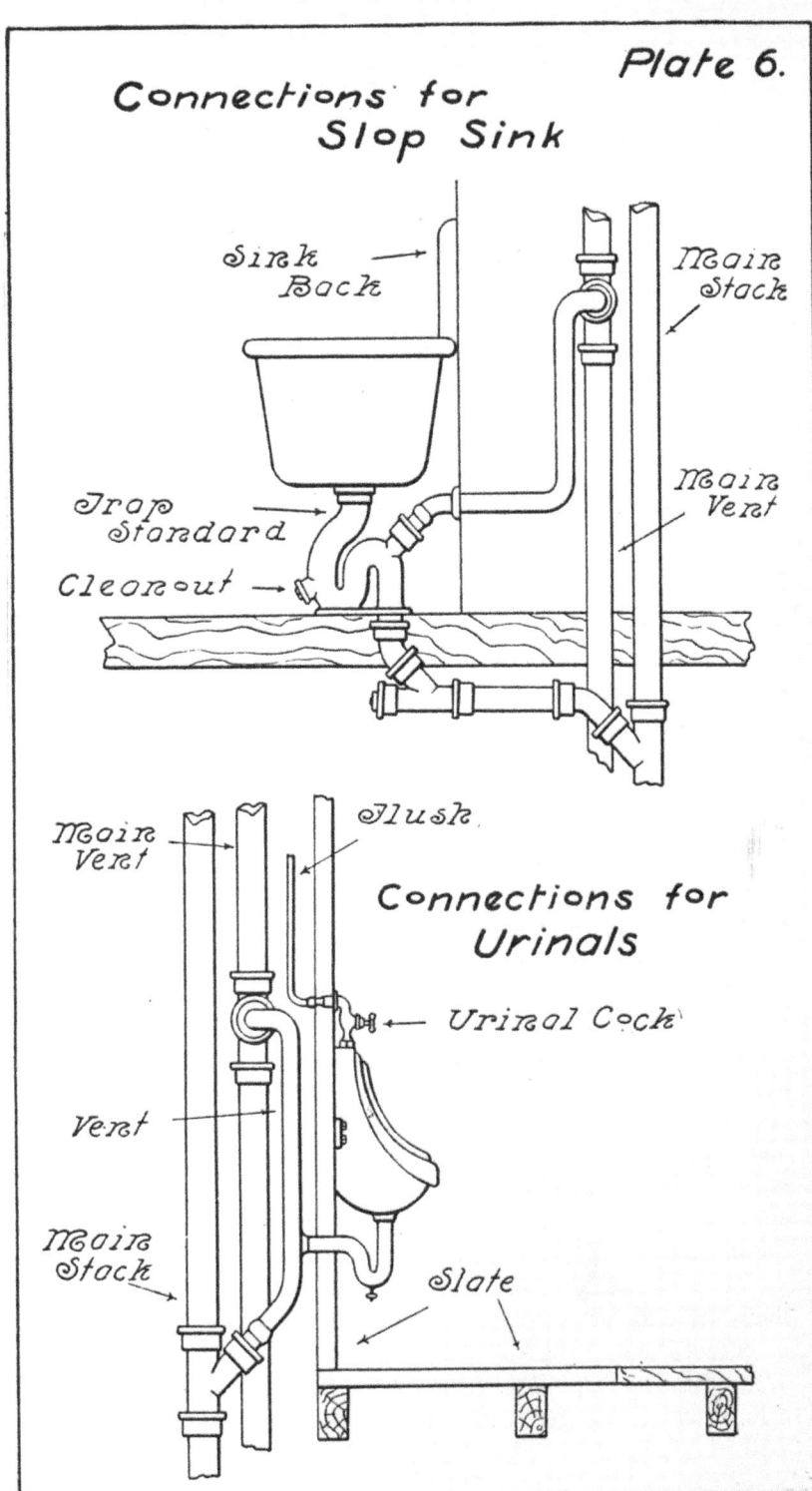

THE SLOP SINK

The best forms of slop sink are those of enamel lined or porcelain ware.

Owing to the nature of the waste which enters it the slop sink becomes a very foul and unsanitary fixture unless properly constructed. The most approved type is that having a flushing rim and provided with a flush tank. As the water enters the slop sink through the flushing rim its entire surface is thoroughly flushed and cleansed. The use of plain cast-iron slop sinks, flushed only by means of a common faucet, is very poor practice indeed. Such a fixture it is impossible to keep in a sanitary condition, and a foul-smelling room must result from its use.

The waste of the slop sink should be 3 in. in size; the size of the vent should be 2 in. The best form of trap for this fixture is one which is enameled over its entire interior and exterior surfaces, and which presents no metal surfaces which may corrode and foul. The slop-sink trap should be provided with a 2-in. cleanout, and it is excellent practice to provide a cleanout, when possible, at the end of the horizontal waste from the fixture, as shown in Plate 6.

The opening of the vent into the slop-sink trap is large and not so liable to stoppage as the vent opening of lead traps of smaller size. An excellent trap of comparatively recent construction is the adjustable slop-sink trap. It is of the half-S pattern, attached to a standard resting on the floor in the usual manner. The height of the outlet above the floor can be adjusted by means of a nipple, to meet roughing requirements, and the trap being of the half-S type, the continuous vent may be used in connection with it. On high-grade work the slop sink is often provided with a local vent.

This local vent should be of the same size as the local vent of the water closet; it should enter a heated flue, and in other respects be installed in a manner similar to the local vent of the water closet. When the slop sink is of the flushing-rim type, and is provided with a flush tank of adequate size and also local vent, it may be made a very sanitary fixture. The size of the slop-sink flush tank should be of 5 gallons capacity. In addition to the type of fixture described above, the waste-preventive slop hopper is used to a limited extent.

This fixture is flushed automatically by the emptying of slops into it, the flushing being accomplished by the creation of a vacuum which produces siphonage. As intimated above, however, this fixture is used only to a limited extent.

THE URINAL

The form of urinal shown in Plate 6 is the Bedfordshire lip urinal with flat back. This is undoubtedly the urinal most commonly in use. This fixture is made in a great variety of forms, several of which are shown in Plate 43.

The waste of the lip urinal should be not less than $1\frac{1}{2}$ in. in size, although a waste 2 in. in size is now sometimes used.

The vent should be $1\frac{1}{2}$ in. in size.

The urinal should be set so that the lip comes about 24 in. from the floor. This height should be less when the urinal is used in toilet rooms for small boys.

All lip urinals should be of the flushing rim type. The flushing rim allows the entire surface of the interior to be thoroughly cleansed at each flush. The lip urinal may be flushed as shown in Plate 6, the flush being under direct pressure, and operated by means of a urinal cock attached to the top of the urinal. It may also be flushed from a tank serving a single fixture or a group. This flush tank may be of the automatic type, flushing the group of urinals at regular intervals.

Owing to the conditions surrounding the use of the urinal, the known carelessness of many of the people using it, and the character of the waste entering it, the partitions, backs, and flooring should never be of wood or of any material which may corrode. When wood is used for these purposes it soon absorbs moisture with its impurities, and in a short time becomes very unsanitary. Slate is the proper and commonly used material for this purpose. A form of urinal, which is not shown in Plate 43, is the waste-preventive urinal, which works in a manner similar to that of the waste-preventive slop hopper. The fixture is of such sensitive action that the

THE BIDET

entrance of urine into the trap acts to form a vacuum which produces siphonage and the immediate operation of the flush. This fixture is not in extensive use, however, although an excellent device.

THE BIDET

The bidet is a fixture of comparatively recent origin, and, although not commonly in use, its use is increasing.

It is a bath-room or toilet-room fixture, and to be found principally in the bath room or ladies' toilet rooms of pretentious residences. The bidet is similar in shape to the water closet.

The waste for the bidet should be $1\frac{1}{2}$ in., and the vent of the same size.

Owing to the purpose for which it is designed, however, the supply to the bidet is of a much different character than that of the water closet. Both hot and cold water should be supplied to the bidet, entering the fixture through its side and rising inside the bowl in the form of a jet and douche.

The supply also passes through the flushing rim in order to thoroughly cleanse the fixture. In connection with the bidet, a mixer, similar in character to the valve on shower baths, is generally used. This allows either hot or cold water, or water of any degree of warmth to be used. Such valves should be of some non-scalding pattern.

Plate VII

THE HOTEL OR RESTAURANT SINK
THE USE OF GREASE TRAPS

Plate 7.

Connections for Hotel or Restaurant Sink

- Main Vent
- Main Stack
- Sink Back
- Cold Water Outlet
- Grease Trap
- Cold Water Inlet

Grease Trap

- Cover
- Cold Water Jacket
- Cold Water Outlet
- Waste Outlet
- Waste Inlet
- Cold Water Inlet

THE HOTEL OR RESTAURANT SINK

The waste and vent pipes of the ordinary kitchen sink are generally 1½ in. in size. The waste and vent of the kitchen sink, when used in hotel, restaurant, boarding house, and club kitchens, or when used in other public or private establishments which call for its almost constant use, should never be less than 2 in. in size. The amount of greasy matter entering such sinks is very great, even when the utmost precaution is used, and it is very necessary to so construct the work in connection with such a sink that stoppage shall have the least possible opportunity. It is a well-known fact that when sewage containing grease comes in contact with a cold surface, the grease will separate from the sewage and adhere to such surface. This often occurs in soil and waste pipes, the pipes running through cellars being cold and therefore well calculated to collect grease. When the grease begins to collect it continues to increase in thickness, until in time the entire bore of the pipe is filled. The collection of grease practically forms a body of hard soap in the pipe, and a stoppage of such nature cannot be dislodged by ordinary means of forcing stoppages, but necessitates taking down the pipe and clearing out each length.

For this reason, on horizontal lines of waste from sinks used in hotels, restaurants, etc., a cleanout should be inserted at intervals of ten feet in the piping.

Money put into cleanouts on such work as this is always well invested, as their use will eventually avoid the necessity of taking down the waste piping, an expensive undertaking.

THE USE OF GREASE TRAPS

When conditions are such that a great amount of grease necessarily enters the kitchen-sink waste, it is necessary to use a grease trap, a form of which is to be seen in Fig. 7, this form representing the best type of such traps.

As already stated, contact with cold surfaces causes the grease in sewage to separate from the liquid, a fact which is made use of in the operation of this or any other grease trap. The body of the trap is surrounded entirely by a water jacket or chamber, with the exception of the top. In addition, the partition in the center of the trap, which is designed to aid in breaking up the sewage and deflecting the grease upward, is also formed into a water chamber.

The water pipe supplying the kitchen sink is connected at the inlet and outlet ends of this water jacket, cold water thus flowing through the jacket constantly and changing whenever water is drawn at the sink. If the jacket were simply filled with water and not changed there would be no cooling effect, but the method described keeps the surfaces against which the waste comes in contact always cool, resulting effectively in the separation of the grease, which rises to the top and is taken out through the removable cover. The trap outlet is made at the bottom of the trap, instead of at the top, to aid in preventing the escape of the grease.

The partition through the center of the trap also helps to prevent grease entering the trap from being carried over into the outlet.

While the water jacket surrounding the trap does effective work, a large part of the results obtained is due to the presence of the hollow partition or deflector. This trap is of cast iron and made in several sizes.

Less expensive and less satisfactory grease traps are made on the same general lines as the trap just described, but not provided with a water jacket. Many of them do very good work, but it is not to be expected that they can hold back as large a part of the grease as the trap does which is cooled continuously by the water supply. There is one point in the use of the grease trap which does not always receive consideration—the amount of money to be derived from the sale of grease coming from the grease trap. In large establishments this is often a very respectable sum of money. Traps similar in design to the one described are also made of wrought steel. Cast iron, however, would seem to be less in danger of deterioration than wrought steel, which is more easily acted upon by acids. The grease trap, on a larger scale, in the form of a catch basin, is sometimes located outside the building, underground, and into this receptacle all the kitchen waste from kitchen sinks, pantry sinks, dishwashing sinks, etc., is discharged. The great advantage gained in the use of such a catch basin is that it is constantly cooled by the moisture of

THE USE OF GREASE TRAPS

the ground in which it is located. It should always be set low enough in the ground to be out of danger of freezing. If it is impossible to so install it, the catch basin should never be used. A serious disadvantage in the use of the underground catch basin is that generally its use necessitates a long line of horizontal waste pipe from the kitchen to the catch basin, and in this pipe and its connections grease has abundant opportunity to collect before reaching the catch basin, resulting in the ultimate stoppage of such pipes.

These pipes generally run in cool cellars and for a distance underground, which favors the collection of more or less of the grease on their surfaces. The better plan would seem to be the use of grease traps under the fixtures in the kitchen, with systematic attention given to the removal of grease that accumulates.

In the case of a line of kitchen sinks or of dishwashing sinks, one grease trap of proper size may be used for the accommodation of the entire number of fixtures. Catch basins for kitchen waste may be of brick or cast iron, and should never be less than 30 in. in internal diameter, tapering toward the top, if desired, to about 22 to 24 in., and provided with a cast-iron cover. If of brick, they should be made water-tight. The drain from the kitchen catch basin to the sewer may be of glazed tile, and should be not less than 5 in. in diameter and provided with a trap having a deep seal.

Plate VIII

REFRIGERATORS—SAFE WASTES—TANK OVERFLOW—SPECIAL WASTES

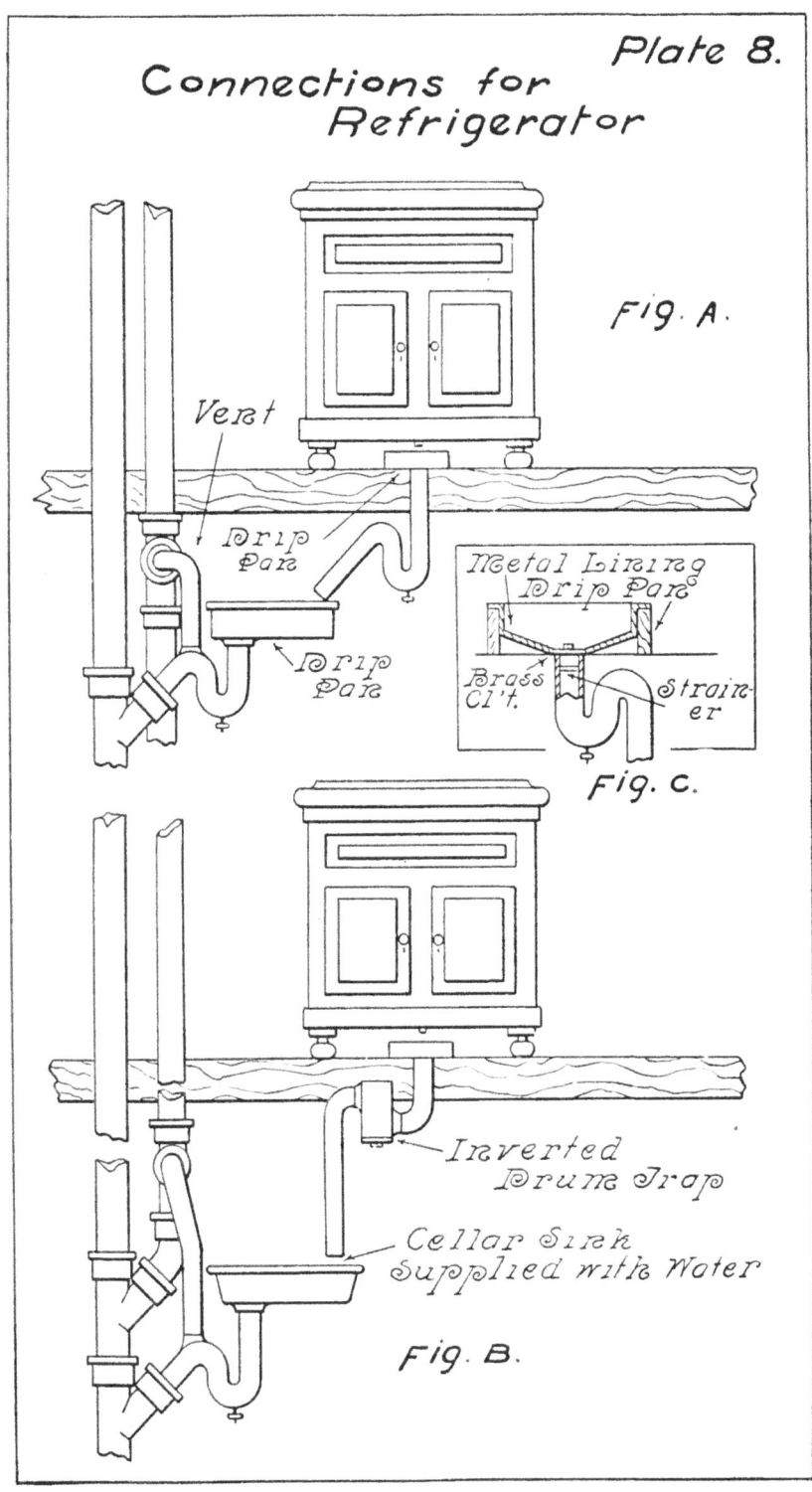

REFRIGERATORS

REFRIGERATORS should never, under any condition, be directly connected to any part of the drainage system.

This restriction makes it necessary to provide connections for the refrigerator on an entirely different principle from those of the regular plumbing fixtures. The refrigerator should drip into a pan beneath it, which should be trapped, the waste from the trap dripping into an open sink.

The sink should be trapped and vented in the usual manner, and may be connected to any soil or waste pipe.

The use of the drum trap is good practice, as it may easily be cleaned of the slime and sawdust which collects in considerable quantity. It also has a much deeper seal to withstand evaporation when the refrigerator is out of use.

The methods shown in Figs. A and B amply protect the refrigerator, for there is not only the trap usually found inside the refrigerator, and the other two traps, but also the two breaks in the connections.

The outlet from the refrigerator trap should discharge as far from the sink outlet as possible. It is preferable to drip into a sink in common use, as the renewal of its trap seal is ensured, but if impracticable, a special sink may be employed.

It is permissible also to discharge the refrigerator waste into a cellar-floor drain, yard drain, or into a trap provided with a receiving funnel. In the latter case it is necessary to provide a brass screw cover or a gate valve for closing the trap when the refrigerator is not in use.

The waste from the refrigerator should never be less than $1\frac{1}{4}$ in. in size. Short wastes and traps may be of lead, but long lines should be of galvanized wrought iron.

The refrigerator waste should have as sharp a grade as possible.

Fig. C represents a desirable form of refrigerator drip pan. The box is lined with metal, formed so that all drippings entering the pan flow toward the outlet, which is provided with a strainer and brass screw cover, the latter for use when the refrigerator is not being used.

The requirements for refrigerators apply also to ice boxes, or any other receptacle for food or provisions which it is necessary to drain.

SAFE WASTES—TANK OVERFLOW

Wastes from safes, drip pans, etc., should not be directly connected to any part of the drainage system.

Such wastes should discharge into a sink or laundry tub, cellar-floor drain, or deep seal trap.

The lower end of such a pipe should have a brass flap valve to prevent the passage of cellar air.

The overflow from the attic tank or other similar tank should not be directly connected to the drainage system, but should be discharged upon the roof or into an open fixture. It is often convenient to discharge this overflow into the flush tank of a water closet on a floor below the tank. This overflow should never be less than $1\frac{1}{4}$ in. in size, and $1\frac{1}{2}$-in. pipe is often better.

FLOOR DRAINS AND DRIPS FROM ICE HOUSES, ETC.

Floor drains, etc., used for the draining of ice houses, refrigerator rooms, storage rooms for provisions, etc., or for draining any room where food is prepared, should not be directly connected to the drainage system, but should discharge into an open catch basin or trapped sink located outside the building, the outer end of the pipe being provided with a brass flap valve.

LAUNDRY WASTE—CREAMERY WASTE

The waste from washing machinery in laundries, from similar machines in breweries and other establishments where a large volume of water is constantly used, and from receptacles and sinks used in creameries, may be discharged onto the floor, provided it is water-tight, properly graded, and provided with a suitable floor drain.

Plate IX

REFRIGERATOR LINES—BAR AND SODA-FOUNTAIN SINKS — EXHAUSTS — BLOW-OFFS, ETC.

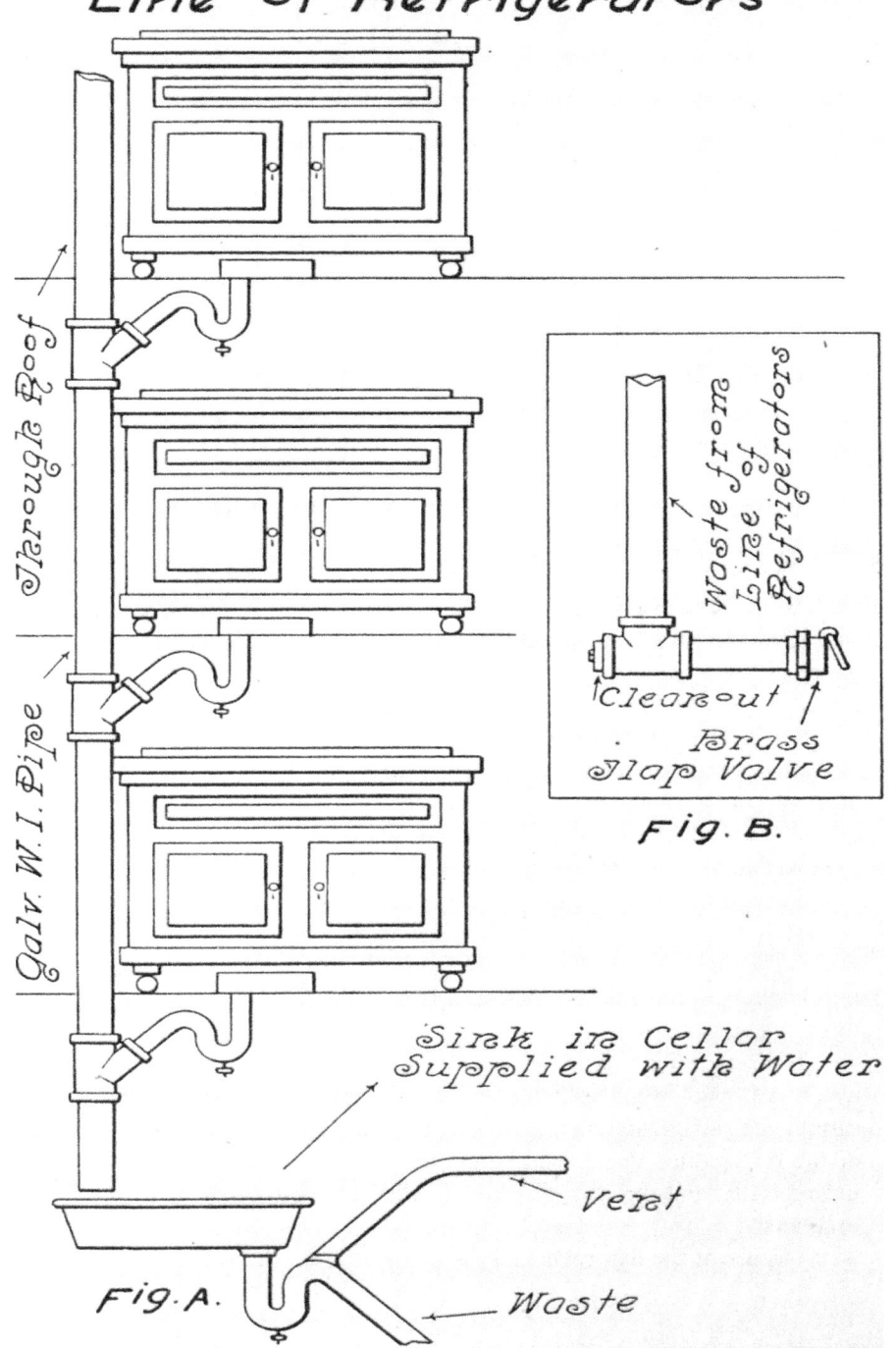

REFRIGERATOR LINES

THE size of a line of waste pipe serving refrigerators on two floors should be at least 1¼ in., for three or four floors 1½ in., and for more than four floors 2 in.

Galvanized wrought-iron pipe is generally used for this work, and all branches from this pipe should be made by means of forty-five-degree Y-branches.

Refrigerator traps do not require venting, as no conditions are present to cause siphonage of their contents.

The waste pipe which serves a line of refrigerators should in no case be connected direct to the plumbing system, but should discharge in the same manner as the single refrigerator, as described under Plate 8. All changes in direction and all offsets on the refrigerator waste pipe should be provided with full-size cleanouts.

Refrigerator pipes should never discharge upon the cellar floor or bottom, and wherever sewage privileges exist they should not drip onto the ground. However, if necessary to discharge upon the ground, such discharge should not take place within three feet of the foundation walls, unless into a tight gutter.

Each refrigerator connecting into a line of waste pipe should be separately trapped, with its branch waste as short and direct as possible. The main line should be carried directly through the roof, and in cold climates it should be increased to 4 in. in size before passing through the roof.

The reason for this is that smaller sizes often close up at their upper ends with hoarfrost, thus stopping ventilation, which in the case of the refrigerator is a most important matter. The cellar end of the refrigerator line should be provided with a brass flap valve, in order that the upward passage of cellar air and odors may be prevented.

The use of the flap valve and the cleanout is shown in Fig. B.

BAR SINKS—SODA-FOUNTAIN SINKS

The bar sink or the soda-fountain sink may be installed, if desired, with an indirect connection to the drainage system, or with direct communication.

When an indirect connection is made for either of these fixtures it may be trapped or not, as preferred, but should always discharge into a fixture or pan properly trapped and located as close to the bar sink or fountain sink as possible.

EXHAUSTS, DRIPS, AND BLOW-OFFS OF STEAM BOILERS, ETC.

The exhaust, draw-off, drip, and blow-off from a steam boiler should never connect directly into any sewer or into any part of the drainage system. These pipes should discharge into a tank or condenser, the capacity of which should be the same as that of the boiler. The tank should be provided with a vent pipe not less than 2 in. in diameter, connecting with the outside air. The tank should connect, through a waste not less than 3 in. in diameter, into the house drain or sewer, preferably the latter. The waste should be trapped and vented and provided with a back-pressure valve. The reason that this class of drainage should not discharge directly into the drainage system or sewer is that the steam rising from it produces sewer pressure, against which all possible precautions should be taken. Water over 120 degrees in temperature should not be discharged into the sewer, owing to the result which may follow in the formation of steam.

The drainage from hot-water heating systems and from low-pressure steam-heating systems may, however, be connected directly into the drainage system, if properly trapped, without entering a condensing tank.

The drainage from hydraulic elevators, lifts, and other similar apparatus which is direct connected, should not be discharged directly into the drainage system, but should first enter a tank, in order that it may be discharged from that point into the sewer without pressure. Tanks used for this purpose should be trapped and vented and provided with a back-pressure valve.

Plate X

THE STALL SINK—HORSE TROUGH—FROST-PROOF WATER CLOSETS

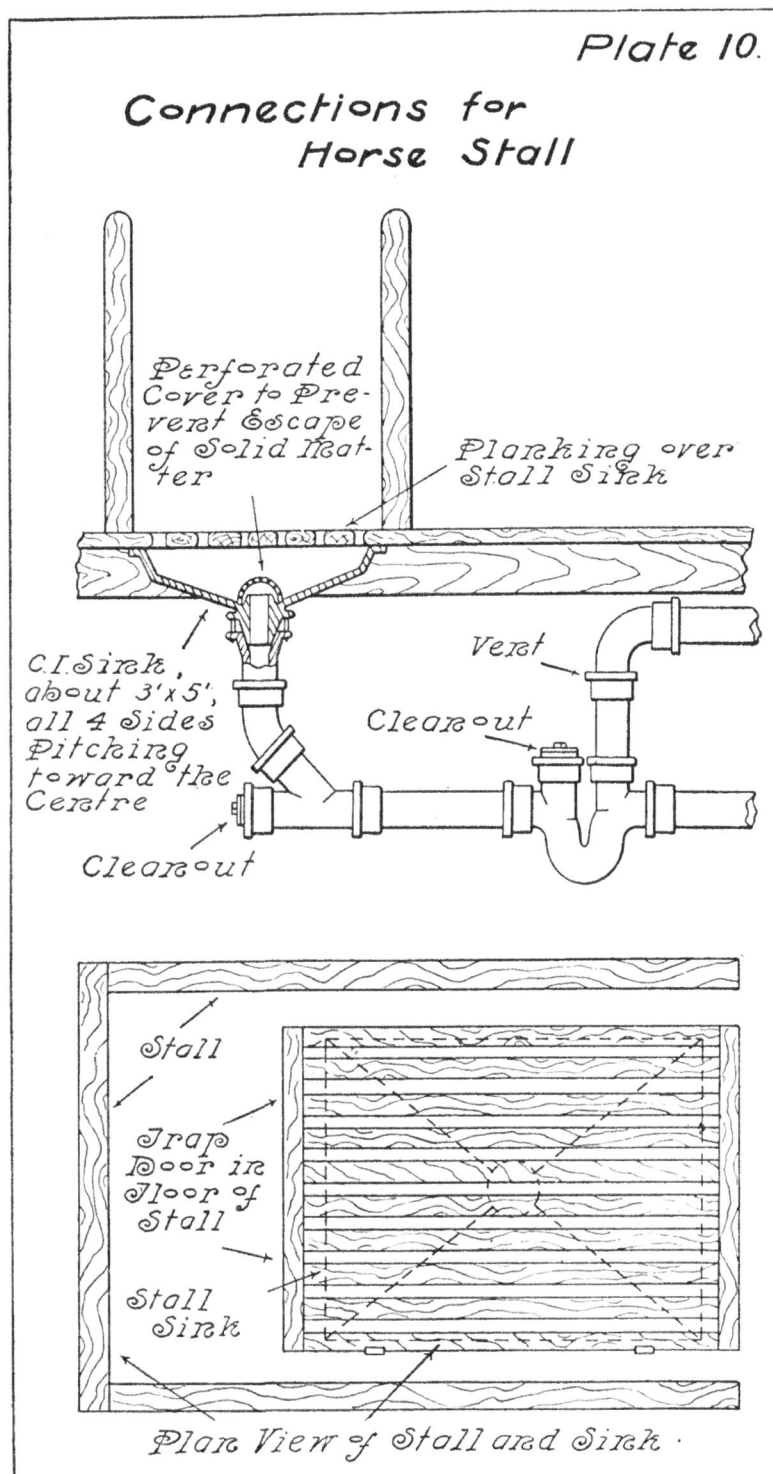

THE STALL SINK

In modern stables much attention is given to the proper drainage of horse stalls. Although not of so much moment when stables are located at a distance from dwellings, or in sparsely settled districts, the horse stalls of stables that are located in sections devoted to residential or business purposes should be provided for in the same manner as any other plumbing fixture. This applies to private stables, livery stables, engine-house stables, etc.

The drainage of the horse stall is best accomplished by the use of a specially constructed cast-iron stall sink, the four sides of which pitch toward the center, from which point the waste is carried off. Below the sink a special fitting is provided which bolts to the sink and caulks into the cast-iron waste pipe. The waste and vent should be of 2-in. cast-iron pipe, cast iron withstanding the action of the acids in the waste much more effectively than wrought iron or steel.

The waste line should enter a trap located as close to the stall as convenient, and provided with two 2-in. cleanouts.

Two cleanouts may be used by taking the vent from a tee located next beyond the trap, instead of from the trap itself, as shown in Plate 10. The use of cleanouts wherever possible on work of this nature, is a necessity, as even the utmost precaution will not serve to entirely prevent the entrance of solid matter into the drain. A cleanout at the end of the horizontal cast-iron waste, as shown, will prove of much value.

A perforated cover is provided with the stall sink, its purpose being to prevent as far as possible, the escape of solid substances into the waste pipe.

The stall sink should be set well toward the rear of the stall, as shown in the plan view, in order to best serve its purpose.

The sink should be covered by a skeleton trap door, through which the liquids may find their way into the sink.

Even when provided with these drainage facilities, the horse stall soon becomes foul smelling, owing to the foul nature of the solids and liquids deposited; but if the sink is thoroughly flushed out with the hose each day, it may be kept in a comparatively clean condition.

THE HORSE TROUGH

The plumbing of the stable is not complete without the properly connected horse trough. The horse trough is generally made of cast iron, and may be provided with a standing overflow to guard against the overflowing of the fixture.

Its waste should be 2 in. in size, and its vent 1½ in. The drainage pipes of stables are generally of cast iron, as the presence of strong acids in the waste soon causes wrought iron to deteriorate.

FROST-PROOF WATER CLOSETS

Several forms of water closet are now made, designed especially for operation in places exposed to extreme cold, such as unheated stables, yards, etc. Water closets for this purpose cannot be of the ordinary style, that is, with the trap combined in the fixture, as the contents of the trap would be in danger of freezing. Therefore long hoppers are generally used on frost-proof water closets, the trap being generally of cast iron and located below the closet at sufficient depth to avoid danger of freezing. Various methods are employed in providing a flush. In some cases the flush is direct connected, while in other cases galvanized cylindrical flush tanks are used. The flush tank is sometimes placed in a pit below the water closet, and sometimes on the wall above it.

In the latter case the tank fills only when the seat is occupied. When the seat is released, a heavy weight attached to it opens the flush to the closet and empties the tank, any water standing in the piping draining through a small pipe into the trap.

When the tank is located below the floor it remains empty except when the seat is occupied. When the seat is pressed down, the tank fills with water to whatever extent the pressure will compress the air. When the seat is vacated the weight attached tips the seat up, closing the inlet to the tank, opening the flush to the closet, and the compressed air forces the flush through the fixture. When frost-proof water closets are located in cellars or basements of such buildings as factories, warehouses, and other buildings occupied, but not used as dwellings, they should be vented and local vented.

Plate XI

CONNECTIONS FOR S-TRAPS—VENTING

Plate II.

Connections for S Traps

Fig. A.

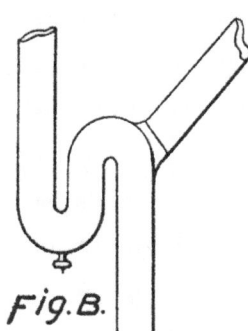

Fig. B.

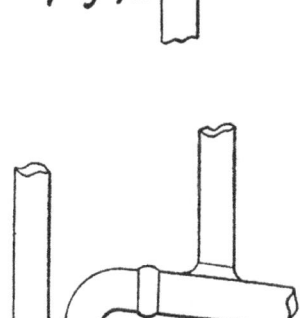

Fig. C.

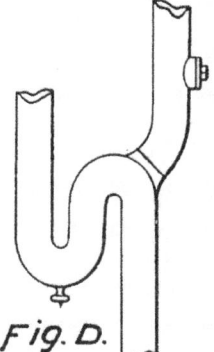

Fig. D.

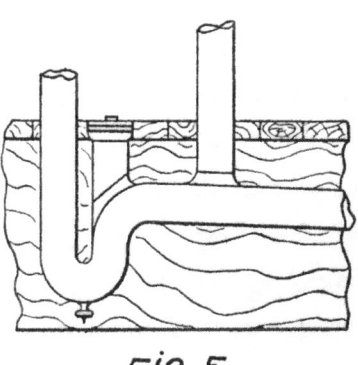

Fig. E.

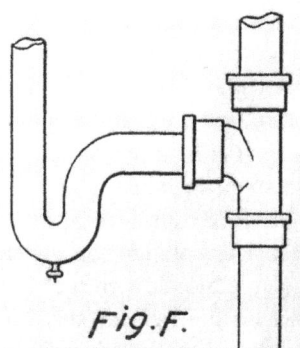

Fig. F.

CONNECTIONS FOR S-TRAPS—VENTING

THE trap and its vent are so closely allied that it is best to consider them under the same heading.

The trap is a vessel containing a body of water, the duty of which is to obstruct and prevent the entrance of sewer air and gases into the house. All plumbing ordinances recognize the necessity of a trap under each fixture, and upon the application of proper principles in its construction, installation, and venting, a large part of the successful operation of the modern system of plumbing depends.

A trap to be entirely satisfactory and sanitary should possess a good seal, be self-scouring, non-siphonable, have the least possible opportunity for the collection of filth, have no partitions within itself, and depend upon no mechanical contrivance to make a seal.

To secure all these features in the same trap is a difficult matter, but the claim is made for several traps now on the market that they meet these requirements, and the non-siphonable requirement having been solved, they require no venting.

If an absolutely non-siphonable trap could be produced, there would be no need of the venting system, and the cost of the average plumbing system would thereby be reduced approximately one-third.

It is true that several traps have been introduced which have withstood severe siphonage tests remarkably well. A very important question arises, however, as to what results these traps will show after they have been in service for a time, become fouled and in other ways reached the trap's normal condition. Some few plumbing ordinances now allow the use of these so-called non-siphonable traps without the use of the trap vent. The vast majority of ordinances, however, still adhere to the venting of the trap as a safeguard against siphonage, and it would seem at the present time a wise stand to take.

Before considering the special subject of S-traps, it will be well to consider some of the general features of the trap question.

By the seal of the trap is meant the depth of water between the outlet of the trap and the dip, that is, the depth of water which prevents the entrance of gases from the sewer.

A safe depth of seal is 2 in.

A much greater depth of seal might be secured for many traps, but the argument against it is that it presents a larger body of stagnant waste than is necessary. A small seal is dangerous, as it may more easily be destroyed by evaporation. Evaporation is a great menace to the trap seals of fixtures which do not have their seals renewed in the everyday use of the fixture; and the conveyance onto the trap seal of air through the trap vent increases the evil.

Internal partitions are dangerous, for sewer gas may pass into the house through defects that may exist in the partition above the water line.

Formerly traps with mechanical seals were much in use, but are now generally prohibited. The mechanical device employed was usually a heavy ball or float, which gave opportunity for the collection of grease and other filth about itself, resulting in the stoppage of the trap.

The trap seal may be destroyed by back pressure, capillary attraction, momentum, evaporation, and siphonage.

The trap seal may be forced by back pressure, that is, the pressure of gases generated in the sewer.

This evil has been practically eliminated by carrying the vertical stacks through the roof, but was a serious matter in the old-style system, in which each stack ended at the highest fixture.

The action of capillary attraction takes place in the trap when threads, pieces of cloth, etc., happen to dip into the seal and extend over into the outlet. By this means, a drop at a time, the seal may be, and often is, broken. There is no remedy that can be applied to this evil, for its existence is never known. A trap may lose its seal by momentum, that is, in flowing out of the trap, the rush of the waste is so strong that it may carry a part of the seal with it.

This is the tendency in some traps working on the centrifugal principle. In these traps the waste inlet and outlet are on a tangent, resulting in a whirling motion which is so strong as to endanger the seal. These traps have great scouring qualities, which is an excellent feature.

Occasionally traps on top floors may lose a part of their seal by its being blown out by gusts of wind passing over the top of the stack.

Siphonage, however, is the worst evil which the trap has to contend with. For the purpose of the consideration of the action of

CONNECTIONS FOR S–TRAPS—VENTING

siphonage it is considered that the trap in Fig. A, Plate 11, is without a vent.

In that case, if a vacuum or partial vacuum were formed by any means in the lower part of the trap outlet, the atmospheric pressure exerted on the house side of the trap seal would force the contents out of the trap into the waste pipe. In other words, the contents would be sucked out of the trap. If conditions are such that a vacuum is produced as above, the only way in which siphonage of the trap can be prevented is by bringing a supply of air into the trap at or near its crown.

The siphon consists primarily of a bent tube, one arm being shorter than the other. After the vacuum has been created, and both arms filled with water, the action continues because the falling of the greater weight of water in the long arm exerts a suction on that in the short arm. If the two arms were of the same length, the weight of each would balance that of the other, and the result would be that the water in each arm would fall by gravity, at once emptying both arms of the siphon. It will be seen, then, that the trap with its outlet, almost always represents the ideal form of siphon, for the middle leg of the trap is short and under atmospheric pressure, and the outlet is generally much longer, and at its lower end often subject to influences which tend to produce a vacuum. In order, then, that the entrance of air may break the siphonic action, the air must be admitted at or near the crown of the trap. That there are many influences in the plumbing system tending to produce a vacuum may be seen in the text under Plate 36, in which this subject is taken up more extensively.

The vent pipe connected at the crown of the trap is the means employed to prevent trap siphonage, and to date it is the only practical means. Various experiments have been tried to prevent trap siphonage without employing an expensive vent system, but to no avail. Having now covered some of the features which apply to traps in general, the consideration of the S-trap will be taken up.

This trap is more extensively used than any other form of trap.

The S-trap and the drum trap may be considered as the fundamental forms of traps, all other traps now in use being based upon one or the other in their operation.

Much debate has arisen as to the relative advantages of these two forms of traps, but it is not the purpose of the author to enter into the controversy. Facts concerning the advantages and disadvantages of each will be given, the reader reaching his own conclusions as to which is the more perfect trap.

The S-trap, owing to its form and to the fact that its passage throughout is of the same size, possesses excellent self-scouring qualities, a most desirable feature in traps.

On the other hand, there is no other trap so susceptible to the action of siphonage as the S-trap, and it would be very unsafe to install this trap without providing it with a vent. Upon the proper application of the vent the successful operation of the S-trap largely depends. The greatest difficulty which the trap vent has to contend with is the accumulation of grease, hair, lint, etc., about the opening of the vent into the trap.

So great is this evil that it is an acknowledged fact that in a very large majority of instances the vents of traps that have been in use for a number of years are undoubtedly inoperative, owing to complete stoppage of the entrance of the vent into the trap.

Patent devices to prevent this have failed. Cleanouts on trap vents, as shown in Fig. D, are seldom used, owing to the fact that the existence of the trouble is usually unknown, and the need of the remedy therefore not appreciated.

The nearest approach to a vent which will not close up is the connection shown in Fig. F, in which the vent is taken from the top of the waste fitting. This method is known as continuous venting, and is of such acknowledged excellence that it is taken up at length under Plates 26, 27, and 28.

S-traps are made in three styles, the full S, three-quarter S, and half S.

In the latter two forms the vent may be taken off at a considerable distance from the seal, as seen in Figs. C and E. Such a connection is preferable to that of either Fig. A, B, or D, for there is not so great a tendency to throw the waste up into the vent as in the three connections named.

There is one other feature which makes the work of Fig. C preferable to that of Figs. A, B, and D.

Air is supplied to the trap seal at such a distance from it, that the rate of evaporation will be materially less than in the case of the other three connections.

CONNECTIONS FOR S-TRAPS—VENTING

The vents in Figs. B and D being taken off further from the trap seal than in Fig. A, their rate of evaporation will be less.

It may be stated, however, that the connection shown in Fig. A is the one most commonly in use. Although evaporation is not so dangerous a factor as siphonage in connection with traps, it is much more to be feared than would appear at first thought.

This is particularly true of traps under fixtures which are seldom used, or traps of fixtures in houses that are vacant, as is often the case during the summer season.

The S-trap, when used to serve the bath tub, is often found very inaccessible when it is desired to clear it of stoppage, for the trap screw, so convenient in most positions, is in this case very difficult to get at.

Flooring must usually be taken up to get at the cleanout.

In Fig. E is shown a very desirable method of providing a cleanout for the bath trap. The cleanout being brought flush with the floor, any stoppage may be removed without taking up the flooring.

The sizes of traps are, viz.:

Traps for water closets,	4	in. diameter.
" " slop sinks,	3	" "
" " kitchen sinks,	1½ or 2	" "
" " laundry tubs,	1½	" "
" " bath tubs,	1½	" "
" " urinals,	1½	" "
" " lavatories,	1¼	" "
" " other fixtures,	1½	" "

Every trap should be provided with a cleanout on its inlet side or below the water level in the trap, and the overflow from each fixture should be connected on the inlet side of the trap. Through carelessness and ignorance the overflow is sometimes found connected to the sewer side of the trap, thereby forming a by-pass through which gases and odors from the drainage and sewer system may enter the house. The trap should always be set level with respect to its water seal. Otherwise the available depth of seal will be lessened, and the seal possibly entirely lost.

Traps located under floors should have cleanouts accessible from above the trap, except in cases where the trap is accessible from the floor below, owing to the form of floor construction, as, for instance, in factory work. The waste from a fixture should never pass through more than one trap before entering the house drain. The effect of passing waste through two traps is to cause air-lock between the two traps, which impedes the natural flow of the waste and results finally in a stoppage of the waste.

Plate XII

CONNECTIONS FOR DRUM TRAPS—PRACTICAL REQUIREMENTS OF VENTING

Plate 12.
Connections for Drum Traps

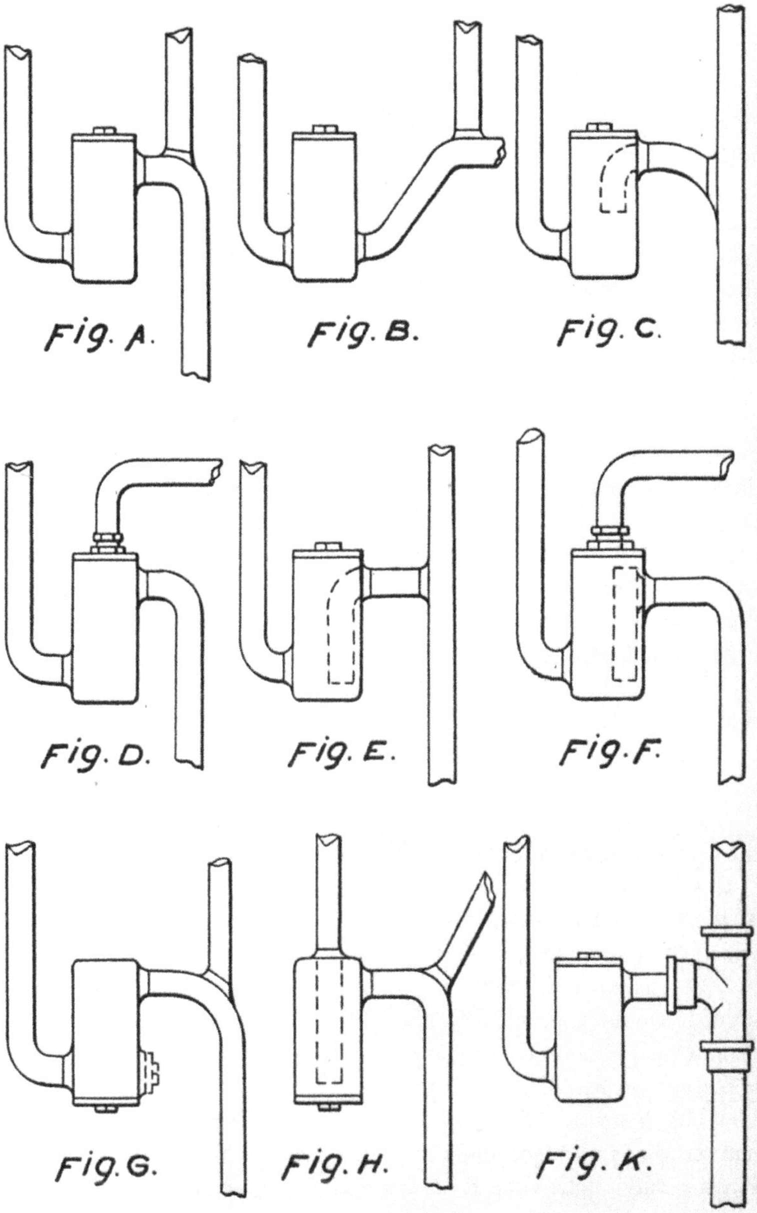

Fig. A.   Fig. B.   Fig. C.

Fig. D.   Fig. E.   Fig. F.

Fig. G.   Fig. H.   Fig. K.

CONNECTIONS FOR DRUM TRAPS

The drum trap for general fixture use is 4 in. in diameter, and into it are wiped the inlet and outlet waste pipes. The trap, then, represents an enlargement in the waste from a pipe of $1\frac{1}{4}$, $1\frac{1}{2}$, or 2-in. diameter to 4 in., and under this condition it cannot be expected that the drum trap will possess the scouring qualities to be found in the S-trap. The drum trap, however, certainly possesses one very strong point. While the S-trap is the trap most easily siphoned, the drum trap is one of the most difficult to siphon. In fact, under any ordinary working conditions the drum trap is practically non-siphonable. Special tests of great severity have shown that at least a part of its seal may be siphoned, but these tests subject the trap to conditions far more severe than they encounter when installed on the plumbing system. The strong point of the drum trap is that, unlike the S-trap, it holds a large body of water, and when subjected to siphonic influence, such action takes place through a passage of the same diameter as the waste pipe, allowing the remaining body of water to fall back and form the seal.

While acknowledging that the drum trap is far less subject to siphonage than the S-trap, it should be vented, in order that every possible precaution may be taken to eliminate this danger and to give the entire system the benefits to be derived from thorough ventilation.

It would seem a poor policy to maintain a radical stand against the use or in favor of either the S- or the drum trap. A better course is to select the form of trap to be used after considering the nature of the fixture which it is to serve, and the special conditions under which the plumbing system acts.

For instance, in country districts, where venting is not always used, it would appear to be good practice to make free use of the drum trap. Wherever the continuous vent can be applied to the trap, however, the use of the S-trap will give excellent results.

The drum trap is of special value in serving the bath tub, as it may be easily cleaned, and very often a better pitch can be secured for the outlet pipe than in the use of the S-trap. It is also well adapted to the laundry tubs, as it will easily receive the inlets from the several compartments, and may be placed in a more advantageous position than the S-trap, often avoiding a long line of horizontal waste extending from the farthest section to the S-trap. The drum trap is often used to serve two or more fixtures, but this is a practice which should not be followed, as each fixture should have its own separate trap.

Connections to the drum trap may be made in a great variety of ways, several of the more common connections being shown in Plate 12.

The connections of Fig. A are no doubt the most common, but the trap so installed is open to an evil which is not often considered. The trap screw is made tight by means of a rubber or leather gasket, and unless this joint is perfectly tight, direct communication with the sewer will exist. It is almost impossible to open this cleanout after the gasket has been in use for some time without destroying it, and a defective joint is very liable to be left. There are a number of ways in which this danger may be avoided. Fig. G shows a method of using the drum trap so that any defect in the cleanout gasket will at once be made apparent by leakage from the trap. The cleanout may be placed at the bottom or on the side, as shown by dotted lines. In either case it is not only submerged, but allows the trap to be cleaned to better advantage. Many ordinances now require the cleanouts of fixture traps to be submerged.

Fig. B shows a trap which is well guarded, having its outlet submerged, in which case, when the trap screw is removed, there is no direct communication.

This method of connection, however, is open to a serious objection. By taking the outlet from the bottom of the trap, where the heavy parts of the sewage collect, and thereby making the outlet pipe form the trap, there is much greater liability of stoppage.

In Fig. C the outlet ends inside the trap, dipping down into the seal, and thereby preventing direct communication with the sewer when the trap screw is removed. Although gaining this point, the part of the outlet inside the trap forms an obstruction, and there is opportunity for the collection of grease, etc., around it. The interior of the trap should always be free from any obstruction.

Fig. D shows a trap in which the vent is connected through the cleanout cover. Many ordinances prohibit a vent connection of this

CONNECTIONS FOR DRUM TRAPS

kind on the ground that no vent connection should be made by means of a union and gasket.

There is still another objection to this form of vent connection.

All traps sooner or later have to be opened and cleaned out, and in this case to remove the cleanout the vent must be bent around out of the way, which is not only an annoyance but harmful to the vent.

In Figs. E and F the outlet pipe is shown dipping down to the bottom of the trap. This is done to prevent direct communication when the cleanout cover is removed, but is a bad practice, for two reasons. In the first place, it takes up space in the trap, and forms an obstruction around which collections of foul matter may form. In the second place, either of these two forms of trap is very much more liable to siphonage than would be the traps in Figs. A and B, for the inlet and outlet openings are close enough together to practically form an S-trap, which is very susceptible to siphonage.

Fig. H shows a trap which is compact in the manner in which its connections are made, but which has the same fault that is found in Figs. C, E, and F.

This trap will siphon more readily than when connected as in Figs. A and B.

Fig. K shows a trap provided with a continuous vent, that is, a connection so made that the vent may be taken off the waste fitting. As stated in connection with S-traps, this method is an excellent one.

It is taken up thoroughly under Plates 26, 27, and 28.

In the case of Fig. K, the fault is the same as in Fig. A, that is, there will be direct communication with the sewer whenever the cover is removed. The same trap reversed, however, so that its cleanout is submerged, overcomes this objection.

Therefore, in summing up, it would seem that the trap shown in Fig. G, connected like that shown in Fig. K, would present the drum trap under the most favorable conditions possible.

PRACTICAL REQUIREMENTS OF VENTING

The matter of venting appears in the plumbing system in several ways. In the first place there is the soil or waste vent through the roof, the main lines of vent into which the individual trap vents connect, the trap vents themselves, the fresh-air inlet, and the local vents of water closets, urinals, and slop sinks. Local vents and the fresh-air inlet have no connection with the system of trap vents, and will not be touched upon under this plate. The soil and waste vents, main vent lines, and trap vents are closely allied, however.

One of the chief steps toward the improvement of the plumbing system was taken when soil and waste stacks were carried through the roof instead of being allowed to end at the connection of the top fixture. Even without the use of trap vents the roof vent was of great benefit, as it was often the means of preventing the creation of siphonic conditions, which meant the siphonage of the unvented traps.

In addition, it proved a successful remedy for back pressure from the sewer, as the latter could not force the seals of traps, for the reason that the roof vents relieved any such pressure.

It is generally through the soil or waste vent that air is brought into the main vent lines of the plumbing system, which in turn deliver the air to the traps through their separate vents.

The trap vent should be as direct in its course from the trap to the main vent line as possible, in order that the passage of air may be secured with as great an amount of freedom as possible.

Each fixture vent or trap vent should incline upward throughout its course, in order that any condensation forming in it may be conducted back into the trap. The trap vent should in all cases enter the main line of vent above the fixture which it serves. When the vent is thus properly connected, and a stoppage occurs in the trap or the fixture waste, the waste from the fixture will back up into the fixture, thus giving warning of the trouble that exists. If the vent pipe is connected below the fixture, however, the waste in the event of such a stoppage will not back up into the fixture, but will flow off through the fixture vent into the main vent line, and thence into the drainage system, thus defeating the purpose of the vent system, and making of the trap vent and main vent a waste pipe for the fixture.

Each fixture trap should be separately vented, but vents from several fixtures may be connected into a single branch vent, provided this branch runs above the highest fixture of the group.

Plate XIII

SOIL PIPE AND SOIL PIPE CONNECTIONS

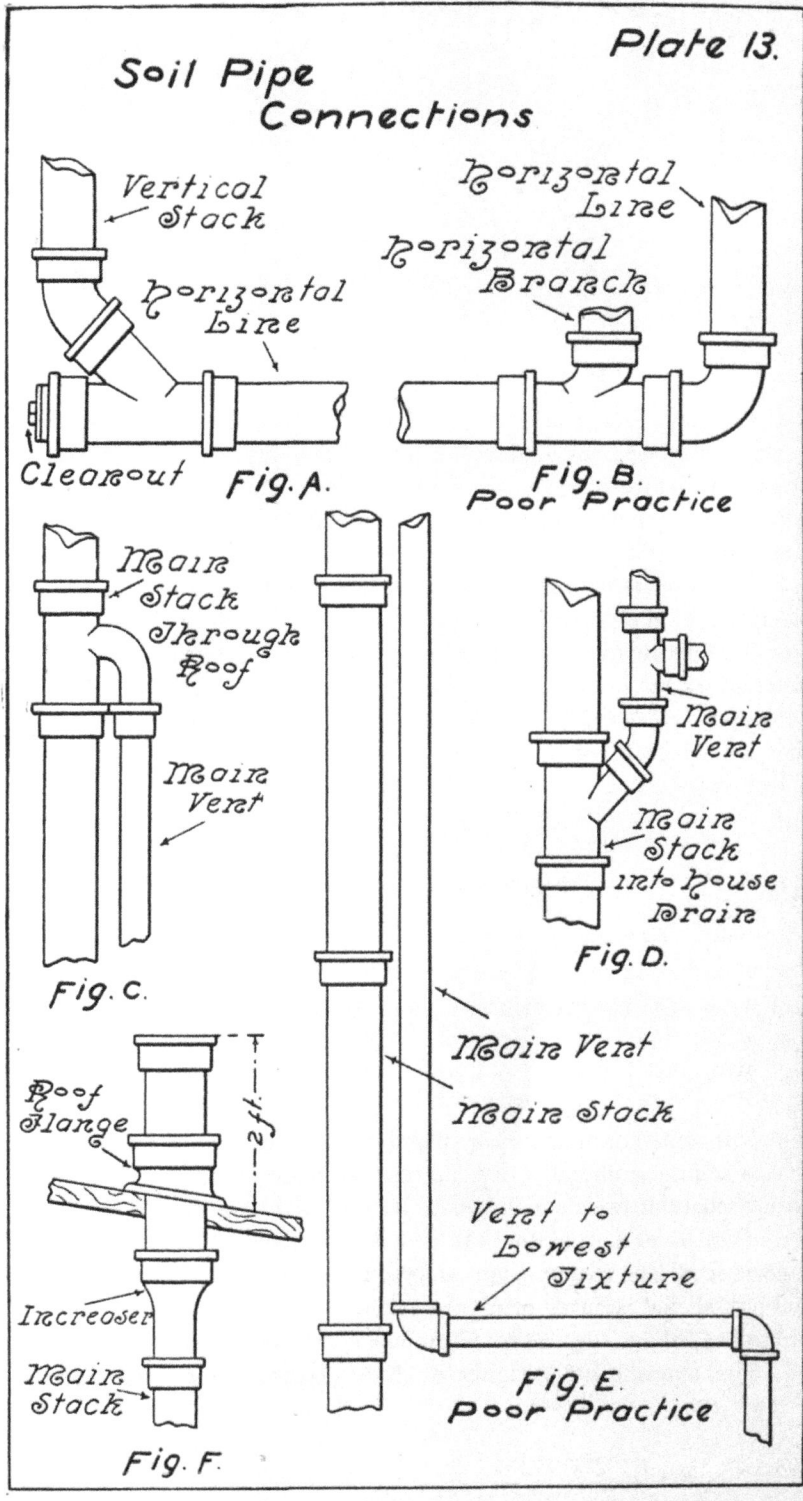

SOIL PIPE AND SOIL PIPE CONNECTIONS

PROPERLY, soil pipe is any pipe through which the waste from a water closet passes, and waste pipe is any pipe receiving waste from any fixture or group of fixtures other than the water closet. The term soil pipe is often used to designate cast-iron pipe of any size and for any purpose in connection with the plumbing system.

The latter is the sense in which it will be referred to in the consideration of the present subject.

Soil pipe is of two weights, "Standard," and extra heavy, the latter being far preferable in general, owing to the fact that it may be cast more evenly, with fewer defects, sand holes and cracks, and that it may be cut and caulked with less liability of cracking pipe and fittings.

WEIGHTS PER FOOT OF CAST-IRON PIPE

Diameter	Extra Heavy	Standard	Diameter	Extra Heavy	Standard
2 in....	5½ lbs.	3½ lbs.	6 in....	20 lbs.	10 lbs.
3 in....	9½ lbs.	4½ lbs.	7 in....	27 lbs.	
4 in....	13 lbs.	6½ lbs.	8 in....	33½ lbs.	
5 in....	17 lbs.	8 lbs.	10 in....	45 lbs.	

It is sometimes required by plumbing ordinances to use soil pipe that is plain and uncoated, it being usually coated inside and outside with asphaltum or tar. The coating often covers defects, which in the uncoated pipe would appear and be remedied. If plain pipe is used it should be coated after being tested. The joints on cast-iron soil pipe should be made of molten soft lead poured onto a firm body of caulked oakum, the lead being caulked even with the top of the hub.

The approximate weights of lead necessary for each joint are, viz.:

MODERN PLUMBING ILLUSTRATED

2-in. caulked joint	1 lb.	8 oz.
3-in. " "	2 "	4 "
4-in. " "	3 "	
5-in. " "	3 "	12 "
6-in. " "	4 "	8 "
7-in. " "	5 "	4 "
8-in. " "	6 "	
10-in. " "	7 "	8 "

It is generally unsatisfactory to give such a table as the above, of the amount of lead necessary for caulked joints of different size, as one workman may use much more oakum than another, and a correspondingly less amount of lead. Therefore it will no doubt be found that the table published will not agree always with the practice of different workmen. There is a rule, sometimes used in estimating the amount of caulking lead, calling for one pound of lead for each inch in size of the respective joints; thus, 3 lbs. for a 3-in. joint, 4 lbs. for a 4-in. joint, etc. In estimating the total amount of lead to be used on the cast-iron piping, it is necessary simply to estimate the number of hubs on fittings of different sizes, and the number of lengths of pipe of different sizes, adding the amounts of each size together and multiplying by the weight of lead used per joint.

Thus a Y or tee would call for two joints, the third joint on the spigot end, being estimated on the straight pipe.

An allowance for waste, shrinkage, and extra fittings, should always be added to the estimated amount of lead.

It is sometimes necessary to make a rust joint on soil pipe. This should be done by caulking into the hub a ring of oakum, and filling the remaining space with a putty made by mixing together sulphur, iron filings, and sal ammoniac.

Connections between cast-iron pipe and lead pipe should be made by connecting the lead pipe to a brass ferrule by means of a wiped solder joint, the ferrule being caulked into the cast-iron hub.

Overcast and cup joints are often weak and imperfect, and should not be used.

Connections between cast-iron pipe and wrought-iron or brass pipes should be made by means of a caulked or screw joint. All horizontal soil pipes, whether for drainage or venting, should, when possible, have a uniform fall of ½ in. to the foot, but never less than

SOIL PIPE AND SOIL PIPE CONNECTIONS 89

¼ in. to the foot. A less amount of pitch brings the pipe nearly level, and stoppage and sluggish flow of waste is liable to result. A grade on vent pipes is necessary in order that condensation may be carried off.

All changes in direction of soil pipe used on the drainage system should be made by means of Y-branches and sixth, eighth, or sixteenth bends.

This connection is shown in Fig. A, Plate 13, and applies whether the change in direction is made vertically or horizontally. A cleanout should always be used in the end of the Y in order to control that section of the piping. The change in direction made in Fig. B is entirely wrong, the quarter bend not being permissible on any part of the drainage system.

It is allowed, however, on the fresh-air inlet, vent lines, rain leaders, and floor and yard drains.

The tee should not be used on any part of the drainage system; the T-Y being allowed on vertical lines when it is impossible to use the Y-branch, but not being allowed on the horizontal piping.

The object in restricting the use of these fittings on the drainage system is to secure for the waste flowing through the drainage system as natural and unimpeded a passage as possible.

Double hubs should not be used on the drainage piping, as in their use a rough end of pipe is always exposed where the pipe was cut off, and on this end, lint, paper, etc., in the sewage is liable to be caught.

The use of double-hub pipe will often avoid the use of double hubs.

The double T-Y is another fitting which should not be used on horizontal work, as the waste entering one side of the fitting will cross and enter the branch on the other side, instead of entering the main line only.

Vertical stacks should be straight whenever possible, but when offsets are necessary they should be made with 45-degree fittings.

Any building in which plumbing fixtures of any description are installed should have at least one stack extending through the roof.

Whenever a vertical line receives waste from a fixture on any floor, it should extend through the roof, if 10 ft. or more from the nearest stack.

The following sizes of soil and waste pipes should be followed:

90 MODERN PLUMBING ILLUSTRATED

Each soil pipe should be at least........................... 4 in.
Main soil pipes for water closets on two, three, or four floors. 4 "
Main soil pipe for water closets on five or more floors........ 5 "
Main soil pipe for tenement houses of more than three stories.. 5 "
Branch soil pipes .... 4 "
Main waste pipe for kitchen sink........................... 2 "
Main waste pipe for sinks, lavatories, or laundry tubs on five
   or more floors .... 3 "
Main waste pipe for six or more fixtures, not less than........ 3 "

The following sizes for main vent lines should be followed:

Main vent for 4-in. soil-pipe line........................... 2 in.
Long branch vent lines .... 2 "
Main vent for stack serving sink, laundry tubs, and lavatories. 2 "
Main vent for line of water closets on three or more floors.... 3 "
Main vents for tenement houses of more than three floors.... 3 "

Additional main-vent sizes will be found under Plate 36.

The main vent line may be run independently through the roof, or it may be reconnected to the main soil or waste pipe above the highest fixture vent. The latter connection is shown in Fig. C, Plate 13, and it has certain advantages over the independent roof connection. In the first place, it saves cutting an extra hole through the roof, and the smaller the number of pipes passing through the roof the less will be the danger of leakage, and the less unsightly will the roof appear. In addition, the circulation of air through the vent system will be better, owing to the influence of the warmer air of the main stack in keeping the air in motion.

This connection may be made into the vent fitting shown in Fig. C, into an inverted Y-branch, and in the use of wrought-iron main vent by means of a tapped fitting on the main stack. When the pipe is to be increased through the roof, the vent line may enter the main stack through an increaser, such as shown in Fig. F, provided with a side hub or tapping. The lower end of the main vent should be reconnected to the main stack, as shown in Fig. D.

This connection allows all condensation and collection of rust and scale to be carried off into the drainage system, and in addition, it gives rigidity to the work, the danger from leakage due to accidental blows, settling, shrinkage, etc., being largely eliminated.

SOIL PIPE AND SOIL PIPE CONNECTIONS

Fig. E shows a very common but undesirable method of connecting the lower end of the main vent to the fixture vent of the lowest fixture.

It will be plainly seen that all scale falling through the main vent will collect in the bend at the foot of the line, and such collections of rust and scale often present a serious difficulty.

In Fig. F is shown a common method of making the roof connection. Some plumbing ordinances require a 2-in. stack to be increased to 3 in. in passing through the roof, and a 3-in. stack increased to 4 in., that is, each pipe less than 4 in. in size shall be increased one inch in size.

Most ordinances, however, allow no pipe of less size than 4 in. to pass through the roof. The latter is the preferable method, for the reason that 2 and 3 in. and smaller sizes of pipe will sometimes entirely close up with hoar frost formed about the opening above the roof, this accumulation being produced from the steam rising through the stack. In increasing the size of pipe, long increasers, such as shown in Fig. F, should be used, and the increaser located not less than one foot below the roof.

Caps or cowls should not be used to cover roof pipes. In the case of roof pipes of tenement houses whose roofs are used by the inmates, the openings should be protected by the use of a wire basket, but under other conditions it is preferable to keep the opening entirely free, as even the wire basket gives opportunity for the collection of frost.

The roof pipe should extend two feet above the roof. Whenever the roof is used by the inmates, all pipes passing through it should be carried up at least 6 ft. above the roof. Roof pipes should terminate not less than 3 ft. above any window, door, or air shaft that may be within a distance of 12 ft., and such pipes should not terminate within 6 ft. of any chimney or flue.

When carried above the roof, pipes should be securely stayed to the roof. Many styles of roof flanges are in use, the most common probably being that of Fig. F, in which the hub is riveted to a flange of sheet copper, which may be slipped under the slate or shingles above the pipe, and over them below it. Adjustable roof flanges will fit a roof of any pitch. A very desirable form is one in the use of which the plumber is not required to go onto the roof to pour the lead joint.

A change has in recent years come about in the use of materials on the drainage and vent systems of the plumbing system. Years ago all piping of the plumbing system was of lead. This was followed by the use of cast iron on both main drainage lines and vent lines, with branch wastes and vents of lead.

Although much cast iron is still used on main vent lines, a large part of the main vents of modern plumbing systems are now constructed of wrought-iron pipe, and the branch vents as well, until at the present time a large majority of trap vents are of wrought iron, excepting in certain sections of the country that still adhere to lead work.

The present tendency, especially on large work in the large cities, is toward the use of wrought iron and brass for fixture wastes, and a very excellent feature to be noted in their use is that cleanouts at bends may be used, whereas this was not done in the use of lead wastes. The use of brass pipe for drainage purposes is excellent practice, but the cost of brass pipe is so great that, excepting on the higher grades of work, its use is limited.

Plate XIV

SUPPORTING AND RUNNING OF SOIL PIPE

Supporting of Soil Pipe

Plate 14.

Fig. A. — hangers

Fig. D. — Poor Practice — hooks

Fig. B. **Fig. C.** — Clamp

Fig. E. — Vertical Stack, Brick Pier

Fig. F. — Vertical Stack

Fig. G. — Pipe-Supporting Fitting

SUPPORTING AND RUNNING OF SOIL PIPE

Too much care cannot be exercised in the running and supporting of soil pipes. They are generally made tight by caulked lead joints, which are easily made defective when moved in any way, owing to the great weight and leverage of the pipe. Few plumbing systems that have been in use for a number of years would show perfect joints under test, and in many cases this condition is due to imperfect supporting of the pipe.

When a vertical line drops to the cellar bottom, it should rest upon a thick flagging or upon a brick or stone foundation, as in Fig. E.

Care should be taken in building such a pier during the winter season that there is no frost beneath it, which would allow the pier and stack to settle when it thawed.

Brick or stone piers should also support a horizontal line running above the cellar bottom, particularly at points where vertical stacks enter it. The use of piers to support horizontal lines running below the cellar timbers is preferable to long hangers, as in the use of the latter the pipe would be inclined to swing if subjected to side pressure.

There are now on the market pipe-supporting fittings, as shown in Fig. G, which can be made to support piping running at any given grade. When there is no firm cement cellar bottom, these supporting fittings should rest on wide flaggings.

Equal care should be used on overhead piping, some ordinances calling for overhead running of all pipes.

In supporting overhead pipes, hangers of the pattern shown in Fig. A should be used, and the pipe should be supported once in each five feet. Some ordinances call for a support in each ten feet, but the above provision is better.

Fig. D shows a practice, generally prohibited, of using hooks for the supporting of pipe.

The hanger is firmly supported at each end, the pipe resting between the two supporting points; in the use of pipe hooks, however, the weight of the pipe, owing to the form of the support, will cause it to sag, and though the sag may often be very slight, it will generally be sufficient to cause defective joints.

All vertical lines of soil pipe should be supported at each floor by iron bands placed just below the hub or under the branch of a fitting.

These bands are made of flat wrought iron, and should have the strength of ½-in. round iron, and should be securely fastened to the timber with screws.

The support should be made on a vertical timber if possible, as the danger of settling or sagging of a horizontal timber is greater.

A practice sometimes followed is to cut the pipe in such a manner that it supports itself on a hub at each floor, as shown in Fig. C.

For hangers for 2- and 3-in. soil pipe, ⅜-in. wrought-iron rod should be used; and ½-in. rod for 4- and 5-in. pipe.

That there is great need of every precaution in running and supporting soil pipe may be seen when it is considered that a 4-in. stack in almost any ordinary residence or dwelling will weigh at least 550 lbs., without taking into account any branches or fittings, and pipe of larger size will weigh very much more.

Furthermore, when the entire system is filled with water during the water test, this weight is raised to a much higher amount.

Stacks passing through the roof and carried several feet above it in order that their upper ends may be above all roof openings or above adjoining windows, should be given special support, as the pressure of the wind against them is at times very strong.

When roofs of tenement houses are occupied and used by tenants, as often happens, there is the additional danger of blows against the pipe. Such pipes should be supported by three or four stout wrought-iron rods firmly secured to the soil pipe, run off at an angle and secured to the roof. A wrought-iron collar placed around the pipe and above a hub, provides a good means of attaching the rods to the soil pipe. Another method is to tap the pipe and secure the rods by bolts.

Vent pipes from cesspools when required to run vertically in the open for a number of feet should also receive special support.

A very good method of providing such support is to set in the ground, close to the cesspool, a heavy pole which will not sway under the pressure of the wind, and run the pipe vertically against it, supporting the pipe under each hub by wrought-iron bands.

SUPPORTING AND RUNNING OF SOIL PIPE

The present excellent practice of connecting main lines of vent pipe to their main soil and waste stacks above the highest fixtures, and below the lowest fixtures, is a good practice, as it ties the work together, giving rigidity to it, and, in the event of settling, allows both lines to settle evenly without resulting in an unequal strain on the two lines that would result to a greater extent if not thus connected. The settling of a line of cast-iron pipe often results in pulling apart the caulked lead joints, especially if the line is not properly supported. For instance, a vertical line that may happen to be well supported in its upper sections, but poorly supported at lower points, is very liable to pull apart from the section that is securely fastened. This sometimes results in pulling the caulked lead joint entirely out of the hub.

The great necessity will thus be apparent, of securing vertical lines firmly throughout their course, and of providing support at the foot of each stack which cannot possibly settle. One of the chief advantages to be gained in the use of wrought-iron drainage and vent piping, in the construction of the Durham system of plumbing, is that the screw joints of such pipes will not pull apart in the settling of stacks, as the caulked joints of cast-iron piping will do when the pipe is not properly supported. As far as a vertical pull on a vertical line of screwed pipe is concerned, it will have no more effect on the joint than on the pipe itself in pulling it apart.

However, if proper precautions are taken, vertical lines of cast-iron pipe may be installed even in high buildings without danger of pulling apart.

Plate XV

THE HOUSE OR MAIN TRAP AND FRESH AIR INLET

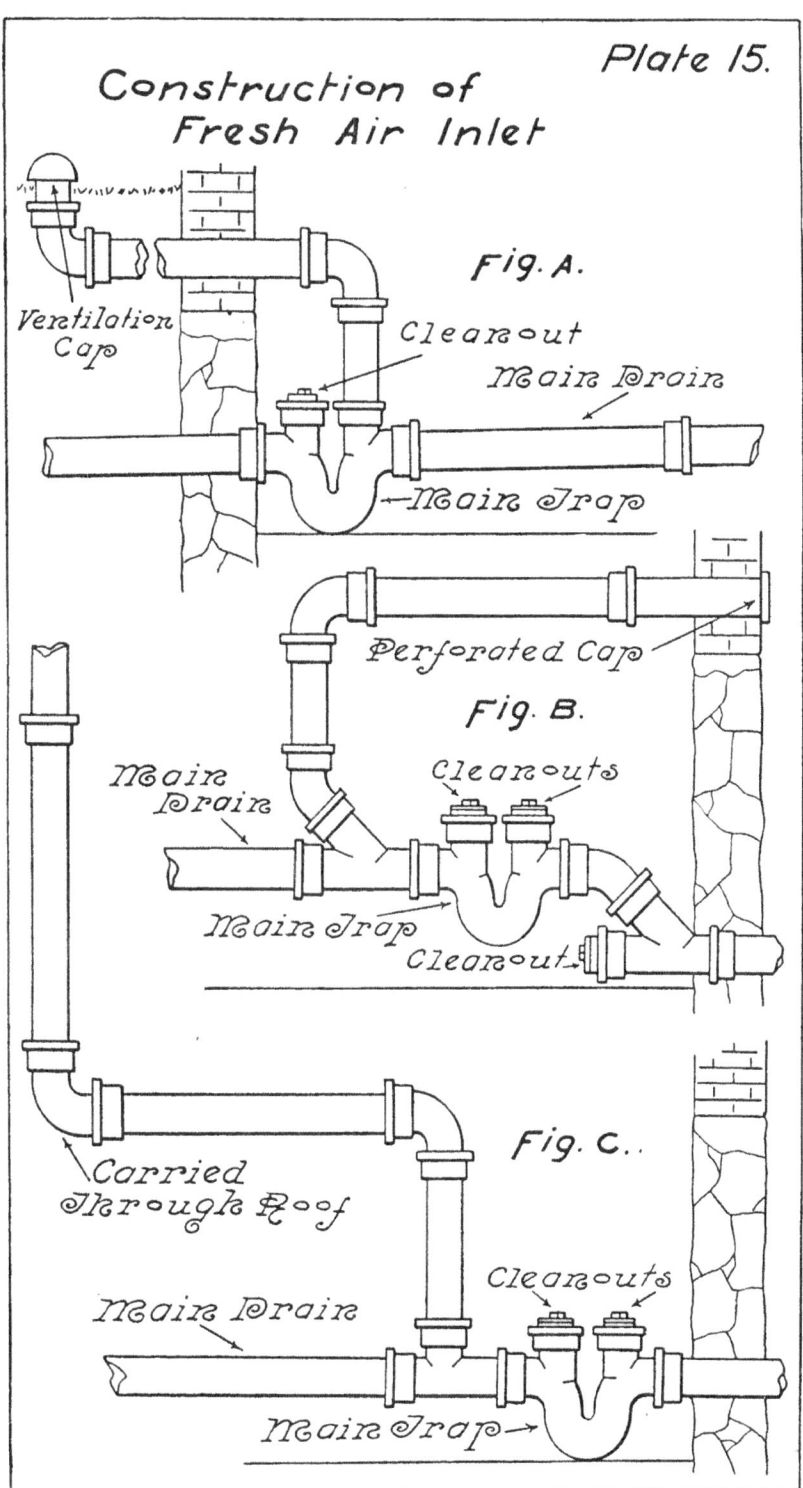

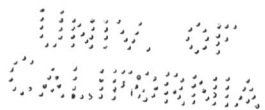

THE HOUSE OR MAIN TRAP AND FRESH AIR INLET

In the construction of any plumbing system, one of the first things to be decided is whether the system shall be protected by a main trap or not.

The question is a debatable one, and has been since the introduction of the trap itself. Plate 15 shows three methods of installing the main trap and its accompanying fresh-air inlet. From these illustrations it will be seen that the main trap is placed on the house drain at a point as close to the place where the drain leaves the building as possible.

The object of this trap is to prevent the entrance into the plumbing system of gases and odors from the sewer.

At first thought, the entrance of gases into the plumbing system would not appear to be harmful, especially as it has abundant opportunity to rise and escape through the roof pipes. However, although the plumbing system of to-day is subjected to rigid test after being constructed under rigid ordinances, there are numerous ways in which gases rising through the plumbing system may enter the house. The settling of floors and foundations may result in rendering soil-pipe joints defective; the soil piping is seldom properly supported, and often settles or sags through its own weight, causing the same kind of trouble. These and other conditions that might be named are of such universal occurrence that it is safe to say that only a comparatively small percentage of plumbing systems that have been in service for a term of years would be able to show perfect joints under test. Even though the plumbing system, with all its various connections, may be perfectly tight, still the danger of entrance of sewer gas is not always eliminated.

Traps of fixtures not in everyday use often lose their seals in a comparatively short time, as do floor drains, cellar drains, etc.

Whenever repairs are to be made on the soil piping or on branch wastes, sewer gas has a free passage until the repairs are completed.

Whenever the water closet is removed for repairs or to be renewed, sewer gas has a free entrance until it is replaced. Many other instances might be given in which the gases and odors from the sewer may find their way into the house.

The main trap is provided as a means of preventing this result.

The opponents of the main trap claim that it obstructs the flow of sewage through the house drain, that the trap will soon stop up, that in cold weather it will often freeze. These objections are not serious, and in many cases are more fancied than real. To be sure, the outflow is somewhat impeded by the trap, but the gain in providing protection to the house would much more than offset such difficulty. The strongest and practically the only real argument against the use of the main trap is that it prevents the ventilation of the public sewer through the roof pipe of the building. The weighing of the questions which arise in this connection is a very difficult matter.

In the first place it does not seem to be right to make a ventilating flue of each stack in each dwelling house, through which the sewer may throw its gases, to escape into the houses through defects and openings.

At the same time, the main drain and stacks present at present the most available means of ventilating the sewers, and are therefore often made use of. The closed sewer should not be tolerated, and the present method of venting the sewer through perforated manhole covers is open to serious objection, as it allows direct communication between the streets and the sewer. Special vent stacks should be erected at high points in the sewage system, through which the sewers might vent themselves, but such means are not provided, and therefore not to be considered.

It is claimed that where a free passage exists between the sewer and the outer air through the roof extension of the plumbing system, a circulation of air will be kept up, by means of which fresh air will be drawn into the sewer through the manhole covers, and the foul air drawn out through the roof pipes. If it were not for the matter of exposing the interior of the house to the admission of sewer gas this would unquestionably be an excellent plan.

Some go even further, and claim that enough fresh air would be drawn in through the manholes to render the gases harmless.

This does not seem reasonable when it is considered what a small area the manhole perforations really represent, and that a large percentage of these holes are closed up with dirt, ice and snow, etc.

If the house could be guaranteed against the entrance of gases, there are certainly many places in which the delivery of them into the air above the houses of the community would be followed by no harmful results.

In our towns and cities, however, with odors and gases escaping through every roof pipe, a heavy atmosphere must force them down to such points that they may often enter windows, light shafts, etc.

In our large cities, also, where low buildings adjoin high ones, it would seem very poor policy to banish the main trap, for without it the pipes through the roof of the lower building are constantly throwing their impurities out, to be drawn into the rooms on the higher floors of the high building.

That they would be drawn in in this way there is no question, as the circulation of the warmer air of the building would often create a suction sufficient to draw in the outer air.

In the case of tenement houses, also, whose roofs in the summer season are occupied by the inmates, the escape of a constant stream of sewer gas would seem to be a thing to be dreaded.

Another, and a very strong point against the employment of plumbing systems having no main trap, is the fact that under such conditions air contaminated with disease germs coming from the human excreta of any infected house on a line of sewers, may find its way through defects in the plumbing systems of other houses on that line, and thus gain entrance into the living apartments of the inmates. Plumbing systems should always be so installed that there may be no opportunity for such occurrences as this, whether in the manner just mentioned or through local vent systems, which have been known to carry infection from one to another apartment in the same building.

For this reason, as well as for other reasons, it is always poor practice to connect the drainage system of one house into that of a neighboring house. Such practices were more or less common years ago, but since the matter of sanitary conditions has begun to receive its proper attention, the connection of two or more houses to the same house drain or sewer has been strictly prohibited.

It would seem that there is an opportunity for the display of good judgment in the employment of the main trap. In sections of a city where the houses are detached, as in the residential sections, it would be wiser to do without the main trap than in the more densely populated sections.

The use of the main trap makes necessary the use of the fresh-air inlet, which, as shown in Plate 15, must be connected on the house side of the trap. The purpose of this pipe is to bring into the plumbing system a supply of fresh air, and to create a circulation of this air through the system and out through the roof pipe. It also serves to prevent air lock between heavy bodies of waste flowing down the house drain and the seal of the main trap.

If the fresh-air inlet were connected on the sewer side of the main trap, it would not only fail of its purpose of supplying air to the system, but would form a direct vent for the sewer at a particularly bad point.

The fresh-air inlet should under no conditions receive drainage of any sort. Formerly the fresh-air inlet was connected to the trap itself, as shown in Fig. A, which method allowed but one cleanout to be used on the trap, whereas two should always be used. Experience proved, however, that this connection had another disadvantage, from the fact that it brought in a current of cold air directly upon the trap seal, which resulted in the chilling and sometimes in the freezing of the water in the trap. Even though not frozen, the chilling of the waste caused the grease to separate from the sewage and cling to the inner surface of the trap, making ultimate stoppage more possible.

The freezing and the stoppage of the trap are two of the arguments against its use, but by the employment of proper means these results may be largely overcome. The fresh-air inlet, when properly constructed, is taken out of a fitting placed next to the trap, on the house side of it. This fitting may be either a tee or a Y, as shown in Figs. B and C. The more bends there are in the pipe, and the more indirect its course, the less will be the possibility of chilling and freezing.

The fresh-air inlet should never end at a point within 15 ft. of any door, window, or cold-air box supplying heating systems. The reason for this is that when heavy volumes of sewage pass through the house drain, a discharge of foul air passes through the inlet. This same trouble also occurs sometimes owing to a heavy atmosphere. When the fresh-air inlet ends at a distance greater than 15 ft. from any opening into the house, it may terminate at the outer face of

HOUSE OR MAIN TRAP AND FRESH AIR INLET

the foundation, as seen in Fig. B. In this case its end must be provided with a perforated cap, or with a bend looking down, in order to prevent different articles, such as stones, etc., from being thrown into it. It must usually be carried out into the lawn or yard to cover the requirement, in which case it is often constructed, as shown in Fig. A, with a ventilating cap covering its end, or ending in a return bend, this bend ending at least one foot above the ground. In business districts, where such devices as the return bend and ventilating cap could not be used, the fresh-air inlet should open into a box, 18 in. square, located below the level of the sidewalk, and at the curb. The bottom of this box should be at least 18 in. below the under side of the end of the inlet pipe.

The box may be constructed of brick or flagging, or of cast iron, and covered with a flagstone provided with a removable iron grating leaded into the flag. The grating should have small perforations in order that refuse may not pass through, and the total area of the perforations should at least equal the area of the fresh-air inlet.

Another method of running the fresh-air inlet is to carry it through the roof, as seen in Fig. C.

In general, this adds considerable expense without giving much added value. An objection to it, especially in the case of the ordinary house where there is but one 4-in. stack, is that the weight of air in the stack and in the fresh-air inlet about balances, with the result that there is but little circulation. This method, however, is but seldom used.

As to size, the fresh-air inlet for traps up to 4 in. in size should be of the same size as the trap.

For traps larger than 4 in. it may be less than the size of the trap.

For 5- and 6-in. traps the fresh-air inlet should be 4 in. in diameter.

For 7- and 8-in. traps, the fresh-air inlet should be 6 in. in diameter; and for traps larger than 8 in. it should be 8 in. in diameter.

Care should be taken that the main trap is set level, in order that none of its seal may be lost. When located below the cellar bottom, it should be made accessible either by setting it in a brick manhole provided with a removable cover, or by making depressions in the cement bottom so that the cleanouts may be easily reached.

The connection shown in Fig. B, whereby it is made possible to use an end cleanout, is an excellent one.

With two cleanouts on the main trap, and this end cleanout, the house drain at this point is well guarded against any possible stoppage. The connection referred to is now demanded by the ordinances of a number of different cities. All connections into the drainage system must be made on the house side of the main trap.

An exception to this rule is made in the case of rain leaders, which are sometimes run outside the foundation walls, in which case they may be connected into the house sewer on the sewer side of the main trap. Such rain leaders must be properly trapped. The main trap is sometimes located underground, outside the foundation walls, in which case it must be made frost proof and accessible. This is done by setting it below the freezing level, in a brick or stone manhole, covered with a flagstone. When so located, the fresh-air inlet should never be taken off the trap, as the passage of cold air would be so direct as to cause trouble.

Plate XVI

FLOOR AND YARD DRAINS—SUBSOIL DRAINAGE—THE CELLAR DRAINER

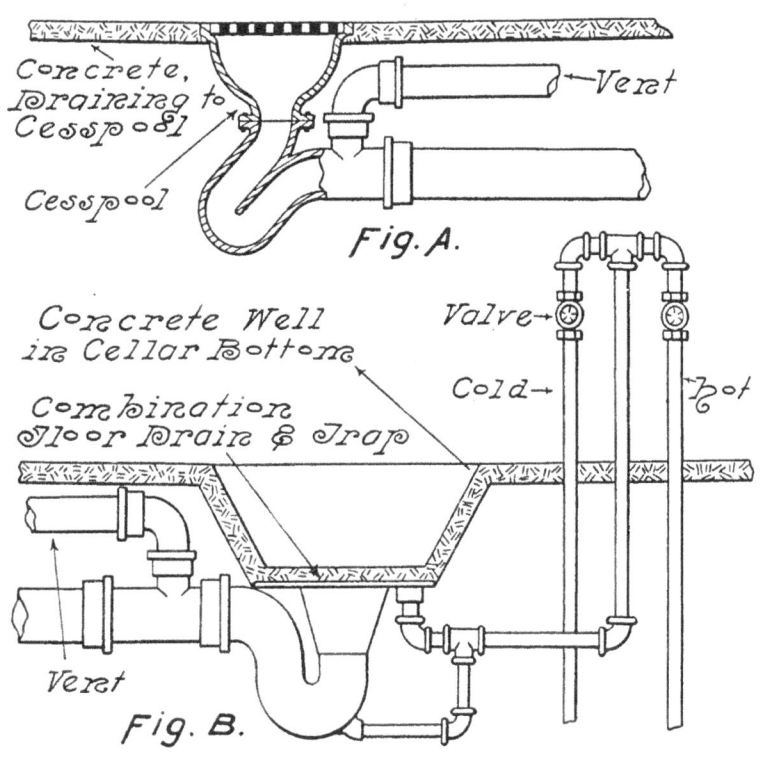
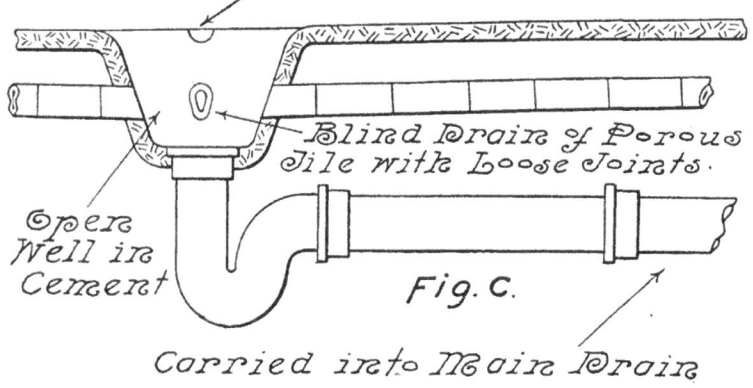

FLOOR AND YARD DRAINS

FLOOR drains are much used and of much value on large work, especially in public toilet rooms for hotels, depots, stables, etc.

The size of floor and yard drains should never be less than 3 in. in diameter, and very often, where there is much service required of them, and where there is any danger of solids of any description entering them, 4 in. is preferable.

The drainage of yards and areas in congested business districts, and in densely populated districts, is a matter of importance to the public health. Under such conditions, all areas, yards, paved courts, and courtyards should be properly drained.

This applies especially to tenement-house districts. The common form of floor and yard drains is of the style to be seen in Fig. A of Plate 40, provided with a removable perforated cover. There are several special forms of drains, such as those shown in Figs. A and B of Plate 16, some of them being provided with a vent connection. Ordinarily, however, drains of this description do not require venting, but may safely be installed without it, as in Fig. C.

Floor and yard drains should always be provided with deep-sealed traps. The deep seal is a special feature of the trap in Fig. A.

An excellent form of trap which will fill this requirement is one made of quarter bends. This trap is generally of the half-S form and may be easily constructed of three quarter bends. The use of a very deep seal on this class of work is not to be feared, as it would be in the case of polluted drainage, for all drainage passing through such drains is composed practically of clear water. In the case of other drainage a very deep seal would allow too large a body of sewage to stand in the trap to putrefy and make the system more impure than there is need of. The drain of Fig. B, with its flushing device, is an excellent one for many purposes, particularly for use in hospitals and on other work where general conditions must be as perfect as possible.

The flushing rim and jet with which the drain is provided allow the entire surface to be thoroughly cleansed, and the cleansing is accomplished without wetting the floor. By means of properly arranged supply connections, the trap may be flushed with hot or cold water, or with both.

The seal of this trap is of much greater depth than that of the ordinary floor drain. The connection of the water supply with drains of this description is an excellent idea, as a very small drip may be provided which will insure a permanent seal in the trap. Yard drains, for instance, in times of drought, and especially when not provided with deep-seal traps, may become a source of danger from loss of the trap seal. This source of danger, by the way, is an argument in favor of the use of a main trap.

Many plumbing ordinances demand that floor and cellar drains shall be water supplied, and this is certainly a needed precaution.

Floor and yard drains need not be separately trapped when one trap can be made to serve two or more drains, or where such drains are so connected as to be controlled by the trap of a rain leader. In fact, the use of a single trap, especially a rain-leader trap, to control one or more floor or yard drains is an excellent means of protection, as the permanence of the seal of such trap is more positive than the seals of separate traps would be.

In many cities a separate system of sewers is used for the disposal of surface and subsoil waters, no house drainage being allowed to enter it. In this case all floor and yard drains, roof leaders, subsoil drains, etc., should enter the surface water system. When these drains enter the house drainage system, however, no drainage which is not of clear water should be allowed to enter them.

Vitrified earthen pipe may be used for stable drains and for yard drains which are not connected with any house drain. Such drains must always be trapped and connected to the house sewer outside of the connection of the house drain to the house sewer.

When drains are of vitrified earthen pipe they should not be less than 5 in. in diameter.

The practice is sometimes followed of using any convenient cleanout opening as a cellar-floor drain, but it is a poor practice, and should not be followed.

The construction of the cellar drain is shown in Fig. C. This drain is naturally located at the end of the cellar at which the house drain passes out, as the house drain pitches in this direction. The cement bottom should be graded from the several sides of the cellar toward the entrance to the cellar drain.

A catch basin or well is generally formed in the cement, and at the bottom of it the cellar drain trap is located. Even though the system is provided with a main trap, a trap should be used on the cellar drain.

Without it, odors from the house drain would pass through the cellar drain and out into the cellar.

The practice of double trapping on this part of the work will not be followed by the troubles that generally follow double trapping, for the passage of water from the cellar drain is seldom of large volume.

It is a good plan to form in the cement bottom a small gutter, following around the entire cellar wall and close to it, this gutter being led into the catch basin of the cellar drain. By means of the gutter, and the grading of the cellar bottom, any water entering the cellar through the upper part of the foundation, or discharging onto the floor through leaks in the water piping, may find its way into the cellar drain.

SUBSOIL DRAINAGE

It is of the utmost importance to the health of the inmates that the cellar be kept as free from dampness as possible.

In the case of damp soil, a system of subsoil drainage should always be employed.

Subsoil drains are constructed of earthenware drain tile, laid with open, uncemented joints. The moisture of the damp soil enters the drain through these open joints. The subsoil drain should be laid completely around the cellar wall, and whenever necessary may have branches running in to the center of the cellar. The drain should be laid on a level with the bottom of the foundation wall, and about six inches inside of it. The subsoil drain should be laid on an even grade, pitching toward the catch basin to which it is to be connected, it being necessary to connect it always into such a catch basin properly trapped and entered into the house drain.

The catch basin is generally constructed of concrete, and made in the form of an open well in the concrete cellar bottom, and covered by a stone or cast-iron cover.

Whenever the sewer to which such a catch basin is connected is known to back up, the trap of the catch basin should be provided with a back-water valve.

THE CELLAR DRAINER

When the house drain is run overhead, it is clear that the cellar and subsoil drainage cannot be disposed of by gravity in the ordinary manner, as just described. The device used in raising the subsoil water is the automatic cellar drainer, and it is also used for removing water from excavations, wheel pits, or other depressions where water accumulates.

The drainer is placed in a pit or manhole below the cellar bottom, into which the drainage to be raised is discharged. As soon as the water collects to the depth of about a foot in the pit, the drainer opens and discharges the water.

As the water rises in the pit, a float attached to the drainer is gradually raised, and when a certain level is reached, the lever to which it is attached opens the valve wide, allowing water or steam pressure to pass through the drainer, and thereby drawing or sucking the water from the pit into the discharge pipe.

The drainer is generally operated by water pressure, this connection being made to any supply pipe. The water passes under full pressure through the drainer point or jet, thus creating the necessary suction to draw the water out. When the water has been removed from the pit, the valve instantly closes, and the drainer again becomes inactive.

The water in passing through the jet of the drainer creates a vacuum, this vacuum being the means of producing the necessary suction. The discharge pipe from the drainer should empty the water of the pit, and the pressure water used in operating the apparatus, into a sink or pan located above the house drain, into which the drainage may then flow by gravity. The sink or pan should be trapped and vented in the same manner as any other fixture.

In general, the cellar drainer requires a water pressure of four or five pounds for each foot through which the water is to be raised vertically. The cellar drainer is not adapted to raising water over 12 ft. usually, and many of them lose much of their efficiency after passing 8 ft.

The drainer may be located in an underground box or barrel. Cellar drainers are capable of raising from 250 to 1,200 gallons of water per hour.

The sizes of supply pipe generally used are ½ in. for small sizes, ¾ in. for medium sizes, and 1 in. and larger for large sizes.

Plate XVII

WATER CLOSETS—FLOOR CONNECTIONS

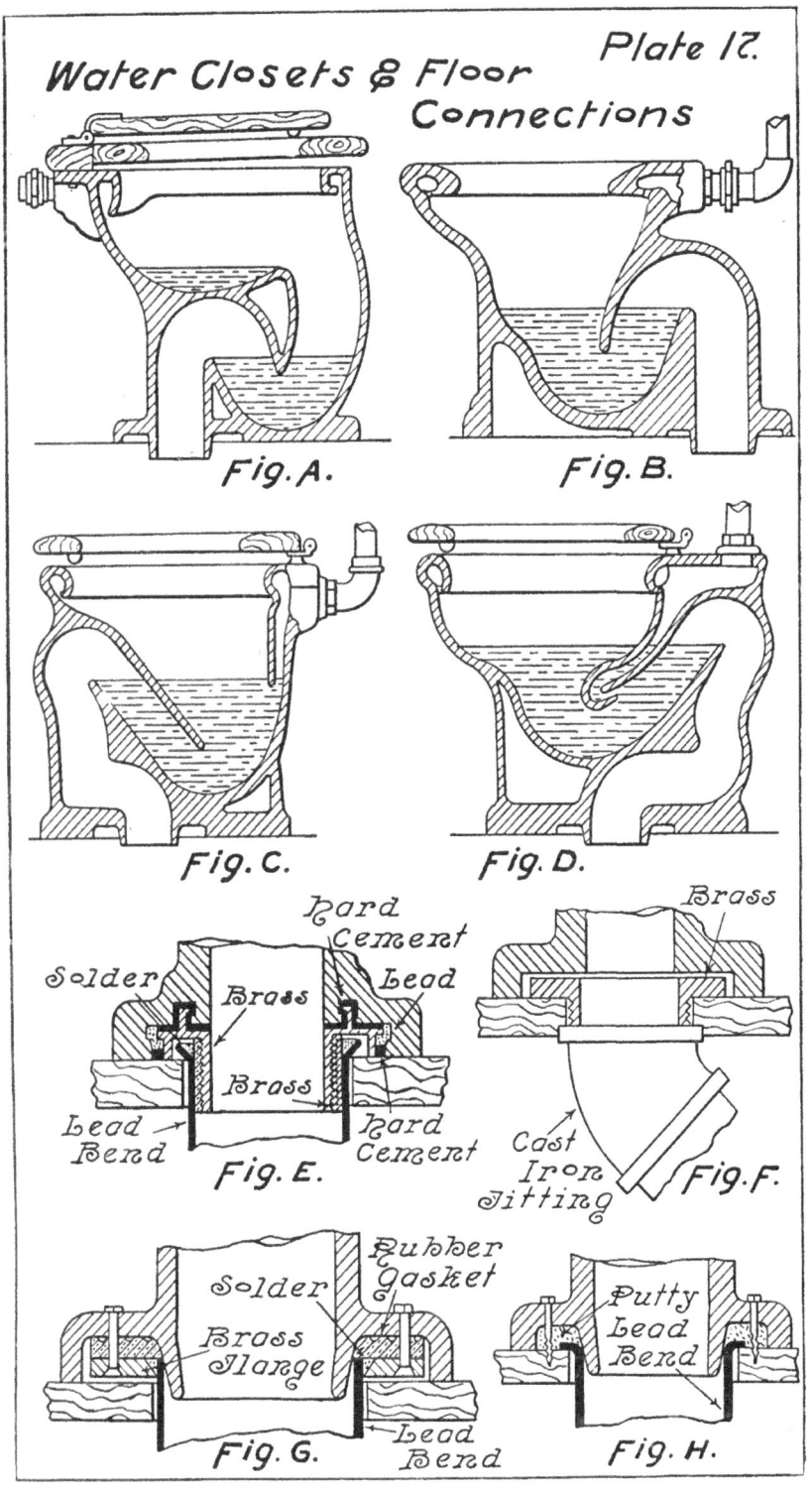

WATER CLOSETS

PROBABLY no other plumbing fixture or device has passed through such great changes and been brought from a most unsanitary condition to a condition of such high excellence as the water closet.

A volume might be written on the changes that have been wrought in its construction, but as this work is designed to deal only with present-day plumbing, only those fixtures now actually in use will be considered.

A water closet to be sanitary should possess the following features: It should be protected by means of a trap within itself, this trap having a good seal; there should be as small an area of surface exposed to contact with soil as possible, and all such surfaces should be thoroughly scoured; the flushing of the fixture should be accomplished as noiselessly as possible, and without unnecessary waste of water; the trap seal should be exposed to view; no mechanical devices should be employed in the operation of the fixture, with the exception of the flush tank; and for flushing the fixture it should never be directly connected to the water-supply system.

Modern water closets are superior to the old-style water closets of the pan, valve, and plunger styles in every respect. They avoid dead ends that are neither provided with water nor with ventilation; surfaces between the bowl and its trap, that in the old fixtures were protected in no way, are now submerged; the modern water closet is provided also with better ventilation, a stronger flush, is more noiseless, and is far more cleanly.

The leading forms of water closets now in use are the washout, washdown, siphon, and siphon-jet, the two first named being used very extensively in many cities on the cheaper class of work.

Since the principle of siphonic action has been applied to the water closet, however, the siphon and siphon-jet fixtures have taken the precedence over all other forms, and it appears to be only a matter of time before they will supplant the less satisfactory forms entirely.

The four water closets mentioned above are illustrated in Plate 17, Fig. A showing the washout style, Fig. B the washdown, Fig. C the siphon, and Fig. D the siphon-jet.

The washout water closet is somewhat different from other forms, from the fact that soil, as it enters the fixture, falls into a shallow pool of water above the trap, from which it must be conveyed by the flush into and out of the trap. The meeting of the flush with the resistance above the trap and with the resistance which the soil presents, impedes its force to a great extent, with the result that the water merely runs over the dip into the trap without much force, losing thereby much of the scouring effect that it would otherwise have.

So much of the energy of the flush is used up in removing the soil from the upper shallow bowl that it has not sufficient energy to perform the work needed in driving out the contents of the trap. This same loss of force is to be observed in the flushing of the old pressure closet, in which the flush is sent around the bowl. There is one advantage that is not often considered that the washout water closet has in having its upper shallow pool. The location of the pool allows excreta to remain in sight, which, in the case of the sick room, is often desirable to the physician and nurse. For this reason the washout water closet is sometimes made use of in private infirmaries.

The washdown water closet is an improvement over the washout, as the action of the flush is more severe and its scouring qualities therefore better.

Surfaces, which in the washout closet are left exposed, in the washdown closet are submerged, making the latter much the more cleanly of the two.

At length, however, the principle of siphonage was applied to the action of the washdown water closet, this step marking a very great advance in water-closet construction.

In the washdown-siphon water closet, the outlet is through a horizontal leg, which is contracted so that its area is considerably less than that of the passage above it. As the flush enters the fixture, and the contents of the trap pass out through the vertical passage, the water in passing through this passage attains a much higher velocity than it has when it reaches the contracted horizontal leg. The outflow being thus retarded, the water completely fills the horizontal leg, and as it passes out creates a vacuum behind it.

With nothing but the water in the trap to resist it, atmospheric pressure exerted on the upper surface of the trap seal, forces the contents of the trap out through the outlet and into the drainage system.

WATER CLOSETS

Atmospheric pressure is approximately 14.7 lbs. per square inch, and it is this amount of pressure that acts to force the contents of the water-closet trap. When the siphon finally breaks, enough water fills into the bowl to fill the trap, when it is ready for another operation.

The application of the principle of the siphon to the washdown water closet allows a larger amount of the surface of the bowl to be submerged than possible to obtain in the same form of closet in which sole dependence is made on a rush of water to operate it. In the siphon closet there is not only a pushing force exerted by the water entering the fixture, but there is also the force of suction pulling the contents of the trap out of the fixture.

The next step in advance in water-closet construction was the application of the water jet to the siphon closet, as seen in Fig. D.

In the washdown-siphon water closet the formation of siphonic action depends entirely upon the filling of the outlet, and until enough water flows out of the trap to accomplish this the action does not take place.

In the case of the siphon-jet water closet, additional aid is provided for the complete filling of the water closet outlet.

At the point where the flush enters the fixture, it divides, a part entering the bowl through the flushing rim, the rest entering a small passage which leads into the trap in such a way that its opening shall point directly up the middle arm of the trap, from which it emerges in the form of a jet. The force with which this jet emerges will help to raise the water and cause it to pass over into the vertical arm. The aid obtained from this jet, in addition to the natural flow of the contents of the trap into the contracted horizontal leg, quickly forms a solid plug of water, a vacuum forms, and siphonage takes place, as seen above.

This entire action is very strong, and in the case of both fixtures shown in Figs. C and D, all surfaces are thoroughly flushed. These excellent features make of these two fixtures the most sanitary and most satisfactory water closets on the market. In addition, there is less annoyance from the noise created by flushing the siphon water closet than others.

The washout water closet, with its shallow seal and its surfaces exposed to the contact of the soil, may be procured at far less cost than the siphon jet, and it may be said that this fact is the only one that makes its use favored by anyone who is at all acquainted with the subject. The washdown-siphon water closet may be obtained at a slight advance over the cost of the washout, the difference being so slight that it would seem that no one desiring proper sanitary conditions would hesitate a second in selecting the siphon closet.

The siphon form of water closet is the only one that should be used in connection with the low tank, the reason for this being that, although the flush inlet from the tank is enlarged to make up for the loss in head which is secured in the high tank, enough water cannot be thrown into the closet from the low tank to make the flushing of the fixture sufficiently strong.

By the aid of the siphon, however, the low tank is able to produce excellent results.

There are numerous other water closets, working on slightly different construction than those shown in Plate 17, which will hardly be worth considering, as those already discussed are most generally in use. The hopper and trap form of water closet, in its various forms, appears, in comparison to the modern high-grade fixture, to be of a very primitive character, and is now generally prohibited.

The use of the offset water closet is a practice which should never be allowed. This form of closet is made for use in connection with the lead or iron trap used with the pan, pressure, long hopper, and other closets.

Very often, when closets of this class were taken out, instead of taking out the trap beneath the floor, it would be allowed to remain, and the offset water closet, which has no trap, set in place of the old fixture. The reason that one of the modern closets could not be used instead of the offset closet was that there would then be two traps on the same fixture. The objections to the use of the offset water closet are that the flush loses its force before it reaches the trap, consequently not flushing the trap to any extent, and that there is a large amount of polluted surface, extending from the crockery into the trap below the floor, which gives off foul and unsanitary odors into the room in which the fixture is located. The offset closet is made in such a manner as to deceive those not acquainted with the subject into the belief that it is a fixture built on modern principles.

The only course to pursue in renewing such work as the above, is to tear out the trap under the floor, replace it with a lead bend, and use a modern type of water closet.

Vitreous chinaware is now used in the construction of all first-

WATER-CLOSET FLOOR CONNECTIONS

class water closets. This ware is formed of compact material, which is subjected to a high heat before being glazed. In the employment of this material there is no danger from the cracking or "crazing" of the glazed surfaces. In former times, before modern processes were employed, the crazing of the water closet was of frequent occurrence, resulting in the absorption of moisture by the exposed surfaces under the glazing, the fixture in time becoming foul and very unsanitary.

All water closets, as well as lip urinals and slop sinks, should have flushing rims, so as to flush the entire surface of the crockery.

Water closets should never be located in dark or unventilated places, and the practice of installing them in cellars, although followed to considerable extent, is not a wise proceeding. Sunlight and air are two powerful purifying agents, and when fixtures such as water closets and urinals are placed where ventilation is not provided and sunlight cannot enter, the conditions must necessarily become unsanitary, and the place where the fixtures are located filled with impure air. For this same reason the open plumbing of the present day is much more sanitary and much more wholesome than the old-style boxed-in plumbing.

WATER-CLOSET FLOOR CONNECTIONS

Floor connections, although often receiving scant attention, are an important feature in obtaining sanitary conditions. Several forms of this connection are shown in Plate 17. Fig. H shows the simplest and probably most common connection, and at the same time most unsatisfactory and unsanitary.

This method consists in flanging the lead bend over onto the floor, filling the groove around the outlet of the closet bowl with a ring of putty, and screwing the bowl to the floor. The putty compresses and forms the joint.

In the event of pressure against the fixture, shrinking or rotting of the floor, this joint will break and allow a leakage of gas into the house. In addition, the oil in the putty often spreads and discolors the flooring around the fixture.

A much better form of connection is to be found in Fig. G. Here the lead bend is brought up through a brass flange, and soldered to the latter, as shown. A rubber gasket is placed between the flange and the base of the water closet, and the whole fastened together and made tight by means of brass bolts. This makes a connection which should never leak, even though there be shrinkage or settling of the floor on which the fixture rests.

Fig. E shows a patented form of floor connection which also makes a good joint. The base of the closet is recessed to receive a brass-screw connection, it being made firmly to the crockery by cement and lead.

A female brass-screw connection is soldered inside the top part of the lead bend, and the closet screwed down into it. The joint formed between the brass and the crockery makes the former practically an integral part of the closet.

Fig. F shows a floor connection for use in connection with wrought-iron soil pipe, such as is used for the Durham system.

A brass floor plate or flange is screwed into the end of the ell or other waste fitting in use, and a tight joint made by using a rubber gasket between the flange and the base of the water closet, the latter being screwed to the floor.

Plate XVIII

LOCAL VENTING

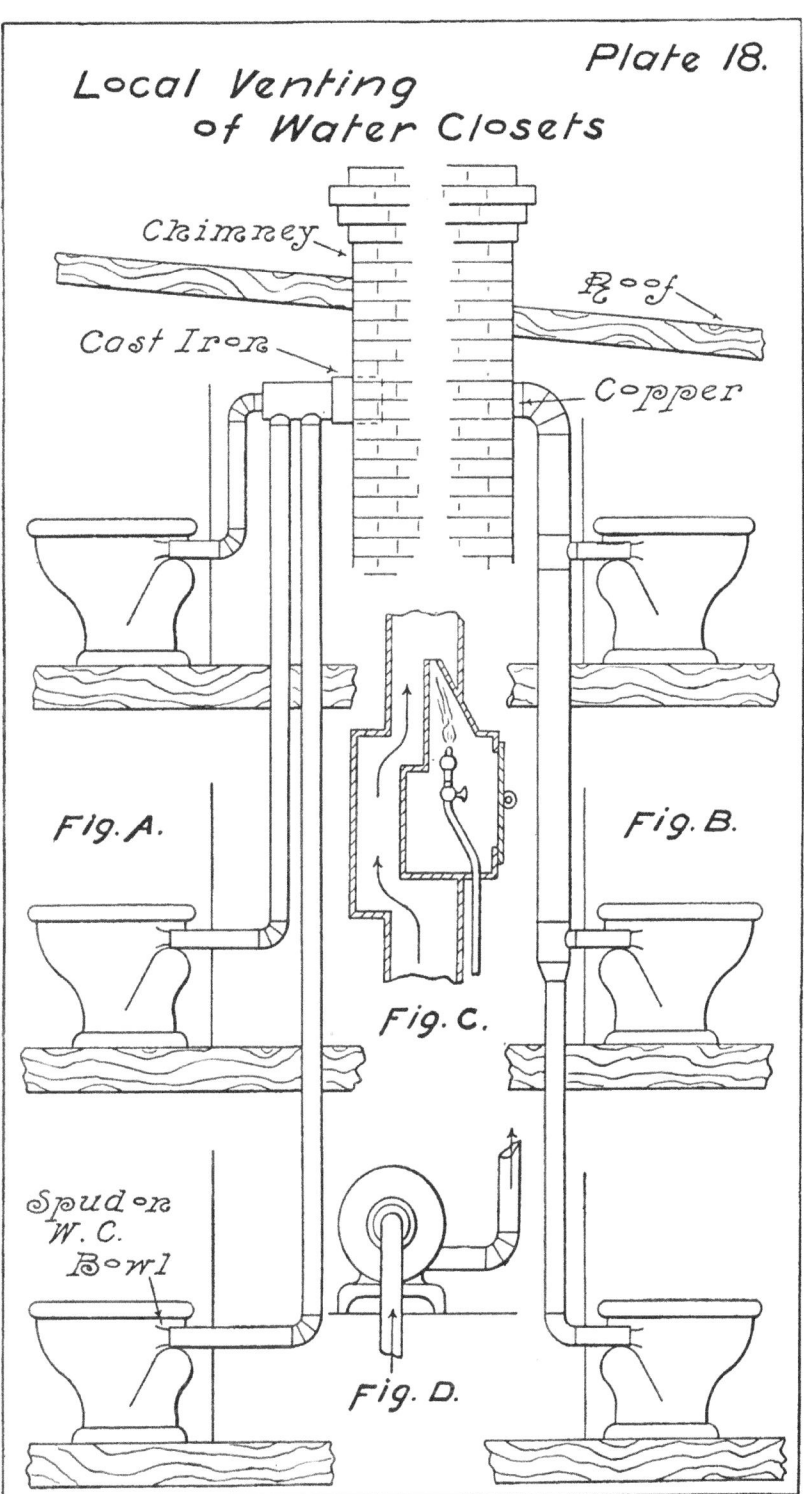

LOCAL VENTING

A LOCAL or surface vent is a vent provided for the purpose of carrying off foul odors incident to the use of the water closet.

This pipe is also applied to the urinal and slop sink to good advantage. The local vent has no relation whatever to the drainage system or to the back-venting system, and may be considered as a measure looking to the comfort of the people making use of the fixtures to which it is applied, rather than as a strictly sanitary measure.

Local ventilation differs in no way from any other form of ventilation.

The system generally in use consists in connecting a pipe from the local vent spud on the water-closet bowl to a heated flue. A good feature of this form of ventilation is that it is accomplished without any expense of operation. As long as a sufficient difference in temperature between the air of the toilet room and the air of the flue exists, excellent results may be maintained by means of this system.

The heated air of the flue being lighter because of being expanded by the heat, rises through the flue, the tendency being to produce a vacuum behind the column of constantly rising hot air. A suction is thus caused on the air in the pipe connecting to the rim of the water closet, and this air is drawn into the flue and forced up and out of it by the current of heated air. The suction is often so strong that small pieces of paper thrown into the water-closet bowl will be forcibly drawn into the local vent pipe and into the flue. The only point against this form of ventilation is the fact that it cannot always be connected to a flue which is heated throughout the year. It is a form of vent which is used principally in dwellings, tenement houses, and other buildings in which the flue to which the local vents are connected is not likely to be heated during the warm months.

On larger work, such as public toilet rooms, other means are used for obtaining ventilation.

However, in most cases where the local vent is applied, no other ventilation would probably be made use of because of the expense of running the mechanical devices used in producing it, and it would therefore seem of much advantage to the inmates to be able to enjoy its comforts during those months when the flues are heated. There is this to be said concerning the months of the year when it might not produce results: the windows at such season of the year are generally wide open, and the need of artificial ventilation not so great as during the period when the local vent does its work thoroughly.

It is certainly true that the toilet room provided with the local vent is far more wholesome than the one which is without it. This vent, sometimes called a seat vent, opens into the water-closet bowl just back of and below the seat, and while the water closet is in use carries off all the odors incident to its use. In addition, when the cover of the closet is down, there is sufficient space for air to enter the bowl and pass into the vent between the seat and the crockery, which are kept apart by means of rubber bumpers on the seat. Therefore the local vent is at all times providing ventilation not only for the water closet itself, but for the entire toilet room.

In order to provide proper ventilation three factors are necessary. There must be an inward passage of fresh air and outward passage of foul air, and a force acting to produce the movement of air which results in the changing of the air. The first factor named is one most likely to be omitted in providing a system of ventilation. Foul air will not pass out of the toilet room unless other air is brought in to take its place. The demand for a supply of fresh air is very largely filled by natural means. Open windows, the entrance of air through window casings, etc., supply in general a considerable amount of fresh air. In addition, it is a fact that air passes through brick walls to a very considerable extent, and through the plastering as well.

Many plumbing ordinances do not make the use of local ventilation compulsory. Even though it is not compulsory to use the local vent in all toilet rooms, there are certain conditions under which it certainly should be used as a sanitary precaution.

In this connection the following requirement is a good one:

All water closets, slop sinks, and urinals should be provided with local vents when located in rooms which receive their light from light shafts, skylights, or courtyards, or when located in compartments not directly connected with the outside atmosphere and sunlight. The application of the local vent may be made more universal by provid-

LOCAL VENTING

ing artificial means of creating a draft when it is impossible to enter a heated flue or a flue which is always heated. Under such conditions an excellent method is to carry the local vents up to an airtight box or compartment heated by means of gas jets, the pipe from which should be carried 3 ft. or more above the roof, ending in an automatic ventilator. Another method of a similar nature is to provide a specially constructed device of the kind shown in Fig. C, Plate 18. This may be inserted in the main vertical line of local vent, and will be found to perform excellent service at only a slight cost for the consumption of gas.

Figs. A and B of Plate 18 show two different systems of local venting. Fig. A gives the separate system of vents, in which the vent from each water closet is carried separately to the point where entrance is made into the heated flue.

The system shown in Fig. B consists of a main vertical line, into which the local vent from each water closet is entered, and is probably more commonly in use than the system first mentioned. The system of separate vents of Fig. A has very decided advantages over the other system.

In the event of the presence in one apartment of a contagious disease, it is possible in the use of the system of Fig. B to communicate the disease to the inmates of other apartments in the building.

This would be especially true of apartments the water closets of which backed up to opposite sides of the same partition. In the same way, in the use of the system of Fig. B, conversation and other sounds may be carried from the toilet room of one apartment into the toilet rooms of other apartments. The separate system of local vents suffers from none of these objectionable features, and although certainly somewhat more expensive to install, the additional outlay should not be considered if the matter of freedom from the evils mentioned is to be secured. The local vent from a single water closet should never be less than 2 in. in diameter. When two, three, or four vents enter a main line of local vent, the main vent should not be less than 3 in. in diameter.

These are the sizes ordinarily used in the local-vent system, and are the sizes generally specified in plumbing ordinances, but are not strictly in accord with the principles that should be followed in securing a perfect system of ventilation.

Providing that a 2-in. pipe is of sufficient size to thoroughly ventilate a single water closet, at the point where the second vent enters, the pipe should be enlarged so that its area shall be equal to the combined area of the two vents which it supplies. When the third vent enters it, the size should be such that its area will be equal to the combined areas of the three branch vents. This gradation in the size of the main local-vent pipe is necessary if each water closet is to receive its full amount of ventilation, that is, if each water closet is to be ventilated as it would be if its individual 2-in. local vent were able to perform its full duties. The area of a 2-in. pipe is 3.14 sq. in.; of two 2-in. pipes, 6.28 sq. in.; and of three 2-in. pipes, 9.42 sq. in. The area of a 3-in. pipe is 7 in., and it will therefore be seen that while a 3-in. pipe is sufficiently large to provide for two 2-in. vents, it is not large enough to provide for a larger number.

The main, in order to properly provide for three fixtures, should be 3½ in. in diameter, and 4 in. for four fixtures. While 2-in. local vents to the several water closets will accomplish good work, single vents of 2½ in. diameter will be found to do better work. When this size is used, it will be found that two water closets will require a main vent 3½ in. in diameter, and three water closets, 4½ in. in diameter. This shows an increase in the main local vent of one inch in diameter for each additional water closet, but after the third fixture has been added the increase in the size of the main need not be so great. Water closets on which the local vent is to be connected should be provided with a spud, which may be on the right or left-hand side, as may be desired. As the local vent has no connection with the drainage system or with the trap-vent system, it is not an essential feature that its joints should be gas tight. For local vents either copper or galvanized sheet-iron pipe is used. Where the vent is exposed to view, and neat-looking work is desired, the copper pipe may be nickel plated. All changes in direction, reduction or increase in size of local vents should be made with long ells, reducers and Ys.

Y-branches and 45-degree bends are preferable to tees, as they make the course of the air currents more easily taken, and thus improve the draft.

The local vent should pitch upward throughout its course, in order to facilitate the work of the vent as much as possible. Heated air naturally rises, and therefore it is always poor practice in running pipes to convey such air in any other way than pitching upward toward the point of delivery. For the sake of convenience local vents are often bent downward to avoid some obstruction, and then carried upward again, a very poor practice when it can by any means be avoided.

Main local vents connected to a heated flue should not have an area exceeding one tenth the area of the flue itself. Local-vent connections with heated flues should always be made at points above the highest opening into the flue. If made below, the foul odors carried in the local-vent pipe may escape into the rooms with which flue openings communicate.

Care should be taken in making the proper chimney connection for local vents. An excellent method is to use copper pipe for connection into the chimney, the local vent lines being connected to the pipe. A cast-iron ferrule may also be used for the purpose, but galvanized sheet iron should not be used, as the soot of the chimney is liable to destroy it after a time.

The chimney connection may be run straight into the chimney, or it may be turned upward, an objection to the latter method being the danger of the collection in the pipe of falling soot.

When so constructed, it is good practice to provide a cleanout at the outer end of the chimney connection, for use in clearing any obstruction.

The pointing downward of the pipe by means of a bend inside the chimney obviates trouble from the soot, but results in checking the draft.

When the chimney connection is run straight into the chimney it should project inside only slightly, as unnecessary obstruction of the flue space is undesirable.

The work which has thus far been described and illustrated relates chiefly to the application of the local vent to residences, dwelling houses, apartment houses of ordinary size, etc.

For larger work more extensive methods are necessary, such as the use of large piping, and the mechanical supply of fresh air and exhausting of foul air.

In the case of public toilet rooms, underground comfort stations, etc., means of ventilation on a large scale are extremely necessary, as the use of such rooms would otherwise result in a public nuisance.

The difference to be noted in the atmosphere of public toilet rooms of hotels, for instance, which are provided with poor light and no ventilation, is great in comparison with the atmosphere of many of our modern, well-appointed toilet rooms of hotels, etc.

It has become a matter of good business to make special effort and outlay in securing proper ventilation for toilet rooms of public buildings, for the public has become educated to the point where they will patronize only those establishments that look after these points.

On the larger work it often becomes necessary to secure greater motive power for ventilating purposes than the heated flue is able to furnish.

For this purpose fans are largely employed, connected as shown in Fig. D. Usually an exhaust fan is used to withdraw the foul air, and another fan to supply fresh air to the fresh-air ducts.

This class of work will be taken up again in connection with the subject of public toilet rooms, as also the local venting of urinals.

Plate XIX

BATH ROOMS

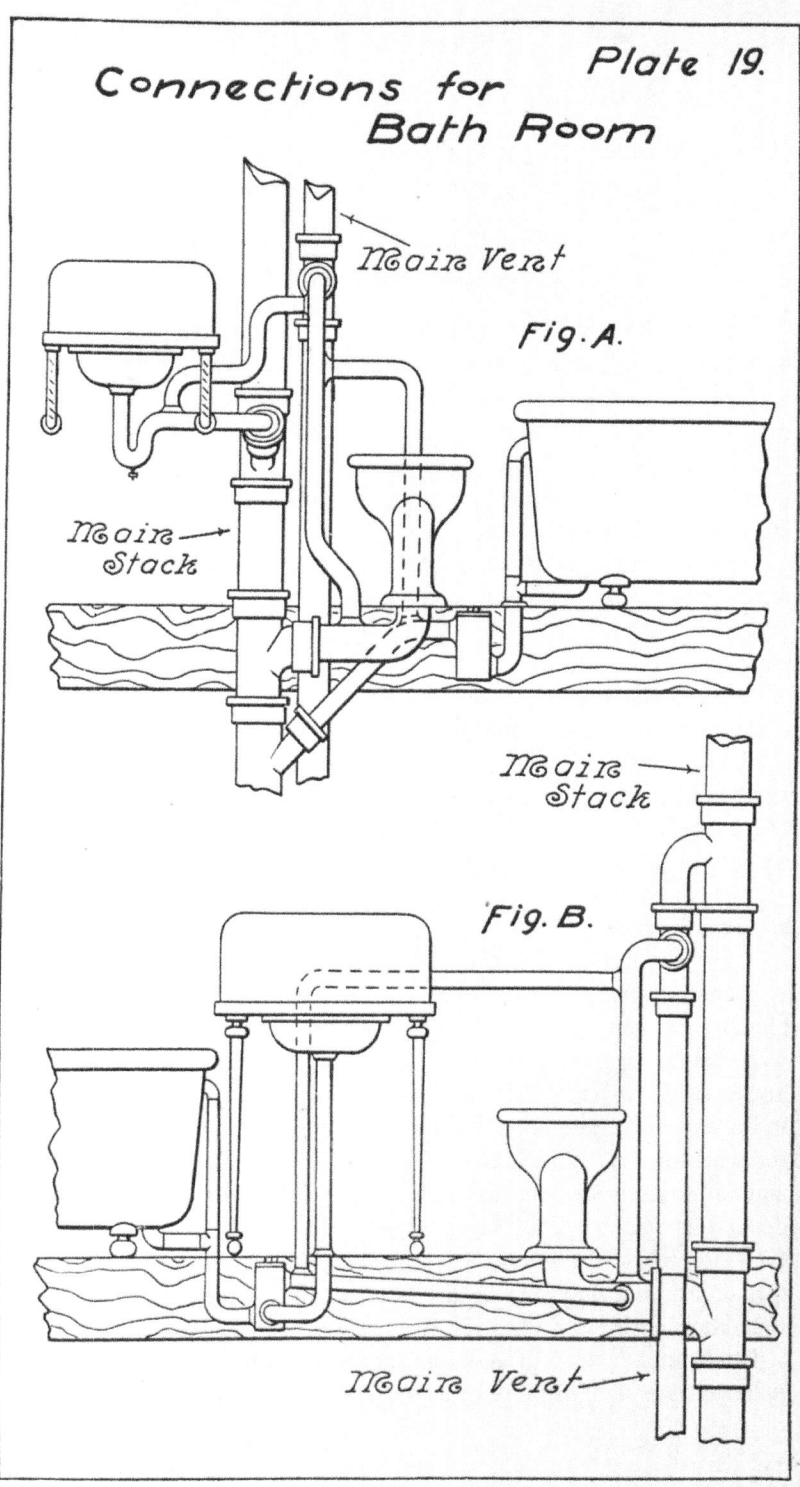

BATH ROOMS

WITH the advent of modern fixtures and modern methods, the bath room of to-day may become, with a comparatively small outlay, a room of great beauty, and when it may be installed regardless of cost, it may become a place of almost marvelous beauty.

No other part of the plumbing system so fully illustrates the many advantages which the open-plumbing system has over the closed or sheathed-in system.

No one attempts to make a comparison of the old-time sheathed-in bath-room work with that of the present day, as far as beauty and artistic effect are concerned. Furthermore, the open system is far more sanitary.

When plumbing fixtures were sheathed in, neither light nor air could circulate about them, with the result that there was constantly a musty, if not foul, odor present. The sheathing absorbed more or less moisture and filth from the careless use of the fixtures, and there was abundant opportunity for the collection of dirt in crevices and corners in the use of sheathing.

The bath room of to-day can indeed be made as clean and wholesome as the parlor.

The connections for the bath room shown in Fig. A of Plate 19 show one point of excellence which is seldom sought for by the plumber or considered by the architect or owner. Each fixture waste has a separate entrance into the soil-pipe line. When fixtures are installed under such conditions, the stoppage of one fixture can in no way affect any other fixture. It will be of interest to compare the work of Fig. A with that of Fig. B. In the latter the lavatory and bath are connected into the same trap below the floor. Without doubt this method often saves expense, but the trap—any trap, in fact—is almost certain to be stopped up at some time, and when this occurs, not only one fixture but two fixtures are affected, both remaining out of use until the trouble is repaired, and thus causing a double annoyance. In addition, the trap which serves two fixtures must become stopped more often than the trap which serves but one.

Furthermore, quite a length of waste must be run from the lavatory before it enters the trap, and the filth of the interior of this trap is bound to give off impure odors into the bath room. To prevent this result as far as possible, each trap should be placed as close to its fixture as circumstances will allow.

The work of Fig. A is free from these troubles, which arise from not entering each waste separately into the stack.

There is another serious objection to be found with the work shown in Fig. B.

The waste after leaving the drum trap, instead of being connected into a Y-branch on the soil-pipe line, is connected into the horizontal arm of the lead bend. Now, if a stoppage occurs in the lead bend, every fixture in the bath room is immediately put out of use, and the waste under these conditions often sets back into the bath tub and water closet. A less number of fittings, and doubtless less labor, is necessary in constructing such work, but if troubles of the nature mentioned do not sometimes occur, it is simply a matter of good fortune.

Usually a slight additional outlay would have made such evils unnecessary. The wiping of the waste into the lead bend is also accompanied by the liability that sharp points of solder have run through inside the bend, forming projections against which paper and other material may catch and form the starting point of a stoppage. The only favorable thing about this lead-bend connection is that in the present instance it is made on the horizontal arm rather than into the heel of the bend, where the connection would be much more likely to be followed by trouble.

It is a fact that many cities operating under strict plumbing ordinances, and maintaining a high standard of plumbing construction, allow both the lead-bend waste connection and the use of a single trap to serve the lavatory and bath. It is also strange that certain cities will allow the kitchen sink and laundry tubs to be served by a single trap, and that occasionally one of these connections is allowed and the other prohibited.

It must be acknowledged that the plumber is often at fault in allowing such connections to be made. However, it must also be stated that it is often almost impossible to gain a separate entrance for each of the three fixtures, owing to lack of working space, location of fixtures, shape and size of the room, etc.

BATH ROOMS

Many times a separate entrance can be provided for the lavatory, if located near the stack, by running the waste back to the wall and using a half-S trap, as shown in Fig. A, the waste fitting coming so much above the other fittings as not to interfere in any way with the rest of the connections.

The architect could, in a great many cases, arrange his work to a great deal better advantage than he usually does.

For instance, the fixtures, with a little study, may be located in such a way that the advantages just mentioned may be obtained. The shape and location of the bath room, the location of pipes, etc., may usually be worked out so that the plumbing may be installed to the best possible advantage. It is not the good fortune of the plumber often to work from plans which show that the architect has given much consideration to, or has much knowledge of, the requirements of the plumbing system.

The plumber often finds, for instance, that in order to run the soil pipe as shown in the plans, an offset on the vertical line must be used, which is always detrimental. He also finds, especially in bathroom work, that he must cut into floor timbers and into uprights in order to conceal his work, and indeed, often cut through timbers and make use of a header to support it; whereas, if the architect knew the requirements and put this knowledge into his work, many of these difficulties might easily be avoided.

The vertical soil piping may sometimes be run in a dark closet adjacent to the bath room, but more often must be run inside a narrow partition, or exposed to view. If it is desired to conceal the soil pipe, it should be boxed in, but the front boarding should be put up with screws, in order that it may be easily and quickly taken down when repairs or changes are necessary on the piping. Unless this provision is made, lathing and plastering must be cut out.

Plate XX

BATH ROOMS

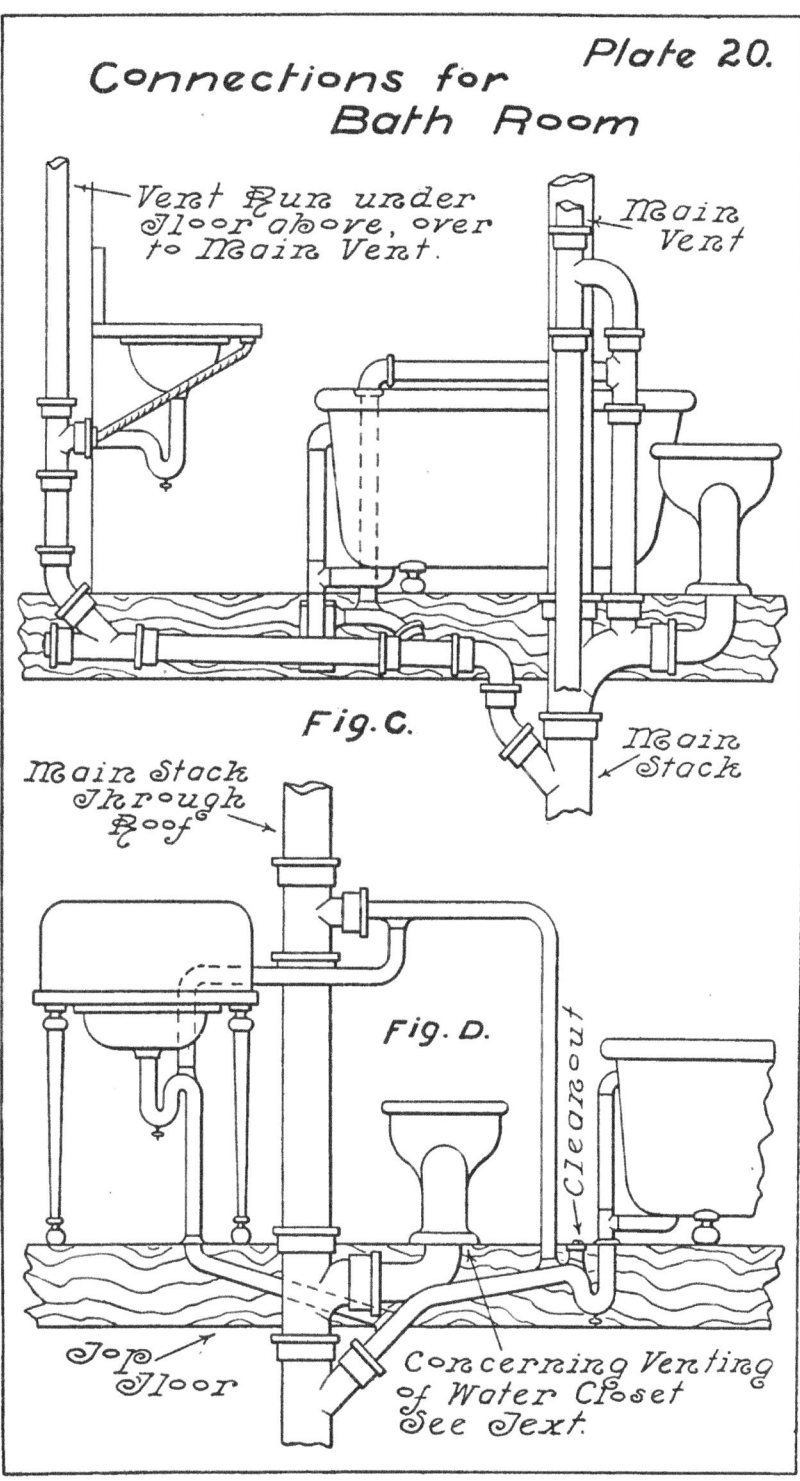

BATH ROOMS

IT will be observed that all the waste and vent connections of the bath-room work shown in Fig. C of Plate 20 are of either wrought or cast iron, with the exception of traps, their short connections, and the lead bend. This is the style of construction that is rapidly displacing lead work. This change in plumbing construction is without doubt as it should be. To be sure, the skill of the expert lead worker is no longer required to any great extent on a large part of the present-day construction work, but the workman of to-day must have a far greater knowledge of physics, hydraulics, and many other subjects which concerned the old lead worker but little.

Whenever a fixture is located at a greater distance than 6 ft. from its stack, it should not have a lead waste. The chief reason for this is that long lines of lead pipe are very liable to sag, thereby causing traps to be formed on the waste pipe.

The lavatory in Fig. C being more than 6 ft. from its stack, a line of cast-iron pipe is run to it, and as the fixture is located on the opposite side of the room from the stack, the vent is carried up to the floor above, and then run over to the main line of vent, a course much preferable to any attempt to run the vent around the sides of the room.

The latter course would often be difficult, as it would generally be necessary to expose the vent to view, and to run it above the height of the fixture, detracting much from the appearance of the bath room. If obliged to run the vent about the sides of the room, it would be necessary to use nickel-plated brass pipe in order to obtain a good-looking piece of work. The vent of the lavatory is known as a continuous vent, and above the waste fitting should be run of wrought-iron pipe.

Separate entrance for the bath waste is obtained into the cast-iron waste, and the cleanout in the end of this horizontal line amply protects it in the event of stoppage. The main vent is shown of cast iron, also the vent for the water closet, which is taken from a vented T-Y, while the vent for the bath trap is of wrought iron, and connected to the cast-iron piping by means of a tapped fitting.

Another method of bath-room connections is seen in Fig. D. While separate entrances into the stack are not provided for the bath and lavatory, the connection of the wastes from the two fixtures into one pipe connected to its own waste fitting is much preferable to the method shown in Fig. B, Plate 19. Of course a stoppage might occur between the junction of the two wastes and the Y, but the chances are against it. Therefore there is not so much danger of a stoppage affecting both fixtures. In this work an S-trap is used for the bath, and a cleanout to the floor provided. If such a cleanout is not used, the flooring over the trap should be put down with screws, in order that the trap may be made as accessible as possible in the event of cleaning.

Fig. D shows a bath room under conditions often to be found, that is, there are no fixtures wasting into the same stack, either above or below the bath room.

Under such conditions no main vent line is required, the fixture vents being connected directly into the stack above the highest fixture, and receiving their air supply through the roof extension of the stack. That part of the stack above the entrance of the highest fixture waste is called the soil vent in the case of a soil stack, and a waste vent in the case of a waste stack.

In the present instance, there being no fixtures either above or below the bath room, there are no conditions present which might cause the siphonage of the water-closet trap, and there is consequently no necessity of venting it, particularly as it is located on the top floor, close to the roof connection. Under these conditions the only reason for venting a water closet would be that the fixture was located at a considerable distance from the stack, in which case venting might be desirable. The question may arise as to the necessity of venting the other fixtures of Fig. D. In the case of these two fixtures conditions are somewhat different, for the water-closet waste enters the stack above the entrance of the waste from the bath and lavatory, and is of sufficient volume to make the possibility of siphonage of these fixture traps strong enough to demand venting, especially as there is an additional danger that the waste from either the bath or lavatory may exert siphonic influence on the other. If, however, the lavatory entered the stack above the entrance of the water closet, through a half-S trap, there would usually be little danger of the siphonage of its trap, and consequently small necessity for venting it.

In the several illustrations of bath rooms shown in Plates 19, 20, 21, and 22, no other fixtures than the three common fixtures, water closet, bath, and lavatory, are shown.

In the modern, well-appointed bath rooms to be found in many up-to-date residences of the wealthy, however, many other fixtures and devices for the comfort of the household are to be found. Many of these bath rooms contain as many as six or eight different plumbing fixtures. Among these additional fixtures may be named the foot bath, sitz bath, child's bath, shower bath, and bidet. The use of two lavatories is occasionally noticed, the pedestal lavatory of porcelain making an excellent appearance.

In addition to the above fixtures, the use of shower baths in connection with the bath tub, and showers in connection with the lavatory, is much in vogue.

Mirrors over the lavatories, porcelain stools, bath seats, and the various nickel soap dishes, sponge holders, etc., also add much to the general style of the bath room.

Nearly all high-grade bath rooms are now furnished with porcelain fixtures, including the lavatory, a very small amount of marble now being used for lavatory work, as compared with its use a few years ago. The porcelain-lined bath so generally used in bath rooms well appointed, but not of the most expensive type, is generally painted some dull color, leaving it to be finished and decorated in the prevailing style of the room.

For the bath room, nothing neater can be devised than pure white, and, if decoration is desired, a narrow gilt band may be used.

Tiling is used extensively in up-to-date bath-room work, including floor, walls, and ceiling.

When the tiling does not cover the entire interior of the room, it is generally carried up on the walls to a distance of four to six feet from the floor, and capped with a half round or O. G. molding.

A very neat innovation in bath tubs is the porcelain or porcelain-lined tub, sheathed on its exposed sides with tiling to conform to the prevailing style of the room.

Plate XXI

BATH ROOMS

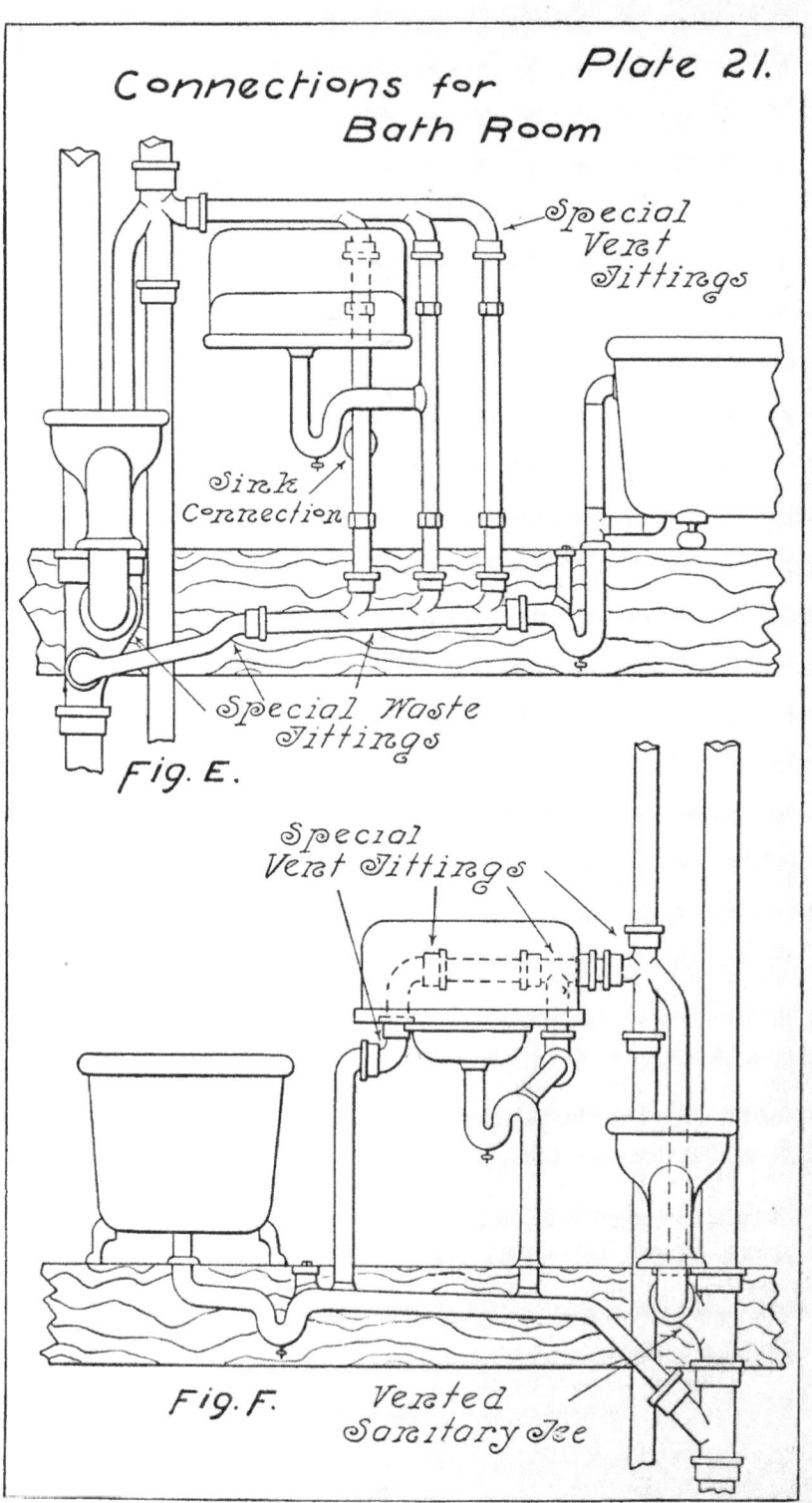

BATH ROOMS

THE bath-room connections shown in Figs. E and F, Plate 21, are designed to show the use of various special waste and vent fittings, which are possibly more useful in bath-room work than on any other part of the plumbing system.

The water-closet waste fitting of Fig. F is along the same line as the vented T-Y of Fig. C, Plate 20, but is a better fitting for bathroom work, inasmuch as the branch is taken spirally into the side of the fitting, allowing the fixture to set closer to the wall. The water closet should set as close to the wall as practicable, as it is less in the way, and less liable to damage.

The water closet is vented from a hub on the waste fitting.

The waste fitting of the water closet of Fig. E is of similar pattern, with a special hub for receiving the waste of other fixtures. The work of Fig. E is almost entirely of iron pipe.

The triple fittings on the waste and vent lines are made in various lengths and with different numbers of openings. By the use of these fittings the vents are so connected to the several traps that there is little danger of stoppage of the vent openings.

The fitting shown on the main vent line of Fig. E is a very useful one, and may be obtained with a short or long arm, with or without the additional vent hub. In the construction of many houses the plumbing is centralized so that the bath room and the kitchen sink may be served by the same stack. This custom is a common one, and is recognized by the triple fittings, which have the third hub for the use of the kitchen sink. It may also be used for a lavatory in a room adjacent to the bath room.

The work of Fig. F is not entirely of iron or made up entirely of special fittings, but is intended to show the use of some of these special fittings on ordinary work. The special fittings shown are very few in number compared to the total number of these fittings. They may be procured for almost any special purpose, or to fit into almost any place.

These fittings are usually more expensive than ordinary fittings, but the practiced eye will easily see how useful they are, and how much work they save, for instance, in the matter of wiped and caulked joints, which are comparatively few, considering the amount of work covered.

The use of special fittings accomplishes two things: it reduces the number of caulked and wiped joints, and it generally allows the use of continuous vents, two very important features.

Too much attention cannot be given to the lighting and ventilating of the bath room. The local vent, which is described under Plate 18, is of very great value in maintaining wholesome conditions in the bath room, as it not only ventilates the water closet while in use, but ventilates the entire room at all times.

In addition to getting rid of the foul air, a good supply of fresh air should be furnished the bath room.

Exterior lighting should always be provided. This may always be done in detached buildings, but in buildings that are built close up to the walls of other buildings it is often a difficult matter. In the bath or toilet room receiving light from a light shaft, the air is usually lifeless and musty, and in such cases all precautions possible in the matter of ventilation should be taken, and the room and fixtures kept as clean and wholesome as possible. The existence of disagreeable odors in the bath room may often be traced to a source over which the plumber has no control, as it is as likely to occur in the plumbing system which is absolutely perfect as in the poorly constructed system.

This trouble sometimes arises from the use of highly scented toilet soaps, toilet water, etc., which are much in use in the private bath room, and but seldom used in public toilet rooms.

When mixed with grease, and waste filled with impurities emanating from the skin, these strong perfumes give rise to heavy, nauseous odors, which are extremely offensive and which are often mistaken for escaping sewer gas. Most of the trouble comes from the slime in the traps and waste connections, but a source which is not often taken into account is the patent overflow of the lavatory bowl. The fact that this is a prolific source for the same trouble, makes it apparent that the same evil often arises in the use of the private lavatory in sleeping rooms, where the presence of foul odors is especially unhealthful.

To remedy this evil, the strainers should be removed from the bath tub and lavatory bowl, and the waste connections and traps thoroughly cleaned out with potash or washing soda and boiling water. As to cleaning out the overflow, the bowl should be taken down and the overflow washed out in the same way. The traps and waste connections may be kept clean by occasionally using the alkali in the bath tub and lavatory, and turning on the hot water.

If this trouble should occur in the bath room of Fig. B, Plate 19, it will be seen that the long, unprotected lavatory waste would be the particular point to look to, as there is a large amount of surface here, which must constantly emit odors into the room. This point further emphasizes the fact that each fixture should have its own individual trap, located as close as possible to the fixture.

A point which may properly be mentioned in connection with bath-room work relates to the painting of exposed soil piping.

When soil pipe is exposed in the bath room it is unsightly at best, and to give it the best possible appearance it should be painted in the prevailing color of the room.

It is not sufficient to cover it with several coats of paint, as the tar will soon strike through and show.

The paint should not be applied until several coats of shellac, such as is used by pattern makers, are applied. The shellac will prevent the tar from striking through.

Another point which may be of value is in relation to the cleaning of marble and porcelain, which often become soiled with rust, oil, and other stains, which may generally be removed by a mixture of 2 parts of soda, 1 of pumice, and 1 of powdered chalk or whiting. These materials should be sifted and water added to form a paste, which should be applied to the soiled surface and allowed to remain for a number of hours, then washed off with soap and water.

Plate XXII

BATH ROOMS

Plate 22.

Connections for Bath Room

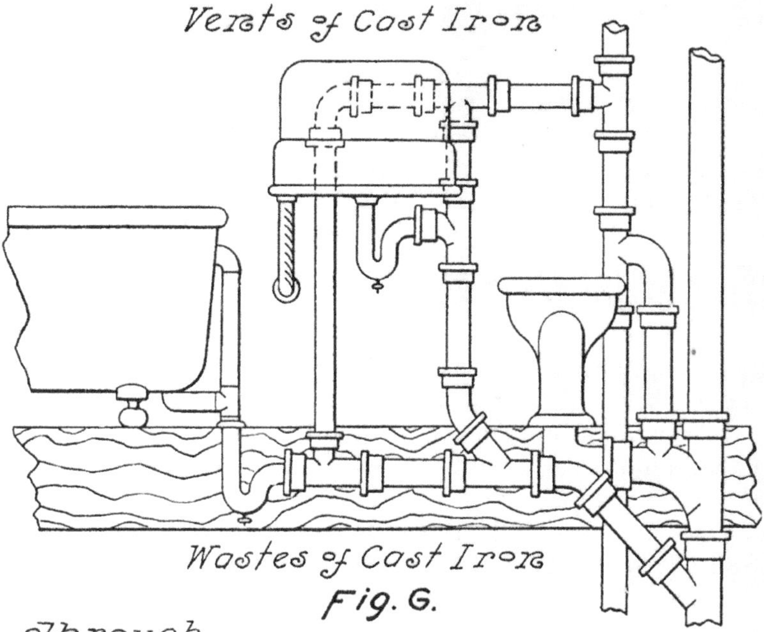

Vents of Cast Iron

Wastes of Cast Iron

Fig. G.

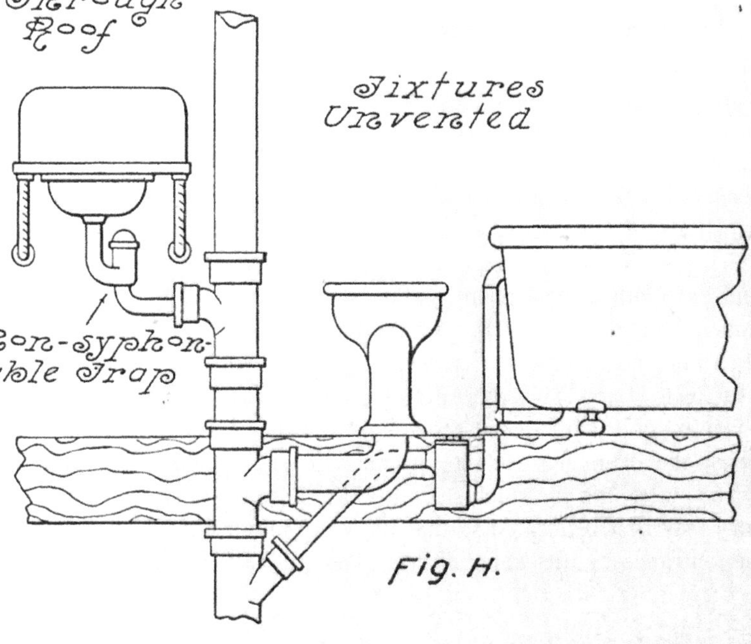

Through Roof

Non-syphonable Trap

Fixtures Unvented

Fig. H.

BATH ROOMS

A SPECIAL feature of the bath room of Fig. G, Plate 22, is that, with the exception of the water-closet bend, no part of the work is of lead.

Fig. C, Plate 20, and Fig. E, Plate 21, also show bath-room connections which are of similar general construction, but in which special and expensive fittings are used.

The work in Fig. G, it will be noted, is performed by the use of common fittings carried in stock by all dealers. The concealed work may be of either wrought or cast iron.

If of wrought iron, the pipe should be galvanized. The traps for the bath and lavatory should be of brass. Another feature of this work is that each trap is served by a continuous vent. Several references have been made to continuous venting, a full description of which is to be found under Plates 26, 27, and 28.

In Fig. H is shown a bath room the fixtures of which are unvented.

While work of this kind is not allowed in many of our large towns and cities, it may be, and is used to a large extent in country districts and in the smaller towns.

If the work is installed in the right manner, it may usually be made quite safe, even though unvented. In the first place, the bath room is usually on the upper floor and close to the roof pipe, features which are of advantage, as the supply of air through the soil vent is quick and direct. There is practically no danger that the lavatory and bath will exert siphonic influence on the water-closet trap, but under the right conditions the flushing of the water closet may exert such influence on them. In the case of the bath tub, it is necessary usually to carry its waste into the stack below the lead bend. In order to give all possible protection to this fixture, its trap should be of the drum pattern or of some non-siphonable make, and the waste outlet into the stack should be as short as possible. The lavatory may best be located so that its waste may enter the stack above the entrance of the water closet. Here it receives the most direct supply of air through the soil vent, and if a non-siphonable trap is used there will be practically no danger from siphonage.

The same general precautions should be taken with other plumbing fixtures of the house. On an unvented system it is poor policy to locate a fixture in the cellar, close to the foot of a stack, and wasting into the horizontal line, as the liability of siphonage under such conditions is fully as great as at any other point in the system.

Before leaving the subject of bath rooms, it will be of interest to many readers, no doubt, to study the fixtures and trimmings for an up-to-date, high-grade bath room.

The water closet should be of the siphon-jet style, and of porcelain, and should have nickel-plated flush and supply pipes, with flush tank finished in the natural wood, or enameled to suit the finish and decorations of the room. The low tank is at the present time more popular than the high tank, and the flush valve, doing away entirely with the flush tank, bids fair to become more popular than either.

The flush valve may be exposed to view or concealed in the wall behind the water closet.

The bath tub should be of porcelain, or at least porcelain lined, and should not be less than 5 or 5½ ft. in length, and provided with nickel-plated waste and supply fittings. The bath may be furnished with a shower and shower curtain.

There is a wide choice in the selection of the bath. The effect of the solid porcelain tub is massive, especially if its base rests upon the floor instead of upon legs. The only decoration that the bath should have is a narrow plain band or other decoration a short distance below the rim.

In lavatories, also, there is a wide range. Porcelain is preferable for fine work, and the one-piece lavatory of enameled cast iron comes next.

If of porcelain, it should be furnished with porcelain legs and back. A very artistic fixture is the oval pedestal lavatory, which is massive and looks well with a heavy bath. The lavatory is much improved with a mirror following in its shape the general style of the lavatory. Nickel-plated legs or brackets may support the lavatory, but do not appear to such advantage as the white porcelain legs. White is by all means the color for the bath room. It is cool and clean in appearance, and obliges frequent attention, as any dust or dirt that gathers shows plainly.

BATH ROOMS

Some fine bath rooms are now provided with fixtures which are supplied with water in such a way that no metal shows in connection with any of the exposed plumbing, the entire effect being of white.

The shower should be provided with a porcelain or porcelain-lined receptor resting on the floor, and nickel-plated combination needle and shower bath, with shower curtain.

The bidet is not in common use, but is to be found in some of the best-appointed bath rooms. It should correspond in style and decorations to the water closet.

The foot and sitz baths should correspond closely in their material, style, and decoration to the bath tub. The best manufacturers now carry the same style, design, and decoration right through the line of bath-room fixtures, so that there is no reason why all the fittings of the bath room should not be in keeping.

Plate XXIII

POOR PRACTICES IN PLUMBING CONSTRUCTION

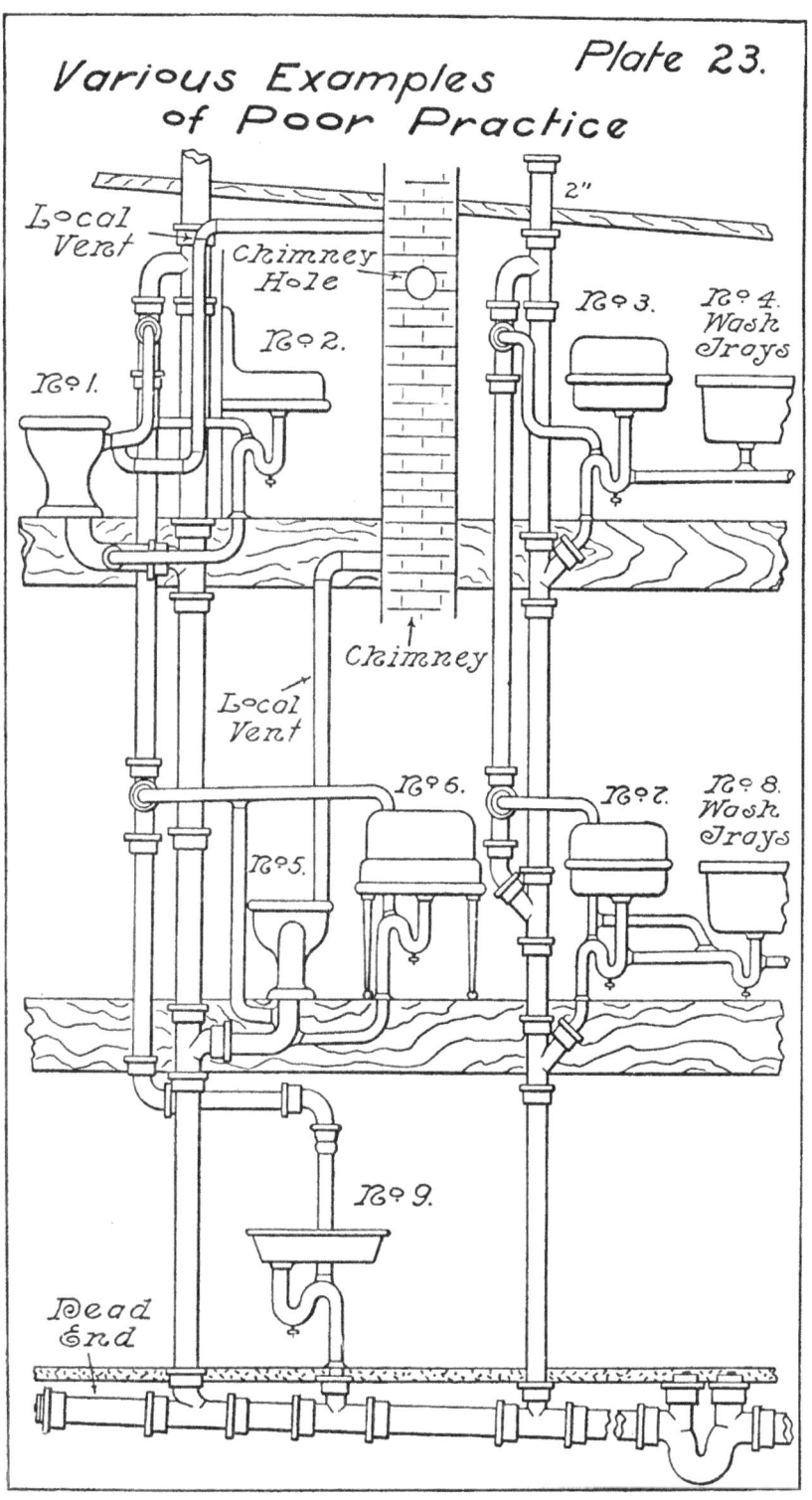

POOR PRACTICES IN PLUMBING CONSTRUCTION

In order that the plumbing system may be absolutely safe, countless points of apparently small importance must be observed. The difference between a strictly high-class plumbing system and one of medium or poor quality is to be found largely in the observance or non-observance of the small points. In Plate 23 are to be seen some of the small points which are often disregarded. The instances of error to be seen in the illustration are not novel or to be rarely seen, but are constantly being made by mechanics who should or do know better. These errors are often made in ignorance, and it must be admitted that they are also often made, especially on contract work, in order that the work may be made to pay bigger profits.

Next to the main trap, a fresh-air inlet should have been provided, as the main trap should never be without it. If the nearest waste stack is near enough to the main trap, it would relieve any air lock, but is in no sense a fresh-air inlet, so long as waste enters it.

The two stacks enter the house drain through tee fittings, whereas the connection should always be made with a Y-branch and eighth bend.

Fixture No. 9 should waste into a Y.

Tees should be used on no part of the drainage system, and T-Ys only on vertical lines.

The continuation of the house drain beyond the soil stack forms a dead end. The main vent for the soil stack should reënter the stack below the T-Y on the first floor, and a trap vent from fixture No. 9 run over into it. The ending of this main vent in the vent of No. 9 allows no opportunity for collections of scale and rust to drain out of the main vent.

The 2-in. waste stack should have been increased to 4 in. before passing through the roof. No stack of less size than 4 in. should pass through the roof.

Taking up the fixtures in consecutive order, according to their numbers, the trap vent of No. 1 should be taken from the lead bend, and not from the vent horn of the closet bowl, and the local vent from the same fixture should not drop after leaving the closet, but should pitch upward throughout its course. No. 2 should have separate entrance into the stack through a Y-branch, instead of being connected into the lead bend, the proper course allowing a shorter and more direct connection. The vent from No. 2 should have entered the vent from No. 1 above the top of No. 2. As it is now connected, if a stoppage occurs on the waste of No. 2, waste from this fixture will run off through its vent, thence through the vent of No. 1, and discharge into No. 1.

Fixtures No. 3 and No. 4 should be trapped and vented independently, and be entered separately into the stack, or into the openings of a Y caulked into the Y already in use.

The horizontal vent from Nos. 5 and 6 pitches in the wrong direction. Vent pipes should always pitch upward after leaving the trap. The vent connection of No. 5 should have been made into the horizontal arm of the bend rather than into the vertical arm, as the latter presents greater opportunity for the collection of refuse in the opening of the vent into the bend.

The waste from No. 6 should have a separate entrance into the stack, but if it must be connected into the lead bend it should be connected into the upper part of the horizontal arm, as the opening of the waste into the heel of the bend is in such a position that soil and other refuse matter may drop directly into it in passing through the bend.

The local vent from No. 5 enters the chimney at the second floor, and at a point below the highest opening into the chimney. When all local vents are not entered above the highest chimney opening there is danger that foul odors carried in the vent may enter rooms into which openings in the chimney communicate. Fixtures No. 7 and No. 8 are double trapped. The waste from No. 8 should be disconnected from the trap of No. 7, and entered separately into the stack, or at least connected to the waste from No. 7 close to the point at which it enters the stack. Numerous errors might be mentioned which do not appear on Plate 23. Some of these errors are the following. Earthenware house sewers are sometimes continued inside the foundation wall, and the house drain connected to it by means of a cement joint.

Cleanouts are occasionally used which depend for a tight joint upon the use of a ring of putty.

POOR PRACTICES IN PLUMBING CONSTRUCTION 157

Drainage is allowed to enter the fresh-air inlet, and the latter is often constructed of too small pipe.

By-passes are a very common form of error, and this particular error often occurs in the connection of the bath overflow to the outlet side of the bath trap, the proper connection being into the inlet to the trap. When thus connected the trap is practically short-circuited, gases and odors passing from the waste pipe through the overflow and out into the room. In the absence of the main trap, a by-pass means that direct communication exists between the house and the sewer. Much poor work is to be found in connection with refrigerator work. Refrigerators are sometimes found connected directly into the drainage system without a trap, and very often found connected directly into the drainage system through a trap, which is not much better than the first-named connection. Local vents may be found connected into main back-vent lines, and trap vents into flues. The blind vent is a deception also often practiced. It consists in running the trap vent back to the wall, or through the wall, and plugging the end, no connection being made into the main vent. This is not so bad in its results as the blind vent with an open end, which is also to be found, and through which direct communication with the sewer exists. The blind vent has every appearance of being honest work, and is no more than open fraud. It will be seen, then, that the opportunities for error are great, and it behooves the owner and inmate of the house to know right from wrong in plumbing construction.

The instances of poor practice in plumbing construction to be noted in Plate 23 are self-evident to the person who has a knowledge of the subject of plumbing. They are errors which the plumbing inspector should not pass over. At the same time there is not an error to be found on this plate which is of an exaggerated nature, and which does not often appear.

Indeed, some of the practices which have been criticised as errors are not looked upon, under some plumbing ordinances, as in any way out of character.

For instance, the practice of connecting the waste from the lavatory, as in fixture No. 2, into the lead bend, is a method allowed in many cities which boast of strict plumbing ordinances.

Poor practices are not alone confined to the methods of making connections, but appear in various other ways.

The use of inferior material is a very common matter, and is to be met in connection with plumbing construction at almost every point.

The use of light cast-iron soil pipe instead of extra-heavy pipe is an instance, as also the use of very light weights of lead pipe, lead traps, bends, etc.

The use of light lead has reached such a point that much of that used on cheap work is entirely unfit for its purpose, inasmuch as it is so thin that it can withstand very little rough usage. In this connection it may be stated that one of the advantages in the rapid displacing of lead pipe, traps, etc., is the fact that stiffer and more durable materials are taking the place of lead.

Many other instances might be named of the use of inferior materials, such as cheaply constructed brass work of poor metal, tanks lined with metal of the thinnest quality, fixtures full of imperfections, etc.

These results have been reached very largely owing to the keen competition of recent years.

It is true that plumbing construction can be made possibly more deceptive than any other branch of building construction. One reason for this is the fact that such a large part of the work is concealed. Frequently, to judge from the neat appearance of fixtures, with their bright nickel work, the plumbing system must be an excellent one, whereas in reality it may be of the poorest description, for the concealed work, which is generally the most important from a sanitary standpoint, may be installed in any but a sanitary manner.

Plate XXIV

"ROUGHING-IN"—USE OF CLEANOUTS

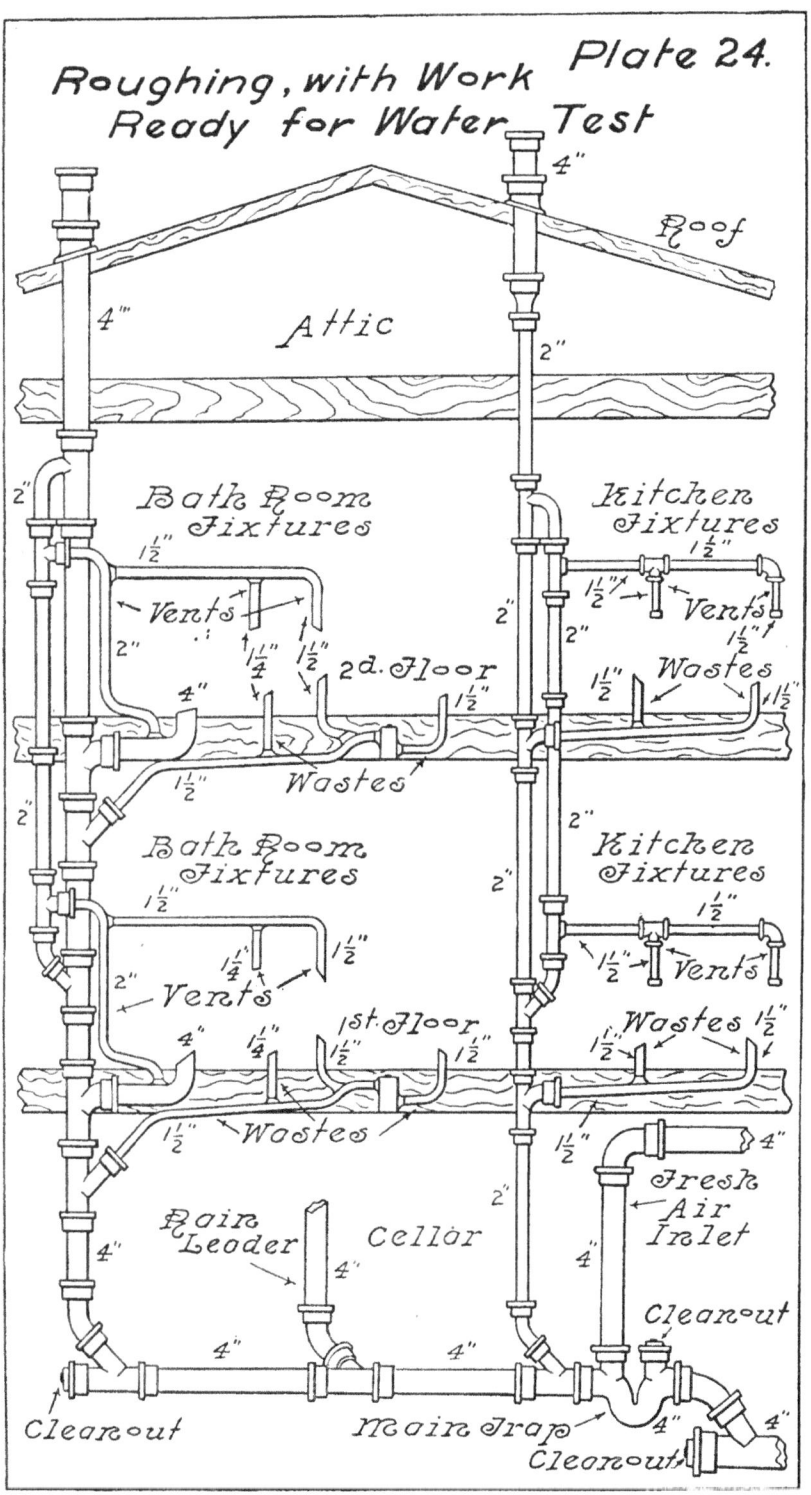

"ROUGHING-IN"

That part of the work on the plumbing system known as the "roughing-in" is shown in Plate 24.

As will be noted, when the work has progressed to this point, all soil piping has been run, from a point 10 ft. outside the foundation, through the cellar, and all stacks run up through the roof, their vent stacks also run and completed, all waste fittings and vent fittings on mains inserted, and all branch fixture wastes and vents completed as far as possible. In the roughing, the fresh-air inlet is included, all cleanouts on the soil piping, rain leaders if they are to enter the drainage system inside the cellar, all floor and yard drains, etc.

In fact, when the roughing is complete, little should remain to be done before the fixtures are set in place. The water test is generally applied to the plumbing at this point. This, when properly applied, is a most thorough test, and a test which cannot be applied after the walls are plastered.

Therefore, in the roughing, just as much of the work should be included as possible, in order that as much of the piping and as many of the joints as possible may be tested with hydraulic pressure.

Therefore, all fixture wastes and vents should be completed if practicable, or brought as near completion as possible.

The vent for the water closet may almost always be completed, unless nickel is to be used. Traps that are located under floors may usually be placed in position, inlet connections made as far as possible, and the outlet into the stack completed. All ferrule connections, whether on the vent or on the drainage system, should be made before the roughing can be considered complete. It will be noted that sizes for all pipes in the plumbing system of Fig. 24 are given, these sizes corresponding to the sizes demanded in most plumbing ordinances.

In the case of the kitchen sink, however, some ordinances now require a 2-in. waste instead of $1\frac{1}{2}$ in., a requirement which is in the line of good practice.

When the fixture wastes are roughed in, great care should be taken that the long runs of lead pipe beneath floors are properly supported.

If not supported, the lead pipe is very sure to sag, thus forming traps in the waste. The best method is to support straight runs of lead waste on boards, properly secured.

Fixture wastes of greater length than 6 ft. should always be run of more rigid material than lead, either of cast or galvanized wrought iron or of brass.

As elsewhere noted, nothing but coated cast-iron pipe should ever be used underground, as the action of the moisture of the earth is very harmful to wrought-iron or steel pipe, and also to unprotected cast-iron pipe. There is really no necessity for coating cast-iron pipe that is not buried, with tar or asphaltum, for, excepting when underground, there is rarely any harmful action that takes place.

CLEANOUTS

The connection shown on the sewer side of the main trap in Plate 24 is an excellent one, and is a practice now demanded wherever possible by many plumbing ordinances.

The chief value of such a connection is that it allows a cleanout to be used in the end of the Y-branch into which the main trap discharges.

This cleanout controls the straight run of house drain into the house sewer, and a considerable length of the latter, while the cleanout at the opposite end of the house drain controls that section of the drain, and the two cleanouts on the main trap complete the entire control of the house drain and house sewer.

Nothing can add more to the worth of the plumbing system than the intelligent and liberal use of cleanouts. The money invested in cleanouts is a good investment always, for their use often saves not only much annoyance, but avoids the breaking into pipes to remove stoppages.

Every trap on the plumbing system, with the exception of water-closet traps and other traps combined in the fixture itself, should be provided with a cleanout. All cleanout screws should be of brass. Cleanouts for use on soil piping are of two kinds, entirely of brass or having the body of iron and the screw of brass.

CLEANOUTS

The latter is known as the iron-body cleanout. The threaded parts of cleanouts should have at least six threads, tapered, and of iron-pipe size. Cleanouts should be of the full size of the pipe or trap which they serve, up to a diameter of 5 in., and not less than 5 in. in size for larger traps.

Cleanouts should always be used in the ends of Ys into which vertical stacks connect, as shown in Fig. E, Plate 14, and in the ends of all horizontal branches of soil or waste pipes. Quarter bends being used on rain leaders, cleanouts used on their traps must be depended upon for cleaning purposes.

A cleanout should be used at each change in direction of horizontal piping. By this means each run of piping is fully controlled in the event of stoppage.

The cleanouts thus far mentioned are known as end cleanouts.

In long runs of horizontal waste and soil pipe it is often necessary to provide cleanouts at intermediate points. Special cleanout fittings are made for this purpose, into which the cleanout cover screws.

They should be placed not farther than 30 ft. apart, and a more liberal use of them can be made with advantage.

All cleanouts should be made tight with a gasket, and no cleanout depending on the use of putty for a tight joint should be allowed.

All cleanouts in main traps that are underground, or any other cleanout that is underground, should be made accessible by means of depressions in the concrete bottom, and cleanouts outside the walls of the house should be located in accessible manholes.

The gasket generally used on cleanouts is of rubber, and if the gasket has been in use for a considerable length of time, it is almost certain to be destroyed in removing the cleanout cover. If not destroyed, it is probable that it has become so hard and lifeless that, if again used, a tight joint cannot be made. Therefore a new gasket should be used on a cleanout whenever the cover is removed, after having been in use long enough to get into this condition.

Another form of cleanout, not extensively used, however, makes tight by means of a ground joint. The advantage of this cleanout is that it is free from the objectionable features incident to the use of gaskets. The ground joint is also often easier to open than the screw joint.

The foregoing remarks apply only to cleanouts used on the large drainage piping.

There are certain additional facts to be considered also, concerning cleanouts on other parts of the plumbing system.

Whenever brass and galvanized-iron pipe is used for waste purposes, cleanouts should be liberally used at points where a change in direction occurs.

All drum traps located under floors should have their cleanout covers flush with the floor, in order to make them accessible without the removal of flooring. Such cleanout covers may be concealed beneath nickel-plated covers or guards screwed to the floor. The cleanouts of all traps should be on the inlet side of the trap, and submerged wherever possible. Submerged cleanouts show an imperfect joint by leakage, whereas the same imperfection in the case of a cleanout not submerged might remain undetected for an indefinite length of time.

Cleanouts on fixture vents are demanded by the plumbing ordinances of certain cities, but in a vast majority of cases it is probably a practice which has little value. The reason for this is that usually use of the cleanout is by the inmates only, who know so little concerning the purpose of the vent and of the cleanout that it is almost never made use of. When there is a stoppage of the waste it makes itself known at once, but a stoppage of the vent opening is never known, and consequently the remedy, by means of the cleanout, never applied.

Plate XXV

TESTING OF THE PLUMBING SYSTEM THE WATER, AIR, SMOKE, AND PEPPERMINT TESTS

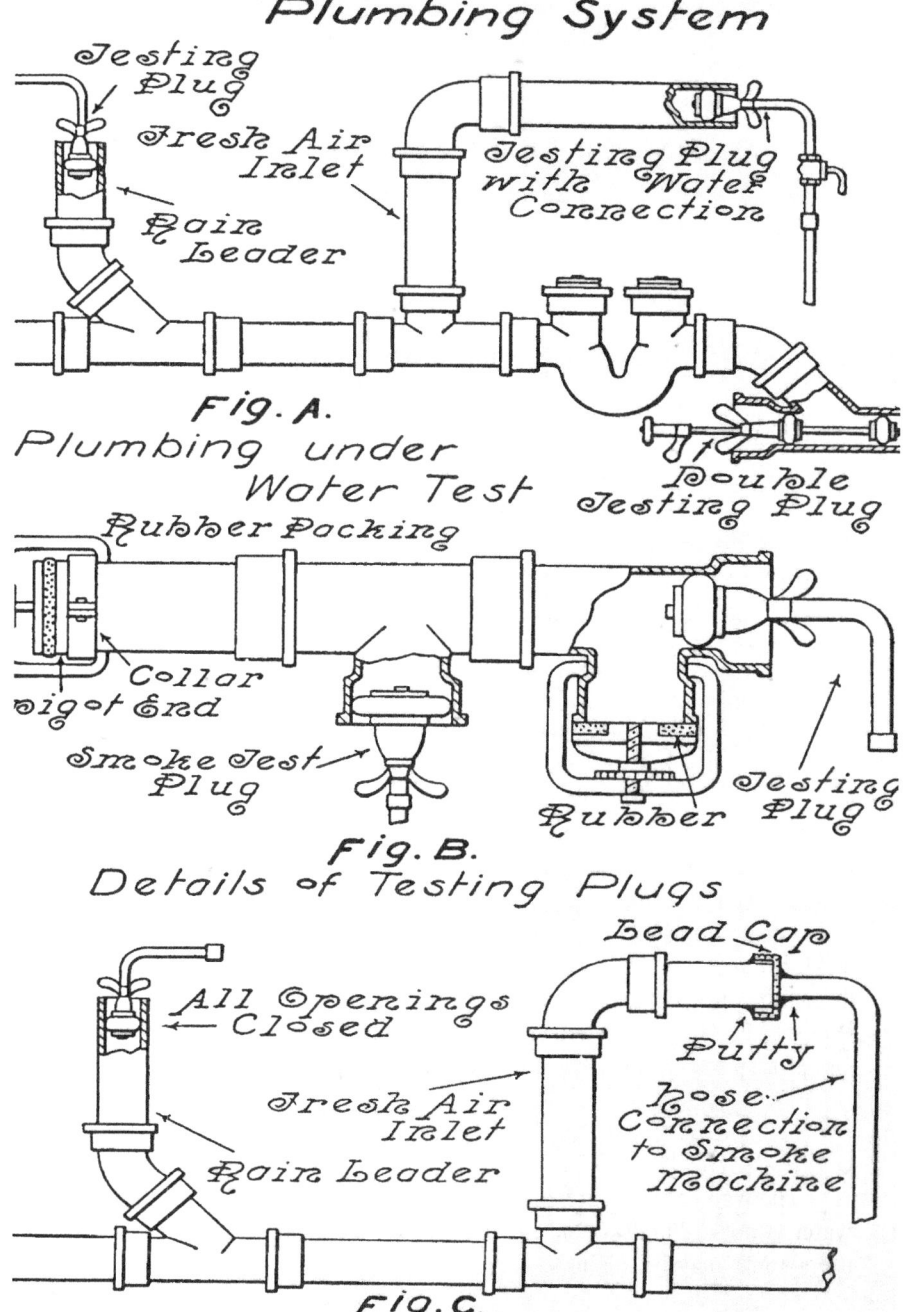

TESTING OF THE PLUMBING SYSTEM

ALL properly arranged plumbing ordinances now demand that two tests shall be applied to each newly constructed plumbing system—one when the roughing has been completed, and the other when the entire plumbing system has been completed and is ready for use. No drainage pipe, vent pipe, or fitting should be concealed in partitions or between floors or buried underground until after the first test has been applied and the work inspected by the proper official.

These tests are for the purpose of ensuring correct work, free from defects arising in construction and manufacture. There are four different methods of testing the plumbing system—the water test, air test, peppermint test, and smoke test. Of these, the water, peppermint, and smoke tests are most commonly used.

The water and air tests are chiefly used as the first test on new work. When it comes to the final test, either the peppermint or smoke test may be applied. Each is thorough when properly applied.

The question as to which is the better test is open to debate, each test having certain advantages and possible disadvantages.

Before the final test is applied, all fixtures should be in position and the system entirely complete, and the traps filled with water.

On old work in residences and other finished and occupied buildings, the water test cannot be applied, owing to the damage that might result. Under these conditions, either the peppermint or smoke test should be used. The testing of old work should be done much oftener than it is, as it is of much value, not only in showing defects in joints and the material for piping and connections, but also in disclosing by-passes and other wrong connections, stoppages, the loss of trap seals, the absence of traps on rain leaders and drains, etc.

THE WATER TEST

The water test is applied to the roughing of all new work, unless water is not at hand or there is danger of its freezing, in which case the air test may be applied.

Plate 24 shows the plumbing system ready for testing. All openings must be closed. Lead bends, traps, and pipes must have their ends soldered, and wrought-iron pipe ends must be capped. The ends of pipes, bends, etc., should be closed when the roughing is completed, without regard to the test, in order to prevent refuse of any kind from entering the system.

Soil-pipe openings should be closed by specially devised stoppers or testing plugs, as shown in the three illustrations of Plate 25.

These openings would include the house-drain outlet, fresh-air inlet, rain leaders, floor drains, etc.

If the stacks do not end above the roof on or near the same level, the shorter stacks should have their open ends plugged.

With the plumbing system thus prepared, water is filled into the system until it overflows from the highest stack onto the roof.

The test is generally made by the plumber, in the presence of the plumbing inspector, and the water is generally required to stand for several hours before being drawn off.

This is for the purpose of exposing leaks which sometimes do not make themselves known for a time.

Defects often do not appear until the water has been standing long enough to thoroughly soak through the oakum. Water may be filled into the system through any opening, the fresh-air inlet often being a convenient point.

Testing plugs are made with a provision allowing water to pass through them, for the purpose of filling the piping. Such a plug, with its connection, is shown in the fresh-air inlet of Fig. A. Several different makes of testing plugs that do good service are now on the market, several forms of which are shown in Fig. B.

The most common form is that shown at the right-hand end. It makes tight by means of the expansion of a heavy rubber ring against the inner surface of the pipe. The ring is expanded between two iron plates brought together by a large hand nut.

Plugs of this description will not generally hold much over 50 lbs. pressure without being blown out.

A very good plug for high pressures is one which clamps around the outside of the hub, making tight by means of a rubber packing forced against the end of the hub. This testing plug is shown in Fig. B.

The same plug may be applied to the spigot end of a pipe by

THE WATER TEST

using a split collar against which the clamp may hold. In Fig. A the use of a double testing plug is shown.

This is a valuable device for the connection shown, and for closing the main-trap outlet.

In using this test, water should be filled into the system slowly, and as fast as defects appear they should be made tight before raising the water higher.

There are two reasons for this. A small leak at a high point may allow water to trickle down the pipe, and thus make it difficult to locate. If the system is quickly filled, a large quantity of water may escape from some large defect before it can be drawn off.

It is sometimes necessary to test certain sections of the system as the work progresses.

In making such tests there should be a column of water at least 10 ft. in height above all parts of the work to be tested.

Very high stacks should be tested in sections of not over 75 ft. in length, as the pressure of water when such a stack is tested entire is very great, and cannot be applied with safety.

To find the pressure that is being exerted at any point on the plumbing system, multiply the vertical distance of this point from the top of the highest stack by .434, the pressure exerted by one foot of water. This will give the pressure in pounds per square inch. Thus, a point 50 ft. from the top will be under a pressure of $50 \times .434 = 21.7$ lbs. per sq. in.

The following table may be valuable in this connection:

TABLE OF PRESSURES OF WATER

Head	Pressure per sq. in.	Head	Pressure per sq. in.	Head	Pressure per sq. in.
1 ft...	.43 lbs.	55 ft...	23.82 lbs.	110 ft...	47.64 lbs.
5 " ...	2.16 "	60 " ...	25.99 "	115 " ...	49.81 "
10 " ...	4.33 "	65 " ...	28.15 "	120 " ...	51.98 "
15 " ...	6.49 "	70 " ...	30.32 "	125 " ...	54.15 "
20 " ...	8.66 "	75 " ...	32.48 "	130 " ...	56.31 "
25 " ...	10.82 "	80 " ...	34.65 "	135 " ...	58.48 "
30 " ...	12.99 "	85 " ...	36.82 "	140 " ...	60.64 "
35 " ...	15.16 "	90 " ...	38.98 "	145 " ...	62.81 "
40 " ...	17.32 "	95 " ...	41.15 "	150 " ...	64.97 "
45 " ...	19.49 "	100 " ...	43.31 "	155 " ...	67.14 "
50 " ...	21.65 "	105 " ...	45.48 "	160 " ...	69.31 "

Head	Pressure per sq. in.	Head	Pressure per sq. in.	Head	Pressure per sq. in.
165 ft	71.47 lbs.	240 ft	103.96 lbs.	330 ft	142.95 lbs.
170 "	73.64 "	245 "	106.13 "	340 "	147.28 "
175 "	75.80 "	250 "	108.29 "	350 "	151.61 "
180 "	77.97 "	255 "	110.46 "	360 "	155.94 "
185 "	80.14 "	260 "	112.62 "	370 "	160.27 "
190 "	82.30 "	265 "	114.79 "	380 "	164.61 "
195 "	84.47 "	270 "	116.96 "	390 "	168.94 "
200 "	86.63 "	275 "	119.12 "	400 "	173.27 "
205 "	88.80 "	280 "	121.29 "	500 "	216.58 "
210 "	90.96 "	285 "	123.45 "	600 "	259.90 "
215 "	93.14 "	290 "	125.62 "	700 "	303.22 "
220 "	95.30 "	295 "	127.78 "	800 "	346.54 "
225 "	97.49 "	300 "	129.95 "	900 "	389.86 "
230 "	99.63 "	310 "	134.28 "	1000 "	433.18 "
235 "	101.79 "	320 "	138.62 "		

THE AIR TEST

When the air test is applied to the roughing, air should be forced into the system through a force pump, until a pressure of 10 lbs. is reached, 10 lbs. representing 20 in. of mercury. The air test is not so convenient and satisfactory to the plumber as the water test, for the location of a small leakage of air is not so easily found as a small leakage of water. Generally, in the case of a small air leak, the plumber goes over the pipe with a lather of soap applied with a brush. The escaping air will form a bubble, thus showing the location of a defect.

However, the air test subjects all parts of the system to the same uniform pressure, while the pressure in the water test varies from zero pressure at the top to a pressure at the bottom depending upon the height of the stack. In applying the air test, all openings are closed. Through any convenient plug, a gas pipe is connected, to which a mercury gauge is attached, and hose connection made to the force pump. The air pumped into the system exerts a pressure on the mercury, forcing it upward in the tube about two inches for each pound of air pressure.

THE SMOKE TEST

In applying the smoke test, a machine designed for the purpose of producing a heavy volume of black smoke is used. Various materials are used in this machine for producing the smoke, among them being oily cotton waste, tarred paper, and oakum which has been soaked in petroleum. Waste is the best material, as it gives off a dense smoke and is not so inflammable as most other materials. In Fig. C, Plate 25, is shown the manner in which the smoke test is applied. Generally the hose connection from the smoke machine is run through a lead cap which is closed up with putty. The smoke-test plug shown in Fig. B is also used, the smoke passing through the plug.

After the whole system is filled with smoke, an air pressure equal to a one-inch water column is applied. Defects are shown by puffs of smoke escaping through them.

The smoke test appears to be displacing the peppermint test, and for work in general, it appears to be the more reliable of the two.

THE PEPPERMINT TEST

If the final test is to be made with peppermint, a mixture of 2 ounces of oil of peppermint to a gallon of hot water is the requirement for an ordinary house.

On large work, 2 ounces of peppermint should be used for each stack up to five stories and basement in height, and for each additional five stories, or fractional part of that number, an additional ounce per stack. The peppermint should be poured into the roof opening and the opening sealed. The person who has handled the peppermint should not enter the building until the test has been completed, as the odor which he carries will spread about the house.

Peppermint has a very penetrating odor, and its fumes quickly reach every part of the system, and by their escape bring attention to defects. A great point against the use of peppermint is that through a large defect the peppermint will pour in sufficient quantity to quickly fill the house with the odor, making it difficult to locate other leaks. Under certain conditions, however, the peppermint test seems to be the more reliable.

For instance, on old work, much of the soil piping is often buried underground. In the event of defects underground, the peppermint fumes will often penetrate through into the cellar, whereas smoke would not.

At the present time there are comparatively few towns of size, or cities, which do not demand the testing and inspection of the plumbing system, and, without doubt, no other factor has resulted in an equal amount of good in the attainment of sanitary work.

Such provision makes it far more difficult for work to be constructed of inferior material and with wrong connections, as between the testing and inspection of the system many of these features are discovered.

It is almost an impossibility to provide country plumbing construction with the advantages of the inspection and test.

The result of inability under the circumstances, to provide such regulation, results in the construction of a considerable amount of poor and unsanitary work in the country.

This condition has been much improved in recent years, however, chiefly through the demands of owners for tests to be made in the presence of architect and owner, and through the effort of many architects to demand these things in their specifications.

Plate XXVI

CONTINUOUS VENTING

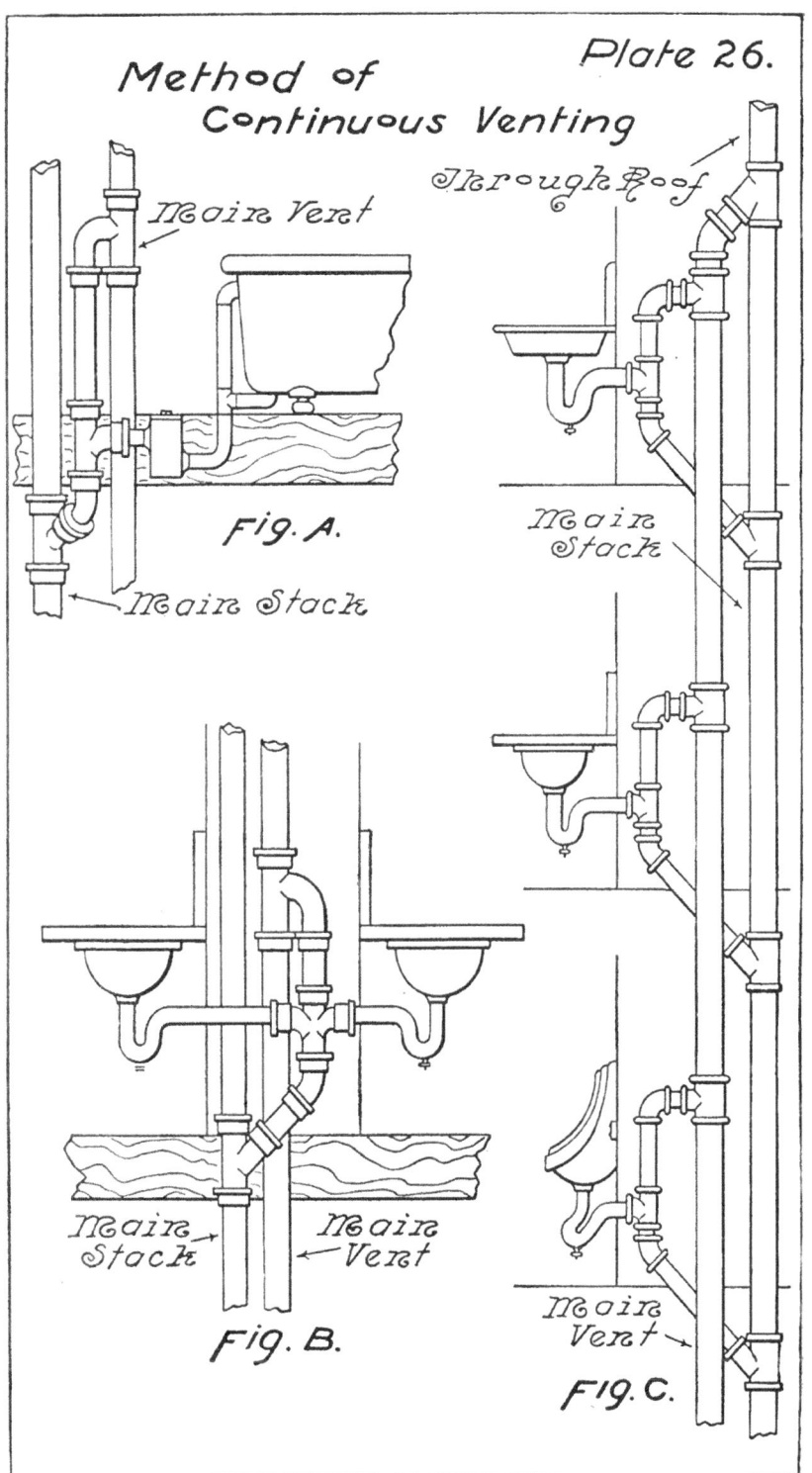

CONTINUOUS VENTING

As previously stated, it is necessary to provide a system of vents to supply air to the fixture traps, in order that they may not suffer from the siphonage of their seals.

The one great objection to the system of trap venting as it now stands, is the fact that a vast majority of vents are found to be almost, if not completely closed, at the end of a few years of service. This result comes about chiefly owing to the location of the opening of the trap vent into the trap. Of necessity the vent of most traps, as ordinarily installed, must be taken off at such a point that this opening readily closes up with grease, lint, etc. If the stoppage came on the waste it would quickly become apparent, but a stoppage of the vent cannot become known usually, for the fixture may be used as readily as if the vent were free, and in many cases the trap may lose its seal owing to the stoppage of the vent, and the fixture still be used, the actual conditions remaining unknown to the inmates.

In the use of the half-S trap, however, the vent may often be taken off the horizontal arm of the trap at such a distance from the trap itself that much less difficulty is experienced from stoppages of its vent opening.

The S-trap or other trap in which the outlet pipe is carried horizontally from the trap, or nearly so, may be used in continuous vent work, but traps of the style of full S or ¾-S traps cannot be used, the reason for which will soon appear.

Plate 26 shows three illustrations of work in which the continuous vent principle is applied. Many attempts have been made to provide special forms of traps whose vent openings would not close up, and mechanical devices have been used for the same purpose, but without satisfactory results. The continuous vent, however, without resort to special contrivances or devices, vents the trap perfectly, and in such a way that there is little, and in fact no danger of the vent-opening closing up.

The three fixtures in Fig. C are provided with continuous vents, the half S-trap being used on each. It consists merely in connecting the outlet of the trap into a waste fitting so located that a vent may be taken off the top of the same fitting. It will be readily seen that the possibility of the stoppage of the openings of these vent pipes is very small in comparison with work of ordinary character, in which the vent is connected to the trap. Wrought iron is generally used for the waste and vent on work that is concealed, while brass is much used on exposed work. Figs. A and B show the same work installed with cast-iron pipe. The objection to the use of cast-iron pipe on this work is that it is not made smaller than of 2-in. diameter. The fittings being so large is another reason for not using it so extensively as wrought iron.

In all continuous vent work the vent is a continuation of the waste line.

As will be seen in connection with several later plates, the continuous vent finds excellent application to groups and lines of fixtures on large work, such as lines of urinals or lavatories in public toilet rooms. The fact that the vent opening is in no danger of stoppage is sufficient to recommend the continuous vent to universal use, even if no other advantages were to be gained. An additional advantage of importance, gained by the continuous vent, is a decreased rate of evaporation of the trap seal. This result is to be expected, owing to the distance of the vent connection from the seal of the trap.

Fig. B shows the continuous vent applied to two lavatories, back to back, on opposite sides of the same partition. For fixtures thus relatively located, the continuous vent is of very great value not only because of the advantages that are gained as named above, but also for the reason that a saving in cost of construction is effected by its use. As far as the waste and vent for the two fixtures are concerned, no more labor or stock is used than in constructing the waste and vent for one alone.

It may not be clear to the reader that traps with other than a horizontal outlet cannot be used on continuous vent work.

As already stated elsewhere, in order to prevent the siphon from operating, air must be brought into it at or near its crown. If air is brought into the long outlet arm of the siphon, it will not break its action. In the same way, a vent taken off the outlet at some distance down from the crown of the ¾-S sink trap, shown in Plate 9, will not accomplish results. In order, then, that air may be admitted on the same level as the trap seal and at a distance from it, a trap of the general design of the half-S trap must be used.

Plate XXVII

CONTINUOUS VENTING FOR TWO-FLOOR WORK

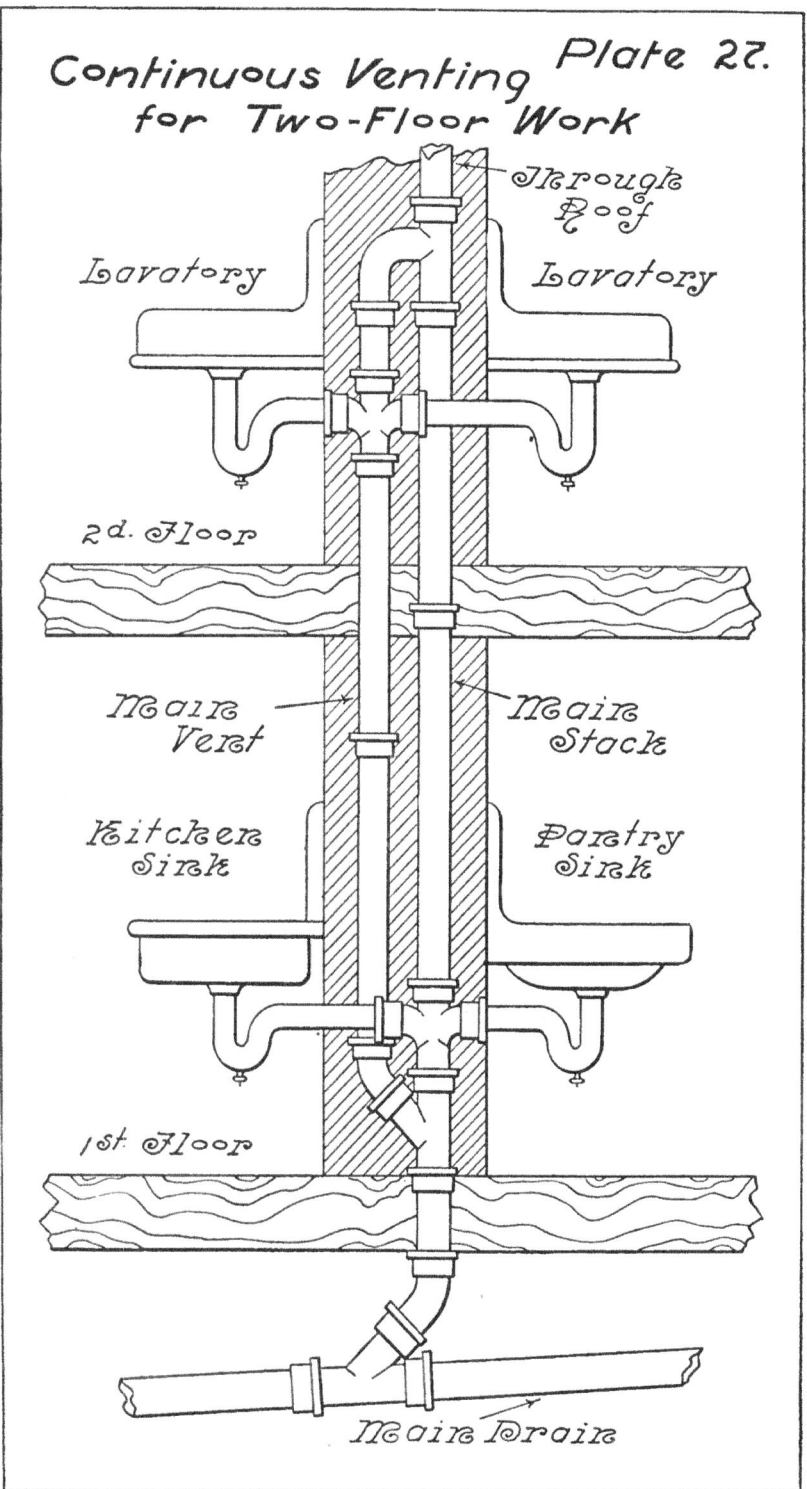

CONTINUOUS VENTING FOR TWO-FLOOR WORK

THE continuous venting of fixture traps is sometimes known as "venting in the rough," the origin of the phrase being easily understood after referring to Plate 27, the connections for which are almost wholly made when the roughing is installed. In many towns and cities double apartment houses, with two flats on each side, are very common, and in buildings of this kind the continuous-vent principle may be applied to very great advantage, after the manner shown in Plate 27.

This same style of work may be used in many other buildings where the plumbing fixtures are on two floors, and assembled in a manner similar to the assembling of the fixtures in Plate 27. So long as the stack serves fixtures on two floors only, it does not matter whether the two floors are consecutive, or whether one or more floors intervene between the two on which the fixtures are located.

In double apartment houses the rooms are generally so planned, and the plumbing fixtures so located, that the stacks may be carried up in the wall which divides the two sides of the building. When so arranged, only half the number of vertical stacks is needed that would otherwise be necessary.

Thus, one stack may serve all four kitchen sinks in the four-flat apartment building, the four fixtures being backed up to each other in pairs, on opposite sides of the division wall or partition, under which conditions the system shown in Plate 27 may easily be applied.

The main waste and vent stacks are run in the usual manner, the two being connected above the highest fixture, and below the lowest waste entrance. A novel departure is made in connecting the traps of the two fixtures on the upper floor. Instead of connecting them into the waste stack in the ordinary manner, they are connected into the line that would ordinarily be the main vent stack.

As the upper-floor fixtures are not connected into the waste stack, the line of pipe above the waste fitting of the lower floor is a vent, and into this vent line the vent line from the other two fixtures connects.

In this style of work, neither vertical stack is entirely a waste stack, or entirely a vent stack. While altogether unlike the regular two-floor work, this style of work is perfectly legitimate.

It can be applied only to two floors, for the third-floor fixtures would have to waste into one or the other of the two vertical stacks, and that stack could no longer be used as a vent line.

A comparison of this plate with Plate 28 will show that this statement must be true, and it will also show that the use of the connections such as Plate 27 shows, calls for much less outlay in stock and labor per fixture than does the ordinary method of continuous venting.

As compared with crown venting, the work of Plate 27 calls for far less labor and considerably less stock.

If crown venting were employed, the main vent line would have to be run and connected with the waste stack above and below, as shown.

A fitting on the main vent line would be required at each floor, while the waste fittings would remain the same.

Separate vents would have to be run from the crown of each trap, necessitating, in the case of lead work, a wiped joint on the trap and another at the vent fitting. This comparison will show that the labor involved in the continuous venting of two-floor work of the style shown in Plate 27 is very much less than on the same system installed according to the ordinary methods of crown venting.

While in general it would seem that continuous venting can be done with less labor, it cannot so often be done with less stock, but its advantages are so great that it would appear that in the higher grade of construction, at least, it would soon come into general use. At the present time its use is demanded by some few city ordinances, and recommended by others.

There is this to be said concerning its adoption: the continuous vent cannot always be applied, and in some cases it could not be applied without considerable additional cost.

Owing to these conditions it would seem unwise to attempt to demand its use without regard to circumstances surrounding the fixture, but at the same time, much good work would be provided for in the future, and a long step taken in advance, if plumbing ordinances would call for the use of continuous venting wherever practicable.

Plate XXVIII

CONTINUOUS VENTING FOR TWO LINES OF FIXTURES ON THREE OR MORE FLOORS—PRACTICAL REQUIREMENTS OF VENTING

Plate 28.
Continuous Venting for Two Lines of Fixtures on Three or More Floors

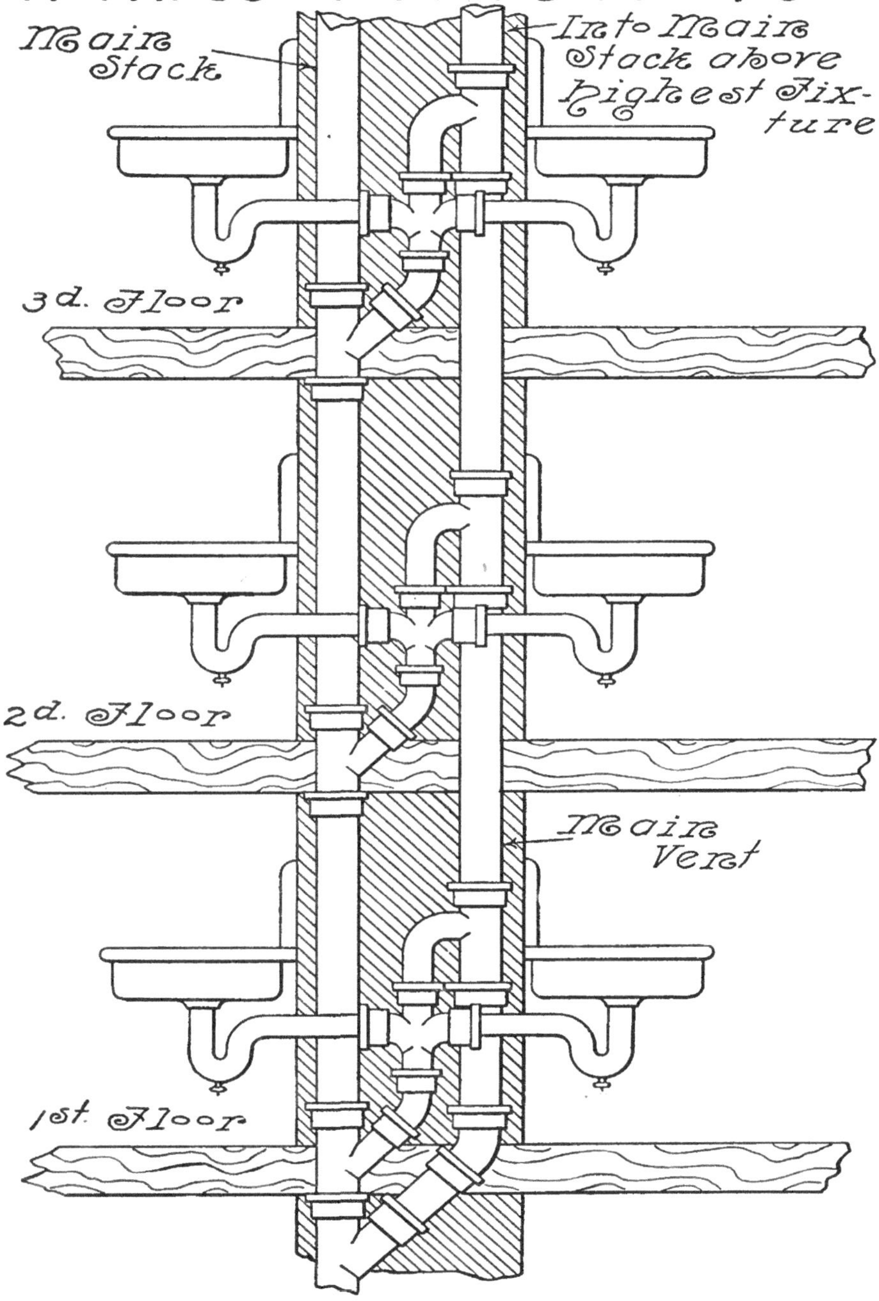

- Main Stack
- Into Main Stack above highest Fixture
- 3d. Floor
- 2d. Floor
- Main Vent
- 1st. Floor

CONTINUOUS VENTING FOR TWO LINES OF FIXTURES ON THREE OR MORE FLOORS

On the preceding plate the continuous vent is shown in a special application to two-floor work for four-flat apartment buildings. In Plate 28 the continuous vent is shown as applied to double lines of fixtures on three or more floors. Such double lines of fixtures are often to be found in double apartment buildings.

In the larger cities such buildings are often many stories in height, and in the towns and smaller cities double apartment buildings of three and four stories are very common.

In office buildings, also, fixtures are often so located that two of them on the same floor, and on opposite sides of a wall or partition, waste into the same stack. The work shown in Plate 28 applies to many cases of similar nature. The waste from each of the two adjacent fixtures is carried into the same waste fitting, from the bottom of which a mutual waste is run to the waste stack, and from the top a mutual vent to the vent stack.

In addition to gaining for each fixture the advantages derived from continuous venting, the work may often, and in fact usually, be done with less labor and material than if installed with the customary crown venting. While the matter of saving in the cost of construction might be questionable in the case of a single line of fixtures, the addition of a second line of fixtures requires no additional material or labor, with the exception of the furnishing of the traps and connecting them to the waste fittings.

The system shown is an excellent one, and without doubt will gradually come into general use, a result much to be desired. The entire system shown is of cast iron, but it may be said that for the main vent, and especially for the fixture wastes and vents, wrought iron is more generally used. In the case of the mutual fixture wastes and vents, wrought iron will effect a saving in expense, as sizes smaller than 2 in. may often be used, and cast-iron pipe is not made in sizes smaller than 2 in.

PRACTICAL REQUIREMENTS OF VENTING

The fixture vent should pitch upward from the trap at all points in order that condensation may drain into the trap, and it should be connected into the main vent line at a point higher than its fixture, so that, in the event of stoppage of the trap or waste, the fixture waste may not pass off through the vent.

To provide against the latter evil, it is good practice in the case of a group of fixtures whose vents connect into a main branch vent, to run this branch so that its lowest vent fitting shall be at least two or three inches above the top of the highest fixture of the group.

Formerly much vent work of lead was used, but the best practice to-day calls for the use of galvanized iron or brass on all branch, main branch, and individual fixture vents of 2 in. or less in size. The use of lead for vent work is fast becoming limited to use in connection with lead traps, short connections being made into the wrought-iron or brass pipe.

Main branch vents should be increased one size in diameter after passing 30 ft.

When a fixture is located 8 ft. or more from the main vent, its trap vent should either be carried independently through the roof, or enter the main vent stack above all fixtures.

Thus, in the case of the lavatory of Fig. C, Plate 20, if its distance is 8 ft. or more from the stack, its vent should be run as above; if its distance is 6 ft. or more, lead should not be used on its waste. Under such conditions the use of the continuous vent for the fixture, as shown, is excellent practice.

Under Plate 13, it was shown that the main vent line might either run independently through the roof or reënter the soil or waste vent above the highest fixture. In many of the large cities this demand is qualified by requiring the running of a main vent separately through the roof, whenever such vent serves fixtures on more than six floors or extends more than 80 ft. above the grade line.

Whenever main vent lines are reëntered into soil or waste vents, no fixture should be located on any floor above such reëntrance, and be connected to the soil, waste, vent, or back-vent pipes from fixtures on floors below.

Plate XXIX

CONTINUOUS VENTING OF WATER CLOSETS—CIRCUIT VENTS—LOOP VENTS

CONTINUOUS VENTING OF WATER CLOSETS—CIRCUIT VENTS—LOOP VENTS

In the system of plumbing shown on Plate 29, the venting of the several lines of water closets is accomplished by extending the horizontal soil line beyond the last fixture, and connecting this extension into a main vertical line of vent at a point higher than the top of the fixtures.

The main vent stack may be at either end of the line of fixtures, but when placed at the end opposite the soil stack the connection of the horizontal lines into the vent stack is usually much shorter and more direct, and installed with the use of less pipe. When placed at the same end as the soil line, the running back to this point of a long line of large-sized pipe would often be a difficult or impossible matter.

This form of venting is not strictly on the continuous-vent principle as shown in the three preceding plates, but being along somewhat the same general lines is often alluded to as continuous venting.

This method is also known as circuit venting.

The system of circuit vents, as prescribed by certain plumbing ordinances, consists in the extension of the horizontal branch soil or waste lines and the connection of these extensions into a main vertical vent stack, the entire system including both main soil or waste stack, main vent stack, and branch soil or waste lines, providing for each line of fixtures a complete air circulation through the branch which serves them.

The advantages derived from this system, as applied to water-closet lines, may also be obtained for other fixtures.

Fixtures of other character, such as the lavatory located on the second floor in Plate 29, are vented as shown in the case of this lavatory. The use of the circuit-vent system is of special value when applied to lines of water closets, such as are very common in public toilet rooms, for the reason that the free circulation of air through the horizontal lines does away with the necessity of venting the individual fixtures in the ordinary manner, that is, from the lead bend. A water closet, however, connected to a horizontal soil line served by a circuit vent, and located 5 ft. or more from that line, should be vented in the usual manner.

It will thus be seen that the continuous venting of lines of water closets by means of circuit vents, provides ample protection to the fixtures against siphonage, and effects a great saving in avoiding the outlay incident to installing a separate vent for each water closet.

The common method of venting lines of water closets is shown in Fig. D, Plate 40. Any branch line of soil or waste pipe serving a line of two or more fixtures may be provided with a circuit vent to the advantage of the system.

When the horizontal soil branch is of not more than 20 ft. in length, measuring from the main soil stack, and the line is not entered by more than four water closets, the vent extension may be reduced to 3 in. from the end of the branch into the main vent stack. When a larger number than four water closets enter the horizontal soil branch, the vent extension should not be reduced in diameter, but should continue of the same size as the soil branch, into the main vent stack.

While not allowable to use quarter-bends on any part of the drainage system, they may be used on circuit vents, as shown in Plate 29. While much used on this work, a better form of practice is seen in the use of a T-Y or Y and eighth-bend, in place of the quarter-bend, thus allowing the use of an end cleanout, by means of which the entire horizontal branch could be controlled in the event of stoppage.

In addition to the circuit vent, there is also what is known as the loop vent. The loop vent is a modified form of the circuit vent, used when a line or group of fixtures on a single floor is to be circuit-vented, and there are no fixtures on the floors above.

In this case the soil or waste branch is extended beyond the line of fixtures, and run up as in the case of the circuit vent, and then looped over the line of fixtures into the soil or waste vent of the stack into which the branch soil or waste pipe connects.

The loop vent may be used for a single line of fixtures, on a floor above which are other fixtures emptying into the same soil or waste stack, by connecting the loop into the main vent stack above the highest fixture of the group.

The loop vent for a 4-in. soil branch may be 3 in. in diameter.

For 5 and 6-in. soil branches, the loop vent should be 5 in. in diameter, and for larger sizes 6 in.

Plate XXX

PLUMBING FOR COTTAGE HOUSE—
GENERAL REMARKS

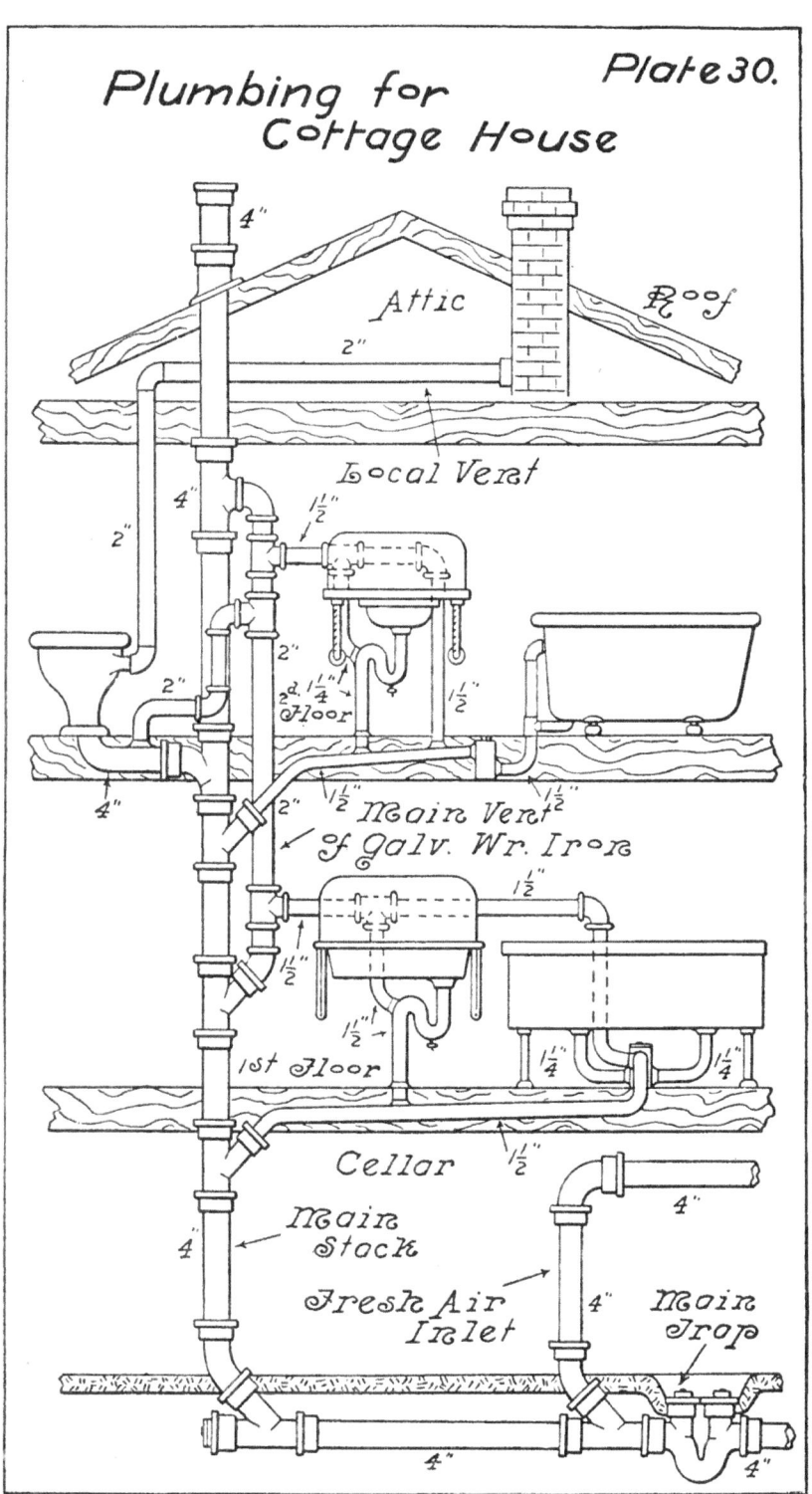

PLUMBING FOR COTTAGE HOUSE—GENERAL REMARKS

The only difference between the plumbing system of a small dwelling, such as the cottage house, and the larger systems to be found in large residences, etc., is that it is of a less complicated nature, the rooms being so laid out and the pipes so located that the plumbing of the house is much more centralized than is possible in larger work. It is quite customary in the construction of the cottage house to so arrange the piping that one stack will be able to serve all the fixtures in the house. For dwellings of any description, this stack must not be less than 4 in. in diameter, for it is to receive the discharge from the water closet, for which nothing less than 4-in. pipe should ever be provided, and as the water closet is to be vented usually, a 2-in. main vent is required.

In the case of two stacks of different size, it is better practice to have the larger one at the house end of the house drain, rather than to reduce after passing the larger stack to the size of the smaller stack.

Thus, in Plate 30, if the house drain were continued to receive a 2-in. stack, and reduced after passing the 4-in. stack, the circulation of air through the system would not be so good as it would be with the 4-in. stack at the end of the line. It is always good policy to centralize the plumbing as far as possible, as any legitimate expedient, looking to the simplification of a system that has now become somewhat complicated, is to be welcomed. It will mean less piping, and therefore less opportunity for defects, stoppages, etc.

The sizes of pipes given in Plate 30 are those which are commonly used, and to which no exception may be taken, unless with the sink and laundry tub, whose waste, according to the requirements of some ordinances, should be one size larger in diameter, which seems to be a wise requirement.

On the plumbing systems of cottages, residences, etc., lead work seems to continue in use to a larger extent than on the work being installed in larger buildings. It must be stated in this connection, that the use of lead is still followed to a large extent in certain sections of the country, the superseding of it by iron and brass being particularly noticeable in the large cities.

For waste pipes the following table of weights may be safely followed:

Diameter of Lead Pipe	Weight per Foot
1 in.	2 lbs.
1¼ "	2½ "
1½ "	3½ "
2 "	4 "
4 "	6 "

The amount of pressure on street mains must determine the weights of lead pipe proper for supplies, but for ordinary pressures the following table is safe to follow:

Diameter of Lead Pipe	Weight per Foot
⅜ in.	1½ lbs.
½ "	2 "
⅝ "	2½ "
¾ "	3 "
1 "	4 "

Sheet lead should never be less than 4 lbs., and 6 lbs. for roof flashings is preferable. The tendency to use light materials, owing to the keen competition of the present day, is very marked, and nowhere on the plumbing system more plainly to be seen than in the lead work. Lead bends and drum traps, for instance, are often used which are so fragile that the workman must be careful that in his handling of them they are not crushed. This is true also of the pipe. The weights given above, however, if obtained, will ensure solid and secure work.

The choice of material for water-supply pipes should always be made with due consideration to the chemical properties of the water supply. This is true also in the matter of range boilers. Some waters will quickly attack wrought-iron pipe and boilers, and make renewal necessary in comparatively few years.

Under such conditions, lead or brass supply pipes and copper range boilers should generally be used.

On high-grade work, brass piping is now being extensively used, and for the best work all changes in direction are made by bending the pipe rather than by the use of elbows.

Plate XXXI

CONSTRUCTION OF CELLAR PIPING—
THE HOUSE DRAIN, HOUSE SEWER, ETC.

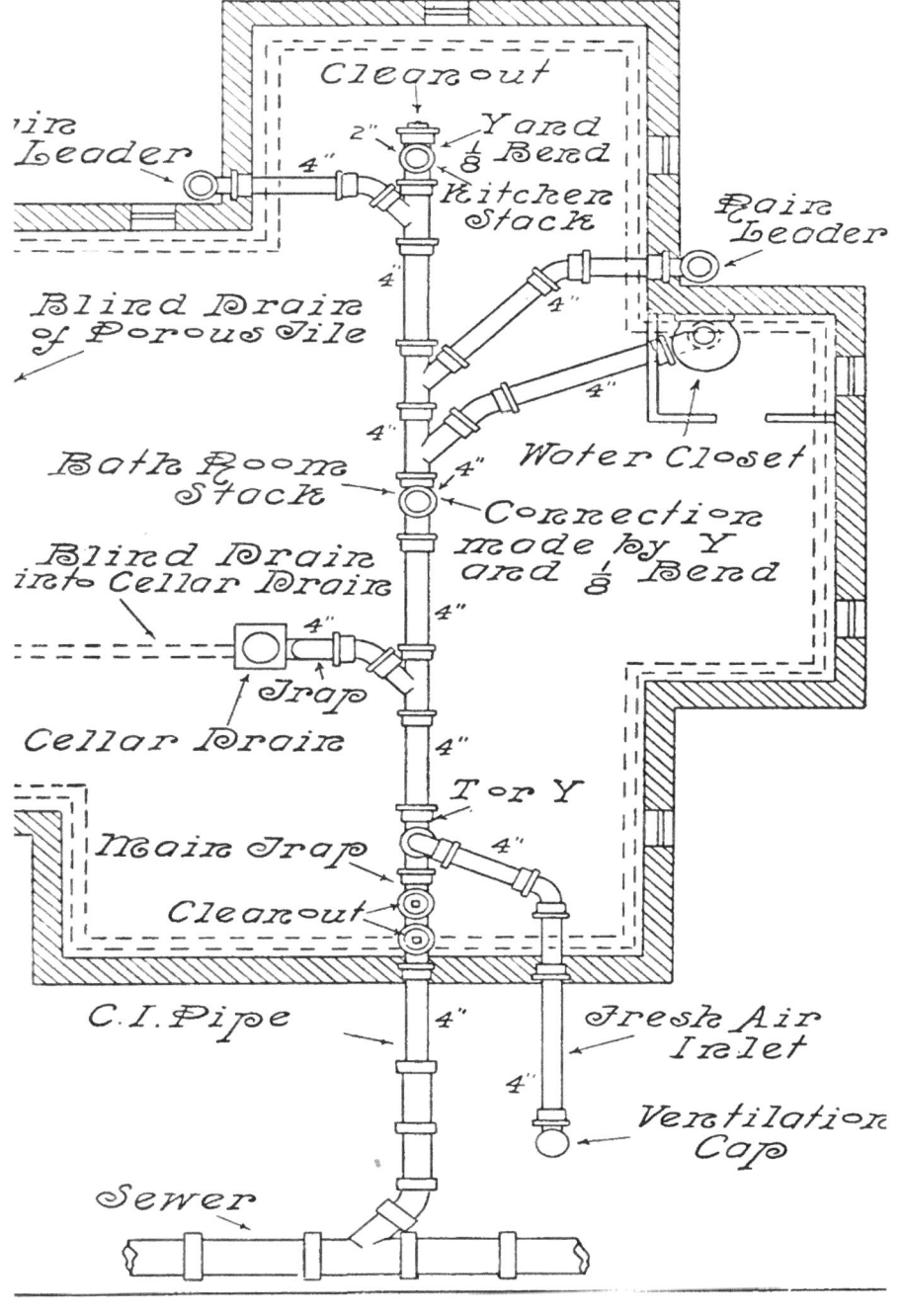

THE HOUSE DRAIN, HOUSE SEWER, ETC.

PLATE 31 shows the general form of the drainage piping in the cellar or basement. Many of the features which appear have been taken up under preceding plates, such as main trap and fresh-air inlet, cellar and subsoil drainage, etc., and will not be again considered here.

Before taking up the consideration of the above subject, it will be well to clearly define the terms house drain and house sewer, concerning which there is often some confusion.

The house drain is that portion of the horizontal piping of the drainage system of any building into which all the soil and waste pipes, whether vertical or horizontal, but inside the building, ultimately discharge. The house drain extends through the foundation wall.

The house sewer is a continuation of the main drain, from the point where the latter ends, to its connection into the sewer or cesspool.

The house drain and sewer, under any ordinary circumstances, should serve but the one building, it being entirely wrong to connect the sewage from any building into the house drain or house sewer of another building. The drainage system of each building should be entirely distinct and separate from all other buildings.

It sometimes occurs in the large cities, where buildings of mammoth proportions are erected, that in order to properly care for the vast amount of sewage collected over large areas and from many floors, it is necessary to make use of two house drains and sewers for different sections of the building, in which case the two systems are entirely separate. More than two house drains and sewers are rarely required. The running of the house drain, whether overhead or underground, is determined largely by the prevailing usages of different towns and cities. For instance, the prevailing construction of some cities is flat houses, in which all plumbing fixtures will be found on the several floors, and none in the basement or cellar, under which conditions the house drain may be run overhead.

On the other hand, the prevailing dwelling houses of another city may have two or three single flats, the laundry tubs for the several flats being placed in the cellar, which necessitates running the house drain underground. The house drain should be of extra-heavy iron pipe, and should be carried to a point 10 ft. from the inner face of the cellar wall. This means that two full lengths of soil pipe are to be used in running from the foundation wall to the house sewer.

The reason for this requirement is the danger of broken earthenware pipe and fittings and cement joints, close to the foundation wall, with the consequent danger of the leeching of escaping sewage through the foundation walls into the cellar. When laid underground, nothing but extra-heavy tarred cast-iron pipe should be used, whether it be the house drain or branches from it. This is required for the reason that uncoated cast-iron pipe is in time destroyed by galvanic action when laid underground, and wrought iron and steel pipe suffers in the same way, but to a far greater extent. On no account should earthenware pipe enter the cellar. The best method of making the connection at the main trap is shown in Fig. A, Plate 25, as the use of an end cleanout is thus allowed, which will control the straight line out into the house sewer in the event of stoppage. If the house drain through the foundation wall cannot be laid low enough for the main trap to discharge into the Y from above, the Y may be used lying on its side.

All entrances into the house drain, or into any horizontal soil or waste branch, should be made through Y-branches or Y-branches and bends.

Into the house drain all floor drains, cellar drains, etc., should be connected.

In the case of rain leaders, they should be connected into the house drain when brought inside the basement or cellar, but may also be run outside the foundation walls and entered into the house sewer. If, however, there is a separate public system for surface sewage, clear waste, such as coming from floor and yard drains, rain leaders, subsoil drainage, etc., should be connected into the house drain of the surface sewage system.

The matter of the use of the main trap is generally determined by plumbing ordinance. The practice is varied, some cities demanding its use, others prohibiting it, and still others making its use optional. When the main trap is used, however, all connections into the main drain should be made on the house side of the trap.

THE HOUSE DRAIN, ETC.

The objection to the use of a main trap, due to the forcing of its seal, has caused a trial of two main traps on the house drain. The use of two traps, however, has not been taken up to any extent.

Whenever two traps have been used, the fresh-air inlet has been taken off on the house side of the trap farthest from the sewer, and in order that there shall be no air lock between the two traps, a vent was taken off a fitting placed between the two traps. The idea of this arrangement was that, in case back pressure from the sewer was sufficient to force the seal of the first trap, the seal of the second trap could never be forced because of the vent between the two traps, and in this way sewer gas would be prevented from entering the house-drainage system. An objection advanced against the use of a single main trap is that it impedes the free outflow of sewage and is subject to stoppage.

The use of two traps would certainly increase these troubles, and their use would seem to be inadvisable. As already stated, simplicity rather than complexity is to be desired in all parts of the plumbing system, and especially at such a point as the main trap, where serious trouble affects the entire system.

As stated above, the house sewer begins at the point where the house drain ends, which is generally 10 ft. from the inside face of the foundation wall, although some plumbing ordinances make this distance only 5 ft. In general, the house sewer is constructed of vitrified earthen pipe, and should be one size larger than the house drain. If the house drain is 4 in. in diameter, the house sewer should be 5 in.

All pipe that is buried deep underground, and therefore not easily accessible, should be of larger size than for the same line when running above ground, whether the pipe be used for drainage or supply purposes. When the house sewer is laid in made ground, or in ground that has been filled in, or is in danger of destruction from roots of trees or from the action of frost, earthenware pipe should never be used. Under these conditions nothing but extra-heavy tarred cast-iron pipe should be used, laid with caulked lead joints, but not with cement joints. When the house sewer must of necessity run close to any cistern, or any source of water supply, it should be constructed of cast-iron pipe.

Joints on the earthen pipe of house sewers should be given as careful attention as joints on any other part of the plumbing system, although this work is often constructed in a most careless manner. Portland cement of the best quality should be used, three parts of clean sand to one part of Portland cement.

The opening between the spigot and the hub should be entirely filled with cement, and whatever cement has squeezed out into the interior of the pipe should be cleaned off and removed before the next length or fitting is laid. A lath is convenient for cutting off the superfluous cement. A stronger and better joint may be made by caulking a ring of oakum into the hub before the cement is put in.

The spigot end should be inserted into the hub so that the thickness of the cement will be uniform around the circumference. Depressions should be cut into the bottom of the trench for the hubs to set into, thus allowing the pipe to rest firmly on its entire length rather than on the hubs only. The bottom of the trench should have a uniform grade of not less than 2 ft. in 100 ft., and more where possible, and in long lines of trench work it becomes almost necessary to have the grade laid out by an engineer in order that the work may be done properly. This is especially true when the total pitch for the entire length is barely sufficient, and must be distributed evenly.

Before trenches are filled in, the earth around pipes should be thoroughly rammed, and no pipe, whether water or drainage, should be covered until inspected by the proper official. Changes in direction of the house sewer, entrances into it of rain leaders, etc., should be done under the same general rules regulating like work in connection with the house drain.

When rain leaders connect into the house drain or house sewer, it should be seen to that these two lines are of sufficient size to handle the large volume of rain water entering them during severe storms. The amount of water which a line of pipe can safely be depended upon to carry depends largely on the grade at which the pipe is laid.

The connection of the house sewer into the street sewer should be made as shown in Plate 31, that is, by the use of a Y-branch on the main sewer and a bend on the house sewer.

This is more satisfactory than entering a tee, just as it is on the house-drainage system. When the street sewer and house sewer are of such levels that a proper grade can be secured, the house sewer should enter the main street sewer above the center of the arch of the latter.

Plate XXXII

PLUMBING FOR RESIDENCES—USE OF SPECIAL FITTINGS—BRASS PIPING

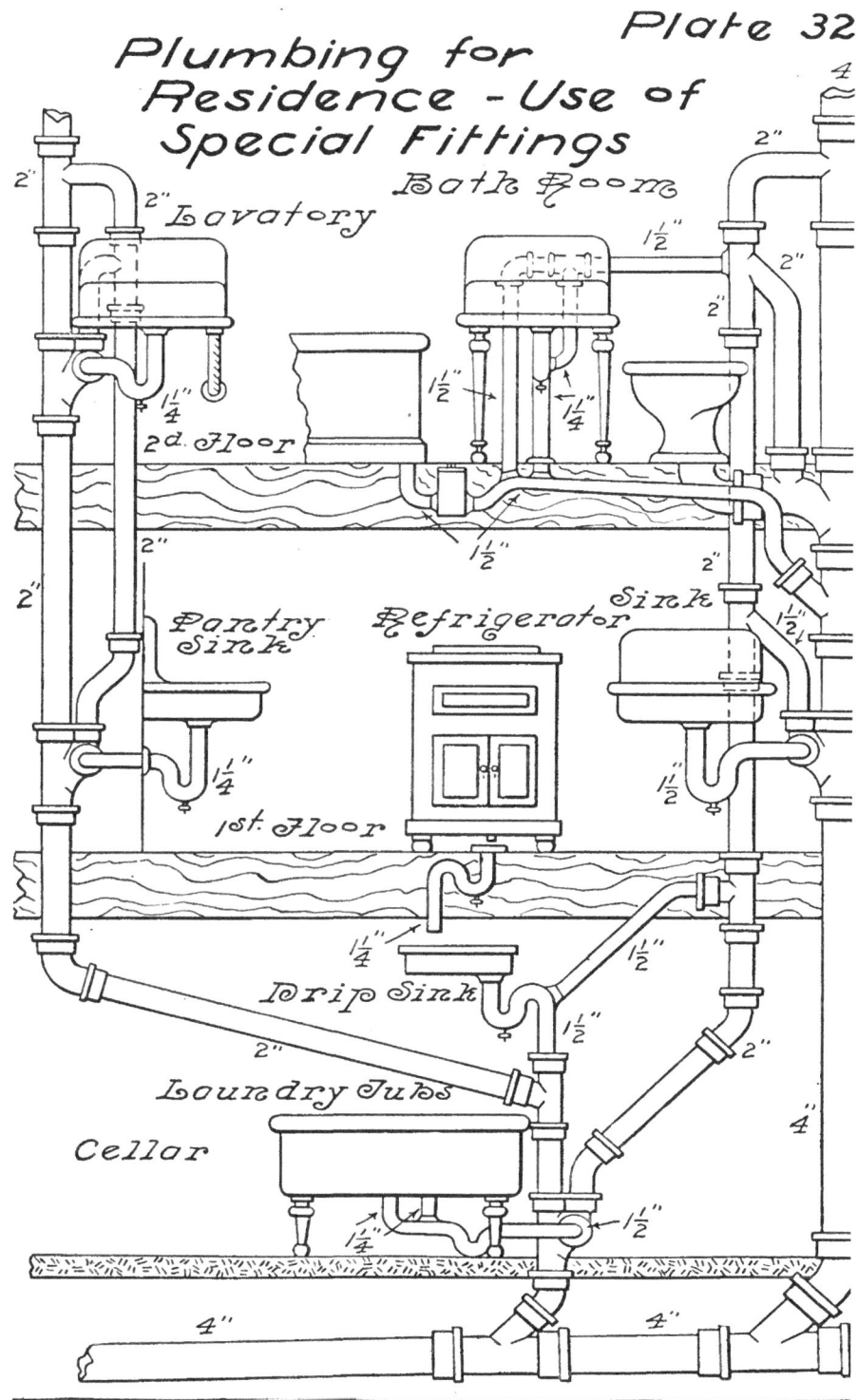

PLUMBING FOR RESIDENCES—USE OF SPECIAL FITTINGS—BRASS PIPING

THE plumbing for a residence, shown in Plate 32, shows the use of various special waste and vent fittings, which are now coming into use extensively on the best class of work. A special advantage gained in their use is that fixture traps may be easily provided with a continuous vent. In previous plates the running of continuous vents by the use of common fittings is to be seen. The use of special fittings often saves the making of one or more joints. In Plate 32 all the fixtures are supplied with continuous vents with the exception of the bath and lavatory in the bath room, and the refrigerator drip sink. It is very rare that a fixture is so located, however, that, by the use of some one of the numerous special fittings or common fittings, it cannot be vented on the continuous principle. It will be noted that sizes of all pipes are given.

For the ordinary residence, double house, two- and three-flat houses, and much other work, a 4-in. house drain and main stack is large enough for the work required of them. It is poor policy in constructing the house drain or the house sewer, or any horizontal drainage pipe, to use a pipe of larger size than is necessary, for it is much better to have the sewage which is flowing through a horizontal line fill the pipe well up on its sides than to have the pipe so large that the sewage flows in a thin stream at the bottom of it. In the latter case, heavy sewage is more liable to lodge in the pipe, while the use of a smaller pipe would have resulted in sufficient scouring action to carry it along through the pipe. It will be noticed that in Plate 32 the laundry tubs are located in the cellar. This is a very common practice. A strong point against it, however, is that, but for placing this fixture in the cellar, the house drain might be run overhead and in sight, which is always preferable to burying it underground.

On high-grade work, such as is to be found in residences, apartment buildings, etc., brass piping is now largely used for waste and vent work.

The proper weights of brass pipe are to be found in the following table:

WEIGHTS OF BRASS PIPE

Nominal Diameter of Pipe	Weight per Foot	Nominal Diameter of Pipe	Weight per Foot
1½ in	2.84 lbs.	4 in	11.29 lbs.
2 "	3.82 "	4½ "	13.08 "
2½ "	6.08 "	5 "	15.37 "
3 "	7.92 "	6 "	19.88 "
3½ "	9.54 "		

Brass fittings used on drainage work should be cast, and of extra heavy weight, and of recessed pattern, similar to cast-iron recessed drainage fittings, as illustrated in Plate 44.

With the various appliances now on the market, there is absolutely no excuse for using on brass and nickel pipes the tools designed for use on wrought-iron pipes. These appliances include brass pipe vises and wrenches of various makes, the use of which avoids all scratching of pipe and tubing, and the crushing of the latter resulting from the use of common vises and pipe wrenches.

Brass pipe work should always be put together with threaded connections of iron-pipe size, but never with slip joints and couplings.

It often happens, both on supply and drainage work, that it is necessary or desirable to make a bend in the pipe rather than to use an elbow. The following is a practical method of performing this work, and the result, when the work is properly done, is a perfect bend.

First fill the pipe to be bent with sand, and securely plug each end. Set the pipe on the work bench, with the point to be bent overhanging. Place a plumber's furnace under the pipe, so that the flame heats the pipe at the bending point. To confine the heat, cover this part of the pipe with a piece of sheet iron, or a shovel, if more convenient. See to it that the pipe does not become overheated.

When it becomes sufficiently hot, the weight of the overhanging pipe will cause it to bend. With care and a little experience, sharp right-angle bends can be easily and neatly made in this manner.

When heated, brass becomes very brittle, and it should not be removed, therefore, until somewhat cooled.

If the overhanging end is too short to provide sufficient weight to cause the pipe to bend, a weight may be attached to the pipe.

Plate XXXIII

PLUMBING FOR TWO-FLAT HOUSE—RAINLEADERS—PLUMBING CONSTRUCTION FOR TENEMENT HOUSES

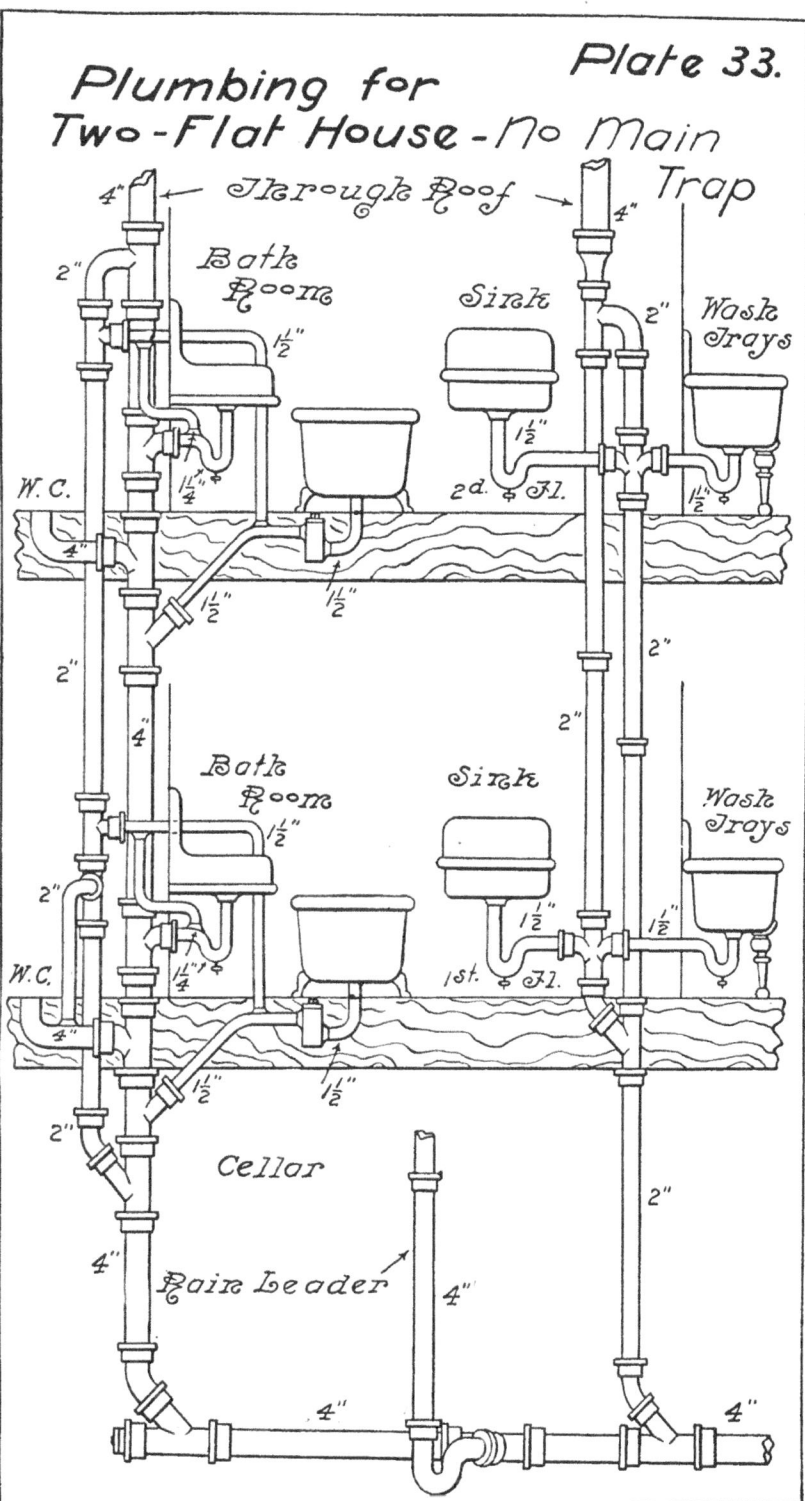

PLUMBING FOR TWO-FLAT HOUSE

The elevation of the plumbing for a two-flat house, with pipe sizes given, is shown on Plate 33. In general, the plumbing on buildings of this class is confined to the kitchen sink, laundry tubs, and three bath-room fixtures. Although not shown in Plate 33, owing to lack of sufficient space, flat buildings of all classes should be provided with refrigerator drainage. Usually in flat houses of two or three stories, a 4-in. bath-room stack and a 2-in. kitchen stack is required, although in some cases the 4-in. stack can be made to serve all the fixtures, obviating the use of a second stack. The use of two stacks is better, however, as separate entrance into the stacks can be gained for each fixture, which would be very difficult if the five fixtures entered one stack. In two- or three-flat houses the laundry tubs are sometimes located in the cellar, against which there is no special objection, if the cellar is well lighted and ventilated, except the matter of inconvenience to the tenants on the upper floors. In Plate 33 all fixtures have separate waste entrances, and it will be noted that the kitchen fixtures are served by the special method described and illustrated in Plate 27.

It will be noted that the water closet on the upper floor is not vented. There is in reality no danger whatever of the siphonage of the water-closet trap when the fixture is located close to its stack, with no fixtures entering the stack on floors above, and therefore there is no necessity of venting it. Most plumbing ordinances acknowledge this fact by not demanding the venting of water closets thus located.

In connection with this plate, the subject of rain leaders will be considered.

RAIN LEADERS

The size of rain leaders should never be less than 3 in., and as much larger as the roof area which is drained should require. Plumbing ordinances differ in trap requirements for rain leaders, some requiring no leader trap when the main trap is used, others demanding leader traps even though the system is protected by the main trap. It goes without saying that each rain leader should be trapped on the system which has no main trap. It would appear wise to use the trap also on systems provided with main trap. There is no danger in this case of air lock from double trapping, for this trouble is obviated by the presence of the fresh-air inlet. The use of the trap prevents foul odors from the house drainage system, and possible back pressure from the sewer, from finding their way through the rain leaders and conductor pipes and escaping through joints and defects in the latter into the rooms of the house through open windows. The usual method is to run the rain leader, of cast or wrought iron, from its connection with the house drain to a point outside the foundation wall, where the galvanized iron conductor enters it. The iron pipe connection should end not less than 5 ft. above the grade level. When run entirely inside the building, they must be of cast or wrought iron, and connected at the roof by means of lead or copper pipe wiped to a brass ferrule and caulked into the top of the leader, the opening being protected by a wire guard or basket. Whenever possible, it is better practice to connect two or more branch rain leaders into one main, and place a trap on this main, rather than to separately trap each leader. This method guards the piping better, for the reason that a trap thus located is more certain of maintaining its seal. In the same way, and for the same reason, the rain leader may be connected into a yard drain, the two lines being protected by one trap.

Conductors run outside should be one size larger than required for a conductor draining the same area when run inside.

When rain leaders pass through the foundation close to a driveway, or where there is danger of being harmed by passing teams, they should be run up in recesses made in the walls, and should not pass through the side of the building at a point lower than 12 ft. above the grade.

If there is no sewer in the street on which the building is located, its roof drainage should be conducted from the leaders into a pipe running below the sidewalk to the street gutter.

If the street is provided with a public surface sewage system, the rain leaders should connect into the surface house drain, and not into the house drainage system. If desired, it is proper to carry the rain leaders outside the house and enter them outside the main trap into the house sewer. When so run, they may be of either extra-heavy cast-iron or glazed-earthenware pipe, and should be provided with traps made accessible by being located in brick or stone wells or manholes. The chief danger that confronts the rain-leader trap is the loss of its seal during a long-continued drought. In traps having only a ¾-in. seal or thereabouts, it can be imagined that evaporation will not be long in causing its destruction. It would be a good idea to construct on all rain leaders, deep seal traps made of quarter-bends, in order that a sufficient depth may be obtained.

The evils of evaporation thus far have been almost impossible to remedy, and the only safe course is to take every possible precaution against it. There is one point that may be advanced in favor of connecting the rain leaders inside the cellar wall with the house drain, instead of running them outside the cellar wall and connecting them into the house sewer. When connected inside, the rain water during a storm enters the house drain in sufficient quantity to thoroughly scour and cleanse the piping.

REGULATION OF PLUMBING CONSTRUCTION IN TENEMENT HOUSES, LODGING HOUSES, ETC.

Many of the larger cities have found that as the crowded conditions of the tenement-house districts increase, special provisions must be made to meet these conditions in such a manner that the sanitary standard of these dwelling places may be kept as high as possible. Other conditions besides that of being crowded, such as the uncleanliness and ignorance of many of the inmates of these districts, make special provisions a necessity. The following requirements with others of similar nature, are therefore now demanded by many of our large cities in their plumbing ordinances.

In all such houses, and in factories and workshops as well, there should be installed at least one water closet, regardless of the small number of occupants, and there should be enough additional water closets to allow at least one such fixture for each 15 persons.

In tenement and lodging houses there should be not less than one water closet on each floor, and whenever more than one family occupies a single floor, there should be at least one additional water closet for each two additional families. In such buildings whenever there are more than 15 persons living on the same floor, there should be an additional water closet installed on that floor for every 15 additional persons, or fractional part of that number. The water-closet compartments of tenement and lodging houses, factories and workshops should be made waterproof, with marble, slate, or tile. In tenement houses, when the water closet is used by a single family only, its base must be not less than 6 in. high, and in all other cases, where it is required, it should be as high as the seat.

Water closet and urinal apartments of tenement and lodging houses should in all cases be provided with a window opening into the outer air, or into a ventilating shaft not less than 10 sq. ft. in area. The partitions separating the toilet from the rest of the floor space should either extend to the ceiling, or the apartment be sealed over. These partitions should be made air-tight, and the outside partition be made to include a window opening into the outer air, into a ventilating shaft or into such a lighted area as may be approved by the proper officials. The interior partitions of such toilet apartment should be dwarfed partitions. The general water-closet accommodations for a tenement or lodging house should not be allowed to be installed in any cellar, and all such fixtures should be open, and free from any inclosing woodwork. Sinks of these houses should also be entirely open, and supported on iron legs or brackets, without inclosing woodwork of any description.

If the water pressure is not sufficient to fill the house tank of such buildings as tenement and lodging houses, factories and workshops, power pumps should be provided. Cesspools should never be permitted in the case of tenement and lodging houses, and the yards, areas, and courts of such buildings should be properly drained into the sewer.

Plate XXXIV

PLUMBING FOR APARTMENT BUILDING SYSTEMS OF HOT-WATER SUPPLY—RANGE BOILERS, ETC.

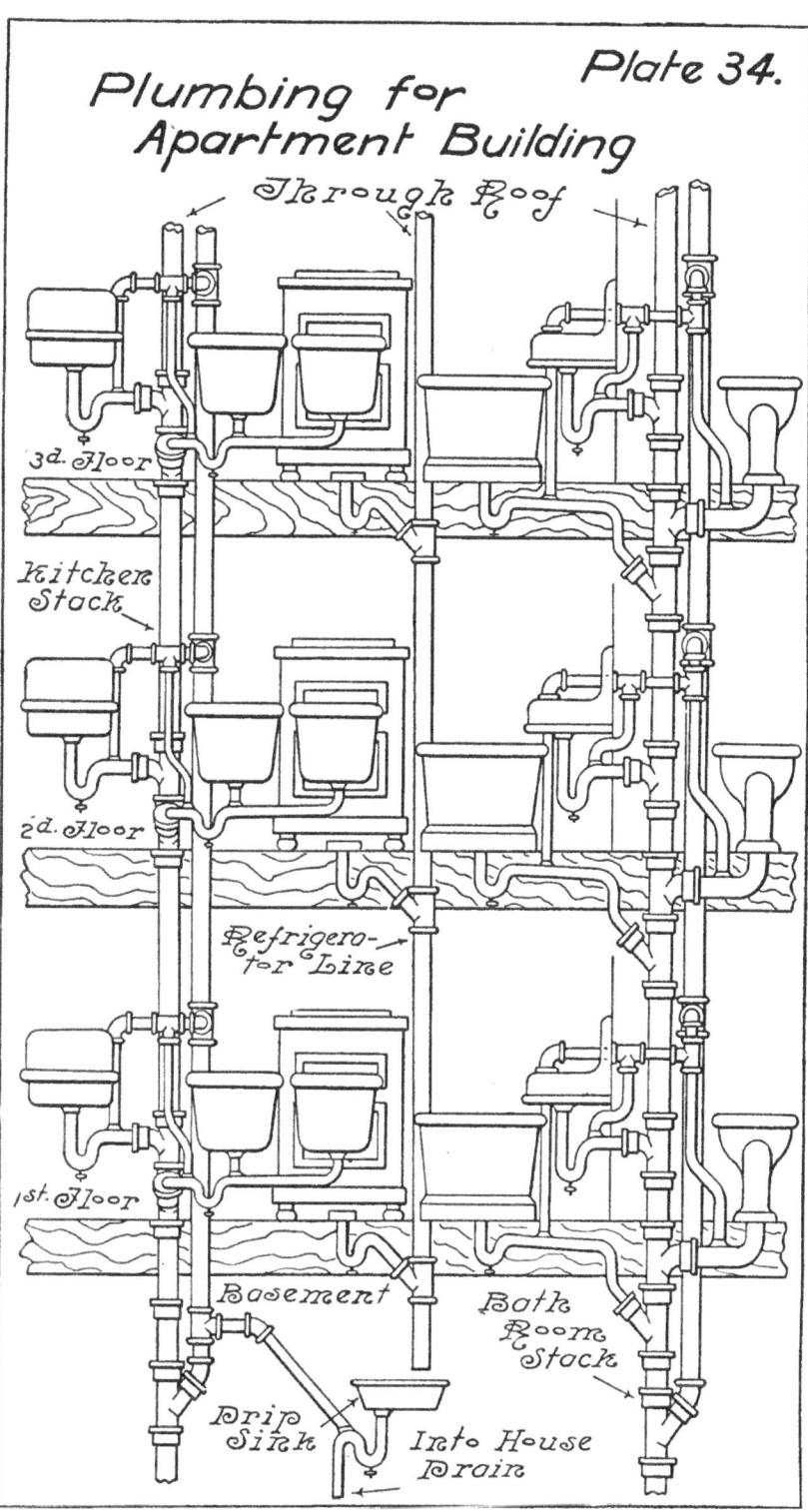

PLUMBING FOR APARTMENT BUILDING—SYSTEMS OF HOT-WATER SUPPLY—RANGE BOILERS, ETC.

It is not the purpose of this work to take up the consideration of either hot- or cold-water supply in a comprehensive manner. There are certain things, however, which many of the readers of this book will desire to know, and some of these will be briefly given at this point.

The range boiler, to be in keeping with the other plumbing fixtures of such work as shown in Plate 34, should be of copper. The galvanized boiler has a great advantage in first cost, but the copper boiler will generally outlast several of the galvanized. On contract work the 30-gallon boiler is much used, but 40 gallons is a better size for apartment buildings having individual range boilers.

For residence work, boilers of larger capacity than 40 gallons are often required. For large apartment buildings, office buildings, etc., it is far more satisfactory and more economical to provide a large tank heated by a special heater. This practice does away with the use of a boiler for each apartment.

A method often followed in the use of the large hot-water tank or boiler, is to provide it with steam coils connected to the heating system, by means of which it may be heated in the winter time, a small heater providing heat for it during the summer time. One of the annoyances in this work comes from carelessness or inattention to the heater on the part of the attendant. This may be avoided by the use of automatic tank regulators, of which there are several makes on the market. By means of such an appliance, the temperature of the boiler heated either by steam coils or coal-burning heater, or by both, may be regulated to a certain temperature.

The size of main necessary to supply the plumbing fixtures for a large apartment building, office building, or other similar building, is a problem that is often difficult to solve. The main and branches, if properly sized, will allow water to be drawn at any fixture or any reasonable number of fixtures, without affecting the free flow of water at other fixtures. When pipes of too small size are used, however, the use of water at a single fixture will result in a reduced flow at other fixtures. The following will be of service in estimating the necessary size of main to perform given amounts of work. In the first place, it must be remembered that all fixtures are not in use at any one time. The chances are that in an apartment such as shown in Plate 34, not more than one fixture in the bath room will be used at any one time, or more than one fixture in the kitchen. Therefore, in the case of apartment buildings, the main will be ample in size if designed to supply two ½-in. fixture supplies per apartment. Thus, if there were 20 apartments, a main having a supplying capacity equal to 40 ½-in. pipes would be of sufficient size. The following table shows the approximate number of ½-in. pipes different larger sizes of pipes will supply:

1 in.	1½ in.	2 in.	2½ in.	3 in.	4 in.	5 in.	6 in.
5	16	32	50	100	200	375	600

Referring to this table, it will be seen that a size between 2 in. and 2½ in. will be required to supply this system. The 2½ in. would be the safer and better size, although 2 in. would no doubt do the work satisfactorily. In a great many systems this question could not be figured out in this way. For instance, in large toilet rooms of hotels, railroad stations, etc., the demand at times is large and at other times small. The main supply lines and branch mains under such conditions must be made to supply maximum requirements.

In supplying hot and cold water to apartment buildings and other similar work, each group of fixtures should be supplied by a separate line. Thus, each kitchen should have its own supply, and each bath room also, each line having a shut-off. This avoids much annoyance, for if otherwise, the making of repairs in one flat might result in the shutting off of the supply in others. On a great deal of high-grade work, faucets for the various fixtures are specified to be of the Fuller pattern, and on public work often of some self-closing pattern. Both Fuller and self-closing work closes very quickly, and water, being almost incompressible, forms a very poor cushion to receive the shock. The common result in the use of these two styles of work is a snapping and jarring of the pipes whenever the faucets are closed. Air chambers properly placed will often entirely remedy this trouble. Compression faucets, however, are much slower in

PLUMBING FOR APARTMENT BUILDING

closing, and from them none of the above annoyances is experienced. Compression work is not only better many times than Fuller' and self-closing work, but it is less expensive.

Two systems of supply are in general use: tank pressure and street pressure. In the use of range boilers on the direct or street-pressure system, supplies are taken directly to the boilers, while in the use of the tank system the supply for the boilers is taken direct to the tank and from that point delivered to the boilers below. The result of the tank method of supply is a uniform pressure, while the direct system gives a pressure which varies greatly according to the demands that are being made upon it. Boilers used on tank systems may usually be of lighter construction than tank boilers, although this is not true in the case of high buildings. The conditions in very high buildings are of a special nature, often requiring special apparatus. For instance, many office buildings, hotels, etc., in the large cities, are of such great height that the pressure on the street mains is not sufficient to force water to the upper floors. Under such circumstances, for those floors not reached by direct pressure, a house tank above all fixtures must be provided, into which water must be pumped.

Large hot-water boilers are generally of the horizontal pattern, hung from the cellar timbers by heavy wrought-iron hangers.

The following is a table of boilers of standard size and make, and their capacities:

Size of Boiler	Capacity	Size of Boiler	Capacity
5 ft. × 12 in.	30 gals.	5 ft. × 30 in.	185 gals.
5 " × 13 "	35 "	8 " × 24 "	192 "
5 " × 14 "	40 "	5½ " × 30 "	203 "
5 " × 16 "	52 "	6 " × 30 "	225 "
5 " × 18 "	66 "	4 " × 36 "	212 "
5 " × 20 "	82 "	5 " × 36 "	265 "
5 " × 22 "	100 "	5½ " × 36 "	290 "
5 " × 24 "	120 "	6 " × 36 "	315 "
4 " × 30 "	140 "	7 " × 36 "	360 "
6 " × 24 "	144 "	8 " × 36 "	425 "
7 " × 24 "	168 "		

For apartment buildings such as shown in Figs. 34 and 35, the construction of circulation work is of very great advantage, as it is in almost any system of plumbing. On ordinary work, the hot-water supply is run from the hot-water main, and ends at the fixture which it supplies. In circulation work, the supply is run from the main also, but it is returned by a circulating or return pipe, into the boiler. The result is that in the first case a long line of pipe filled with cold water must often have to be drawn off before the water will run hot, while in the use of the circulating pipe, the water will run hot almost at once. The latter naturally causes much less annoyance to the person desiring to draw hot water. The first cost of circulation work is greater than that of ordinary work, but if the water is metered and paid for by the cubic foot, it will be found that circulation work generally figures out a good investment.

In installing hot- and cold-water supply systems for large buildings, it is usual to supply headers which are connected with the boiler. Separate headers are used for the cold supply, hot supply and return. The street supply is connected with the cold-water header, and from it all cold-water supply lines are taken out. The flow pipe from the boiler is connected into the hot-water header, and from the header all hot-water supplies are taken off. All return or circulation pipes are connected to the return header, and the latter connected to the boiler return. Each line of pipe connecting with each header should be provided with a stop and waste cock close to the header, a small waste connection from each cock being connected into a main line of waste, which should empty into some convenient basement fixture. Such a waste should not be connected directly into the drainage system. Each line of hot- and cold-water supply, and each return pipe should be provided with a metal tag, showing what fixture, or group of fixtures, and what floor it serves.

A keyboard, as the above arrangement is called, is a very convenient thing, especially on large work, and is much used in nice residences, apartment buildings, office buildings, etc.

In the event of bursts or other emergencies, the keyboard shows at once the valves that control the piping that is to be shut off, and often saves damage to the property that would result if the proper valve could not be found quickly. The use of the valve waste allows the contents of the pipe to drain off into the fixture without discharging onto the cellar bottom.

The foregoing, as already stated, is not meant as comprehensive in any way, but is given simply in a suggestive manner, in connection with the general subject of drainage of different classes of buildings.

Plate XXXV

PLUMBING FOR DOUBLE APARTMENT BUILDINGS—FILTERED WATER SUPPLY

Plate 35.
Plumbing for Double Apartment Building

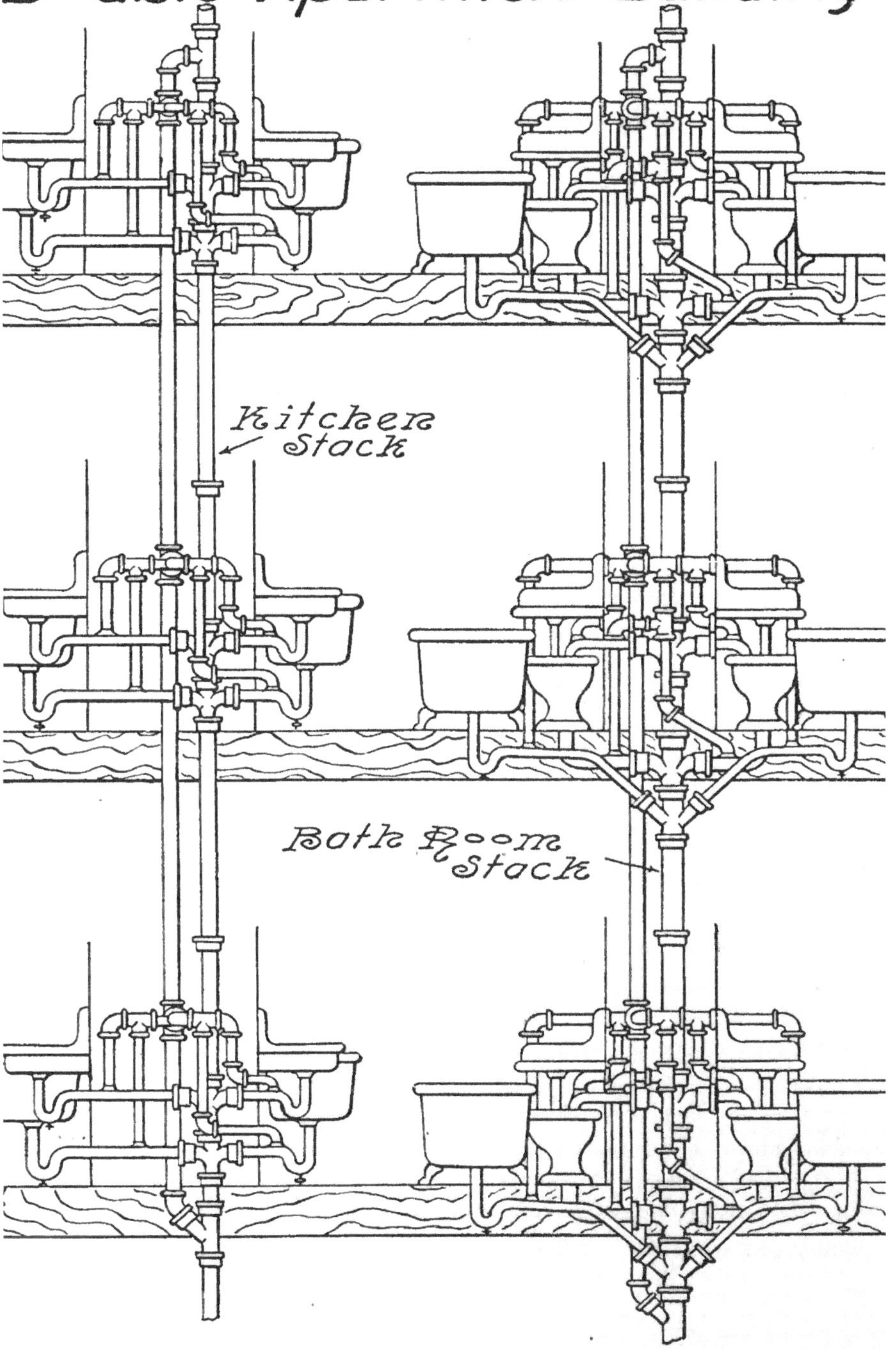

Kitchen Stack

Bath Room Stack

PLUMBING FOR DOUBLE APARTMENT BUILDINGS

IN Plate 35 are shown two stacks serving the fixtures of a double apartment building, one stack for the kitchen fixtures, the other for bath-room fixtures.

The main lines of soil and waste pipes in buildings of this class may often be run in the mutual wall or partition which divides the building at the center. This method centralizes the plumbing, and allows the work to be installed at the lowest possible cost of labor and material.

Lack of space prevents showing in this system a line of refrigerator waste, which should always be provided in buildings of this class. In the more pretentious apartment buildings a pantry sink is often provided for each apartment and sometimes one or more bed-room lavatories.

Connected with the general plumbing arrangements for apartment buildings, office buildings, etc., the matter of a filtered water supply is now demanding much attention, as also for residences, and a brief consideration of the subject will not be out of place at this point.

FILTERED WATER SUPPLY

There is a constantly growing demand for filtered water supplies for city buildings of nearly all classes, the demand increasing as the country grows in population, and as a consequence hitherto pure supplies of water become polluted.

There are two forms of filtration, that which clears the water of all mechanical impurities, such as rust, sediment, etc., and that which not only clarifies the water, but frees it of all germ life and renders it free from the danger of producing such diseases as typhoid fever. For commercial purposes, for the bath room, etc., the first-named form of filtration is sufficient, but for drinking and culinary purposes, the latter form should be required. It is a mistaken idea that the ordinary filtration plant which filters the supply for an entire building in every case purifies the water of disease germs. The water coming through such apparatus is certainly rendered purer as far as inorganic matter is concerned, but a filter working under pressure cannot deliver water so free from the more dreaded disease germs as the filter which operates by the gravity of the water passing through it.

An ideal provision for the supply of filtered water would include the installation of a pressure filter on the main supply of the building, to clarify and purify the entire supply for the building outside of the supply for drinking purposes, and the installation of a gravity filter supplying a separate system of piping for drinking and culinary purposes. In place of the latter, a form of filter of excellent construction, described as follows, may be used. The common form of the filter referred to is made in different sizes for domestic use, filtering enough water during the twenty-four hours of the day to provide a liberal supply of drinking water.

The apparatus is briefly as follows: Connection by means of block-tin pipe is made to the supply pipe, the water being conveyed to a sheet-metal tank hung on the wall, inside of which, and attached to a collecting device, are unglazed porcelain tubes filled with bone-black or animal charcoal. The water is admitted to the tank through a ball cock, which admits it only as fast as drawn. The water, by means of its own gravity only, filters through the tubes and their contents, and flows into the collector to which the tubes are connected by rubber connectors. From the collector the filtered water runs down into a glass globe attached to the bottom of the tank, from which the water may be drawn as required.

In most of the large cities will be found companies operating this and other domestic filters, who inspect, clean, and sterilize the apparatus each month. Upon the periodical attention given to filters depends their satisfactory operation. If no attention is given them, after a time the tubes clog up and refuse to filter, or if filtration continues it is under very unsafe conditions, as all water passing through must come in contact with the thick covering of sediment and impurities collected on the outside of the tubes. This same style of filter in a modified form, can be made to produce any amount of pure water desired per day, and is made use of extensively for providing the drinking supply of hotels, restaurants, hospitals, and other institutions which desire nothing but a pure quality of drinking water.

On large work, the empty tubes are placed in large copper tanks,

FILTERED WATER SUPPLY

supplied through a ball cock, and the water after filtering through the tubes is conveyed from the collectors into other smaller tanks filled with animal charcoal. The double filtration is done entirely by gravity, and produces a perfectly pure water. The animal charcoal is placed in separate tanks on large work, simply to economize labor in cleaning. If the water delivered to filters of this class first passes through the house pressure filter, much of the heavier matter in suspension, sediment, etc., will be taken out, rendering less frequent attention to the gravity filter necessary.

Pressure filters are of various form and make, using many different materials for the filtering medium. When stone or porcelain of a fine quality is used as the filtering medium, a very large percentage of the germ impurities may be removed. A very important feature of all pressure filters is the matter of frequent cleansing, which is absolutely essential. Certain makes of pressure filters depend upon large masses of bone-black for their filtering material, and experimental tests show this to be one of the most effective filtering mediums.

One form of bone-black filter consists of two separate cylinders filled with bone-black, but so connected that by the use of a device known as a manipulator, the entire filter may be switched off from the house it supplies; or the water supply may be divided and sent through each cylinder equally; or the water may be sent through each cylinder in succession, thus filtering the same water twice; or the water may be filtered through either cylinder alone without effecting in any way the supply of filtered water to the building supplied. Thus in this filter, as in the one previously described, each cylinder may be washed by filtered water from the other, and while the entire filter is thus being cleaned, the supply to the house is not cut off or affected in any way.

Experiment has shown that the effectiveness of a filtering medium depends directly upon the amount of air space contained between its particles. This is the reason that porous stone, porcelain, and such materials do such excellent filtering. Sand contains a great deal of air also, but it is claimed that bone-black contains nearly twice as much as sand, owing to the packing together of the latter. The action of filtration depends upon the action of infinite numbers of bacteria which live and multiply in the air spaces of the filtering medium. These bacteria must have air in order to perform their work, and air will not penetrate in sufficient quantity through sand to feed them at a depth of more than three or four feet. Air will penetrate much more thoroughly through bone-black, it is claimed, and therefore this material is preferable for filter use.

The bone-black filter described above is cleaned by forcing compressed air into the mass of bone-black, thus breaking it up into particles, after which the flow of filtered water is sent through the material, thoroughly cleansing it, and carrying it off into the waste.

In the use of sand in pressure filters, it is necessary to use a coagulating agent, owing to the closeness with which the sand packs. For this purpose alum is generally used, and its action is to coagulate the sediment and other impurities of the water into such large masses that they cannot pass through the sand. While the use of alum is not ordinarily harmful, it is not desirable, and it makes the water hard, which is undesirable for many manufacturing purposes.

A great many forms of pressure filters are now made, most of them using either sand, bone-black, porcelain or stone as the filtering medium, and being provided with a variety of apparatus and methods for cleansing.

There are three methods of providing a storage of filtered water, each having advantages of its own.

Storage by means of the closed overhead tank is mostly used. The delivery pipe from filter to tank also answers as the down supply for the building, thus effecting a saving in pipe. An air vent at the top allows air to pass into and out of the tank, but prevents overflow. In this system no impurities can reach the water, which is not true of the open-tank system.

Storage by the open gravity tank is often the most convenient to install in houses already provided with an attic tank.

The open gravity tank is used when the filtered supply must be forced into it by a pump.

The pressure, or compression system is also much used. Only pressure tanks should be used for this work, as others will not hold air sufficiently well to produce the desired compression.

The pressure tank is placed close to the filter into which the latter delivers filtered water, and from the tank the house supply is taken, under pressure. When the tank is filled to its full capacity with water under air compression, the compression stops the action of the filter until water is drawn. The chief drawback to the use of this system is the use of tanks of too small capacity to provide a sufficient reserve supply of filtered water.

Plate XXXVI

PLUMBING FOR OFFICE BUILDINGS

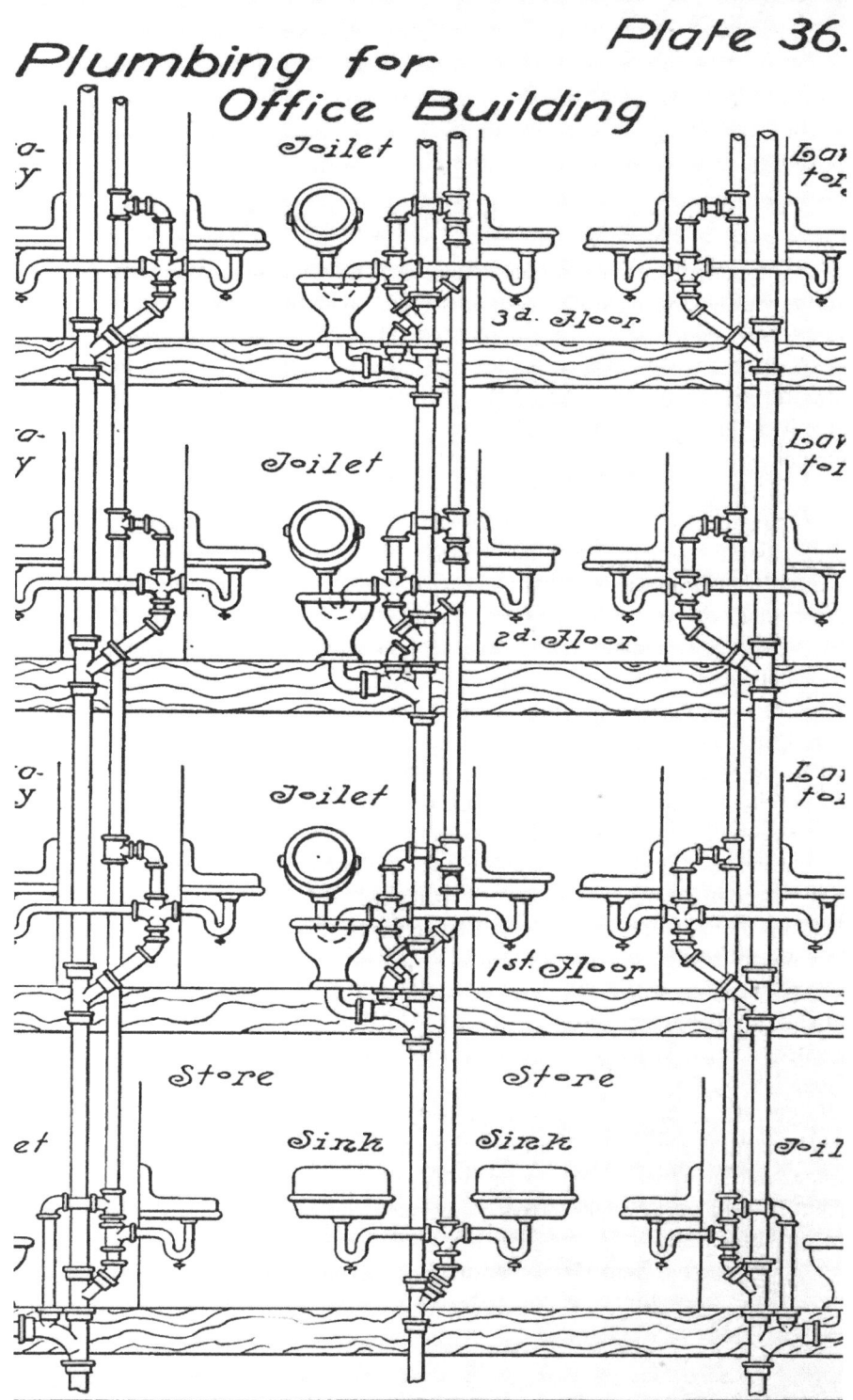

PLUMBING FOR OFFICE BUILDINGS

The plumbing for office buildings is naturally varied, but consists largely of lines of lavatories and toilet rooms, both public and private, successive floors often being duplicates. The continuous vent principle may often be applied to lines of fixtures in office buildings to the benefit of the plumbing system and with a saving over common methods in both material and labor. In office buildings and other buildings containing many stories, the following limitations in the size of soil-pipe stacks should be observed.

Regardless of the small number of fixtures that may enter it, a soil-pipe stack in any building between five and twelve stories in height should not be less than 5 in. in diameter, and in buildings of more than twelve stories, this size should never be less than 6 in.

For sizes of main vent lines, the following regulations should be adhered to:

Main vent lines for water closets on three or more floors should not be less than 3 in. in diameter; a main vent line for fixtures other than water closets on less than seven floors should be not less than 2 in.; for less than nine stories 3-in. main vent; for nine to sixteen stories, 4-in. main vent; for sixteen to twenty-two stories, 5-in. main vent; for twenty-two stories and up, 6-in. main vent should be used. These requirements result in centralizing the plumbing, as it would become an expensive matter to run large stacks through many stories simply to provide for a few fixtures.

Whenever water closets are located on different floors, as in Plate 36, they should each be vented, with the exception of the top water closet. When two water closets, however, are located close together on the same floor, it is not essential to vent both fixtures if they waste into the same Y branch. It is sufficient to prevent siphonage, to vent only the water closet that is the farther from the stack. When two water closets discharge into a double fitting, a mutual vent may be taken from a hub near the junction of the two branches. Fittings of this kind are easily obtained, and it will be seen that the one vent taken from this point vents both the fixtures.

Many plumbing ordinances call for the venting of all water closets except a water closet above which no other fixtures enter. As a matter of fact, it is very difficult to siphon a water-closet trap even partially, by the discharge of other fixtures than water closets. Therefore, it does not seem necessary to vent any water closet which is the only fixture of its kind on the stack, provided the water closet is within 3 ft. of the stack. For the same reason it does not seem necessary to vent either of two water closets discharging into a double fitting, and located on the same floor close to the stack, if other water closets do not discharge into the same stack. Judgment must be used in these instances, however, for batteries of fixtures such as lavatories might be located on the same stack as a single water closet, and be able to throw enough waste into the stack to endanger the water closet.

If it could be depended upon that people of high intelligence were always to install the plumbing system, and also that in every case they could be depended upon to install the work honestly, there are many conditions constantly arising under which a safe piece of work could be constructed without the necessity of venting, whereas venting under the circumstances is required by ordinance. Because dependence of this nature cannot be made, iron-clad rules must be adopted to make the attainment of perfect work a surety.

Plate XXXVII

PLUMBING FOR PUBLIC TOILET ROOMS CAUSES OF SIPHONAGE IN THE UN-VENTED PLUMBING SYSTEM

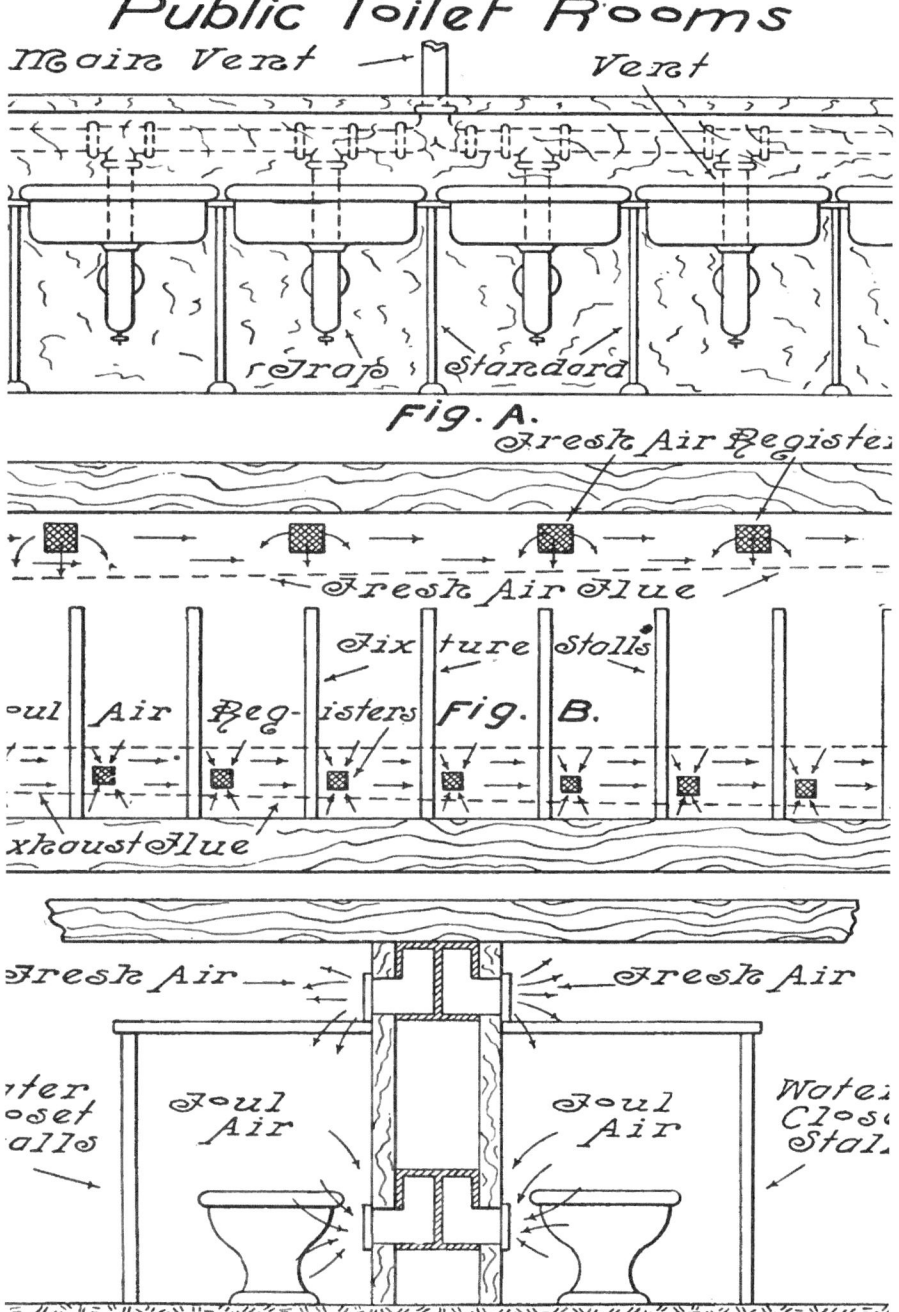

PLUMBING FOR PUBLIC TOILET ROOMS

THE public toilet room of to-day is a far more sanitary institution than that of a few years ago. This is due not to one thing only, but to several.

The methods and practices of installing such work are superior to those of times past; the manufacturer has improved the construction and quality of fixtures in a wonderful manner; and a plentiful supply of light and thorough ventilation are provided.

The floor of the public toilet room, formerly of wood, which soon became reeking with filth, is now of tile or waterproof material, and adds beauty to the room. To provide for the thorough washing out of the room, one or more floor drains should be installed in each such room. For this purpose, an excellent device is that shown in Fig. B, Plate 16. It can be flushed thoroughly with hot water when desired, and thus kept in a clean condition. An important feature of the sanitary public toilet room is the thorough ventilation of the room. In order to succeed in providing perfect ventilation, means must be provided for bringing in a supply of fresh air if foul air is to be drawn out. In Fig. B of Plate 37 is shown a method much employed in providing this ventilation. It will be seen that the foul-air duct is run at the bottom of the room, each fixture stall or compartment being connected to it by means of a small register opening into the flue.

This flue should be connected with a flue constantly heated, or may be provided at its outer end with an exhaust fan. As the foul air is thus exhausted, fresh air enters the room at various points near the ceiling, through registers opening into a fresh-air duct.

If sufficient fresh air does not enter through the flue by natural means, a fan may be employed to force in a sufficient supply. Fig. C shows in section the arrangement of flues, from which it will be seen that they are generally run in a space behind the partition, against which the fixtures are set. Very often the tanks for the water closets and urinals are also concealed in this space, as shown in Plate 38. In the case of large toilet rooms, these flues may be continued for any desired distance, and on different sides of the room.

It will be found desirable to allow openings in both foul- and fresh-air ducts at intervals during their course outside of the fixture-stall openings. In this way a perfect exhaust of foul air and entrance of fresh air may be maintained, and the air of the room kept as nearly pure as possible for the air of a room of this character to be kept. In rooms of this nature, a change of air once in fifteen minutes should be provided for. In proportioning the area of these ducts, about 24 sq. in. of duct area should ordinarily be allowed for each urinal, water closet, and slop sink, and about one half this amount for such fixtures as lavatories, and the effective area of ventilation through the registers should be of the respective amount for each fixture named. It is better practice to raise all partitions of fixture compartments off the floor in public toilet room work, as there is then no opportunity for the collection of dirt and filth about the bases. If located in such a place that outside light cannot enter the toilet room, it should be lighted as thoroughly as possible from a light shaft or skylight, through windows opening into a lighted room, or by artificial means. Water-closet compartments are generally about 7 ft. in height above the floor, and urinal stalls about 4 ft. and 6 or 8 in. The best practice in the construction of toilet rooms to be used by the public, such as to be found in hotels, schools, factories, etc., calls for the use of the individual water closet. The range water closet as constructed and provided for to-day, is certainly far superior to the old style construction, but the fact remains that in its use there is greater danger of infection, and it is more difficult to keep the air of the room pure when ranges are used, as excreta must remain in the bowl until the automatic flush acts, whereas in the use of individual tank water closets this is carried away immediately after the fixture has been used. If the range is to be used, however, a large foul-air flue should be provided at the end of the range, and entered into a heated flue capable of producing a strong draught on the foul-air flue.

It is quite customary to provide public comfort stations and toilet rooms with drinking fountains placed in close proximity to other fixtures. It would seem preferable and more cleanly to place this fixture outside of the toilet room, where it will not be in the midst of foul and impure odors.

The only sanitary drinking fountain is that in which no drinking cup is required.

Drinking fountains of this type are now much used, the water

CAUSES OF SIPHONAGE

issuing through bubbling cups which may be adjusted to give any desired amount of water. The user simply places his mouth over the stream coming from the bubbling cup, his mouth coming in contact with nothing but the water. The ordinary fountain with its common drinking cup is unsanitary and a successful agent for the spreading of many diseases. These fountains are made singly in pedestal form, and in batteries of any number of bubbling cups, the latter being especially desirable for school use.

In the installation of long lines of lavatories, each lavatory should be provided with its own trap, and separately vented. The use of a common waste pipe extending the whole length of a long battery of lavatories to a trap at the end is to be considered very poor practice. It leaves a long line of foul waste pipe to send its odors into the room through each waste connection into it.

In order to economize space, it often becomes necessary to locate a double battery of lavatories at the center of the public toilet room, a matter that is usually difficult owing to the impossibility usually, of running the waste and vent pipes concealed, as is desirable in work of this kind. Fig. A shows a method of accomplishing this result, which is considered further in connection with Plate 38.

CAUSES OF SIPHONAGE IN THE UNVENTED PLUMBING SYSTEM

Under the subject of venting, taken up under Plate 11, it was seen that the trap seal may be lost by siphonage, the latter action following the formation in the drainage system of a vacuum or partial vacuum. Some of the ways in which this vacuum may be formed in the drainage system that is not provided with a system of trap vents, are considered in the following.

Siphonage of a trap may be caused by the outflow of the waste from its own fixture, the momentum of which is sometimes sufficient to suck out a large part of the seal. When two fixture wastes branch into the same pipe, the passage of the waste from one fixture may fill the pipe sufficiently to produce a vacuum behind the column of waste, and thus siphon out the seal of the other trap.

A fixture having a long line of horizontal waste is often endangered by a partial temporary stoppage in the horizontal part of the waste. When this stoppage is relieved, the waste filling the pipe may flow off so strongly as to produce a vacuum behind it and cause siphonage. This is true even of the water closet. The passage of a heavy volume of waste down a vertical stack may produce a partial vacuum at the entrance into the stack of another fixture, causing the trap of the latter to lose its seal. Fixtures at the foot of a stack are more open to the danger of trap siphonage than those nearer the top of the stack. As the lower floors are reached, more waste fills the stack than at points farther up, and as this heavy volume of waste strikes the horizontal line it is naturally impeded, and more nearly fills the pipe, with a consequent greater danger of producing a vacuum followed by the siphonage of trap seals.

These conditions that have been described are the cause of many of the rules regulating the construction of plumbing, such as the prohibition of quarter-bends on the drainage system, for instance, the use of which would impede the outflow of waste far more than the Y branch and eighth-bend form of connection between vertical and horizontal lines.

Plate XXXVIII

PLUMBING FOR PUBLIC TOILET ROOMS

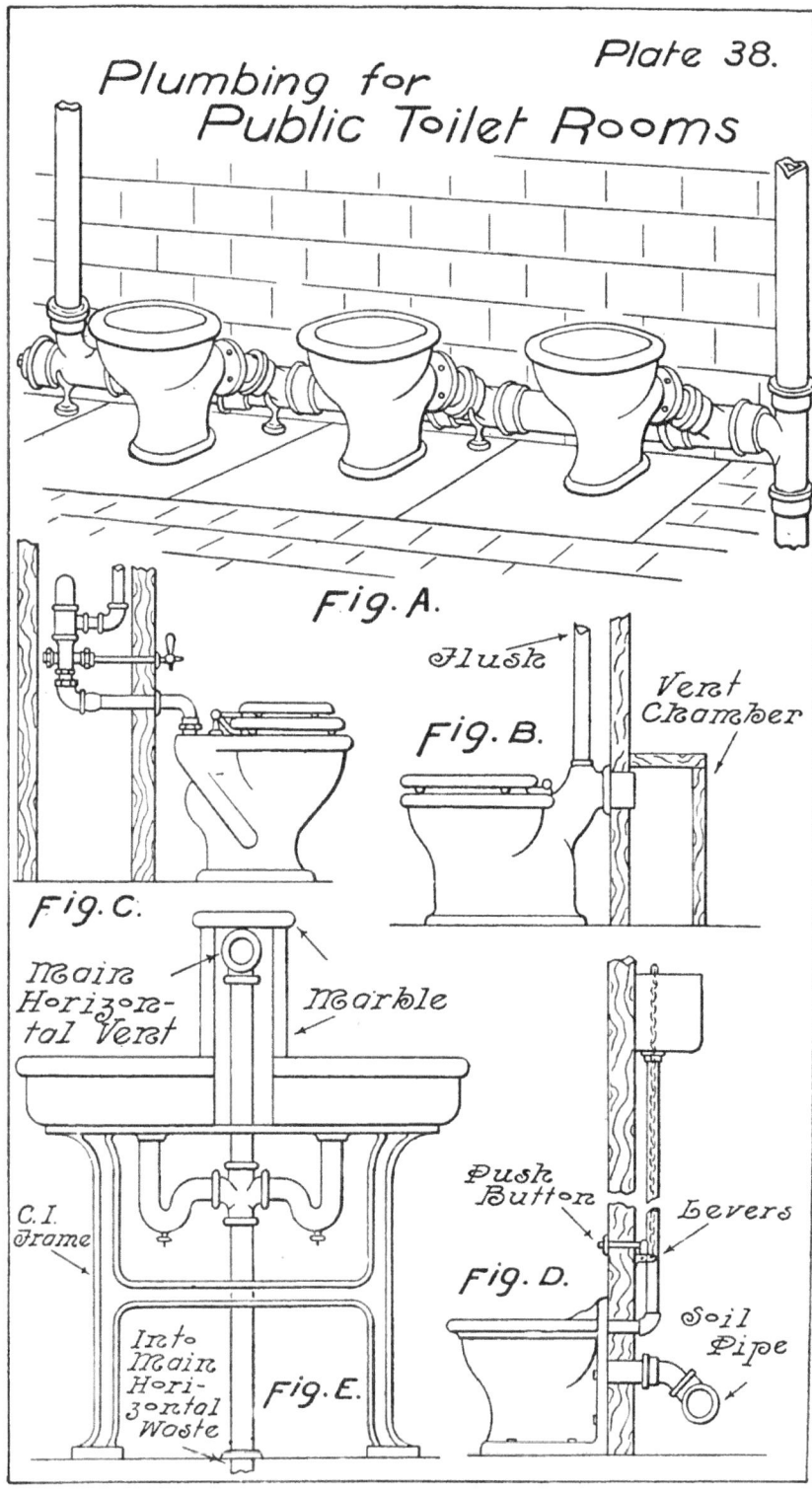

PLUMBING FOR PUBLIC TOILET ROOMS

In Fig. A of Plate 37 and Fig. E of Plate 38 are shown two views, front and end, of double batteries of lavatories installed at the center of the public toilet room, or in such location that no partition may be used for concealing the waste and vent piping.

Each individual lavatory is separately trapped and provided with a continuous vent, this work showing the principle of continuous venting applied somewhat differently than in Plates 26, 27, and 28, though with equal effectiveness. In Fig. A, Plate 37, it is intended to show the main horizontal waste pipe run above the floor, while in Fig. E, Plate 38, the main is run below the floor, and branch wastes connected from each fixture.

Either method that is most desirable may be used. The chief feature of this work is the concealment of the main vent line and branch vents inside a box formed by the marble backs of the two lines of fixtures, and a piece of marble set on top. The marble box runs the entire length of the line, which may rise vertically to run to a vertical vent stack at any intermediate point, as in Fig. A, or at either end. The lavatories in both illustrations are of porcelain or porcelain-lined ware, and supported on cast-iron standards. In Fig. A, the marble backs run down to the floor, allowing all but the traps to be concealed in the space between the two marble back slabs, while in the case of Fig. E the space below the lavatories is open, and a part of the work is in sight.

The use of continuous vents is of great advantage in this instance, as it not only allows the work to be done in a more sanitary manner, more neatly and compactly than by ordinary methods, but at far less cost of labor and material. This last advantage is gained in the use of continuous vents on nearly all work where fixtures back up to each other in pairs, whether under such circumstances as these or on opposite sides of a partition.

Under ordinary circumstances, it is not difficult to so construct the toilet room that much of the work may be concealed in open spaces behind partitions.

In Fig. C, for instance, the flush valves for a line of water closets may be thus concealed, and as in Fig. D, the flush tanks, whether high or low, and the horizontal soil pipe may both be concealed.

Concealment of working parts, such as flush valves and tanks, with their chains and pulls, is often very desirable, especially in school and factory work, where there is danger of damage due to mischievous tampering with such devices. When so concealed, however, the working parts should be made accessible for repairs and inspection.

The use of the circuit system of venting is often of much advantage in public toilet rooms, especially in connection with lines of water closets. It is applied in the case of Fig. A, and might be applied to equal advantage in Fig. D.

The choice of water closets for public toilet-room work is almost unlimited, if the matter of expense is not to be considered. Fig. D shows a very desirable form in many respects. It is so constructed that it fits squarely into the corner made by the partition, and may be made much more firm and secure against accidental blows by being bolted both to the floor and to the partition. It has a rear outlet which allows the soil pipe to be run above the floor. This method of running the soil pipe and connecting the water closets is of special value in fire-proof buildings and for public buildings of various kinds. The soil pipe is supported on standards, the entire work presenting a very neat appearance. In Fig. B a very convenient form of water closet is shown, provided with a large local vent connection, which is a part of the bowl itself. This local vent connection gives a much more finished appearance to the fixture than a connection made with metal pipe. The connection is designed to project into a foul-air flue located back of the partition against which the water closets are set.

When water closets of public toilet rooms are flushed by individual flush tanks, the capacity of the latter should not be less than for other uses, that is, not less than of 5 gallons capacity.

When supplied from an automatic flush tank, however, the latter should be of such capacity that each water closet on the line shall be flushed by at least four gallons of water at each discharge of the tank.

All lip urinals, water closets, and slop sinks used in public toilet rooms should be of the flushing-rim type, this form of fixture being flushed and cleansed more thoroughly than others.

Plate XXXIX

PLUMBING FOR BATH ESTABLISHMENT
TANKS FOR STORAGE AND SUPPLY

Plumbing for Bath Establishment

Plate 39.

Toilet Room

Bath Room

Shower Baths

Concrete Gutter

Floor Drain

Swimming Pool

Shower Baths

To Toilet

Concrete Gutter

PLUMBING FOR BATH ESTABLISHMENT

SYSTEMS of plumbing such as that shown in Plate 39 are to be found in Turkish-bath establishments, clubs, Y. M. C. A. buildings, and in other like institutions. Such a system usually includes a number of shower-bath compartments, other compartments for tub baths, swimming pool, lines of lavatories, and ample toilet arrangements.

A very important feature in the bath establishment is the liberal use of floor drains, for a great deal of water naturally falls upon the floors; and in addition, abundant opportunity must be provided for flushing and thoroughly cleansing. Owing to impurities washed from the skin, the bath rooms of an establishment of this kind may become exceedingly filthy unless constant attention is given them. For this reason many such bath rooms are supplied with flushing-rim floor drains provided with hot- and cold-water connections, which are very effectual in keeping such drains in a sanitary condition.

All floors and walls of bath establishments should be of tile or waterproof material. The walls and ceilings should never be covered with any material that may absorb moisture and odors.

Generally the waste from a line of shower baths is carried off in a gutter at the rear of the stalls, the stall floors being graded so that all water will flow into the gutter.

The gutter may be formed in the floor itself or of slate or marble set into the floor for this purpose, or it may be of cast iron. The gutter should be graded to its outlet. The outlet should connect into a cast or wrought-iron waste line, and be provided with a trap, the size of which should be determined by the number of shower baths which are served, the size generally being from 2 to 4 in.

This trap should be provided with a 2-in. vent and cleanouts.

The plunge or swimming pool should waste through a 4-in. trap, provided with a 2-in. vent and cleanouts of the same size as the trap. The bottom of the pool should be graded toward the outlet end. The swimming pool should be provided with ladders reaching down into it, and a brass hand rail running completely around it.

The water of the swimming pool, when constantly in use, should be changed at least once in seven hours.

Although not seen in Plate 39, the swimming pool should be provided with an overflow. The plunge bath is now to be found occasionally in the basement of fine residences, and the use of shower apparatus of extensive nature has become a common feature of high-grade and well-appointed bath rooms. In some sections, where the water supply is not remarkably clear, the filtering of the water used in the bath establishment will be found to add much to its luxuries. As in the case of other public toilet rooms, it sometimes becomes necessary to provide a storage of water to be used at such times as the regular supply is inadequate.

Concerning the use of tanks, the following remarks may be of value:

TANKS FOR STORAGE AND SUPPLY

Formerly the attic tank, which supplied the house with water under tank pressure, was of large size, holding several hundred gallons. To-day, however, much smaller tanks are used for this purpose. They are supplied with a ball cock, thus allowing water to enter the tank at the same rate that it is drawn out.

The storage tank, although it may be used for the same purpose and in the same way as the common attic tank, is generally used as an auxiliary to the pressure system of supply, and may be of any size, from a capacity of a few hundred gallons to many thousands. These tanks should be of wood or iron, or of wood lined with heavy tinned sheet copper.

The best materials for wooden tanks are cypress, white and yellow pine, cypress being the most satisfactory.

The storage tank should be supported on heavy iron beams which will not sag under the immense weight of the tank and its contents.

In many cases the storage tank must be placed above the point that the pressure supply can reach. Its supply must then be pumped into it. In high buildings it often happens that during the day time, when the mains are being heavily drawn on, the street pressure is not sufficient to force water into the tank, but during the night it is sufficient. A supply can thus be stored at night for use during the day time on those floors not reached by the city pressure.

Tanks should always be covered in order to keep out dust, foul gases, and odors.

Plate XL

PLUMBING FOR ENGINE HOUSE AND STABLES—FACTORY PLUMBING

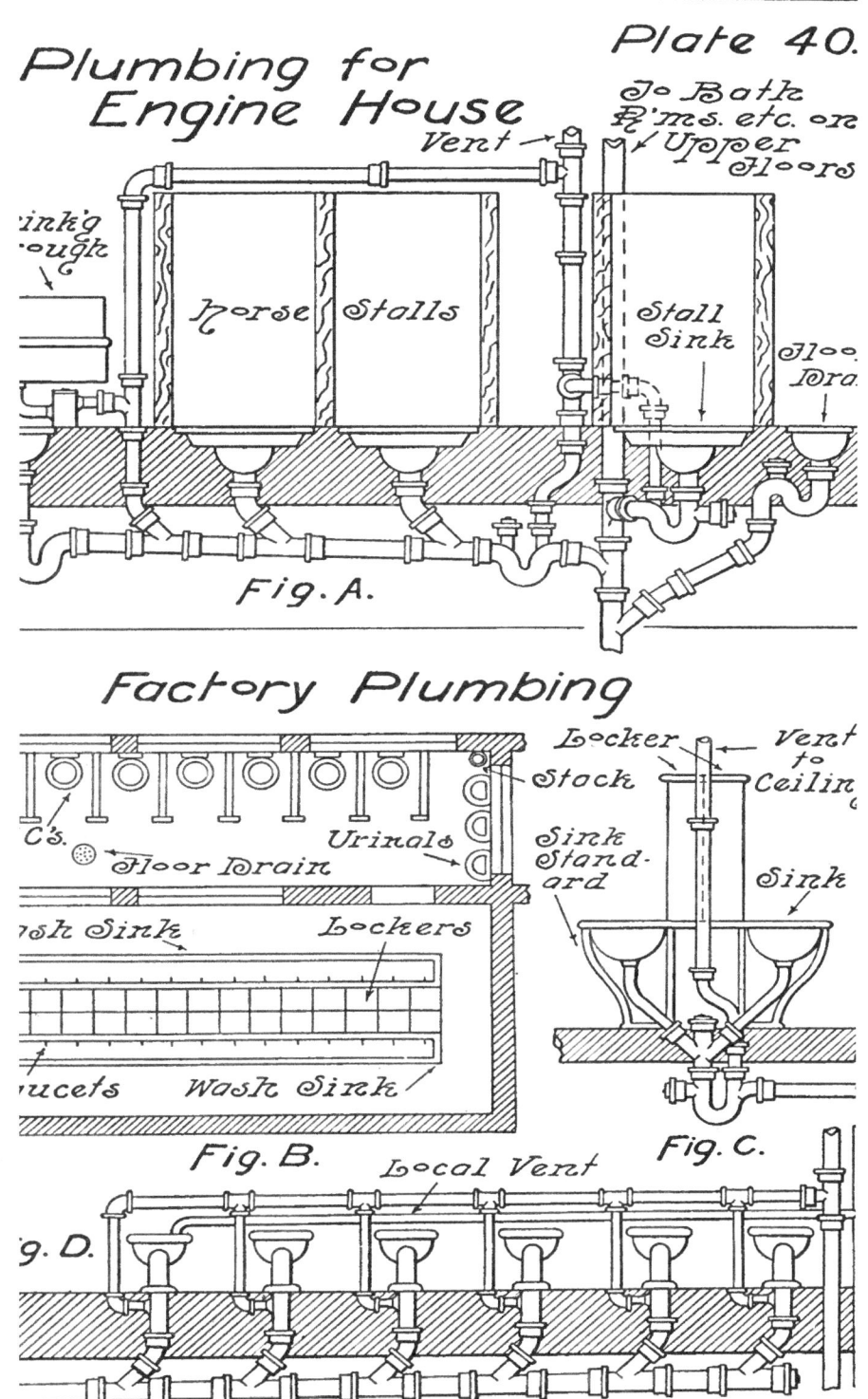

PLUMBING FOR ENGINE HOUSE AND STABLES

In Plate 40 is shown the elevation of a system of plumbing for an engine house. The same style of work may also be used in private stables.

In addition to the connections shown, there are usually toilet accommodations for the hostler, in the case of the stable, and bath rooms and toilet fixtures for the engine house. Floor drains should be placed in the apparatus room, wash rooms, hose tower, etc. The construction and connection of stall sinks is shown in detail by Plate 10. Two adjacent stall sinks may be served by the same trap.

The plumbing system for a stable should be provided with the same sanitary features as for the house system. A separate main drain should be provided for it to the street sewer, which should not be connected with the house drain of any building.

Even under the most favorable conditions, more or less solid matter from the stalls will find its way into the drain, and the following provision is of advantage. All wastes from stables, including waste from wash rooms, manure pits, etc., may, before entering the street sewer, be discharged into a catch basin located underground outside of the stable. The catch basin may be constructed of brick or of cast iron, and should be water-tight, with a tight cover, and properly vented. The outlet from the catch basin may be connected to the stable sewer or street sewer.

FACTORY PLUMBING

The sanitary arrangements of well-appointed factories of the present day are of as high an excellence as for schools and other institutions. There is no reason why they should not be of a high standard, but it is true that, until within a comparatively few years, they have often been given scant attention.

The ventilation of the toilet room should be on the same scale and as thorough as that of other public toilet rooms. In Fig. B is shown a floor plan of part of a factory toilet room.

As will be seen, it is thoroughly lighted from outside windows and also by inside windows, the latter admitting light from the outside to the wash room. The floor should be constructed of waterproofed concrete, and provided with a floor drain, as the thorough flushing out of such rooms is very essential.

A sill cock, conveniently located, will be found convenient in supplying water for this purpose.

In Fig. D is shown the common method of venting such a line of water closets and the connection of the main horizontal vent line into the main vent stack. The use of the circuit-vent system, as shown in Plate 29, is advantageous in such work, and results in reducing the cost of installation.

In buildings of factory construction, horizontal waste and soil lines may be run on the ceiling of the floor below, thus making such lines, with their cleanouts, accessible from the floor below. It may be stated that, in using the circuit and loop vents, it is desirable to run the horizontal soil line as close to the bases of the water closets as possible. The line of water closets shown is provided with local vents. Ventilation by means of fresh and foul-air flues and fans, as described in Plate 37, is preferable for large toilet rooms to the system shown in Fig. D, as it is more thorough, purifying the air of the entire room more effectually. The wash sink for factory use is an important matter.

In Fig. B a double line of wash sinks is shown, and in Fig. C an end view of the same. The sinks shown are of enameled cast iron, cast in sections, thus allowing any length of sink to be used. They are supported on cast-iron standards, and made in a variety of forms. The waste may be arranged as in Fig. C, which shows a short waste connection above the floor, leading into a trap which serves both lines, the horizontal waste being of cast or wrought iron and hung on the ceiling below. In factory and school plumbing systems it is well to have as little piping exposed as possible, owing to the rough and careless usage given it.

The size of the waste from the factory sink should not be less than 2 in., and 3 in. for sinks of great length. The trap should be vented with 2-in. cast- or wrought-iron pipe, which is carried vertically to the ceiling, and then horizontally into the nearest vent stack.

Plate XLI

AUTOMATIC FLUSHING FOR SCHOOLS, FACTORIES, ETC.

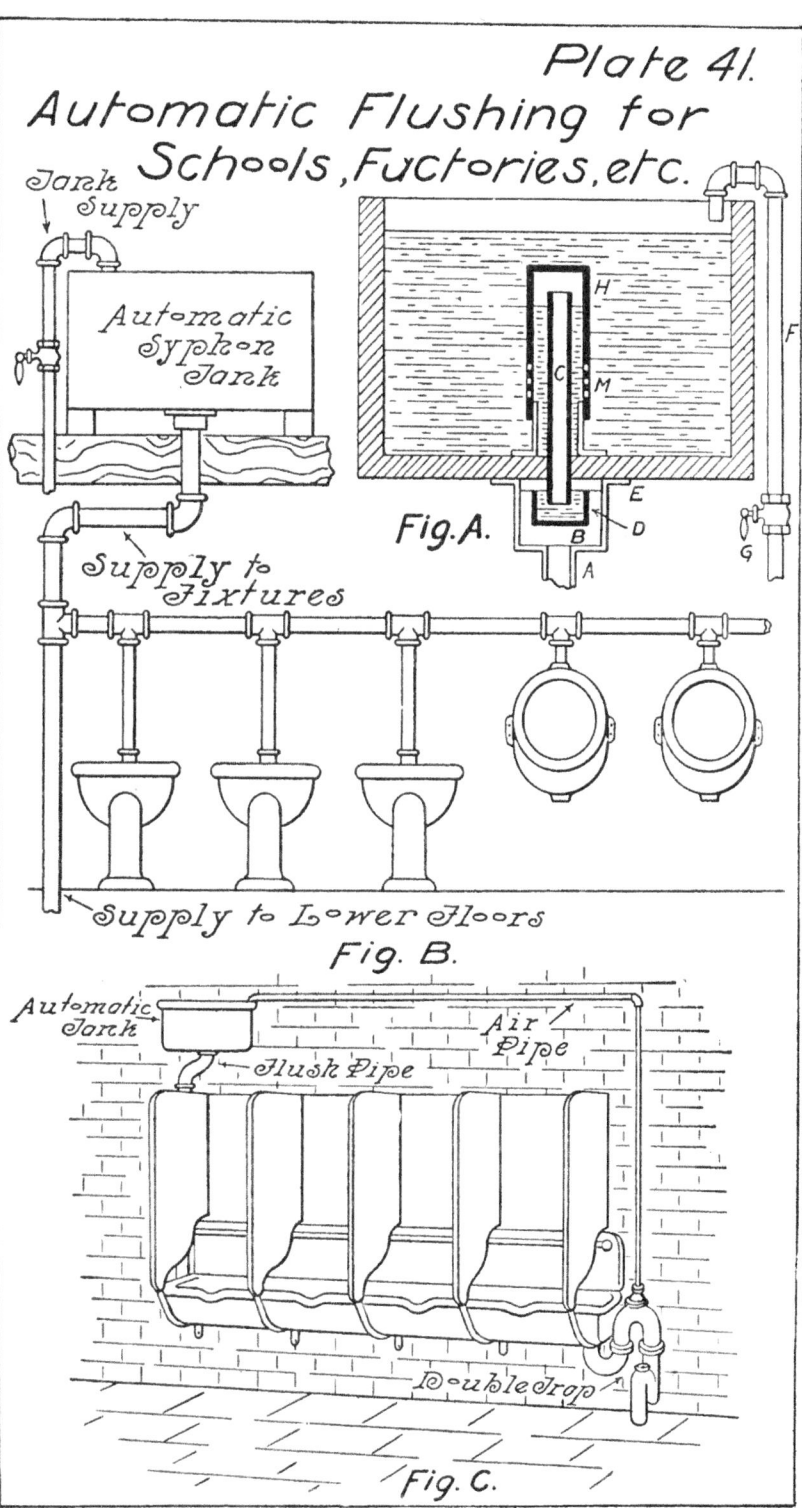

AUTOMATIC FLUSHING FOR SCHOOLS, FACTORIES, ETC.

It is often desirable to provide groups of such fixtures as water closets and urinals with automatic flushing, such provision being specially valuable in school and factory use, and often in public work, such as railway-station toilet rooms, public comfort stations, etc. In the use of any toilet room for the accommodation of the public, the fixtures are bound to be used by many people who are ignorant or careless in the matter of flushing fixtures after having used them. In the matter of urinals, especially, the flushing of them is often left to the attention of an attendant who may be careless in performing this duty. In school houses particularly, small children using the fixtures cannot always be expected to understand the necessity of flushing water closets. Owing to these circumstances and many others, the periodic and automatic flushing of fixtures is of much advantage in maintaining wholesome toilet rooms.

In Fig. A, Plate 41, is shown a sectional view of a form of automatic flush tank, the action of which is as follows:

The admission of water to the automatic tank is not controlled by ball cock, as the supply must be constant. The interval between flushes depends upon the amount of water flowing into the tank, which is regulated by the valve G. The principal working parts of the flushing device consist of a circular vessel D, which is supported by several wires attached to the outer circular compartment B. The vessel D, is filled with water, into which a tube C, projects. Outside of C is a hollow cylinder H, closed at its upper end, and supplied with holes at the bottom, through which the water may enter. As the water rises in the tank, it fills the space between the tubs C and the cylinder H, the air in the tube and at the top of the cylinder being confined between the rising level of the water and the water seal of D. This air becomes more and more compressed as the water rises, until the pressure exerted is sufficient to force the water out of D. This produces a vacuum at the bottom of the tube, and the compression being relieved, atmospheric pressure on the surface of the water in the tank will force it into the tube C, and into the flush pipe A, which conveys it to the different fixtures to be flushed.

This siphonic action continues until the water in the tank drops to such a point that air is admitted through the holes M, when the action stops, the tank again beginning to fill for the next flush.

Fig. B shows the general plan of connections between the tank and the fixtures.

The principles governing the construction, locating, etc., of storage tanks also apply to automatic flush tanks, and are to be found under Plate 39. Successive flushes should not be more than seven minutes apart. A great objection to automatic flushing is that whenever water closets or urinals are used, the excreta entering them must remain in the fixture, giving off impure odors into the toilet room, until the next flush takes place. For this reason it is necessary to provide each water closet and each urinal of an automatically flushed system with strong-acting local vents.

The automatic flush tank should be of sufficient size to discharge into each fixture at least four gallons of water at each flush. The copper lining for the automatic flush tank, and for all other flush tanks, should not be less than 10 ounces. This weight is ordinarily used for tank linings, but a heavier grade of metal is preferable.

Another disadvantage in the use of the automatic flush tank is the large amount of water used, which is a matter of importance if a metered public supply is to be used, owing to cost of water. In many instances however, institutions, factories, and hotels have a large private supply, the use of which is not restricted. When used in connection with many systems, the periodic flushing must go on without interruption, but in the case of school buildings the supply to the tank may be shut off when school is not in session. In connection with plumbing systems automatically flushed, water closets and urinals in private toilet rooms and bath rooms may not be connected to the automatic flush if it is desirable to keep down the cost of water used.

Fig. C, Plate 41, shows a form of automatically flushed urinal, of excellent design.

It is made of porcelain, or porcelain-lined material, is free from exposed metal parts which may corrode, and is well adapted to public toilet rooms.

A cross section of a urinal of this type may be seen in Fig. E,

AUTOMATIC FLUSHING

Plate 43, from which it will be observed that a large body of water always stands in the fixture, the tank after completing its flush always providing this body of water, which stands in the urinal until the succeeding flush. A double trap is provided on the outlet of this urinal, one trap being above the other. When the tank flushes, the air in the upper trap becomes rarefied—that is, partially exhausted—sufficiently to set in action a strong siphon which draws the entire contents of the urinal out of the fixture and into the waste. When the water in the tank drops to a certain level, air is admitted to the pipe running from the tank to the crown of the upper trap, the admission of this air to the trap breaking the siphon.

When the siphon breaks, the water at that time in the urinal, remains there until the next flush. No water is wasted in starting this siphon, every drop of water passing out of the tank being used in cleansing the fixture. A horizontal perforated pipe at the back of the urinal, and connected with the vertical flush pipe from the tank, thoroughly flushes and cleanses the back of the urinal. This same action is applied in the flushing of water-closet ranges. Both range and urinal can be installed of any number of compartments and supplied with a tank of size to correspond.

Slop sinks, in addition to water closets and urinals, may be automatically flushed.

There is a sink for factory use, made of slate, or wood lined with sheet copper, and of any desired length, which is comparatively self-cleansing.

The sink is made with an outer and inner compartment, the latter running through the center of the sink, with space for washing on either side. There is also a narrow space at the end of the inner compartment, between it and the outer compartment, in which a standing overflow is located, connected into the waste. A line of supply pipe runs above and over the center of the sink, and is provided with sprays which throw the water down into the center compartment, from which it overflows into the main body of the sink. Thus the first washing may be done in the outer compartment, with clean water always in the inner compartment for use in face washing.

In factories employing a high grade of help, the line or battery of lavatories shown in Fig. A of Plate 37, and Fig. E of Plate 38 is much in use.

Plate XLII

THE USE OF FLUSHING VALVES

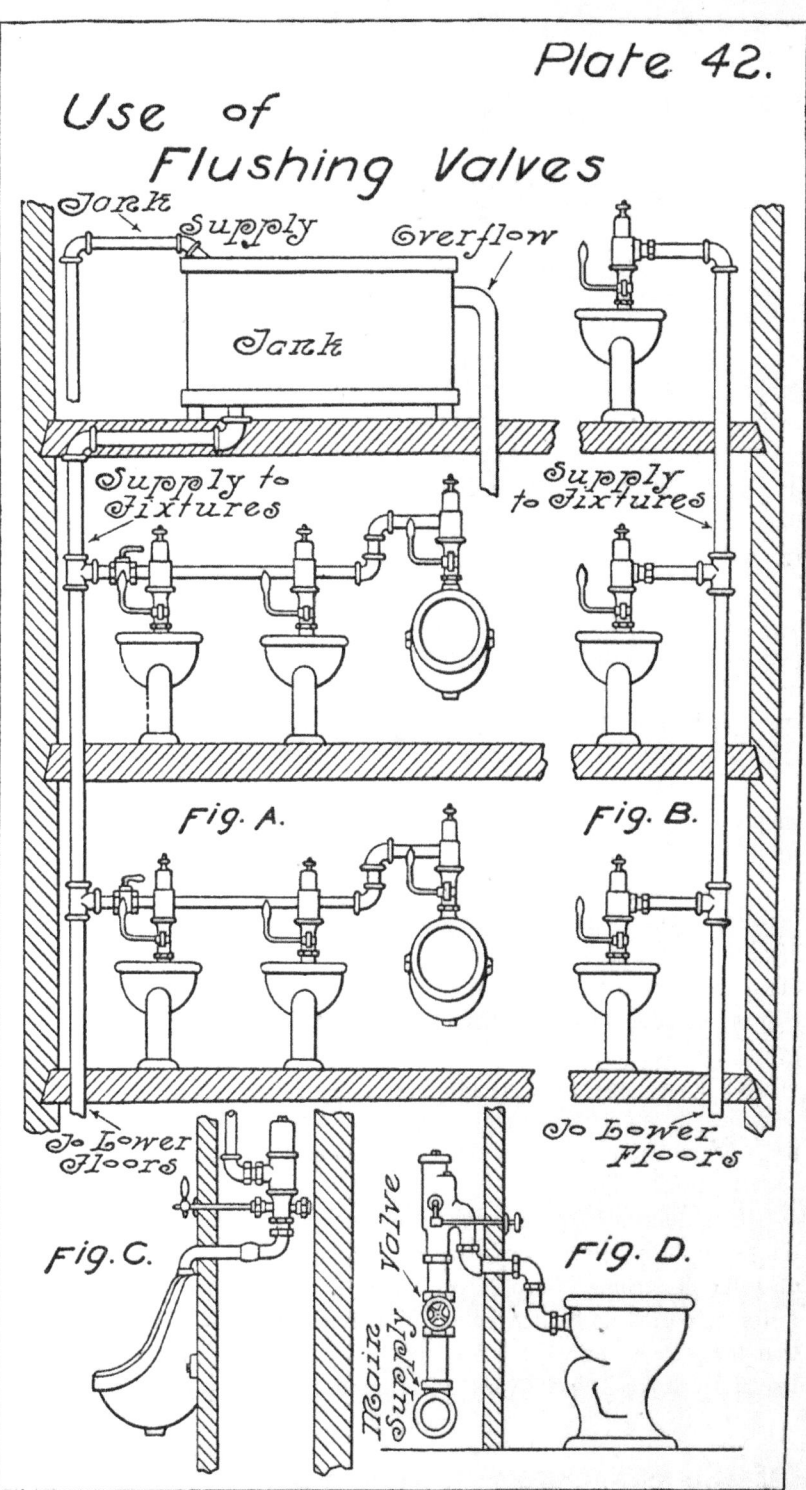

THE USE OF FLUSHING VALVES

FLUSH valves are used in place of tanks in the flushing of water closets, urinals, and slop sinks. They may be placed directly back of and above the fixtures which they serve, or may be concealed behind partitions, as shown in Figs. C and D of Plate 42.

Flush valves may be operated either under direct pressure, as in Fig. B, or under tank pressure, as in Fig. A. The operation of flush valves under tank pressure is generally the more satisfactory method, as there is always a storage of water in the event of an interruption of the public supply, and the pressure is more positive and reliable. The tank pressure is always uniform, while direct pressure is extremely variable, which is an undesirable feature in not only this work, but in all branches of supply work. When a storage tank is used, the height of the tank above the highest flush valve should not be less than 10 ft. if good service is to be expected.

Flush valves may be obtained that are to be connected with the supply pipe coming directly through the wall back of the valve, or for either right- or left-hand side connection.

The operation of most flush valves is similar in its general features. This action is as follows: When the handle is released after flushing, the valve is closed automatically by a jet of water discharged from the pressure side of the valve into and through a by-pass to the valve chamber beyond the piston head, which it gradually forces onto its seat. This by-pass is one of the sources of trouble, as any sand or other solid substance will clog up the passage and stop the passage of the water jet into the valve chamber. Some valves are provided with a device for holding back any such harmful solids.

It is difficult to state definitely proper sizes of pipes and connections for flush valves, as this information, given by manufacturers of different forms of flush valves, varies greatly, depending upon the different forms and construction of valves and upon the pressures that they are designed to work under. Some manufacturers advertise flush valves which work under pressures between 10 and 200 pounds, and are not affected in their operation by a variation between these two points.

Other makes of flush valves, however, are made in different styles, for different pressures. Owing to inability to give absolutely definite data which will cover all makes of flush valves, the following information is given in general, and may or may not be correct in the case of certain makes. Generally a pressure of 8 to 10 pounds is required for the operation of flush valves under direct pressure, and supply pipes serving buildings in which flush valves are used should be of such sizes and so installed that the drawing of water at fixtures will not reduce the pressure at any flush valve below the amount named.

In general, the size of service pipe for flush valves is from $1\frac{1}{4}$ to $1\frac{1}{2}$ in., when operated by direct pressure, for valves up to four in number, and these sizes should be increased for larger numbers.

When working under tank pressure, a main line of supply pipe is run down to the several floors, branches being taken to the different fixtures to be supplied.

A $1\frac{1}{2}$-in. main is ample for from one to four fixtures. If there is more than this number of fixtures, it is well in ordinary buildings to carry a 2-in. supply down from the tank 10 or 15 ft., reducing to $1\frac{1}{2}$ in. for the rest of the distance, and if the building is ten stories or more in height, the lower floors may be reduced to $1\frac{1}{4}$ and 1 in.

Flush valves for urinal use are often smaller in size than those designed for water-closet use, and have smaller supply connections. For low pressures a $1\frac{1}{2}$-in. connection to the flush valve is used, and for ordinary pressures $1\frac{1}{4}$ in. is the general size.

The storage tank for use in connection with flush valves should have a capacity, whenever possible, of about 6 gallons per fixture. This capacity is the requirement when a small number of flush valves are installed. On large systems, where a large number of valves are used, it is not necessary to provide such liberal storage, as the amount named per fixture allows for two successive flushes, and in large work it is almost impossible that all, or anywhere near all, of the fixtures served will be flushed at the same time. Therefore the size of the tank may be reduced from the capacity named, as may be correct for each separate system. A liberal capacity of storage is always desirable, however.

Plate XLIII

URINALS FOR PUBLIC TOILET ROOMS

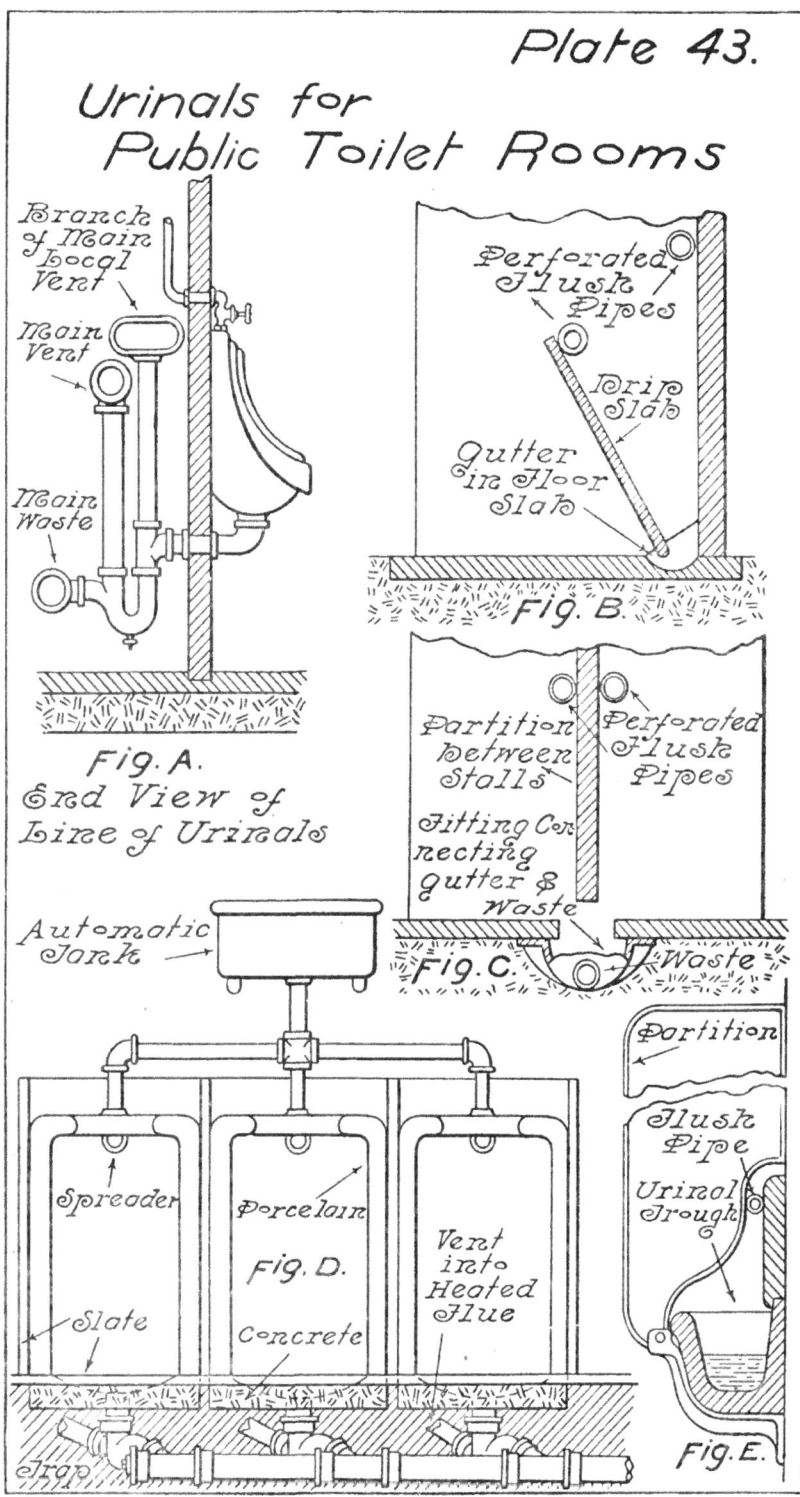

URINALS FOR PUBLIC TOILET ROOMS

OWING to the nature of the waste that enters the urinal, it is the most difficult of all toilet-room fixtures to keep in a clean and sanitary condition.

The foul air noticed in many public toilet rooms that are not properly provided for and attended to, is due in a large measure to foul urinals, this cause no doubt, being greater than the use of water closets. The local vent may be very effectively applied to the urinal, and results in lessening the nuisance mentioned very perceptibly. In Fig. A, Plate 43, is shown a method of applying the local vent to the single urinal or to groups of them when of the lip pattern. The piping for the urinal is concealed behind the back urinal slab or behind a partition. From the house side of the urinal trap the local vent connection is made, it being connected directly into a main horizontal local vent line, which should be carried into a heated flue under the same conditions as prescribed for the local vent serving a line of water closets. The main should be proportioned in size so that at any point its area shall be equal to the combined areas of the branch vents that have been connected into it. A strong draft in the heated flue will result not only in drawing the foul odors out of the connections, but from the fixture itself, and from the room. It is very necessary that a heated flue should be used, and for the ventilation of large toilet rooms a special flue should be used and kept heated the year round. The connection of the local vent does not interfere with the connection of the trap vent, which is, of course, taken off the other side of the trap, and may be connected into a main vent line above the floor, the trap entering a main line of waste either above or below the floor. In Fig. D is shown a system of local venting applied to another form of urinal. These vents should also enter a heated flue. In order to better show the remaining connections, the trap vents have been omitted in Fig. D. The local venting of urinal traps has the disadvantage of producing on the seals a higher rate of evaporation, but when used in public toilet rooms the urinals are more or less constantly in use, and the loss of seal thereby continually renewed. In the case of a urinal seldom used, it would be unwise for this reason, to apply the local vent.

As to the form in which the urinal is made there is a great variety of choice.

One of the most common forms is the lip urinal, shown in Fig. A, which is supported on a slate or marble back by means of bolts, and receives its flush through a urinal cock by direct pressure or from a tank located above it, which may or may not be of automatic action. In Plate 44 is shown a line of these fixtures, from which it will be seen that such a line may be provided with continuous vents to advantage.

The various forms of slate urinals are also very common. Figs. B and C show two of these forms, the latter showing a double line with single dividing partition. In the urinal of Fig. B, the waste, striking the two drip slabs, is washed down into a gutter, formed in the concrete floor, by means of water discharged from two perporated flush pipes running lengthwise. This flush keeps the slabs wet at all times, all liquids being washed away as they fall upon the slab. More commonly in use than this type of urinal, however, is that shown in Fig. C, which consists of a vertical drip slab with perforated flush pipe, the waste liquids being washed into the cement gutter or into a cast-iron gutter. The ends of such gutters should be provided with metal connections and cast- or wrought-iron trap of not less than 2 in. diameter connected into the waste. All urinals should be provided with slate or marble floor slabs, and any wall surface that is exposed and within 5 ft. of a urinal should be constructed of Portland cement or other impervious material. The urinal gutter should also be constructed of like material.

In connection with the cast-iron urinal gutter mentioned above, it should be added that to be strictly sanitary the gutter should be lined with enamel, in order to prevent any corrosion due to the presence of the urine in the waste. All lip urinals should be of the flushing-rim pattern, in order that all surfaces of the urinal may be as thoroughly scoured and cleansed by the flush as possible. In Fig. D is shown a set of three porcelain urinals, flushed by means of an automatic flush tank.

The porcelain urinal is a massive fixture and especially adapted to the service of public toilet rooms and comfort stations, which demand the most perfect sanitary conditions possible, usually without

URINALS FOR PUBLIC TOILET ROOMS

question of expense. The flush pipe is concealed in the fixture itself, the flush entering each urinal through a spreader, which throws it upon every part of the exposed surfaces, these surfaces being so formed as to allow the flush to cleanse them to the best advantage. An excellent feature of this form of urinal is that no metal parts or trimmings are exposed, and thus there is nothing which may corrode by contact with the urine. The addition of the local vent completes in this fixture the highest sanitary excellence to be found in urinal construction. The porcelain trough urinal shown in elevation in Fig. C, Plate 41, and in section in Fig. E, Plate 43, has been fully described under the former plate, and is to be considered an excellent fixture for public toilet-room work.

The pedestal urinal of porcelain, is one of the latest types of urinal to appear on the market, and is also of much excellence. Another recent urinal of high-grade construction is the siphon-jet urinal, supplied from a tank. In this fixture, a heavy body of water is at all times maintained. When the tank is operated, the flush enters through the flushing rim and through a jet, in the same manner as in the siphon-jet water closet. This action results in siphoning the entire body of water out of the fixture, which is of the lip pattern.

Flushing valves may be applied to the urinal to advantage, as shown in Plate 42. These valves may be concealed, as in Fig. C, or exposed, as in Figs. A and B.

Automatic flushing of urinals, as illustrated and considered in Plate 41, is along the line of good practice. When the flushing of this fixture is left to the user of it, this important matter is often neglected, the result being a foul-smelling toilet room. Automatic flushing does away with much of the nuisance arising from this cause.

In Plate 44 a line of urinals is shown in connection with the Durham system. The drainage of this system is entirely of wrought-iron or steel pipe, upon which the action of the acids in the urine passing from the urinals is especially harmful. This action is far less serious on cast-iron pipe, and presents additional argument in favor of the use of the latter material for drainage purposes.

As elsewhere intimated, the public toilet room should be provided with the advantage of good ventilation and with an abundant supply of light. Without these advantages the urinal becomes a foul and unsanitary fixture.

Plate XLIV

THE DURHAM SYSTEM—THE DESTRUCTION OF PIPES BY ELECTROLYSIS

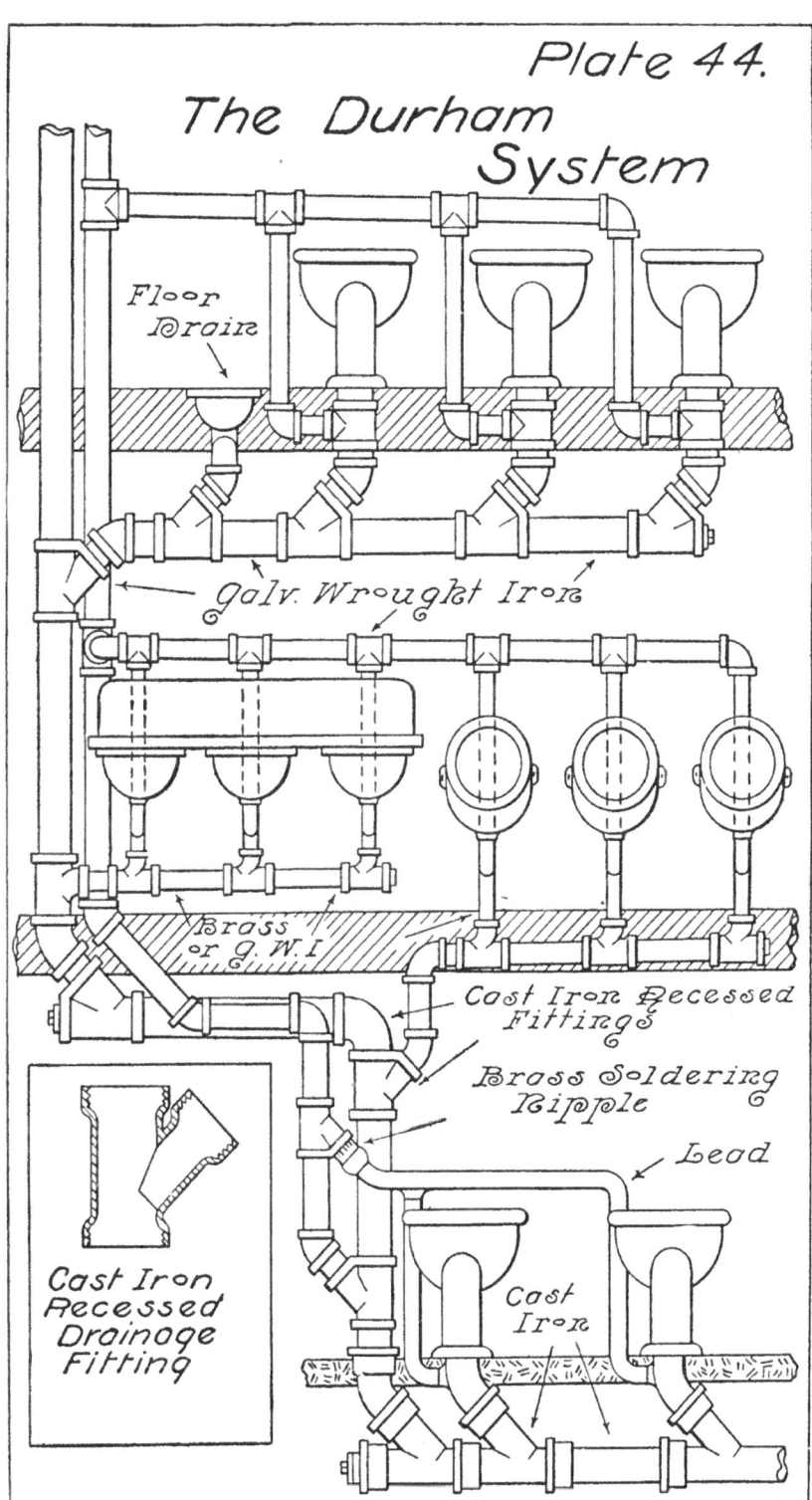

THE DURHAM SYSTEM

There is no difference in the principles of construction between the Durham system and the plumbing system as ordinarily constructed. The only difference in the Durham system is that it is constructed entirely of wrought-iron threaded pipe and cast-iron fittings.

On the Durham system all joints are made with screw threads, no caulked lead joints being used. The Durham system is shown in Plate 44, with a detail in section, of the style of cast-iron fitting used on Durham. Fittings of other than recessed construction should not be used on any part of the drainage system. On vent work in connection with the Durham drainage system, galvanized, cast, or malleable steam and water fittings of ordinary make may be used. The purpose in using recessed fittings is that the alignment of the inside surface of drainage pipe and fittings may be as even as possible, with no ends of pipes that screw into fittings presenting shoulders against which solid matter flowing in the waste may find lodgment.

The use of cast-iron pipe and fittings is free from this trouble, for the hubs are sufficiently recessed to allow an even inside alignment. In the use of common steam and water fittings on cast-iron drainage work, there being no recesses in such fittings, the ends of all pipes entering fittings present shoulders against which lint and other materials in the waste may collect. It may be stated, however, that this trouble is experienced in a greater degree in connection with Durham work than in cast-iron soil piping. For this reason, special care should be taken in cutting wrought-iron pipe for drainage use, and all burs on the ends of such pipes should be reamed out. The weights of wrought-iron pipe for drainage purposes should not be less than the following:

Diameter of Pipe	Weight per Foot	Diameter of Pipe	Weight per Foot
1½ in.	2.68 lbs.	5 in.	14.5 lbs.
2 "	3.61 "	6 "	18.76 "
2½ "	5.74 "	7 "	23.27 "
3 "	7.54 "	8 "	28.18 "
3½ "	9 "	9 "	33.7 "
4 "	10.66 "	10 "	40.06 "
4½ "	12.34 "		

All fittings used on Durham work and on all vent work should be galvanized. Short nipples, in which the unthreaded part is less than 1½ in. long, should be made of weight and thickness known as "extra heavy" or "extra strong." This provision is to guard against crushing and splitting, which is liable to happen in the use of nipples made of ordinary pipe.

Joints on the Durham system should be made up with red or white lead, applied to the male part of the thread. When thus applied there is less opportunity for the lead to squeeze through into the interior of the pipe and form an obstruction.

Care should be taken that all such obstructions are removed when the joint is made. When wrought-iron or brass pipe is connected into cast-iron pipe, the connection may be made by a caulked lead joint or by a screw joint.

Connections between lead and wrought-iron pipes may be made by means of a brass ferrule caulked or screwed into the cast iron, the lead connection to the ferrule being made by means of a wiped joint.

An advantage claimed for the Durham system by its friends, is that a screw joint, being as strong as the pipe is, there are no weak points in a line of such pipe, whereas it would be folly to claim any such thing as this regarding a line of cast-iron pipe with its caulked joints. This argument is followed by the claim that the above being true as regards a vertical line of wrought-iron pipe, so long as it rests at its base on a firm foundation, there is no necessity for side supports, and that it may be carried thus, through the height of the tallest buildings. This would not seem plausible, for the reason that any line of drainage pipe, whether vertical or horizontal, of cast or wrought iron, should be given lateral support in order that it may be rigid and not subject to any lateral movement. Even though the screw joint is a strong one, lateral motion in a long line of pipe will often result in snapping the pipe at one of the screw joints or in breaking a fitting. Furthermore, if a vertical line of cast-iron drainage pipe be given the support that it should receive, it will not sag or settle so that the caulked joints will be forced out of the hubs, a claim that is made against the use of cast-iron pipe. It is true that in the construction of the plumbing system the proper supporting of heavy piping is not given the attention that it should receive, damage to caulked joints often resulting thereby. It is also true that lines of

THE DURHAM SYSTEM

cast-iron pipe properly provided for, suffer no more from broken joints than wrought-iron lines, and are free from certain serious evils which wrought iron is subject to. The Durham system, which has received its name from the inventor of certain patents on the application of wrought-iron pipes to drainage systems, is now extensively used in high city buildings, mainly because of the advantages thus claimed for the system, and it is a question whether such extensive use would have resulted if the cast-iron system had been properly handled. It has often been placed in high buildings with not much more provision being made for supporting its great weight than is made in the system of a private residence, and it is mainly due to this cause that cast iron has been somewhat superseded in very large work. There are many uses to which iron piping is put, in which the use of wrought iron for drainage purposes is preferable. Greenhouse work is an important instance. In this work, where there is much expansion and contraction due to changes in temperature, the caulked joint will not stand nearly so well as the screw joint. This is also many times true in the case of factory work, where constant and severe vibration tends to start the caulked joints of cast-iron piping.

A very strong argument against the use of the Durham system is the fact that wrought-iron pipe has a much shorter term of life than cast-iron pipe, particularly when buried underground. This fact is testified to very strongly by the demand made by all plumbing ordinances dealing with the subject of the Durham system, that whenever pipes connected with the system are to be run underground, such pipes shall be of cast iron. This feature appears in the illustration in Plate 44. Regarding the life of wrought-iron pipe, it may be stated that under certain unfavorable conditions, plain wrought-iron piping that has been installed not longer than eight to ten years has had to be renewed, owing to its deterioration.

Steel pipe is much used in place of wrought iron, many times indeed, under the impression that it is wrought iron.

This material is far shorter lived than even wrought iron, and is entirely unsuited to the plumbing system, which should be expected to render service almost as long as the house in which it is placed.

The only way in which either wrought-iron or steel pipe can be used with any degree of safety is by coating it with a non-corrosive substance such as galvanizing, which is demanded by all ordinances on plumbing. Even when so protected, there will be thin places in the coating, and whenever the pipe is cut, the coating at the ends of the pipe is more or less damaged, so that the steel or wrought iron is left bare. At such points corrosion gets in its work. A scale is formed by this galvanic action, over the exposed surface, which in time exposes a fresh surface to be acted upon, the scale forming again, and again falling off. Thus the action continues until a hole has been eaten entirely through the pipe. The action of gases and acids in the sewage, and in the vapors and steam that rise from the sewage, tends to increase this corrosive action in a marked degree. Cast iron, however, is much more free from such corrosion, for it simply rusts over on any exposed surface, but does not scale, the rust actually forming a sort of protection for the piping.

An important agent in the corrosion of wrought iron and steel is the condensation of vapors on the sides of the pipe in the form of drops of water, which quickly oxidize any exposed surface which they come in contact with.

Mild steel is especially objectionable, as it is so filled with impurities that it rapidly decays wherever they exist.

The vent system is open to the injurious effects of corrosion to an even greater extent than the drainage system, for the latter is often covered with a slime which acts as a protection against such action.

While the screw joint is the strong arguing point in favor of the Durham system, it is right at this point that the most serious trouble may be expected, both on the drainage and on the vent lines. Wherever a thread is cut, the material of the pipe is entirely exposed, and whenever threads project out from the joint, which often happens, there is not only abundant opportunity for corrosive action to take place, but there is a large surface to act upon, because of its being threaded, and owing to the depth of the thread there is less thickness of metal to be eaten through, before the pipe is punctured. In the case of mild steel, especially, it takes only a few years to accomplish such a result under the above conditions.

It is a very easy matter for most users to be imposed upon in deciding from the appearance of pipe, whether it is wrought iron or steel. A very large part of the pipe now turned out is of steel.

The following shows some of the differences between iron and steel. Iron pipe looks rough and has a heavy scale, while the scale on steel pipe is much lighter and in the form of small bubbles, with a smooth and rather white surface beneath.

Steel pipe, when spread out, seldom breaks, while iron pipe breaks easily. A break in the former shows a very fine grain, while that of the latter is much coarser.

Steel pipe is not hard and its threads tear rather than break. Dies that are used on steel pipe may also be used on wrought-iron pipe, but blunt dies that work satisfactorily on wrought-iron pipe will tear the softer threads of steel pipe.

A few remarks concerning the length of life of wrought- and cast-iron pipes under actual working conditions, and the conditions which act to protect or destroy them, may be of interest. A case is on record of the complete decay of an entire underground wrought-iron gas-supply system in eleven years, the cause being in this case traced entirely to external conditions and not to the gas which the pipes were carrying. In the same town experience shows that wrought-iron water-service pipes have a life generally of about seven years. Cast-iron pipes have been known to fail through softening of the metal after a period of use underground of from thirty-five to fifty years. This action, however, is very rare, and the failure of cast-iron pipes, when laid underground, may generally be traced to defects in manufacture.

A few years ago in the city of Los Angeles, the cast-iron water mains were uncovered in over three hundred places, and the pipes, which had been laid nearly thirty years previous, were found to be in almost perfect condition.

It was found that the coating of asphalt had almost entirely disappeared, that in sandy soil the bare pipe had not rusted, and that in other moist soil it had rusted somewhat but was almost uninjured. In conclusion, it would seem advisable to use cast-iron pipe for drainage purposes wherever possible, and that when impossible or impracticable, nothing but wrought-iron pipe heavily galvanized should be used. Steel pipe should never be used.

DESTRUCTION OF PIPES BY ELECTROLYSIS

In recent years great damage has been done to all kinds of underground piping by the action of electric currents, chiefly from electric railway systems. This damaging action affects water mains and service pipes, gas mains and service pipes, the lead sheathing of underground telephone and telegraph lines, and in fact any line of underground piping, regardless of the nature of the metal of which it is made. In the action of the ordinary galvanic battery, such as is used for house bells, two metallic plates are used, one of these generally being zinc, and the other some metal which will not oxidize so readily as zinc.

When two such plates are immersed in a saline solution, and a circuit completed by connecting a wire from one plate to the other, it is a well-known fact that the more easily oxidized plate will be acted upon chemically and decomposed. It is for the reason that this chemical action in time destroys the zinc plate that battery zincs must be replaced in batteries at longer or shorter intervals. This destruction of a metal by means of the passage of an electric current, is known as electrolysis, and is an action which is constantly going on underground, in the vicinity of trolley tracks.

It is the practice in the operation of most electric-railway systems to carry the electric current to the end of the line through large wires, and to carry it back to the dynamos through the rails. As the rails are not separated or insulated from the surrounding earth in any way, there is nothing to prevent a part of the current from escaping from the rail and passing into and through another near-by conductor. An electric current will always take the path that is easiest for it; that is, the path that has the least resistance. Whenever an electric current passes a point where it may take either of two or more paths, it will always divide, a part of it passing through each path that is open to it, and the path that presents the least amount of resistance to its passage will receive the largest part of the current. If the rails of the trolley system were welded together and therefore one continuous conductor, the action of electrolysis would be much less prevalent. As it is, however, the rails must be bonded, and at these joints the greatest resistance is to be met. Even though two rails might have their ends pressed together as closely as possible, there would still be at this joint a resistance to the passage of the current many times greater than the resistance it would meet at any intermediate points in the rail. Even when the rails are connected together by means of copper wire attached to the rails in the most approved manner, the resistance at the points of connection will be very great. It is at such points of resistance as these that the electric current will jump from the rail to some other conductor which offers

DESTRUCTION OF PIPES BY ELECTROLYSIS

less resistance, and this easier path for the current is often supplied by a near-by line of underground piping. If the current would only continue in the pipe, and not leave it, the pipe would not be damaged, any more than the rail is damaged by having the current pass through it.

It is at the points where the electric current jumps from the pipe to the rail again, or to some other conductor, that the damage comes, and also at fittings. The current in passing from the pipe, through the joint and into a fitting, does specially harmful work. It is not at the point where the current enters the pipe, or at intermediate points along the pipe that the pipe is destroyed, but at those points where the current leaves it. This point is not generally understood.

While all kinds of piping are subject to the action of electrolysis, and valves as well, cast iron is probably less harmfully acted upon than the other metals, although there are many instances where cast-iron water mains have been very seriously damaged.

There are, however, several instances recorded, where serious damage was done to wrought-iron and lead pipes, while the cast-iron mains, which were apparently subject to the same conditions, were practically unharmed. An explanation of this result is not clear, although it has been suggested that in the casting of the iron pipes in sand moulds, a sort of silicious coating forms over the pipe, which acts as a protection to it. The plumber is naturally much interested in the methods that may be employed to prevent the action of electrolysis. It may truthfully be said that there is really no practicable remedy which may be applied at an expense which is not prohibitory. The owners of electric-railway systems may often considerably reduce the cause of damage, but that is not the part of the question in which the plumber is interested. If the pipe that is affected can be surrounded by some suitable non-conductor, the trouble may be remedied, but it is a most difficult matter to provide a suitable non-conductor. Many materials that above ground might be used as non-conductors, cannot be used underground for the same purpose, as they absorb moisture and become conductors. The use of asphaltum, resin, wax, and other substances has been tried, but they are not generally practicable, as a coating of such material is liable to crack and fall off, and in addition is too expensive to apply. In some cases, about the only thing that can be done is to provide for taking out sections of pipe, that are being constantly destroyed, in as easy a manner as possible. Sometimes it is well to encase the pipe in another pipe, in which case the current will often act on the outer pipe only.

The action of electrolysis has caused the plumber an endless amount of annoyance in a great many instances, as one pipe after another has often been destroyed, and the cause many times being unknown, the plumber has been blamed for results that are practically beyond his power to remedy.

In addition, the gas and water and telephone and telegraph companies have suffered enormous losses. In the case of the gas and water companies, especially the former, the loss has not been entirely on the piping, but loss of great extent has occurred in the waste of gas or water carried in the pipes.

The action of electrolysis is not confined alone in its destructive action to underground piping. The steel frames of large city buildings, the steel framework of elevated railways, and much other construction work of a similar nature has also been very seriously impaired from the same cause.

The great losses due to the action of electrolysis, and the danger attending the results of such action, have become of such importance that a very large amount of money has been offered by a leading scientific institution for a practicable remedy that will overcome its effects.

Plate XLV

CONSTRUCTION OF WORK WITHOUT USE OF LEAD

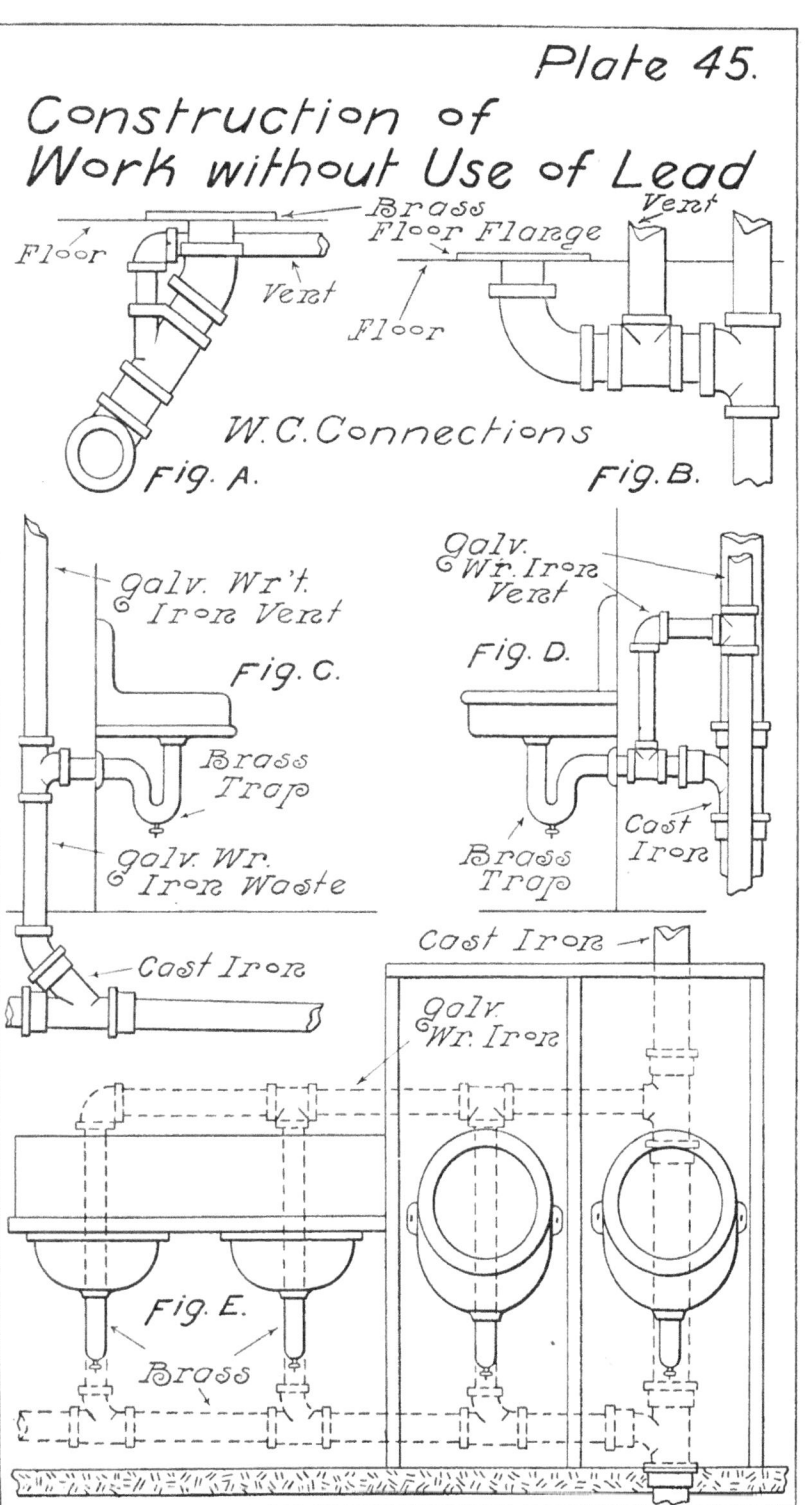

CONSTRUCTION OF WORK WITHOUT USE OF LEAD

THE present tendency of plumbing construction is toward the use of other metals than lead, cast and wrought iron, brass and copper being the materials commonly used; whereas in former times the entire drainage system was of lead, including the soil piping. This practice has reached such an extent that many plumbing ordinances restrict the use of lead to short branches of soil and waste pipes, closet bends and traps.

Plate 45 shows several illustrations of this class of work, Figs. A and B showing work in connection with the Durham system, while the three remaining illustrations show brass and wrought-iron work in connection with main lines of cast-iron pipe. It is entirely feasible to construct the entire plumbing system without the use of any lead whatever, and numerous buildings may be found which are so provided. Figs. A and B show two methods of installing water-closet connections without the use of lead. In the latter, the long-turn elbow takes the place of the lead bend. The connections in Fig. A are very satisfactory for water-closet work, giving a quick discharge of the waste into the main. Very often in connection with a line of water closets, the connections of Fig. A may be used without the vent, and the end of the horizontal main extended in the form of the circuit or loop vent. In such work the horizontal line may be brought considerably closer to the fixtures than in Fig. A.

In Fig. C the lavatory is served by a brass trap and vented by a continuous vent. When such a fixture is located at a distance from a main line of vent, this method is very convenient, as the vent can be carried to the ceiling above, or under the floor, and horizontally to the desired point.

Fig. D shows the manner in which a fixture connected in the ordinary way may be installed without the use of lead. In Fig. E a group of urinals and lavatories is connected in a manner which is very satisfactory and now much used. The main horizontal waste line is generally run above the floor, and directly above it and above the highest fixture, the main horizontal vent is run. Back of each fixture the main waste and vent lines are connected by a 1½-in. vertical pipe, and into these vertical lines the fixture wastes are connected by a horizontal trap outlet, into a fitting of the T-Y pattern. This provides a continuous vent for each fixture, and effects a saving in cost of installation over the ordinary methods.

The waste connections into the horizontal waste are ordinarily made through T-Y fittings, but it is preferable to use a Y branch and eighth bend, the waste passing off by this means more smoothly than through the T-Y fitting. In the use of wrought-iron pipe on the drainage system, the work may often be put in more compactly than with cast iron, owing to the fact that fittings and hubs take up less room. This will appear from Fig. A. In Figs. A and B the brass floor flange for the water closet is screwed into the cast-iron elbow. Fig. F, Plate 17, shows a detail of a water-closet connection when the soil pipe is of wrought-iron and no lead bend is used. All cast-iron fittings used in connection with wrought-iron drainage pipes should be recessed fittings, whether the entire system is of Durham construction or only branch wastes, as in Fig. C.

When the Durham system is used, and it is desired to connect lead pipe into the wrought-iron pipe, it may be done by means of a brass soldering nipple or brass ferrule caulked or screwed into the wrought iron, as shown in connection with the water closets in the basement, in Plate 44.

Brass ferrules should be of extra heavy cast brass, not less than 4 in. in length and 2¼, 3½, and 4½ in. in diameter.

The weights of brass ferrules should not be less than the following:

Diameter	Weight
2¼ in.	1 lb.
3½ "	1¾ lbs.
4½ "	2½ "

Soldering nipples should be of brass pipe, iron-pipe size, or of extra-heavy cast brass. Cast-brass soldering nipples should not be less than the following in weight:

Diameter	Weight
1½ in.	8 oz.
2 "	14 "
2½ "	1 lb. 6 oz.
3 "	2 lbs.
4 "	3 " 8 "

CONSTRUCTION OF WORK

On several of the foregoing plates, illustrations are shown of work constructed without the use of lead. For instance, on Plate 43, Fig. D shows a line of porcelain urinals constructed in this manner.

For urinal work, cast iron and brass are preferable to wrought-iron, steel, and lead pipe, for certain acids and gases in the urine which enters the connections of this fixture act destructively on the three last-named materials, and this action is often very rapid.

There is a considerable amount of work installed in which the only lead used is the lead bend. The bath-room connections of Fig. E, Plate 21, are an example of this style of work, in the use of special fittings.

Fig. G, Plate 22, shows the same class of work performed by the use of common fittings.

Figs. B and C of Plate 26, and the illustrations of Plates 27 and 28, show plumbing construction provided with continuous vents, in which brass traps may be used, thus avoiding the use of lead. These illustrations show clearly that continuous vent work favors the use of other materials than lead. Plate 36 shows an entire plumbing system in which the only lead material used is the lead water-closet bends, and, if desired, other materials may be used in place of these.

Fig. E, Plate 38, shows connections of wrought iron for a line of lavatories which give satisfaction and make a very neat appearance. Thus it will be seen that lead has but a small place in the construction of present-day plumbing in the larger cities, and on large work especially.

The displacing of lead in plumbing construction by such materials as cast and wrought iron and brass is attended by results both favorable and unfavorable, some of which may be seen from the following. The great objection to the use of lead, as stated elsewhere, is that when run of considerable length it will sag and form traps, owing to the softness of the metal. This objection is certainly not encountered in the use of wrought- and cast-iron and brass piping.

There are many places where lead will give better service, however, than material of a stiffer nature. For instance, lead will stand sudden strains and concussions better than cast- or wrought-iron or brass pipes. For this reason it is always advisable to use lead on the suction pipes of pumps, water lifts, etc. On such work as this, lead pipe does not develop the leaks that other materials do. In connection with the use of lead for suction pipes, it may be stated that in the event of a leak on the suction pipe it is far easier to locate it if the pipe is of lead than if of wrought iron.

The reason for this is that the sound made by the passage of air through the leak telephones along the length of the wrought-iron pipe to a much greater extent than through lead pipe, the result being that it is difficult ofttimes to locate the exact place where the defect exists, while in lead pipe the noise can be heard only indistinctly at distant points.

The objections to the employment of wrought iron and steel on the drainage and vent systems are considered thoroughly under the subject of the Durham system.

It may be stated that while certain disadvantages exist in connection with the use of lead, wrought-iron, and steel pipes for drainage and vent purposes, there is almost nothing that can be said against the use of cast iron and brass for the same purposes.

Plate XLVI

THE DISPOSAL OF SEWAGE OF FIXTURES LOCATED BELOW SEWER LEVEL—AUTOMATIC SEWAGE LIFTS—AUTOMATIC SUMP TANKS

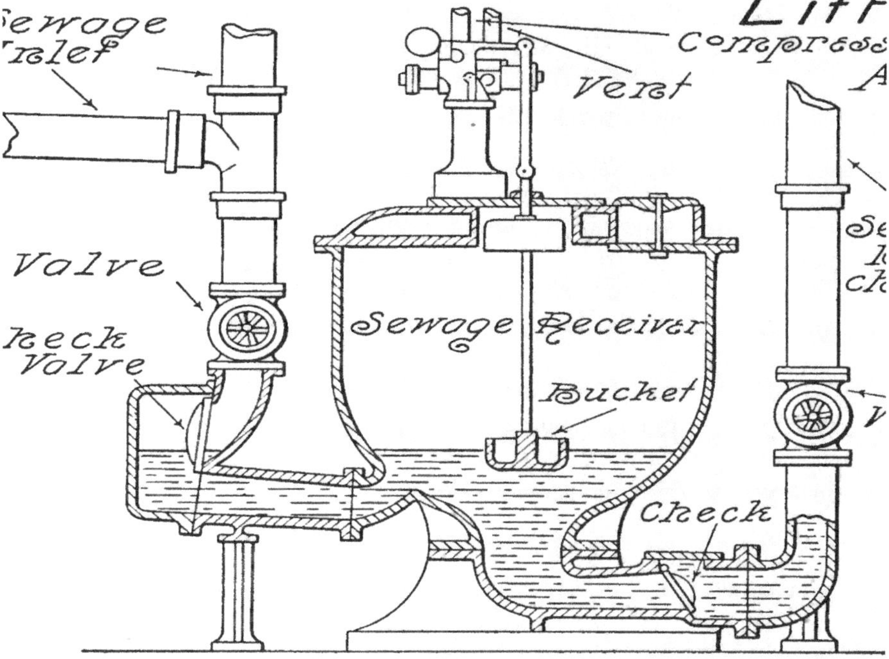

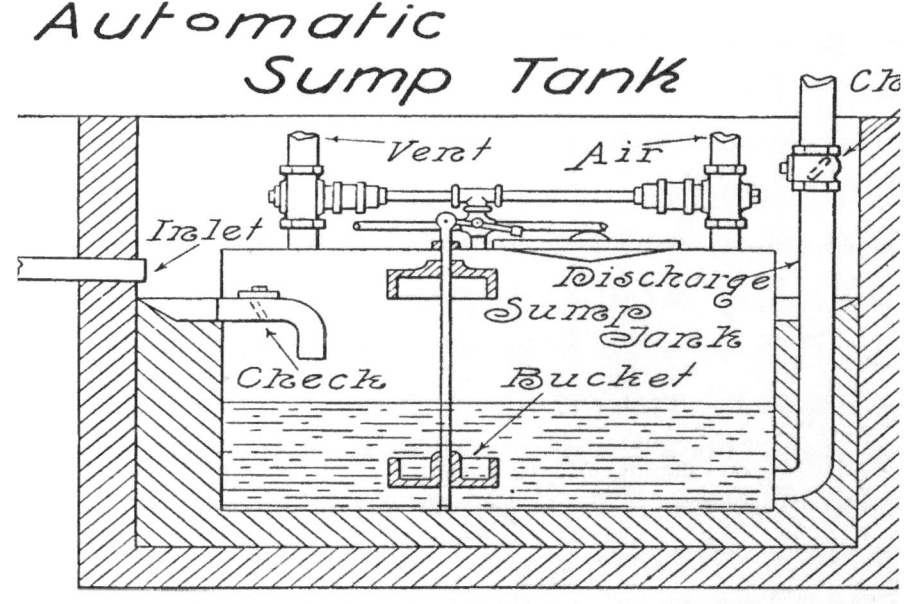

THE DISPOSAL OF SEWAGE OF FIXTURES LOCATED BELOW SEWER LEVEL—AUTOMATIC SEWAGE LIFTS—AUTOMATIC SUMP TANKS

In the larger cities there are many instances where plumbing fixtures are located below the level of the street sewer, in which case it is obviously impossible to discharge the waste coming from them, into the sewer by gravity. Such conditions must be dealt with in the sub-basement floors of numerous tall city buildings, underground toilet rooms or public-comfort stations, and in underground or subway passenger stations.

Briefly stated, the method of handling such sewage is to convey it by gravity through the ordinary soil and waste lines into a receiving tank, from which it is pumped or ejected by other means, into the house sewer of the gravity system.

In addition to fixture drainage, the matter of subsoil drainage, which is often a very considerable matter in underground work, must be taken care of.

There are several methods of raising the low-level sewage into the gravity house drain.

It may be done by pumps of different kinds, or by means of automatic sewage lifts, several of which are now on the market, and operated by compressed air or steam.

A sectional view of such a sewage lift or ejector is to be seen in Plate 46.

When pumps are to be used, the low-level sewage is discharged into a receiving tank located below the level of the lowest fixtures, each soil or waste inlet to the tank being trapped, and the trap supplied with a vent, which may be connected into any main vent of the gravity system.

A tank of this kind should be large enough to hold the sewage collecting during several hours, if the discharge from it is automatic, and if not, it should be large enough to hold the sewage entering it during twenty-four hours.

As nearly above the tank as possible, a centrifugal pump is set, which is operated by an electric motor. A float inside the tank is arranged to rise with the sewage in the tank, and when it has filled to a certain point, the rising of the float locks an electric switch which controls the motor. The motor is thus set in action, operating the pump, and the latter quickly draws out the contents of the tank and forces them into the house sewer of the gravity system. The suction of the pump should reach down to the bottom of the tank in order to draw out all the heavy matter. To the tank a fresh-air inlet should be connected, not only to serve the ordinary purpose of the fresh-air inlet, but to relieve the tank while it is filling and to aid the pump by admitting air when the latter is in action. The pump may also be set on the same level as the tank, and, in fact, works to better advantage when so set, as no primer is necessary, and the apparatus is thereby considerably simplified. Piston pumps are also used in raising sewage from low levels.

The centrifugal form of pump is best adapted to large volumes of sewage which are not to be raised very high, while piston pumps will raise smaller amounts through much greater distances.

In the use of piston pumps, however, it is necessary to prevent anything but clear sewage from entering, as the coarser and gritty matter works destructively on the working parts of the pump.

The great objection to the use of pumps in disposing of low-level sewage is the cost of operating.

The use of automatic sewage ejectors, however, is accompanied with small running expenses, and they have many advantages over the use of pumps, chief among which is the fact that there are almost no working parts to get out of order, and very few auxiliary devices, which are expensive to operate, as in the case of electric motors used on pumps.

In Plate 46 is shown such an apparatus, operating automatically, and designed especially for this kind of work.

There are several other makes that may be obtained, all working on more or less similar principles. Compressed air has proved the most satisfactory motive power, but very often these machines are provided with appliances by means of which steam or water may be used to operate them in the event of an interruption in the compressed-air apparatus.

The action of the automatic sewage lift is the following: Sewage from the levels below the crown of the sewer is conducted, through various lines of soil and waste pipe, into a sewage tank or receiver.

DISPOSAL OF SEWAGE

Inside the receiver an open bucket rests upon the surface of the sewage, rising as the latter rises. When it has risen to a certain point, the rod to which it is connected, and which passes through a stuffing box at the top of the tank, by means of a lever attachment trips a valve on the compressed-air supply pipe, the same action closing a valve on the vent pipe of the apparatus. Compressed air is at once admitted upon the surface of the sewage in the receiver, and is sufficient in pressure to raise this sewage through the outlet and into the house sewer of the gravity system.

A pressure of 2 pounds should be provided for each foot in height through which the sewage is to be raised.

When the pressure of the compressed air is exerted on the sewage, it closes the check valve on the inlet to the receiver, and opens the check valve on the outlet, and as the closing of the vent pipe closes the only other path for the sewage, it must pass out through the proper outlet.

As the water in the receiver falls, the bucket, which is weighted with the water which it holds, follows with it, and when it reaches a point near the bottom, the lever attachment shuts the valve which controls the compressed-air supply, and opens the vent valve, thus venting the air confined in the receiver. The ejector is now ready for another operation. It will be seen that the ejector acts as a trap, and therefore the use of a main trap is unnecessary in connection with it.

The receiver of the ejector should be vented, such vent usually being connected into some convenient main vent on the gravity-drainage system. Air compressors and a storage tank for compressed air are necessary features of a plant of this kind.

The valves on the inlet and outlet pipes of the ejector are for use in the event that it is desired to disconnect any one of several sewage lifts that are connected together on the same system. The automatic sewage lift is generally installed in a brick or iron well and made accessible in case of inspection and repairs. In handling the low-level sewage of some of the immense hotels of the large cities, apparatus must be used which is able to discharge many thousands of gallons of sewage each hour.

This may be accomplished by means of ejectors of the type shown in Plate 46, by connecting several of the lifts together.

When so connected, combination lifts working under either compressed air or steam are generally used, in order that in the event of a breakdown on one source of motive power, the other may at once be made use of. It will readily be seen that no chances can be taken in providing against a mishap which may totally disable an entire system of this kind, for it is a question of handling a great many thousands of gallons each hour, and when this cannot be done, and the sewage constantly accumulates at this high rate, the situation becomes very serious.

When several ejectors are connected together, the main sewage inlet divides the sewage between the different ejectors, and each one discharges into a main.

Some of the advantages of this method of disposal are the following: No pumping apparatus, with working parts to get out of repair, is necessary; there are practically no working parts in the lift to get out of order; the receiving tank, in which the work of the apparatus is chiefly performed, has no finished surfaces or parts on which the coarser matter in the sewage may act injuriously; and the tank acts as a trap to protect the building against the entrance of gases from the sewer.

In addition to the matter of caring for fixture drainage, subsoil drainage, floor drainage, etc., must also be provided for. This drainage is usually disposed of by other apparatus than that used in connection with polluted drainage, the apparatus being known as the automatic sump tank, an illustration of which appears in Plate 46. This tank is installed in a water-tight catch basin or pit, constructed of brick or iron. Subsoil, floor drainage, and any other clear-water drainage that must be taken care of, should enter the pit through inlets provided with check valves, as shown, all drains being trapped in the usual manner. The tank should be air-tight and vented, generally into some convenient main vent in the gravity system. The action of the automatic sump tank is similar to that of the automatic sewage lift already described.

When the bucket is raised by the drainage in the tank to the right height, it opens the compressed-air supply valve and closes the vent pipe, the admission of compressed air forcing the contents out of the tank and into the main gravity line.

A wise provision in the installation of automatic sewage lifts on large work, is that they shall be provided in pairs, each being large enough to hold the drainage accumulating from the fixtures during an hour. The two ejectors should be so connected that they will operate alternately. When water closets discharge into sewage ejectors, the vent from the apparatus should not be less than 4 in. in diameter, and when other fixtures only are connected into it, the vent should be of the same size as the main waste pipe serving such fixtures.

There is another form of ejector sometimes used, which discharges low-level sewage into the house sewer of the regular system, also by means of compressed air.

The compression of the air in this apparatus, however, is accomplished by the head of the sewage in the gravity system discharged into a large tank. Water from the public water supply may also operate this system, and this water afterward be used in supplying fixtures on the floors below the sewer level. This system, while not particularly well known, has the advantage of disposing of the sewage without apparatus which entails expense in installing and in operating.

Of the several different methods mentioned or described for raising low-level sewage, the automatic sewage lift, operating by compressed air, with steam as an auxiliary, is, in general, the most desirable.

In order to determine the size of lift needed for any given plant, the amount of waste entering it must be known, and to estimate this it is necessary to know the number and character of all plumbing fixtures below the sewer level, the number of floor drains, and the character and size of all other drains and apparatus from which waste of any description is discharged.

It is also necessary to know the size of the gravity house sewer, and the kind of power that is to operate the lift, with full data concerning pressure, etc., relating to such motive power.

In addition to its use in connection with underground floors of high buildings and underground public toilet rooms, there are several other uses to which the automatic sewage lift may be put.

It often happens that small villages or hamlets, situated in level country, which has no advantages for disposing of public sewage by gravity, are in a perplexing situation. The sewage lift may be used to advantage under such conditions.

By installing it in a pit underground, as low as desired, enough pitch can be obtained to allow the discharge of the public sewer into it. The lift may discharge the sewage into a septic tank at a higher level, and this tank in turn onto filter beds, the latter delivering the clear sewage which results, into underground distributing pipes. More concerning the septic tank, filter beds, and underground distribution will be found under following plates.

If other sources of motive power are not available, the lift may be operated by water.

The sewage lift is used in many marine plumbing systems also. The apparatus is located below all fixtures, which discharge into it by gravity, the lift discharging the sewage into the sea.

This is an important application, as the disposal of sewage of large steamships, as well as other vessels, is a matter of importance and difficulty.

Plate XLVII

COUNTRY PLUMBING—WATER SUPPLY

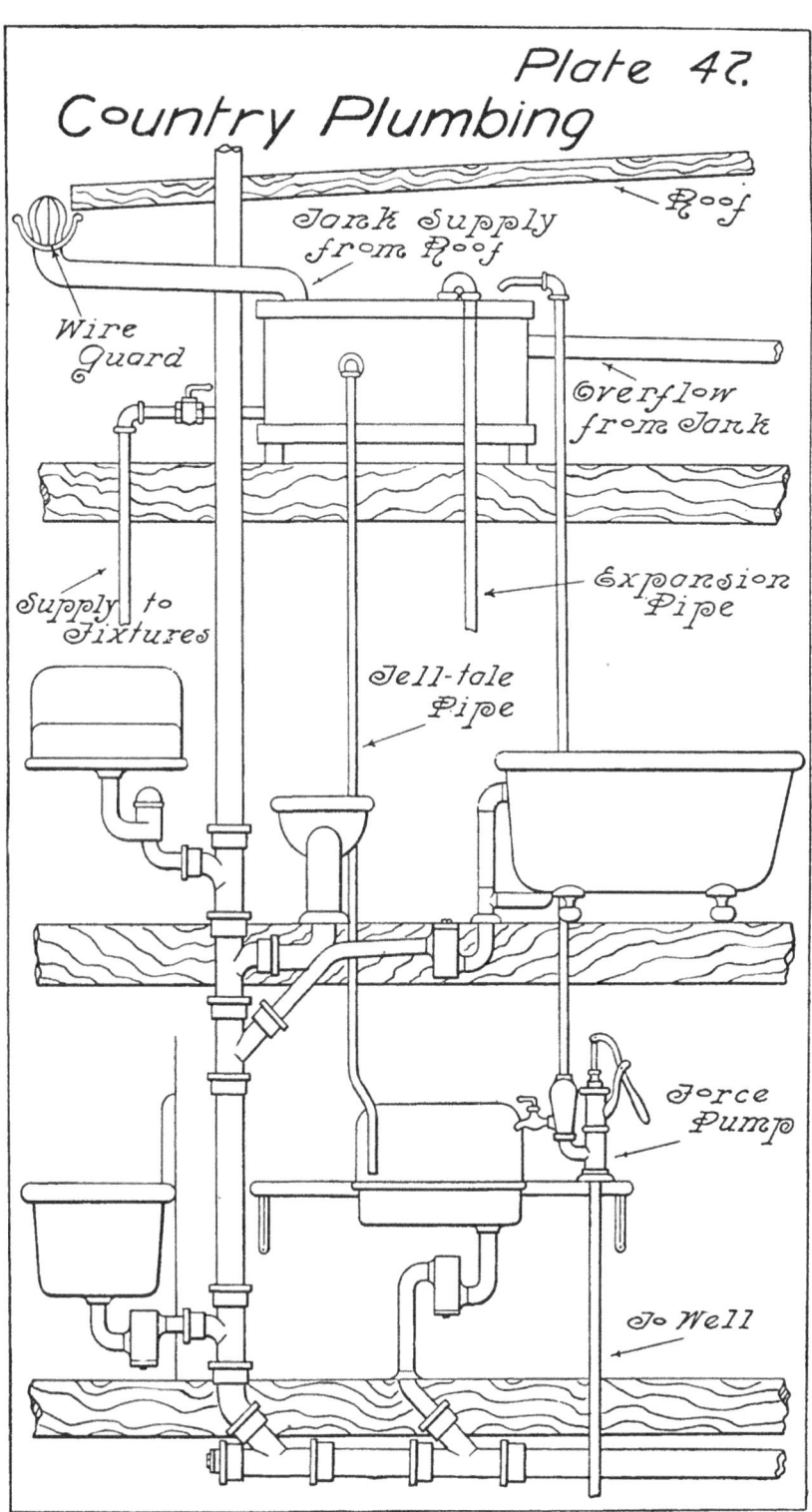

COUNTRY PLUMBING

The subject of country plumbing differs in many respects from the plumbing of cities and towns. The difference arises principally because of the fact that usually the plumbing system installed in the country cannot enter a system of public sewers, and a water supply cannot be secured from any public system of supply. These conditions make it necessary to study each individual plumbing system, and to provide for it as conditions require.

Another feature that also influences the installation of the plumbing system, is the absence of any regulation or inspection of plumbing work. As a consequence, many houses in the country, of ordinary style, are provided with an unvented plumbing system. This, however, in many cases need not be a serious matter, as on small systems special provision may often be made for making the work as safe as is possible to make it when the traps are not vented.

Plate 47 shows such a plumbing system.

In many cases one stack serves all plumbing fixtures of the house, including usually the three bath-room fixtures, kitchen sink, and, possibly, laundry tubs. The use of S-traps on such work is poor practice, as this form of trap is easily siphoned, unless provided with a vent. The use of drum traps and approved forms of non-siphonable traps is much better practice. As far as possible, long, horizontal runs of lead waste pipe should be avoided in an unvented plumbing system, as siphonage often results from the backing up of waste in these long runs. The connections from bath-room fixtures into the stack can usually be arranged as shown in Plate 47, with the lavatory waste entering above the water-closet connection. If the lavatory connection is below the closet connection, the liability of siphonage of the lavatory trap will be greater, owing to the passage of a heavy volume of waste from the water closet past the lavatory waste opening.

The passage of the stack through the roof is a great safeguard for any system of plumbing, especially in the case of an unvented system. When the country plumbing system empties into a cesspool or septic tank, a vent should be run from such receptacle. The septic tank or cesspool, stands in the same relation to the country plumbing system that the public sewer system does to the city plumbing system.

If the cesspool or sewer is not vented, gases will generate and produce a pressure that will force the seal of the main trap.

The soil vent or roof connection relieves this pressure, which is a duty of much importance, for if not thus relieved, the fixture traps will also be forced, and poisonous gases from the cesspool thus find entrance into the house. The use or non-use of the main trap does not appear to be a matter of so much importance in connection with the country plumbing system as with the city system. One reason for this is that in the country districts there is no danger of contaminating the surrounding air by venting the cesspool, whereas in the city the venting of the sewer through the soil vents of a building only a few stories in height may throw foul odors and gases into the windows of a high building next to it.

There is one reason why the main trap is of much value to many country systems. There being no regulation by ordinance, or inspection of plumbing, much poor work is installed that remains undiscovered, which a test would quickly reveal; and, moreover, standard soil pipe is generally used, which is easily split in handling, and which has more defects than extra-heavy pipe. Consequently, sewer gas would have a much greater opportunity to find its way through defective pipe and joints than in work of a higher grade, and the main trap will prevent much of this trouble, by preventing the entrance into the plumbing system of the house, of gases from the cesspool.

The subjects of cesspools, sewage siphons, septic tanks, etc., are considered more thoroughly under the two plates following.

WATER SUPPLY

The manner in which the water supply for the country house shall be procured is always a matter of importance, and usually depends largely upon the natural facilities that exist. The methods commonly in use, are pumping by hand from wells or by power—such as windmill or pumping engine—supply by gravity, by siphonage, or by the use of a ram. In the use of a gravity supply, the source of supply must be at a higher elevation than the point of delivery. The siphon is used in procuring water from a higher point than the point of delivery, when a hill or other obstruction intervenes between the

WATER SUPPLY 287

two points, and over which the supply line must be carried. The ram can be used only when the source of supply is lower than the point of delivery, and when the supply is so located that the ram may be placed at a point below it. . Thus it will be seen that in procuring a water supply, local conditions must usually govern the matter. In order to provide a head which shall deliver the water at the several points where it is to be used, an attic storage tank is generally used. A tank of 300 to 500 gallons will be found to be large enough for the ordinary country home. The tank when filled, represents an immense weight, and care must be taken in giving it a proper support. This is easily done in installing a tank in a house in course of construction, but is often a difficult matter in an old house. The tank should be located where it will not freeze, near a chimney often being a good location. The top of the tank should be covered, in order that dust and dirt and odors may not reach the water, and a ventilating pipe should also be provided.

The tank may be filled in many ways—by hand or power pump, windmill, pumping engine, or ram. Plate 47 shows the discharge pipe from the pump delivering to the tank over the top, the supply pipe to fixtures being taken out of the bottom. Another very good method is to connect the pump pipe into the bottom of the tank and use this same pipe as the down supply to the fixtures.

This will save the necessity of running a separate supply pipe to the fixtures, and answers the purpose as well.

If a hand force pump is used, as shown in Plate 47, a faucet on the pump may be used to advantage. Drinking water may· be pumped direct from the well through the faucet, and when this is closed it may be pumped into the tank.

A tell-tale should always be provided, which should end, if possible, at the point where the pump is located, in order that the person operating the pump may know by the escape of water, when the tank has been sufficiently filled. The tell-tale may enter the side of the tank, as shown, or pass through the bottom into a standing overflow.

The attic tank should have an overflow either of $1\frac{1}{4}$- or $1\frac{1}{2}$-in. pipe, which, if possible, should empty onto a roof. It may be carried into a fixture on a floor below. It is often convenient to discharge the overflow into the water-closet flush tank.

When the attic tank is used, the hot-water supply for the house is under tank pressure, and in order to provide for expansion, an expansion pipe should be taken from the highest point of the hot-water system and carried over the top of the tank, into which any expansion may vent itself.

Under the tank a safe or drip pan should be placed, to take care of any leakage from the tank. From the safe a drip should be run into some open fixture in common use, in order that, by the escape of leakage through the pipe, warning of trouble may be given as quickly as possible. Sheet lead is generally used for drip pans or safes, while sheet copper is now mostly used for tank linings. When the attic tank is filled from a pump or ram, the ball cock and valve are not used, but when a supply by gravity is used, the ball cock and valve are necessary in order to regulate the flow of water as it is needed.

A great objection to many well waters is their excessive hardness, which make them objectionable for kitchen and laundry purposes. When the natural supply is of this nature, the rain water falling on the roof of the house is collected and used for these purposes entirely, or as far as possible.

Rain water may be discharged directly from the roof into the attic tank, as shown in Plate 47, the objection to this course being that a large part of the water must be lost through the overflow, and in the event of the stoppage of the overflow during a heavy storm, the house would be in danger of being flooded. Instead of discharging the overflow upon the roof, it may be carried into a cistern, and all the water needed, thus saved. If desirable, the rain water may not be connected directly into the attic tank, but may be discharged into the cistern.

In either case of using the cistern, a pump must be used to force the water into the attic tank. When the rain water is thus utilized, wholly or in part, the pump connection with the well may be allowed to remain as shown in Plate 47, to be used whenever the cistern water gives out, and for providing through the pump faucet, a supply of drinking water.

In the use of the faucet, there will often be sufficient storage of water in the pipe between the pump and the tank, without having to pump.

It is best to use a cistern capable of holding a month's supply of rain water, in order that when a rainy period comes, enough water

WATER SUPPLY

may be stored to last until it will probably be renewed. When entire dependence is made upon rain water, storage should be provided for a period of six weeks, if possible, at the rate of about twenty-five gallons per day for each inmate of the house. To some this rate of water use may seem excessive, but it is low rather than high, as extended experience shows.

When the water supply must be economized, a much lower amount may be figured on, but when plumbing fixtures, such as water closets, are constantly in use, the rate increases rapidly.

If possible, rain water should be screened before entering the attic tank, as leaves, twigs, slate, etc., enter the cistern in considerable quantity. Filters are sometimes used for clearing the water, and screens of various kinds are employed. Devices known as rain-water separators may also be procured, which prevent the first washings of a rain storm from entering the tank or cistern.

Well water is no doubt used to a far greater extent in the country than any other source of supply. Whether it is a well or spring or other source of supply, the greatest care should be taken in providing against its contamination in any way. It is popularly considered that the country is free from all manner of impure conditions, but it is true, nevertheless, that in the past, the death rate in country districts, where, apparently, living conditions are perfect, has been as great or greater from such diseases as typhoid fever than in cities.

Generally a case of this dreaded disease in the country, may be traced to a contaminated well or other supply. For this reason every precaution should be taken.

The well should never be located near a leeching cesspool, it being well to have at least 300 ft. separate them. A tight cesspool should not be located within 30 ft. of any well or other source of supply.

In running a line of earthenware drain pipe, it should be kept as far away from any source of water supply as possible.

Whenever possible, a cesspool or drain-pipe line should be located at a lower elevation than the well, in order that the natural drainage may carry any leakage away from, rather than toward, the well.

The location and common use of wells within a few feet of privies, is a practice which may be seen in almost any country district, and is a practice which has been the direct cause of a large part of the typhoid-fever cases in the country.

It is claimed that contaminated water in running through a comparatively few feet of soil, will purify itself, and on the strength of this claim, many are willing to take chances in the use of drinking water coming from exposed sources.

While this fact may be true under certain circumstances, it has little in it to cause a lessening of precautionary measures, as the contaminating source is usually a permanent one, and the action of purification by filtration is not to be depended upon at a depth of more than three or four feet, as the admission of air, upon which the action depends, is not sufficient at greater depths.

Wells are of three kinds, those which are dug, driven wells, and bored wells.

The first named is the most common, and the driven well next.

Even the driven or bored well is by no means proof against contamination, as impurities may enter the water at considerable distances from the well.

Many waters of sparkling appearance, and apparently absolutely pure, are very far from being what they appear, and too much attention cannot be given to the matter of precaution in securing a supply for country use which is absolutely pure, and then seeing to it that it is not contaminated later.

Plate XLVIII

CONSTRUCTION AND USE OF CESSPOOLS

Plate 48. Construction of Cesspools

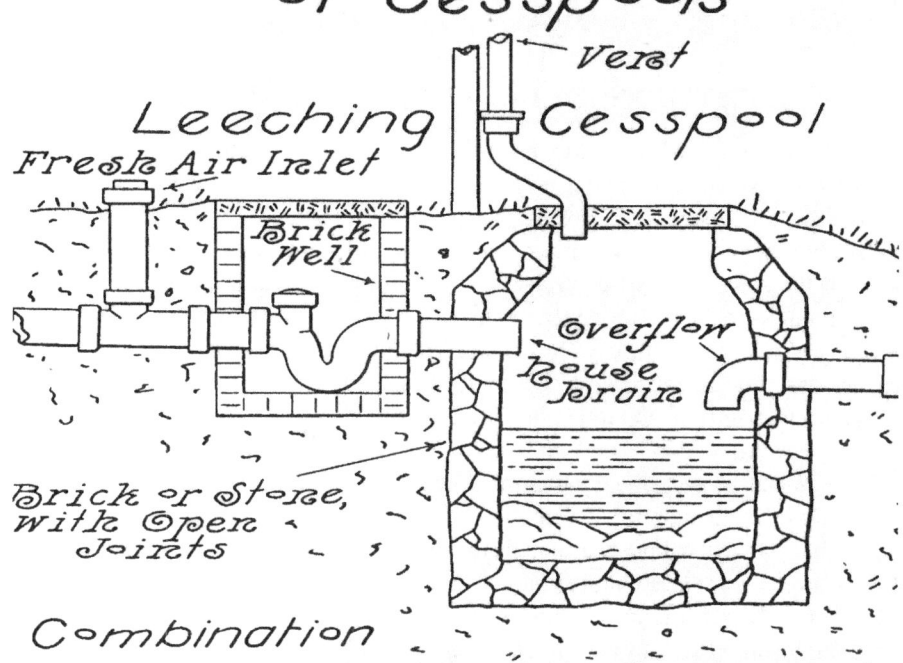

Leeching Cesspool

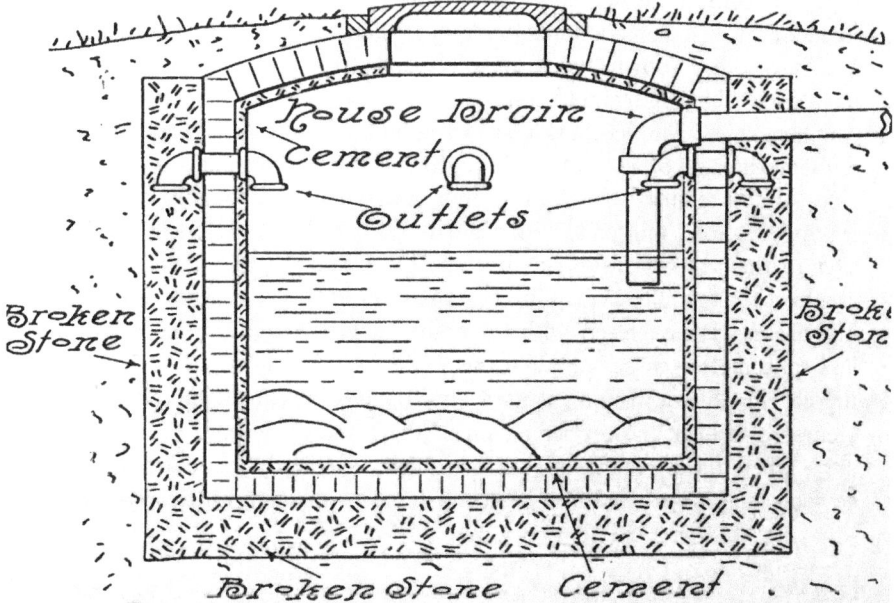

Combination Leeching & Tight Cesspool

CONSTRUCTION AND USE OF CESSPOOLS

THE cesspool is made use of only in the absence of public sewers. Whenever entrance may be made into a public sewer, the use of the cesspool should be discontinued entirely. After public sewers have been constructed, cesspools are sometimes connected into the sewer instead of replacing them entirely, with a direct connection from house to sewer. This is extremely poor practice, for the cesspool should always be considered simply as a makeshift, made necessary by the absence of better facilities. The worst feature that presents itself in country plumbing, is the disposal of the soil in house sewage.

When, as occasionally happens, the sewage of a house may be discharged into a running stream, the difficulty may be solved in the case of that particular house, although for all points lower down on such a stream, the water is polluted and should not be used for drinking purposes. Therefore this method is usually out of the question, even though such a stream is at hand. The only other practical method is to discharge the house sewage into a tank, from which the liquids may escape into the surrounding soil, the tank retaining the solid matter, including soil. Such a tank or compartment is called a cesspool. In Plate 48 are shown two forms of cesspool, the leeching and combination leeching and tight cesspools. The former is by far the more common type. The leeching cesspool is built of loose brick or stone, without the use of cement. Through the crevices or joints in the sides of the cesspool, the liquids leech out into the surrounding soil, leaving the solid matter to remain in the cesspool. A serious objection to the use of this form of cesspool is that, after a time, the crevices become filled with soil and other solid matter, and the leeching process is interfered with. Another objection is that more or less solid matter passes off with the liquid into the surrounding soil, thereby in time destroying it as a filtering medium, upon the effectiveness of which, the proper action of the cesspool depends. To be sure, when these results have come about, the liquids entering the cesspool may be carried into a second cesspool through an overflow, in which case the first cesspool will continue to retain the solid part of the sewage, and the second cesspool to dispose of the liquids, somewhat in the manner of the septic tank.

When the first cesspool has become filled it may be emptied, and its use continued. Instead of discharging into one cesspool and overflowing into a second one, it may be more desirable, when the first cesspool is no longer able to perform its duties satisfactorily, to abandon it, disconnect the house drain from it and reconnect into a cesspool located in new soil.

The only proper location for a leeching cesspool is in light or sandy soil, into which the liquids may leech and purify themselves by filtration. Sand is a recognized filtering medium. Filtration depends upon the action of certain bacteria which exist in the soil, their numbers being far greater in light soils than in those which are heavier, as in the former, air has an opportunity to reach the bacteria, without which the bacteria are unable to live.

Therefore, at considerable depths, the action of filtration is not nearly so strong as at points nearer the surface, and for this reason, cesspools of comparatively small depth will give better service.

While the employment of the leeching cesspool in the manner described above is the common method, a better method is to discharge the house drainage into a tight cesspool and connect it by overflow into a second cesspool of the leeching type, the first retaining the solids, which may be cleaned out, and the second cesspool leeching the liquids into the surrounding soil. The water-tight cesspool should ordinarily be about six feet in diameter by ten feet in depth, and is usually built of brick, one brick thick, laid in Portland concrete, and provided with a 24-in. cast-iron cover and frame. A tight cesspool should not be located within two feet of any boundary line, or within ten feet of any house or rain-water cistern, or within thirty feet of any source of water supply. A leeching cesspool should not be located within 100 feet of any house or cistern, or within 300 feet of any source of water supply.

The house sewer should be trapped before entering a cesspool, and the trap provided with a 4-in. fresh-air inlet, which should be governed by the regular limitations surrounding the construction of fresh-air inlets. The cesspool, whether leeching or water-tight, should be vented by a 4-in. vent pipe, carried at least 10 ft. into the air. A convenient method is to carry this vent line on a stout pole

CONSTRUCTION OF CESSPOOLS

or post, set for the purpose. The ground above the cesspool should be banked with turf, in order to shed surface water and prevent its entrance into the cesspool.

Rain water should not be discharged into a house sewer connecting with a cesspool, as the latter will be flooded and called upon to take care of drainage which is not harmful to discharge upon the surface of the ground if properly provided for. It will be seen that the leeching and water-tight cesspool each has its own particular advantages, which, in the main, are not held in common.

A most excellent form of cesspool, combining the features of these two types, is the combination leeching and tight cesspool shown in Plate 48, the construction and action of which are as follows:

An excavation of proper size having been made, a heavy layer of broken stone is filled into the bottom, and upon this as a foundation a common brick, water-tight cesspool is built, a wide space being left between it and the sides of the excavation, which space is filled with broken stone. Overflow outlets at several points around the cesspool, and exactly on the same level, are then constructed, which will allow liquids to pass over into the broken stone and leech into the soil, the heavy matter remaining in the water-tight cesspool, from which it may be removed at intervals. This form of cesspool takes up but little more room than an ordinary cesspool, is as efficient as the use of the tight cesspool overflowing into a leeching cesspool, and is in every way a very satisfactory arrangement for handling the drainage of a country house. The outlets should be on the same level, in order that the liquid may be distributed evenly into the broken stone.

If these outlets are not placed on the same level, the lower ones will get nearly all the waste from the cesspool, and that part of the filtering material into which they discharge will after a time become filled with impurities, and thus be unfit to perform the duties required of it; whereas, if each outlet is made to take care of its proportional part of the work, the cesspool can be made to do good work for a much longer period.

Notwithstanding that the main part of the solid matter remains in this cesspool, a small part at least of the solids is carried out into the broken stone. Instead of outlets of the style shown in Plate 48, very good outlets may be obtained by using half-S lead traps in an inverted position.

The sewage should be brought into the cesspool in such a way that its contents will not be stirred up any more than possible.

If the contents are disturbed, a greater amount of solid matter will be carried out through the overflows. By carrying the inlet pipe well down into the cesspool, the sewage will enter with less commotion than otherwise.

While there is a great difference between the efficiencies of the several types of cesspools, it should always be remembered that this device at best is only made use of as the most practicable method of solving a difficult problem, at the least possible expense. In other words, the cesspool should be considered only as a necessary evil, to be used only when other methods cannot be employed.

City plumbing ordinances make acknowledgment of this fact by prohibiting the use of cesspools in all sections of the city that are provided with public sewage facilities. A very great improvement over the cesspools, as shown in Plate 48, is to be found in the septic tank.

This subject is one of very great importance, and is taken up under the following plate.

Plate XLIX

CONSTRUCTION AND ACTION OF THE SEPTIC TANK—UNDERGROUND DISPOSAL OF PARTIALLY PURIFIED SEWAGE—AUTOMATIC SEWAGE SIPHONS

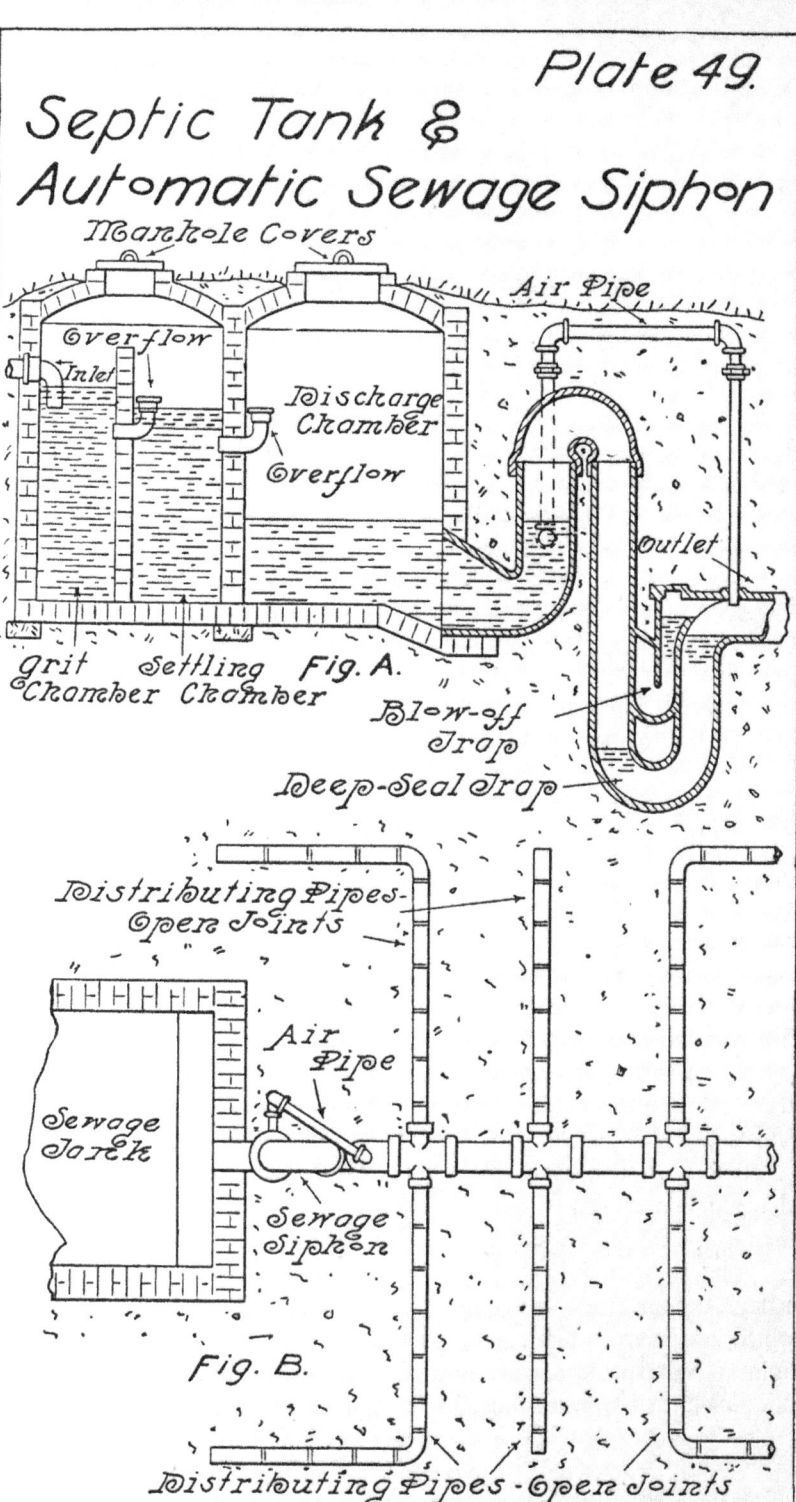

CONSTRUCTION AND ACTION OF THE SEPTIC TANK

As stated under the preceding plate, the use of the cesspool is a practice to be followed only as a last resort, when no better method can be employed. At best, however, the cesspool is a crude, filthy affair, although in times past it has served an important purpose. The use of the septic tank is to-day leading to the disuse of cesspools, and it seems to be only a matter of time when the latter will be largely a thing of the past.

One form of septic tank is shown in Fig. A, Plate 49. The house sewage is discharged into the first of the three compartments of the septic tank, this compartment being commonly known as the grit chamber, and in which the most important action of the tank takes place. From the grit chamber the liquid portion of the sewage overflows into the second, or settling chamber, and from this into the third or discharge chamber, from which the effluent may be disposed of in a number of different ways, which will be considered later.

All three compartments of the septic tank are necessarily watertight, the leeching process not being employed in connection with the septic tank. The action of the septic tank does not result in separating the solids from the liquids by mechanical means, the action being entirely of a chemical nature. The reduction of sewage by means of the septic tank is by the action of certain bacteria which live and multiply in all fresh sewage. By means of this bacterial action, all forms of organic and vegetable matter are transformed from solids into liquids known as nitrates. Ordinarily this action effects the change from solid to liquid within a few hours. Even substances of such hard nature as bones, leather, etc., may be thus changed in form, although the time required is very much greater than in the case of substances of softer nature.

The septic tank is made generally of sufficient size to hold about a day's accumulation of sewage. The action of the class of bacteria which act upon sewage requires neither light nor air; in fact, both light and air should not be allowed to enter the septic tank. A certain amount of warmth must be maintained in order to provide for the proper action of the bacteria, although no special arrangement to provide heat is necessary. There is considerable heat present in all house sewage, and the sinking of the tank underground provides an additional amount, as also the action of the bacteria itself. To secure the best results, the sewage which enters the septic tank should be well diluted.

The presence of a supply of air in the septic tank not only stops the action of the bacteria, but allows the contents to putrefy, as in the use of the cesspool. Without the presence of air, obnoxious gases do not form, and therefore, even when opened for a short time, the septic tank does not throw off foul odors and gases in any amount.

In starting a septic tank there is nothing to be done of a special nature, after the plant has been made ready, beyond the admission of sewage to it. For the tank to reach a high state of efficiency, however, requires a sufficient length of time to elapse for the bacteria to breed and form in sufficient numbers. This period varies with conditions that are present, from one to three weeks. On the surface of the sewage standing in the tank, a thick coating or scum of vegetable and animal matter soon forms, in which the bacteria breed and perform their work of disintegration.

Upon the under side of this scum their action is particularly strong, the solids being transformed within the space of a few hours into liquids, which are in the form of ammonia compounds.

The scum on the surface of the sewage varies greatly in thickness, but is sometimes of such an amount and so compact that the weight of a person can be sustained upon it. The bacteria also form upon the sides of the tank, thus attacking the sewage from every direction.

The numbers of these bacteria are so great as to be inconceivable, millions of them being present in a very small volume of the sewage.

In order that the best results may be obtained, the bacteria should be disturbed as little as possible. They adhere to almost any rough substance, but upon glass and similar surfaces they do not seem to be able to gain a hold. Great care should be taken against breaking or disturbing the scum in any way. Therefore, the inlet, as it enters the grit chamber, should discharge through a bend to a point well below the surface of the sewage, as shown in Fig. A.

Metallic and other substances upon which the bacteria are unable

THE SEPTIC TANK

to act, settle to the bottom of the grit chamber, which should be cleaned out occasionally, and for this purpose each chamber of the septic tank should be provided with a 24-in. iron cover, fitting tightly into an iron frame securely embedded in the masonry.

From the grit chamber the liquids collecting in that compartment overflow into the settling chamber. This overflow should be so constructed as to transfer the liquids with the slightest possible disturbance of the contents of the settling chamber. The method of overflow shown in Fig. A is a good one to follow, as it allows the liquid to trickle over as it collects. The process of disintegration is continued in the settling chamber, although to a much less extent than in the grit chamber, for the reason that the sewage has been so far purified in the latter that there is not the substance present in the settling chamber to give life to the countless numbers of bacteria that exist in the settling chamber. In many plants, a third chamber is added, into which the effluent overflows before reaching the discharging chamber, the septic action being less in each successive chamber, owing to the increasing purity of the liquids.

From the last settling chamber the effluent overflows into a discharge chamber usually, although in some cases it is discharged directly from the settling chamber to the final place of disposal.

A great factor in the successful operation of the septic tank is the formation of the scum on the surface of the sewage. This scum not only provides working ground for the bacteria, but aids in preventing the penetration of light and air when the cover is removed, and holds the heat contained in the sewage and prevents the striking through of colder air. This scum sometimes reaches a thickness of over a foot and a half. After the effluent reaches the discharge chamber, or in some cases the last settling chamber, the method of final disposal must be determined, the decision being made with due regard to the existing local conditions. If a running stream or ravine is convenient, the solution is often easily made by discharging the sewage into such a natural disposing medium or ground.

When the effluent reaches the discharge chamber, it has been purified to a great extent, but not entirely, and unless some natural means of disposal, such as a stream, is at hand, it is necessary to make provision for the carrying on of this final purifying process, which is commonly known as filtration.

A method quite commonly employed, consists in discharging the effluent into a specially prepared trench close to the surface of the ground, or with its upper face open.

For ordinary residences, a trench 18 to 20 ft. in length and 3 or 4 ft. in depth should be sufficient, the trench being made of correspondingly larger dimensions when greater amounts of liquid must be cared for. At the bottom of the trench a thick layer of broken stone should be filled in, and above this a layer of gravel. Above the gravel a layer of coarse sand is sometimes used. Into this trench the liquid from the septic tank is discharged, and provision should be made for distributing it as evenly over the filtering bed as possible, in order that no one part of the trench may be called upon to perform a greater amount of work than is its share. If too large an amount of liquid is delivered at one point, it cannot be properly cared for by the filtering material, and is therefore not properly purified.

This form of disposal is sometimes carried further, by collecting the water filtered through the trench into an under drain, and from this pipe discharging it into a second filter. From the second filter the water may be pumped out onto the surface instead of allowing it to leech away into the soil. When pumped from the second filter, the sewage which entered the septic tank, has been transformed into an absolutely pure form. That this is true may be seen from the fact that such pump water has in some instances been used for drinking purposes.

Sometimes the liquid discharged from the discharge tank is deposited over the surface of the ground, where filtration and the purifying action of the sun's rays complete the final purifying operation.

This practice is not generally practicable, however, for various obvious reasons, among which are the lack of sufficient exposed surface of light soil, the proximity of other dwellings, the difficulty of securing an even distribution over the surface, etc.

UNDERGROUND DISPOSAL OF PARTIALLY PURIFIED SEWAGE

As a general thing, the most practicable method of final disposal of partially purified sewage, is obtained by discharging the contents of the discharge tank into an underground system of distributing pipes. Such a system is shown in Fig. B, the illustration showing a plan view of the system.

If the soil is light and porous, there is no difficulty in the use of this method of disposal, but it is not so satisfactory in its results when used in other soils.

Good judgment should be used in determining the method of providing for final disposal of sewage. In the case of a moist soil, which is unfit for filtering purposes, the system mentioned above may be employed to advantage; that is, by the use of filter beds placed underground, the final filtered product being pumped out onto the surface. The underground disposal system, irrespective of the means of discharging the contents of the discharge tank into it, consists of a connection from the discharge tank into a main distributing underground pipe, from which a number of branches are taken out, the object of the piping being to distribute the liquid as evenly over the area used for disposal purposes as possible. These branch lines of pipe should be of unglazed earthenware, laid with open joints, so that through them the liquids may escape. These pipes may be laid in any way to conform to the shape of the distributing area.

Laterals may be constructed of 2-in. pipe, and it is well to allow an opening of nearly a quarter of an inch at each joint.

If such a joint is unprotected, sand will find its way into the pipe and gradually choke it up. Therefore it is well to use a thimble or collar of some sort to cover each joint. This collar may be a short piece of earthen pipe of a larger size than the pipe to be protected. Generally the branch distributing lines should be laid from $3\frac{1}{2}$ to 4 ft. or more apart, in order that too large an amount of liquid may not be deposited over a given area.

The pipes should be graded, for otherwise the liquid will escape in larger quantity through joints nearer the main, and those farthest from it will have comparatively little to do. If the soil is moist or of clay, the laterals should be run farther apart than in sandy soils. Experience shows that about one to one and a half feet of porous, loose-jointed tile is necessary to properly handle a gallon of liquid, according to the nature of the soil, and for heavy soils a greater length. Therefore, in providing underground disposal for a discharge tank holding 500 gallons of liquid, from 500 to 750 ft. of 2-in. pipe would be demanded for its underground disposal.

In grading the main distributing pipe, as well as the laterals, there is one point that should be guarded against. The pitch should be very gradual, as, if much pitch is given them, the liquid will quickly flow to the farthest ends of the main and laterals, and overburden such areas, while not giving other areas a sufficient share.

Common fittings should not be used in connecting the laterals with the main, as the branch in such fittings is from the middle, and this would not allow all the liquid in the main to pass into the laterals. Special fittings are made for this kind of work, in which the branch is dropped below the center of the main fitting, sufficiently to allow all liquid in the main to escape through the branch.

Unless these fittings are used on the main, the latter should be run with open joints, in order that at each discharge of liquid the entire volume may be able to escape into the soil. In order to give perfect results, the area covered, and the length of pipe used, should be sufficient to thoroughly dispose of one discharge of liquid before another is received.

This final purifying action of filtration is the result of the action of a class of bacteria which are of entirely different character to those which do such effective work in the purifying process that goes on in the septic tank. While the latter operate out of contact with light and air, the action of the bacteria in the filtration purifying process, depends entirely on the presence of air and light.

These bacteria exist in countless numbers in the air spaces which sand and other porous substances contain, their existence in such materials depending on the fact that air is easily admitted, upon which they depend. The better a filtering medium is for its purpose, the more porous it will be found to be. As air is admitted more easily to the soil near the surface, at these points bacteria will be found in the greatest number, and as greater depths are reached, the number of these bacteria rapidly decreases until their number is insufficient to accomplish satisfactory work.

Therefore, the nearer the surface the underground distributing pipes are run, the greater the efficiency of the system. If possible, these pipes should be laid about a foot from the surface. Owing to frost, however, they must generally be laid deeper.

If areas used for underground disposal are turfed over it will be found that the turf will afford considerable protection against frost. While the bacteria in the septic tank change the complex forms of sewage into simple chemical compounds, the action of the bacteria of the sand again changes the chemical nature of the liquid, the change being from nitrites into nitrates, and resulting in chemically pure water.

When first passed through primary or contact filter beds of broken stone and gravel, the liquid is broken up, and its particles exposed to the oxidizing action of the bacteria, and the action in the sand filter is similar, although more thorough.

The entire change from sewage in the most extreme condition of contamination into pure water, is made by these simple processes, there being no outlay for expensive apparatus of any kind, or any demand for outlay in running expenses. A plant constructed on these lines may be, and often is, used for the reduction of the entire sewage of villages and small towns, which could otherwise dispose of the public sewage only with great difficulty, and doubtless far less efficiently, and with much greater expense.

The same system, on a smaller scale, may be employed for a residence, and with safety, even in thickly populated districts, for all the apparatus may be located underground, and, as already explained, its nature is such that it is in no way a menace, such as the cesspool always is.

The whole plant for a small residence may usually be located in a back yard of ordinary size.

While in many locations the close proximity of the septic tank to the house is not objectionable, in the use of it in cities certain restrictions are advisable, for it is not certain that it will receive proper attention, that leakage from the different chambers may not occur, etc.

Therefore, except in the case of houses surrounded by a considerable extent of private grounds, it should not be used in thickly populated districts unless unavoidable. Its use in such places, however, is not often called for, owing to the presence of public sewers.

AUTOMATIC SEWAGE SIPHONS

After the introduction of the septic tank it was seen that ordinary methods of discharging the contents were not desirable.

For instance, in the employment of underground systems of disposal, an ordinary constant discharge from the septic tank would give poor results, as the liquid entering the main distributing pipe would be of such small amount that it would escape through the nearest joints, and never reach those farthest away. This would result in giving all the disposal work to a very small area, an amount greater than it could accomplish. In addition, a period of rest following a period of work is necessary in order that the supply of air to the bacteria may be renewed. To solve this difficulty, it was seen that intermittent discharges of the full contents of the discharge chamber were necessary, the interval between successive discharges being a number of hours in duration.

The automatic sewage siphon is the device employed for this purpose. There are numerous varieties on the market, depending for their action on more or less similar principles.

In Fig. A of Plate 49, a very desirable form of sewage siphon is shown, attached to the outlet end of the discharge chamber of a septic tank. Its action is the following, depending upon the confining of air between the liquid standing in the outlet of the siphon and the seal of the large trap: As the liquid rises in the discharge chamber, this confined air becomes constantly more compressed, until the pressure is great enough to blow the water out of the blow-off trap, thereby relieving the air, which is immediately followed by a heavy flow of water from the discharge chamber, of sufficient volume to quickly fill the long vertical arm, and start the siphon into full action, which continues until air enters the siphon from the outlet pipe through the air pipe.

Air enters the air pipe only when the siphon has drawn the liquid in the tank so low that the siphon does not fill the outlet. A quick passage of the contents of the discharge chamber into the siphon is provided for by enlarging the outlet from the tank.

Plate L

PNEUMATIC SYSTEMS OF WATER SUPPLY
—HYDRAULIC RAMS—PUMPS—WATER
SUPPLY BY SIPHONAGE—PUMPING
BY WINDMILL—CAPACITY OF
TANKS — PROTECTION OF
SUPPLY PIPES AGAINST
FREEZING

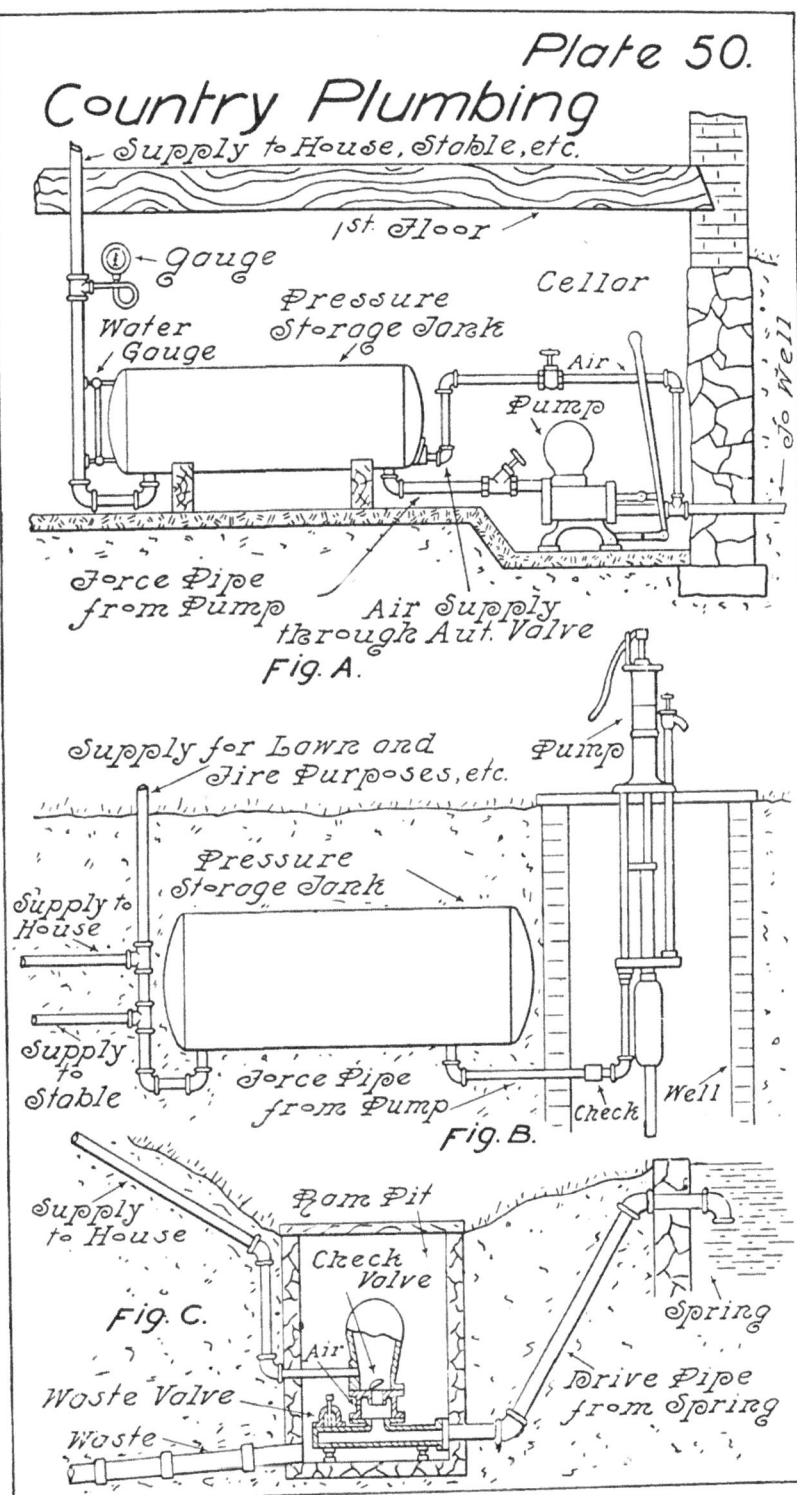

PNEUMATIC SYSTEMS OF WATER SUPPLY

In considering the general subject of country plumbing under a previous plate, allusion has been made to different methods of procuring a supply of water for use in the country, where there is no system of public supply. In addition to the attic-tank system, which is so generally used to supply country houses, there is another system, known as the pneumatic system of supply, which has many advantages over the old method. This system is of comparatively recent introduction, and depends in its operation upon compressed air. The use of this system is dependent only on the ability to procure a generous supply of water from a well, cistern, spring, or other source from which it may be pumped. A very important feature of this system is the fact that the tank may be located anywhere, either in the cellar, stable, underground, or at any other point where there is no danger of frost.

This allows a pressure to be maintained on the water piping, without the necessity of using an attic tank, with all its attendant evils, such as the danger of leakage, straining of timbers under its great weight, etc. The tank is of wrought iron or steel, air tight, and is generally filled by a power pump, pumping engine, or windmill pump, although, excepting as a matter of labor and convenience, it may be filled by the use of the hand pump.

Either a vertical or horizontal tank may be used, as most convenient.

There are several systems of pneumatic water supply on the market, the principal difference being in the methods employed in providing for the admission of air into the tank. In Plate 50, Fig. A represents the pneumatic tank located in the cellar, and Fig. B the tank located underground. The latter shows the use of a hand pump, and the former shows a lift-force pump operated by means of a brake. In both systems, which, by the way, are made by different manufacturers, it will be noted that both the force pipe from the pump and the supply pipe to fixtures, etc., connect into the bottom of the tank. A check valve between the pump and the tank is necessary, to hold the pressure in the tank when the pump is not in operation.

When the pump is in operation, a certain amount of air is pumped into the tank at every stroke, through a special form of automatic air valve. As the water rises in the tank, the air becomes more and more compressed, and when the tank has been filled about two-thirds full, it will be found that the air pressure is sufficient to force the water to any height ordinarily desired. In connection with the tank in Fig. A, a water gauge, seen at the left, serves to show the height of water in the tank, and a pressure gauge shows the pressure which the water is under, and indicates to the operator at the pump, when a sufficient pressure has been reached.

A pressure of 75 lbs. may be reached with the pneumatic system, and the manufacturers will guarantee a pressure of 50 lbs. The latter pressure is sufficient to raise water 100 ft., and as 20 lbs. or so is sufficient to raise it to the third floor or attic, it will be clear that 50 lbs. is ample for country use of almost any character. Manufacturers also guarantee to deliver water by means of this system through horizontal lines of pipe a mile in length.

The advantages of a pneumatic system are many. It not only does away with the attic tank, but allows the apparatus to be located conveniently to the pump, where it may be watched while the pump is running; the danger of freezing, common to elevated tanks placed out of doors, is avoided, also the expense of erecting towers to hold such a tank. An advantage to be gained in placing the tank underground, is that water delivered by it, is very nearly of a uniform temperature during all seasons of the year. The application of the pneumatic system of water supply covers a wide range, for it may be used in connection with a farm, for instance to provide a supply of water not only to the house, but also to the stables, carriage wash room, milk room, and may be used for lawn and garden purposes and in case of fire. The latter is a protection which country houses have always been sadly in need of, without the opportunity of filling the need. This same system has a much larger application in supplying institutions, factories, and even entire villages.

If the demand is not too great, one large tank may be used. Otherwise one pump working continuously, or during certain periods, can be used to fill as many tanks, located in different houses, as desired. For ordinary house use—that is, where the supply is to be used only for household purposes—a tank holding 400 or 500 gallons will be found satisfactory. Tanks for pneumatic supply purposes are generally tested under at least 150 lbs. pressure, and are therefore strong enough to produce any desired pressure.

The pressure produced in the use of the attic tank, however, is simply of an amount due to its height above the level at which water is delivered.

It may be stated that, in the use of a windmill pumping into a pneumatic tank, a regulating cylinder may be used, which will stop the action of the windmill whenever any given pressure in the tank is reached.

HYDRAULIC RAMS

The use of the hydraulic ram is the solution of many an otherwise difficult problem in securing a supply of water in the country. It is only under certain conditions that the ram can be made use of, but when feasible it serves a valuable purpose without further cost than that of installing it.

In order to use the ram, the spring or other source of supply must be situated so that the ram may be located below it, with an opportunity for the waste water from the ram to be carried away from it. Such a location is usually to be found on a side hill.

The operation of the hydraulic ram is based on the following principle: When a body of water is discharged downward through a pipe running at an angle, and its passage out of the end of the pipe is suddenly stopped, the momentum which the body of water has gained, will force a part of the water to a much higher level than that of the water before it passed into the pipe. The connections of the hydraulic ram are to be seen in Fig. C of Plate 50.

In this case the source of supply for the ram is a spring located above it, as necessarily required. The water enters the ram from the spring, through a pipe which is called the drive pipe, its passage being checked by the waste valve when it attempts to escape. The momentum acquired by the water in falling through the drive pipe, forces whatever water is not lost through the waste valve, up into the air chamber, compressing the air in the latter. A check valve at the entrance to the air chamber prevents any escape of the water in a backward direction, and the compressed air of the air chamber forces it through the only other outlet, that is, through the force pipe, which carries it to the point of delivery. It is necessary to maintain a supply of air in the air chamber of the ram, and this is accomplished by an air valve, which admits air at each stroke, at a point below the air chamber.

The proper operation of the ram depends entirely on the working of the waste valve. When this valve is properly arranged, the action of the ram is continuous so long as it is supplied with water. In order that the valve shall be properly arranged to be self-acting, it should be weighted heavily enough to overbalance the pressure against its lower face. When a volume of water flows down the drive pipe from the spring, its weight and momentum is sufficient to suddenly close the waste valve. When this occurs the water in the drive pipe is for an instant without motion, and the force against the valve face is not great enough to keep it closed.

The valve therefore opens, the water in the drive pipe is again set moving, and in seeking to escape through the valve, again closes it. This alternate opening and closing of the waste valve thus continues without intermission, each descent of the water through the drive pipe forcing water up into the air chamber and thence to the point at which it is to be delivered. An overflow should be provided to the spring or whatever source of supply is used, in order that the water may always stand at the same height above the waste valve. If otherwise, the weight on the waste valve will not be properly adjusted, and the ram, therefore, not self-acting.

The air valve is an important feature of the ram. In all supply work, air is taken up mechanically by the water, and all air chambers in time lose their air by this means, and become waterlogged.

This would be a serious matter in the use of the hydraulic ram, as the operation of the weighted waste valve without an air chamber, would cause a violent shock at each stroke, which would be felt throughout the supply piping, resulting in a loud cracking and rumbling noise, and possibly in the destruction of the piping as well.

The air enters by virtue of the creation of a partial vacuum at the inner face of the valve, which allows atmospheric pressure to open the valve at each stroke and force in a small quantity of air, thus renewing any loss that the air chamber may have sustained.

Rams may be operated with a difference in level between the

waste valve and surface of the source of supply of only 16 in., although a greater difference is desirable for good results. It is better practice to use a fall somewhat greater than actually required to perform the work, but not much greater, as an excessive fall means greater momentum, with a consequent greater wear and tear on the ram and piping. Five to 10 ft. is an amount of fall on the drive pipe that can generally be depended upon for good work. Manufacturers of the common makes of hydraulic rams claim that the ram will deliver approximately one-seventh of the water entering the ram, to a height approximately five times the difference of elevation of the waste valve and surface of the spring, and to a height twenty times such difference in elevation, one-fourteenth of the water entering the ram. The greater the height through which the water is to be raised, then, the greater will be the waste of water.

This waste of water is the one great obstacle, in many cases, to the use of the ram, as it generally requires a considerable supply to operate it. Rams or hydraulic engines are now made, for which the manufacturers claim a much higher rate of efficiency than can be obtained in the use of the common ram. While the action of the common ram depends upon the opening and closing of a heavily weighted valve, the valve in the modern hydraulic engine is made very much lighter, its opening resulting from the creation of a vacuum below the valve, and the weight on the waste valve being so regulated that the latter almost balances. This results in the rapid opening and closing of the valve, which in turn results in a quicker stroke. These and other improvements guarantee, as claimed by the manufacturers, 30 ft. of elevation of the water in the delivery pipe from the ram, for each foot that the water descends in entering the ram from the source of supply. This result, it is claimed, is accomplished with much less waste of water. The modern hydraulic engine will operate under any fall on the drive pipe, from 18 in. to 50 ft., will force water to a height of 500 ft., and is made in sizes capable of pumping any amount of water up to 1,000,000 gallons, during twenty-four hours.

The waste water should be carried away by a drain as fast as it collects in the ram pit, for if not, it will back up and prevent the operation of the ram.

The drive pipe of the ram should be about twice the diameter of the force pipe; it should run on an incline without other bends than the one necessary to carry it into the ram; and this pipe should be air-tight. The end of the drive pipe in the spring, should be submerged to keep out air, and be provided with a strainer to prevent entrance into the ram of foreign substances, as the lodgment of such substances on the valve may prevent its proper action.

In order to provide an unbroken incline of the drive pipe to the ram, when it is impossible to do so in the ordinary manner without making a very deep excavation, a tank or stand pipe with open end may be placed on the pipe at some point between the ram and the place where it is necessary to bend it, such tank or stand pipe being of sufficient height to allow water to stand in it at the same level as in the original source of supply.

A form of ram known as the double-acting ram is now built, and is of much value when the supply of pure water to be used for water supply is limited, and a poorer quality of water is also at hand. By means of this ram the poorer water supply is utilized to operate the ram, the latter delivering to the house-supply system only the pure water. The ram has a great variety of applications in country work, and is very generally in use not only for private supplies, but for supplying institutions, factories, etc., and even on public supplies of towns and villages.

PUMPS

The simplest form of pump is the suction pump, and this is the form most commonly in use. Its action depends upon atmospheric pressure, which at sea level is approximately 15 lbs. to the square inch, and therefore capable of raising water to a height somewhat over 33 ft. in a perfect vacuum.

The suction pump is provided with an upper and a lower box. When the pump piston moves upward, it creates a more or less perfect vacuum behind it, and as a consequence the atmospheric pressure exerted on the surface of the water in the well, forces in water to fill this vacuum.

When the piston descends, the lower box closes and the upper box opens, allowing the water in the pump to pass through the upper box into the barrel of the pump, and be emptied out of the spout when the piston is next raised. By means of the suction pump, water can never be raised through the entire theoretical height of

PUMPS

33 ft., as a perfect vacuum cannot be produced in the pump, and because of the friction of the water in passing through the pipe.

The lift pump is another common form of pump, especially useful in driven wells.

The barrel of this pump, and the lower valve, are set below the surface of the water in the well, the upward stroke of the piston lifting the water without the help of atmospheric pressure as in the suction pump.

The lower cylinder is made small enough to fit into the bore of a driven well, and provided at its lower end with a strainer.

When the cylinder is not of sufficient length to reach into the water, a suction pipe may be connected to it, the pump then delivering water both by suction and lifting.

A third form is the lift-force pump. It has the same upper and lower valves that the suction pump has, but has a tight top provided with stuffing box, through which the pump rod works. At a point above the upper box, a force or delivery pipe is connected, in which is a check valve. As the water is raised above the upper box by suction, it opens the check valve in the force pipe, and passes into it. On the down stroke this check valve is closed by the water above it, thus allowing the force pipe to hold all the water that enters it. These pumps are always provided with an air chamber on the force pipe, which produces a steady stream instead of a broken one, and also prevents any strain on the pump and piping.

There is also the double-acting force pump, which delivers water on each stroke, whether upward or downward. This is a modified form of the common force pump, contains four valves, and gives a constant stream, which is very desirable for fire and other purposes.

For providing a large supply of water for small public-supply systems, for factories, institutions, and fire purposes, a system of driven wells may be used to great advantage, according to methods similar to the following, providing such supply is of sufficient amount. Below the surface of the ground, and below the frost line, a line of main pipe is laid, from the middle of which a smaller pipe of proper size is run up to the surface and connected to the power pump as a suction. At intervals along the line of main horizontal pipe, these intervals depending on the amount of the supply that exists underground, connections are taken to numerous driven pipes. These pipes connect to driven wells located several feet from the main, the entire system of driven wells covering sufficient area to enable the requisite amount of water to be obtained. Generally the driven wells are sunk at irregular depths. Such a system, operated by a power pump or pumping engine, will deliver a very large supply of water.

A few remarks on driven wells may be of value.

When water has been struck, it is necessary to know how much of the strainer is submerged, to find which information, a string with a small weight attached may be let down into the drive pipe, and when withdrawn, the length that has been wet, noted. If the strainer is entirely submerged, the water should be tested, and if found of undesirable quality the driving should continue until a satisfactory supply is obtained. An old pump is then screwed onto the drive pipe and operated until the water issuing from it comes clear and free of sand. The strainer on the drive pipe may not become clogged for a period of twelve or fifteen years, or possibly longer. When this happens, it becomes necessary to draw out the old pipe and replace the old strainer with a new one, or, if unable to withdraw the pipe, to drive a new well.

WATER SUPPLY BY SIPHONAGE

When the source of a water supply is at a higher elevation than the point at which the water is to be delivered, and there are no intervening obstructions between the two points, the supply may be delivered by gravity.

When there is a hill or rise of land between the source and the point of delivery, however, the only method that may be employed is to convey the water by means of siphonage.

If the intervening elevation rises above the source to a height to which atmospheric pressure cannot force the water, the siphon cannot be made to work. Theoretically, the siphon will raise water to a height somewhat above 33 ft., but in actual practice, owing to friction and the lack of an absolutely perfect vacuum, this height cannot be reached by several feet. The great obstacle to obtaining a supply of water by siphonage is the accumulation of air at the high point or points on the supply line. This trouble may be remedied by the use of cocks located accessibly at the high points, through which to vent the collections of air. They must be opened frequently in order that the siphon may operate properly, and such constant atten-

WATER SUPPLY BY SIPHONAGE

tion is always a matter of inconvenience. If not given frequent attention, however, the siphon will soon cease entirely to deliver water.

There is comparatively little trouble experienced from air-lock in siphons that lift water through distances of 10 ft. or under, and empty it at a point low enough to develop a strong flow. Under such circumstances, the air mixed with the water is carried along with it. In the case of lifts much greater than 10 ft., however, air begins to give trouble, the trouble increasing rapidly as the lift is increased, especially when the crown of the siphon is sharp and unable to contain much air. Under the latter conditions, the siphon will cease working in a very few hours. Another method sometimes employed to relieve the siphon of air, is the placing of an air pump on the crown of the siphon, for use in pumping out the air that may have collected. The interval between successive operations of such a pump cannot be definitely stated, as the nature of the water sometimes affects this matter, as well as the height through which the water is raised.

There is still another method, more effective than either of those already described, which may be applied as follows. A connection should be made at the top of the siphon into a galvanized sheet-iron tank of 2 or 3 gallons capacity. Between this tank and the siphon a shut-off is located, and also one above it, a funnel being soldered into the upper end of it. Close the lower cock and open the upper one to allow water to be poured in, which should fill the tank and the funnel.

If the upper cock is then closed and the lower one opened, the water will drive out the air in the siphon and maintain the siphon in this condition until the tank becomes empty. When the tank has drained out, close the lower cock, open the upper one, and refill the tank. Now again open the lower cock and close the upper one, and the tank is prepared to perform its work as a receiver for the air that accumulates at the crown of the siphon.

By the use of such a device as this, the siphon may be kept free of air for a considerable length of time. The larger the tank used, the longer the interval between the successive fillings. Galvanized wrought-iron pipe and galvanized cast-iron fittings are better suited for siphons than other materials.

The use of cast iron with caulked lead joints for large siphons, is very poor policy, as experience shows that much difficulty is experienced in keeping it air-tight, a very essential feature in the proper operation of a siphon.

The siphon may be made to cover a very wide range of work, as siphons of large size may be used as successfully as those of smaller size. In the use of large-pipe siphons, however, it is necessary to use special starting apparatus and to provide for constant attention to the removal of air at all high points. These siphons have been made to carry water through distances of many miles. The same principle is successfully applied to the disposal of sewage under similar circumstances, large amounts of sewage being thus handled.

PUMPING BY WINDMILL

The following suggestions on windmill pumping may be found of value. One of the most desirable features in this work is the efficiency of the plant in light winds. A pump used in connection with a windmill should be of smaller size than when operated by hand.

When water is pumped by hand, a pump must be used which will perform the greatest amount of work in the shortest time.

The requirements are different in the use of windmills, however, for generally the windmill need not run more than three or four hours of the day to supply the tank with all the water that is necessary. During certain seasons of the year there are many days when the wind is very light, and at such times the windmill should work under as light a load as possible in order that it may be certain of performing some work continuously under such adverse conditions. Therefore a small pump, even though unable to furnish more than half the water that could be pumped by hand during a given time, will prove most satisfactory.

The use of a small pump will allow the windmill to work a greater number of hours during light winds, and will be found to pump more water during the entire twenty-four hours of the day than a larger pump would.

A great mistake is commonly made in building the windmill tower too low. It should be of such height that the wind may reach it freely and without being interrupted in any way. Neighboring buildings, trees, hills, etc., determine the height at which it should

CAPACITY OF TANKS

be built. If such obstructions are met with, the tower should rise 10 ft. above them.

Another point to be considered is that when such obstructions exist, they are liable during high winds to be the means of producing eddies and counter currents, which result harmfully to the windmill. Moreover, the currents of air at elevations farther away from the ground become more steady and uniform, allowing the windmill to work more efficiently and with less wear and tear. For the reasons above mentioned, windmill towers should ordinarily be constructed not less than 30 ft. in height, and of sufficient strength and firmness to give the windmill as great stability and freedom from vibration as is possible. The following information is necessary in giving intelligent data concerning the selection and installation of a windmill proper for the work required:

The character of the well and its depth should be known—whether it is a driven, drilled, or dug well; if drilled, the inside diameter of the casing must be known; the height and distance through which water is required to be raised, these dimensions being taken from the foot of the pump to the bottom of the storage tank.

The amount of water entering the well during the dry seasons should be known, also the size of tank used, and the amount of water required for an entire day's use, and the height necessary to construct the windmill tower to provide free access of wind to the windmill.

CAPACITY OF TANKS

In connection with windmills, rams, etc., which pump to storage tanks, it is often required to estimate the dimensions of tanks to hold certain amounts of water, or to find how many gallons are held by tanks of certain dimensions.

These tanks are generally either rectangular or cylindrical in shape. In either case the cubic contents of the tank in cubic inches, divided by 231, will show the number of gallons which the tank is capable of holding, 231 representing the number of cubic inches in a gallon. If the dimensions of the tank are in feet, the capacity may be found by multiplying the cubic feet of contents of the tank by 7.476, this quantity representing the number of gallons in a cubic foot.

The following rules will give the capacity in gallons of rectangular and cylindrical tanks.

To find the capacity of a rectangular tank: Multiply the internal length, breadth, and depth in feet together, and multiply this result by 7.476. Or multiply together the three interior dimensions in inches and divide the result by 231.

To find the capacity of a cylindrical tank: Multiply the square of half the interior diameter in feet by 3.1416, multiply this result by the depth in feet, and this result by 7.476. Or multiply the square of half the interior diameter in inches by 3.1416, then multiply this result by the depth in inches, and divide this result by 231.

If a tapering cylindrical tank is used, add the large and small diameters together, and find half this amount. This will give the average diameter, and the contents may then be found by the regular rule for cylindrical tanks.

Thus, the capacity of a rectangular tank measuring $4 \times 5 \times 6$ ft. will be found in the following manner:

$$4 \times 5 \times 6 \times 7.476 = 897 \text{ gallons,}$$

or

$$(48 \times 60 \times 72) \div 231 = 897 \quad \text{``}$$

The capacity of a cylindrical tank 5 ft. in diameter and 6 ft. deep will be found as follows:

$$2.5 \times 2.5 \times 3.1416 \times 6 \times 7.476 = 881 \text{ gallons,}$$

or

$$(30 \times 30 \times 3.1416 \times 72) \div 231 = 881 \quad \text{``}$$

The capacity of a cylindrical tank tapering from 5 ft. in diameter at the bottom to 3 ft. in diameter at the top, and 5 ft. deep, will be found as follows:

$$(5 + 3) \div 2 = 4 \text{ ft.} = \text{average diameter,}$$

$$2 \times 2 \times 3.1416 \times 5 \times 7.476 = 470 \text{ gallons,}$$

or

$$24 \times 24 \times 3.1416 \times 60 \div 231 = 470 \quad \text{``}$$

PROTECTION OF SUPPLY PIPES AGAINST FREEZING

Many attempts along various lines have been made to solve the question of protection of water pipes against freezing, with greater or less satisfactory results.

In some cases the covering of supply pipes with prepared covering, such as used in steam and hot-water heating, is effectual, although its use is not so satisfactory as might be supposed. If the pipe is exposed to extreme cold, as would be the case if run in an unprotected place out of doors, there is possibly no more effective protection than that afforded by the following:

Around the pipe, and about one inch from it, build a wooden box of the length of the exposed section, and outside this box construct a second box, with an inch air space between the two. Four or five of these boxes will afford ample protection for a pipe, although more of them can be used to great advantage if the exposure is extreme.

The boxing may be of rough boarding if it is desired to save expense. It is not the boarding that affords the protection to the pipe so much as the air confined between the several boxes.

Pipes laid at the bottom of streams are generally well protected, and also when laid in turfed ground they are very much better protected than when laid in uncovered ground. Another method that is often effective is to lay the pipe in trenches surrounded with hot horse manure. The heat of the manure will keep the frost from affecting the piping. The same method may be followed above ground by running the pipe in a box filled with manure.

The manure must be renewed usually each year, however, as it loses its strength in that time, then affording no protection. Sawdust cannot usually be depended upon as a protection for piping, as it absorbs moisture.

Hair felt closely packed about an exposed pipe acts as a strong protection. The latter material is of special value in pipes inside the house when passing through partitions or floors, the spaces between which are cold.

Plate LI

WATER SUPPLY FOR COUNTRY HOUSE
DOUBLE-ACTING RAM—CISTERN FILTERS—HOT-WATER SUPPLY

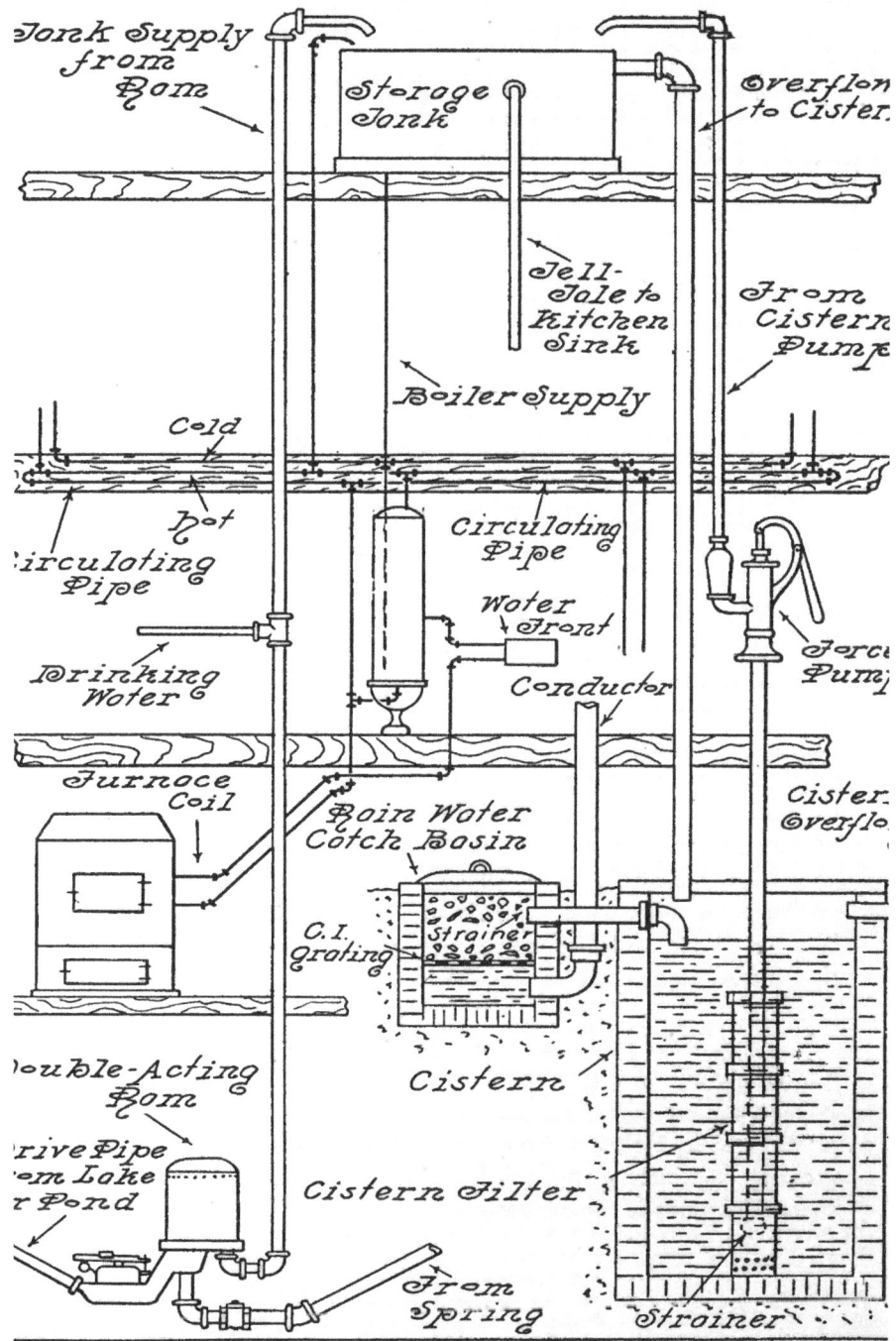
Plate 51. Water Supply for Country House

WATER SUPPLY FOR COUNTRY HOUSE

In the foregoing pages reference has been made to several of the features shown in Plate 51. This illustration gives a general system of supply, showing several details of value.

DOUBLE-ACTING RAM

The double-acting ram is of very great value under certain circumstances; for instance, when a limited supply of pure spring water is obtainable, but in too small quantity to operate the ram continuously. Under these conditions, any other water supply of inferior quality from a pond, lake, or stream properly located may be employed to operate the ram, its arrangement and connections being such that nothing but the pure water supply will be pumped. This machine is of comparatively recent origin and is very effective

CISTERN FILTERS

One of the chief features of Plate 51 is the work in connection with the cistern.

The collection and storage of rain water is very necessary as a means of providing a supply of soft water when the natural water supply is hard. Under such conditions it is sometimes necessary to use rain water for drinking purposes.

The storage of drinking water in tanks and cisterns is not advisable if better methods can be employed, but is sometimes necessary, and when this is the case too much attention cannot be given to providing the best possible conditions. To place the water coming from the roof in proper condition for drinking purposes it is necessary to filter it.

If rain water could be stored without taking up any impurities, it would be the purest water supply that could be obtained, but in falling upon the roof it not only carries with it such things as twigs, pieces of slate, etc., but also things which are much worse, such as decaying vegetable matter, bird manure, and dust and dirt which contain all kinds of impurities.

These things not only make the water impure, but discolor it to some extent, and cause it to give out foul odors.

It will thus be seen that before being pumped from the cistern into the house tank the water should be purified, and filtration is the easiest and most practicable way of performing the work. There are many forms of cistern filters.

A simple form of filter may be built in the following manner. Only a small part of the cistern is needed for the filter chamber, which should be of brick, extending from the wall about two feet into the cistern. It is practically a brick box built up from the bottom of the cistern about two or three feet, the top of the box also being bricked over. The bottom of this brick box should have a thick covering of gravel or broken stone and charcoal. Narrow openings should be provided at the bottom of the brick box at different points around it in order to allow the water of the cistern to pass through into the filter, and at these openings coarse wire cloth should be used to prevent the gravel and charcoal from working out. The top surface of the filtering material should also be protected in the same manner.

The brick box should not be covered with any coating to make it water-tight.

The suction pipe of the pump should end inside the filter box, resting firmly above the filtering material. It is also well to provide an air pipe of ½- or ¾-in. pipe, connecting into the filtering chamber and ending above the surface of the water in the cistern. The cistern water will filter through the filtering material and also through the bricks of the filter chamber, and when pumped from the latter to the house tank will be entirely suitable for drinking purposes. Porous stone and brick, by the way, make excellent filtering materials, as they are filled with minute air spaces, which is a necessary feature in any material that is to be used for filtering purposes. After having been in use for two or three years the filter chamber should be torn out, the filtering material renewed, and the bricks thoroughly cleaned before being used again, or new ones used, which would be better, as the pores of the bricks will have become more or less filled in this length of time. If the old bricks are to be used again, it will be a good plan to bake them, thus destroying any impurities that may exist in them.

While the filtering arrangement just described is efficient and

CISTERN FILTERS

satisfactory, it is an excellent idea in such work as this to prevent as far as possible the entrance of impurities into the cistern in the first place, and to filter the water also in some manner similar to the method described.

A sort of catch basin, such as shown in Plate 51, three or four feet in each of its three dimensions, or three or four feet in diameter and of about the same depth, if built in cylindrical form, may be used to hold back from the cistern much of the coarser substances, and thus prevent the cistern filter from becoming so quickly clogged.

This catch basin may be built against the cistern or separate from it, its top reaching to the surface of the ground and provided with a removable cover. A cast-iron grating should cover the full area of the catch basin, and be set securely a few inches from the bottom of it. Above the grating, and reaching nearly to the top of the catch basin, gravel or broken stone should be filled in, and from the upper part of this material an outlet of the same size as the conductor pipe is carried into the cistern. The conductor pipe from the roof is carried into the catch basin to a point below the iron grating. Therefore, to reach the cistern, all rain water must pass through the broken stone or gravel, which is easily renewed when necessary. It should be borne in mind that this catch basin should be used only as an aid to the cistern filter.

Another very good and simple form of cistern filter can be constructed as shown in Plate 51.

In the center of the cistern several lengths of large-size porous tile should be securely joined together, the bottom being cemented to the bottom of the cistern. The tile should be completely filled with broken stone and charcoal, and the suction pipe of the pump connected to the top. At the bottom of the tile, holes should be drilled through it in sufficient number to allow water to pass into the filtering material. The cistern water also filters through the tile. The connection of the suction pipe into the filter should be so made that it cannot break the tiling or the cement joints, and thus destroy its effectiveness by allowing unfiltered water to be pumped.

If desirable, this same filter may be laid on the bottom of the cistern, with the filtering holes in the end opposite the suction-pipe connection.

In Plate 51 the filtered cistern water is pumped into the attic storage tank, and an overflow from the latter run to the cistern. From the cistern an overflow is run to the surface of the ground.

It is necessary always to provide an unfailing supply of water, and the use of the double-acting ram, together with the use of rain water, present means of doing this. If it is desired to use cistern water at the pump, a faucet devised for this purpose may be attached to the pump at the bottom of the air chamber.

In the use of tanks for rain-water storage, it is better to use tin-lined sheet copper for the lining than sheet lead, as rain water will often attack lead. It is a fact that a pure water will more often attack metals than a water containing a large amount of impurities.

HOT-WATER SUPPLY

In connection with the supply work shown in Plate 51 there is also shown a system of hot-water supply, in which the kitchen-range boiler is heated both by the kitchen range and by a coil in the furnace. This is a very common practice not only in country work, but in the city also. Very often a small bath-room radiator may be heated from the hot-water supply.

The hot-water supply system is represented by the single heavy lines. There are several methods of heating a range boiler from the kitchen range and another heating source below it, and the method shown is probably the most satisfactory. It will be noted that in this method the course of the circulation of hot water is continuous, the hot water from the furnace passing through the range water-front, thence to the boiler and to the fixtures, and, when it has cooled, returning to the furnace coil. Two lines of circulation are shown, each being brought together on the return.

The use of circulating pipes, if properly installed, insures a constant supply of hot water close to the fixtures supplied, and naturally obviates the necessity of drawing off a long line of cold water before the water will run hot, as must be done in work unprovided with circulation.

This saving in the use of water is a matter of importance wherever water is metered or limited in amount.

Whenever the house supply is from an attic tank the hot-water supply must be under tank pressure, in the use of which system an expansion pipe is necessary.

Plate LII

THAWING UNDERGROUND WATER PIPES BY ELECTRICITY

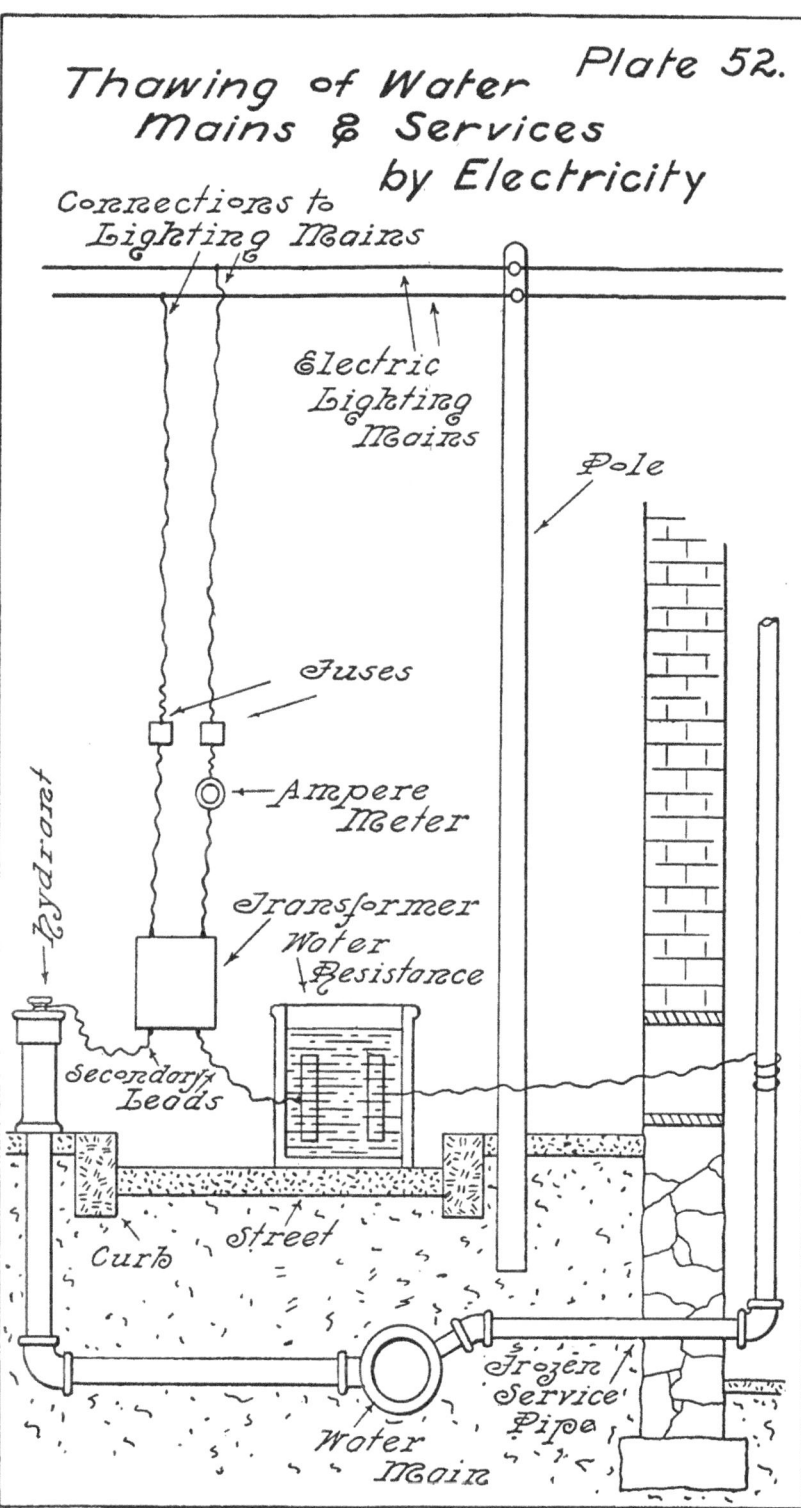

THAWING UNDERGROUND WATER PIPES BY ELECTRICITY

A SUCCESSION of severe winters has had the result of establishing the practice of thawing frozen water mains and service pipes by means of electricity. In some sections during the winter of 1903-4 water mains 7 ft. underground were frozen, and the old method of digging up the frozen ground to expose the affected pipe was found to be a matter of great expense, especially as several thousands of freeze-ups occurred in some of the large cities.

The principle upon which this method works is the fact that an electric current, in passing through a conductor which offers considerable resistance to its passage, develops a great amount of heat in the conducting material.

In passing an electric current through a frozen water pipe there is sufficient resistance encountered to generate the heat necessary to thaw the pipe. The ice itself offers great resistance, it being a poor conductor, while the pipe, especially at its joints, offers a considerable amount also. With this principle to work upon, the thawing of pipes may be accomplished if the means are at hand for providing a large enough current, in this work the securing of a large amount of current being of most importance, just as in the use of water for some purposes, the volume which may be obtained is of greater importance than the pressure which it is under.

Many different and successful methods have been made use of in supplying the electric surrent. In sizable towns and in cities, the most convenient source of electricity for this work has been the electric-lighting mains, most of which are now alternating circuits.

In employing alternating currents it is necessary to use what is known as a step-down transformer. Such a device consists essentially of two coils of wire adjacent to each other, but not connected together in any way. The ends of the primary coil are connected to the lighting mains, and the passage of the current through this coil induces a current in the secondary coil. The step-down transformer takes a current from the mains at a high voltage or pressure and delivers it through the secondary coil under a much lower voltage.

Currents under various voltages, up to several thousand in amount, have been used on the primary and transformed generally to about 50 volts on the secondary.

An electric circuit is made up of three factors—current in amperes, voltage, and resistance. As the resistance increases, the amount of current decreases, and vice versa.

The thawing apparatus is generally placed upon a wagon or sled, and consists principally of the transformer and what is known as a water resistance. The latter is usually in the form of a small barrel filled with salted water, in which two copper plates are immersed, each being connected to a wire.

After this apparatus has been taken to the place where the thawing is to be done, the primary leads are connected to the electric-light mains, proper fuses and an ammeter for measuring the current being provided.

The secondary leads or connections are then attached at either end of the frozen section, and the water resistance placed at any point in the secondary circuit, with the copper plates far apart. When in this position the resistance is great, and the amount of current small. When it is seen that a larger amount of current is necessary, it may be obtained by reducing the resistance, that is, by moving the plates closer together. Various amounts of current are required, depending on the conditions of each individual piece of work. For service pipes, which are naturally more often affected than the mains, currents of an amount between 200 and 300 amperes are generally used.

Long leads are used on this work, and when possible the connection may be made most easily by attaching one of the secondary leads to the nearest hydrant, and the other to a faucet or to the piping inside the house, the current thus being allowed to pass through the frozen section. Attention should be given to making as good connections to the hydrant and faucet as possible, as a poor contact at either place may result in burning the metal.

When there is no hydrant conveniently located, connection may be made to the piping of an adjacent house, and if the latter is too far distant it sometimes becomes necessary to dig down to the pipe to make the connection.

When the service pipes of two or more adjacent houses are to be thawed, the several water services may be connected in series, and a single application of the current answer for thawing all of them.

By using long secondary leads, frozen service pipes of several houses may often be thawed without changing the primary connections to the lighting mains.

So universal has the practice become of thawing frozen mains and service pipes by electricity, that apparatus designed especially for such work may now be procured of manufacturers of electrical apparatus.

In some cases, where it was impossible to use lighting or power circuits, portable outfits have been used in this work, consisting of a steam or gas engine connected to an electric generator. Storage batteries have also been made use of. The time used in thawing pipes depends so largely on conditions, size of pipe, length of frozen section, amount of current available, etc., that it is difficult to make any estimate of it. Under favorable conditions, however, service pipes of different sizes have been thawed out in from ten to twenty minutes, and long lines of water mains, as large as 10 in. in size, in two or three hours.

The plumber, being ordinarily unacquainted with electrical work, should always seek the advice or the services of competent electricians before attempting this class of work, as errors in connections on his part might result seriously.

The workman inexperienced in electrical work might easily make a mistake which would not only result in considerable damage to apparatus, but which might also affect the lighting circuit to such an extent as to render it useless until repaired. In addition, there is the danger of serious or fatal injury to the workman.

The matter of caring for frozen mains and services has in many cities been taken over by the city water department, the thawing operations being performed by them, in combination with the electric-lighting companies. This would appear to be by far the best method under the circumstances.

Plate LIII

DOUBLE BOILERS

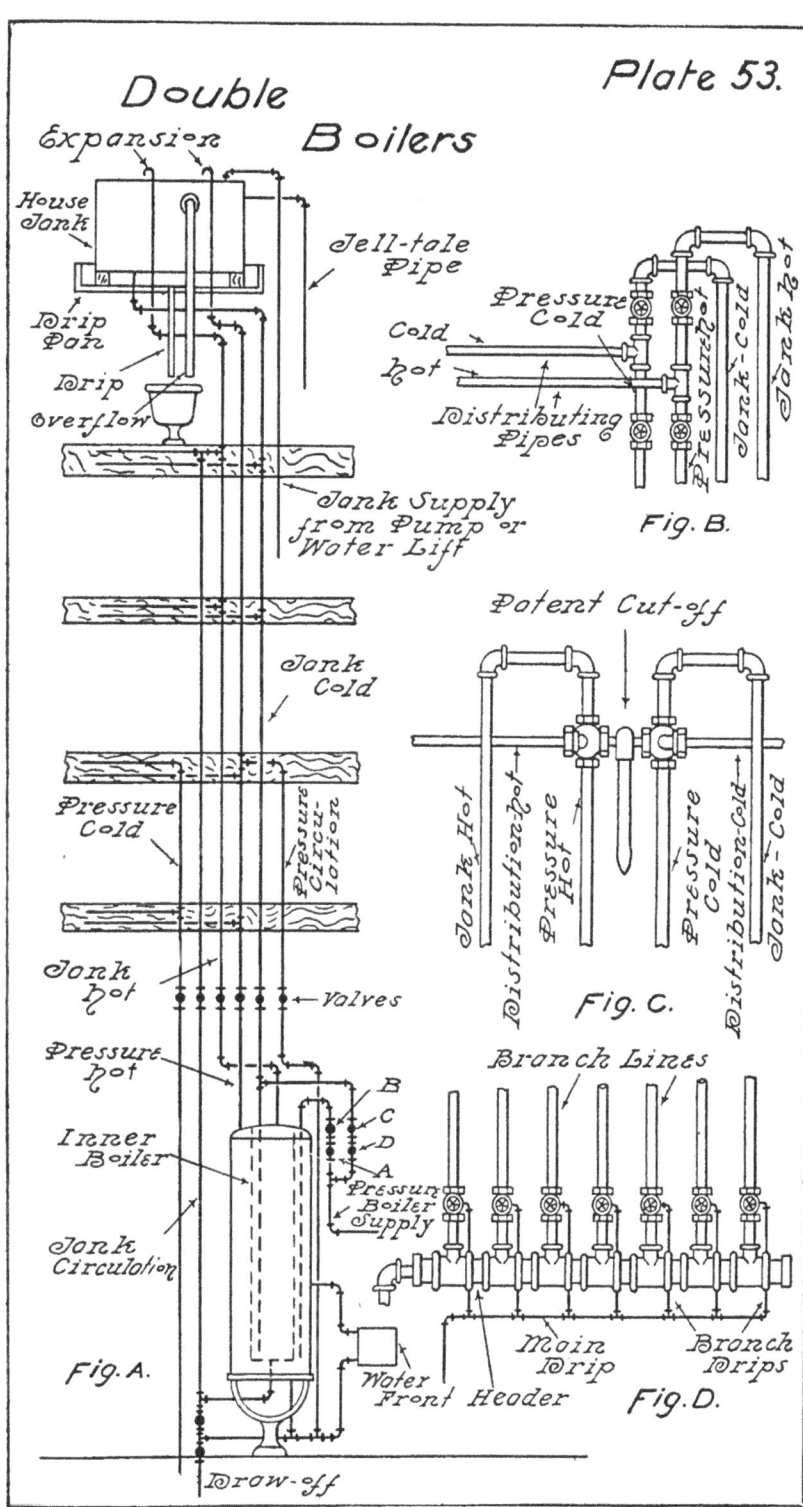

DOUBLE BOILERS

WHILE the principle of the double boiler is simple and its connections straightforward, there are comparatively few who understand the manner in which it should be installed. The double boiler is used in city buildings of such height that the water under city pressure will not at all times reach the upper floors.

It consists of two boilers, one inside the other, the outer boiler being connected in the usual manner with the heater, and the inner boiler receiving its heat from the hot water in the boiler which surrounds it.

This form of boiler is much used in large residences, and often in apartment buildings.

In most of the largest buildings, however, where very large amounts of hot water are required, the water is pumped into the house tank, and the entire hot-water supply for the building delivered under tank pressure.

The outer boiler is supplied by city pressure, while the inner boiler is under tank pressure. The lower floors, which can be reached by city pressure, are supplied from the outer boiler, and the upper floors, which cannot be reached by city pressure, are supplied from the inner boiler. The connections for the double boiler are to be seen in Fig. A, Plate 53.

The hot-water supply line from each boiler should be provided with an expansion pipe taken from the high point on the line and emptying over the house tank.

The supply to the latter is delivered by a pump or water lift. From the tank an overflow should be carried, generally into some open fixture which has a sufficiently large waste to insure the passage of all overflow water that may enter it. A tell-tale pipe should also be run from the tank to a fixture conveniently located, so that the pump operator may be warned when the tank has been sufficiently filled. Beneath the house tank a drip pan should be provided to collect any leakage that may come from the tank, and from this pan a drip pipe delivers such leakage into some open fixture.

In the event of a breakdown of the pump, or from other cause, there is always danger that the house tank may lose its supply. If this condition should continue for some time, it might result in danger to the inner boiler, to guard against which a connection is made from the pressure supply to the outer boiler, into the tank supply to the inner boiler, a check valve, C, being used on this connection. When the system is working normally the check valve remains closed, owing to the pressure of the tank supply, but when this is withdrawn, as would happen after a time if the pump were not in operation, the street pressure will open the check valve, and thus keep the inner boiler supplied with water. A check valve, B, prevents the siphonage of the contents of the outer boiler in the case of a break in the service pipe. It is the use of this check valve that necessitates the use of an expansion pipe on the hot-water supply from the outer boiler, the check valve cutting off the natural means of expansion.

The valves A and D control the use of these two lines. If circulating pipes are used, as they should be on such work as this, the tank circulating pipe should connect into the return of the inner boiler, and the pressure circulating pipe should connect into the return to the heater.

Special attention should be given to properly draining the double boiler. If the inner boiler is drawn off first, there may be danger of collapsing it, due to the creation of a partial vacuum inside it and street pressure outside of it. This danger is eliminated by arranging the draw-off in such a way that the outer boiler must be drawn off first or both boilers drained at the same time. This is accomplished by the proper placing of valves, as shown in Plate 53, Fig. A.

CUT-OFFS

Under some conditions street pressure will not at all times of the day raise water to the highest floor which is intended to be supplied by city pressure. It then becomes necessary to use a device, known as a cut-off, by which tank pressure may be supplied to the floor. Fig. B shows the simplest form.

The two cold-water pressures are connected together, also the two hot-water pressures.

By opening the two upper valves and closing the two lower ones the floor may be provided with tank pressure, and vice versa. The

HEADERS

objection to the use of this crude form of cut-off is that confusion may result from the use of valves.

In Fig. C a patented form of cut-off is shown, in which this trouble is not present. By throwing the lever up or down either tank or street pressure is turned on.

HEADERS

In large hot-water supply systems the cold-water lines connect into a header, the hot-water lines into another, and the circulation pipes into another.

This makes the work very systematic and easily cared for. Fig. D shows the general arrangement of a header, with its branches, each supplied with a shut-off, and each branch also provided with a drip connecting into a main drip, the latter emptying into an open fixture.

The same general arrangement of headers, branches, drips, valves, etc., may be, and often is, employed to great advantage in connection with the hot- and cold-water supply of a residence.

In connection with high-grade residence work, a very neat and artistic piece of work can be performed on these headers by using polished brass pipe and fittings, and additional neatness in appearance may be obtained by bending the pipes at changes in direction, instead of performing the work with fittings. Better results can also be obtained from this method for the reason that there is less friction encountered in smooth bends than in bends made with fittings.

The employment of these methods is almost a necessity on large work, as in such work the supply piping is of such a complex nature that it cannot safely be installed other than in the most systematic manner.

Plate LIV

HOT-WATER SUPPLY FOR LARGE BUILDINGS

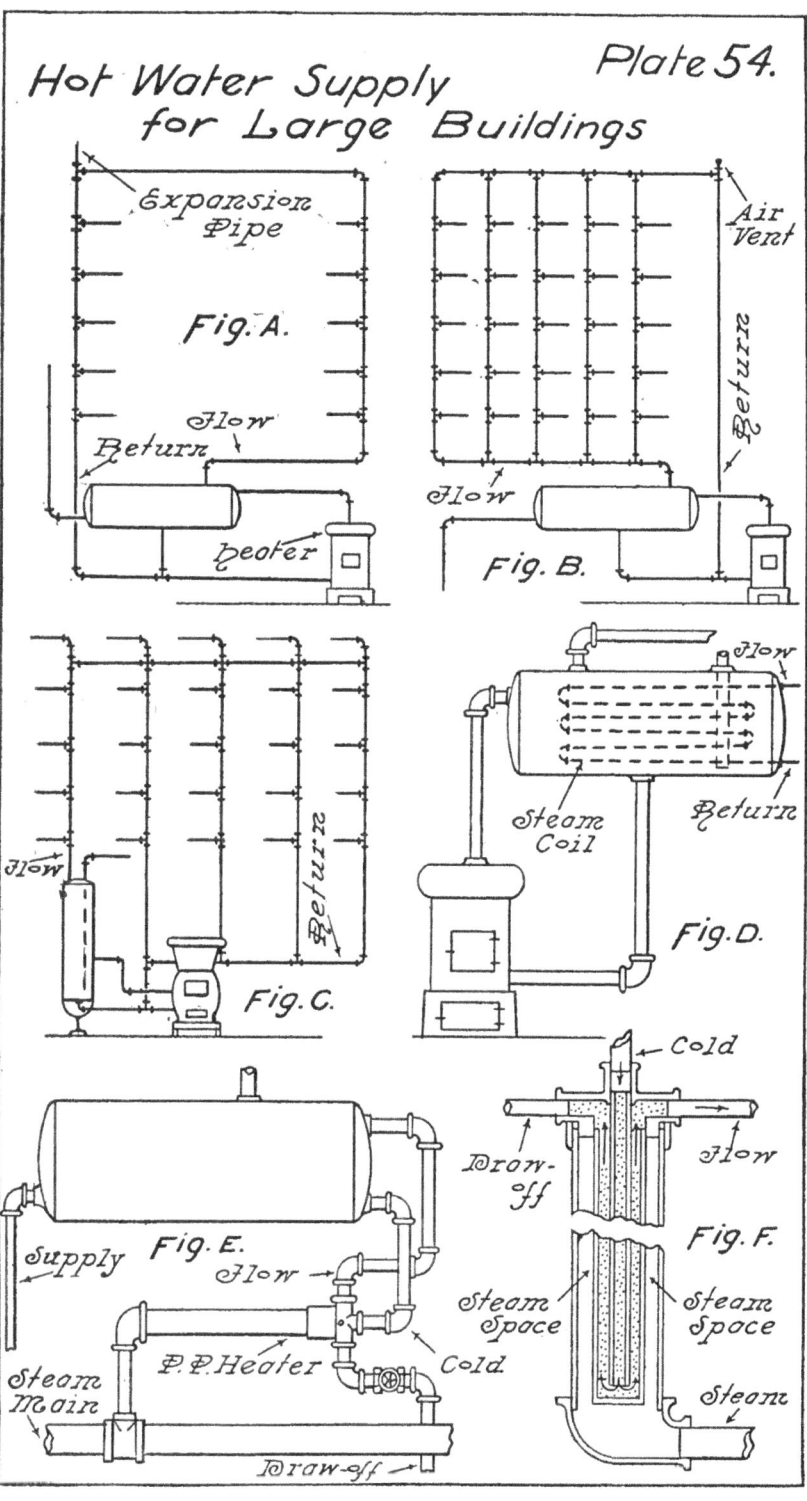

HOT-WATER SUPPLY FOR LARGE BUILDINGS

IN the supplying of hot water for large buildings the boiler is generally of the horizontal style, hung by wrought-iron hangers from the cellar timbers, although vertical boilers are sometimes used. The source of heat for such boilers is generally a special tank heater. Live and exhaust steam are also much used by means of steam coils placed inside the boiler. A combination often used to advantage includes both tank heater and steam coils, the heater being used during the summer and the coils during the winter season, when the heating plant of the building is in operation. The use of the tank heater and steam coil is seen in Fig. D, Plate 54.

In addition, special heating devices or auxiliaries are used in this work, one of them, known as the P. P. Heater, being shown connected to the boiler in Fig. E, and a sectional view of the same in Fig. F, Plate. 54. As seen from the latter, the device consists essentially of three pipes, one inside the other. Cold water is conducted through the innermost pipe, from which it passes into the pipe or tube next outside, this pipe being closed at its end.

Steam is conveyed into the space between the middle pipe and the outer one, thus entirely surrounding the cold water that enters.

The flow connection is made to the middle pipe, also the draw-off connection. It is claimed that the heating of water by means of this heater is very rapid, and that even in the form of steam vapor it will heat the water more rapidly and in greater quantity than it can be heated by a water front with a hot fire.

The heater may be connected with the steam piping of the building, as shown in Fig. E.

The heater is made in several sizes, ranging from the kitchen-boiler size to sizes suitable for large work. The size of hot-water boilers naturally depends on the character and use of the building, the number of apartments, and number of fixtures supplied with hot water. In the case of apartment buildings it is generally a comparatively simple matter to approximate the boiler capacity necessary, but in the case of many buildings, experience and judgment are necessary in arriving at a proper size.

A very common method, and one that is ordinarily a safe one to follow, is to estimate about 20 gallons of boiler capacity for each full set of fixtures that would commonly require hot water in an apartment. These fixtures would include the kitchen sink, wash trays, bath tub, and lavatory. If any of these fixtures are omitted, or others are added, a due allowance may be made.

Reckoning on this basis, the following table shows the boiler capacity necessary for different numbers of apartments, and the standard sizes of boilers having the respective capacities.

TABLE OF HOT-WATER BOILER CAPACITIES

No. of Apartments	Capacity of Boiler	Size of Boiler
4	100 gals.	22″ × 60″
6	120 "	24″ × 60″
8	180 "	30″ × 60″
10	215 "	30″ × 72″
12	250 "	30″ × 84″
16	365 "	36″ × 84″
20	430 "	42″ × 72″
24	575 "	42″ × 96″
36	720 "	42″ × 120″

Another table which will be found of value is the following, which shows the number and size of steam coils necessary for the several sizes of hot-water boilers specified in the foregoing table.

TABLE OF STEAM COILS FOR HOT-WATER BOILERS

Capacity of Boiler	Size and Number of Coils
100 to 120 gals.	4 1-in. pipes.
180 " 215 "	6 1-in. "
250 " 365 "	6 1¼-in. "
430 " 575 "	4 1½-in. "
720 "	6 1½-in. "

In Figs. A, B, and C, of Plate 54, are shown three different methods of installing large hot-water supply systems.

Of the three systems, probably that shown in Fig. A is least satisfactory, for the reason that the supply at different points is less evenly heated than in the case of the other two systems. For instance, the hot-water branches taken out of the return will not deliver such hot water as those on the flow line. However, the choice of a hot-water supply system must often depend upon the character and construction of the building to be supplied. All things being equal, the overhead system shown in Fig. C will probably do as satisfactory work as any of the others shown, although the system in Fig. B is an excellent one. The latter should be provided at its high point with an air vent, while the former needs none.

Plate LV

AUTOMATIC CONTROL OF HOT-WATER TANKS

Automatic Control of Hot Water Tanks

Plate 55.

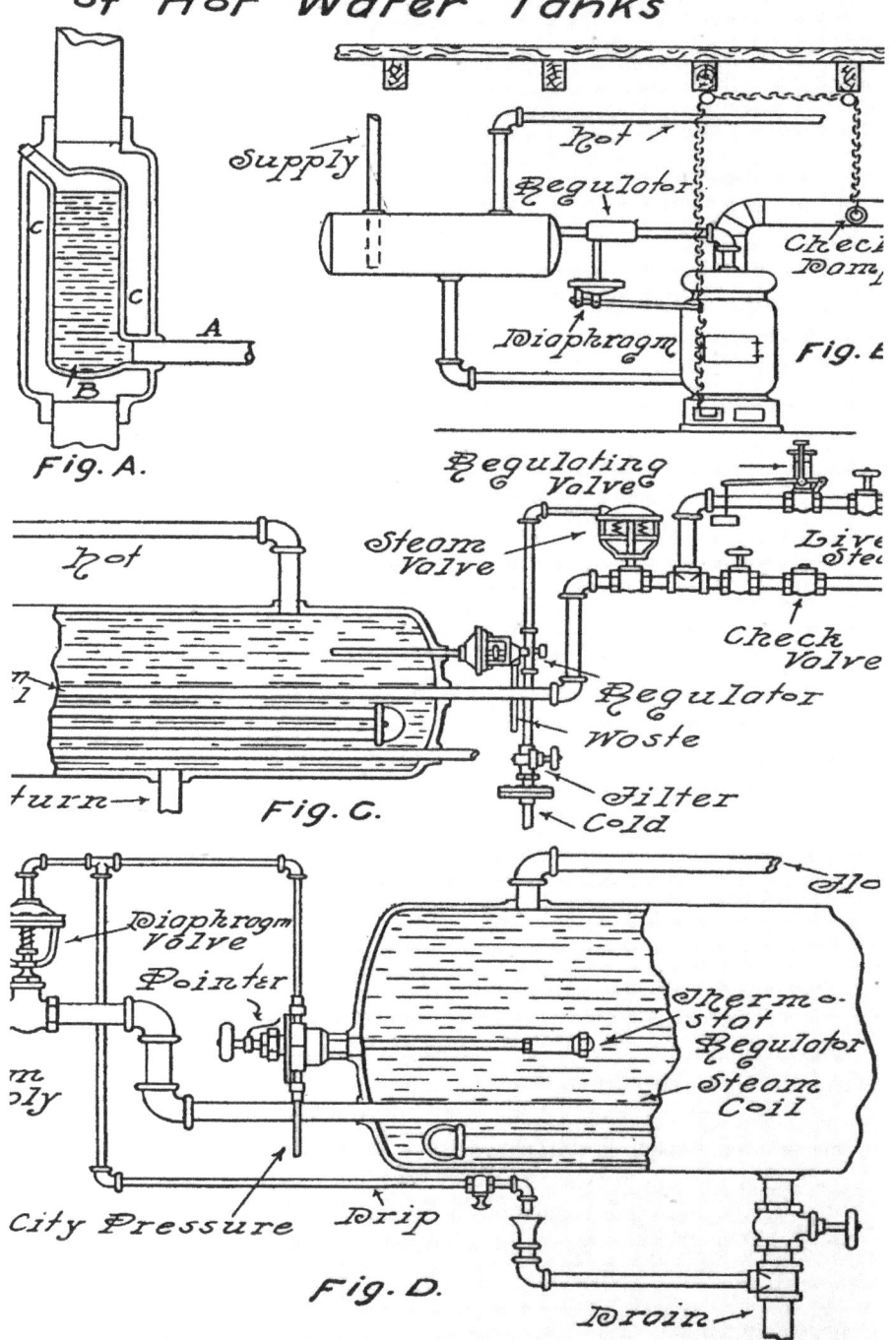

AUTOMATIC CONTROL OF HOT-WATER TANKS

On large work it is essential to satisfactory service to provide automatic control for the hot-water tank. On smaller work, also, automatic control may be used to advantage. When the supply system is under the attention of a painstaking attendant the necessity of automatic regulation is not so great, but in general constant attention to the necessary requirements cannot be depended upon, in which case control of the temperature of the hot-water supply by automatic means avoids all trouble.

There are several excellent systems of regulation now on the market, two of which are shown in the several illustrations of Plate 55. Fig. A represents a sectional view of one of these regulators for use in connection with boilers heated by kitchen range or special tank heater. Fig. B shows this regulator in use in connection with a boiler heated by tank heater. The regulator should always be connected to the flow pipe, and may be in either a horizontal or vertical position. In using this regulator, the part B is filled with water through the opening D, which is closed by means of a plug. About a cupful of water should be drawn out through a small tube, and this liquid replaced by an equivalent amount of gasoline.

The hot water of the flow pipe which passes through C, C, heats the contents of B to the temperature of the hot water itself.

Gasoline has a somewhat lower boiling point than water, and will boil just before the water in B and C, C, reaches the boiling point. The gasoline in boiling exerts a pressure which is transmitted through A to a diaphragm, which in turn, by means of a lever, operates the chain which will close the draught damper and open the check damper. When the temperature of the water has dropped sufficiently, the diaphragm will react, opening the draught damper and closing the check.

The regulator may be set at any convenient point in the flow pipe, the only requirement being that it be set so that the plug D shall be at the top, in order that it may be filled.

Fig. C shows the regulation of live and exhaust steam to the steam coils when the boiler is to be heated in this way.

The regulator is connected into the end of the boiler and about three-quarters of the distance up from the bottom. This regulator should be set horizontally, with the tube running into the boiler. A diaphragm steam valve is placed on the steam-supply pipe, at a point between the boiler and the live-steam connection, in order to control both live and exhaust steam. City pressure is connected to the regulator, and thence to the steam valve. Before reaching the regulator the water supply is reduced to the proper pressure by a filter. As the temperature of the tank water rises, the expansion of the tube inside the boiler operates the regulator, which allows the water pressure to reach and close the steam valve, thus shutting off the supply of exhaust steam to the coil.

When the water cools, the regulator acts in an opposite manner, the city pressure is shut off, and the water carried away from the steam valve through the waste.

On the live-steam connection the regulating valve is adjusted to open at a lower temperature than that usually carried in the exhaust-steam pipe. Thus, when the latter falls below its normal point, live steam is admitted through the steam valve.

If a tank heater is also connected to a boiler thus supplied, the regulator shown in Fig. B may be used in conjunction with the regulating apparatus of Fig. C.

The regulator of Fig. D is of another make, but working along similar lines to the regulator of Fig. C. By means of this regulator any desired temperature of the water may be obtained by moving the pointer toward " cooler " or " warmer."

By means of a diaphragm similar to that shown in Fig. B, this regulator can be made to control the temperature of hot-water tanks heated by tank heaters.

Plate LVI

THE THREE-PIPE SYSTEM OF SUPPLY

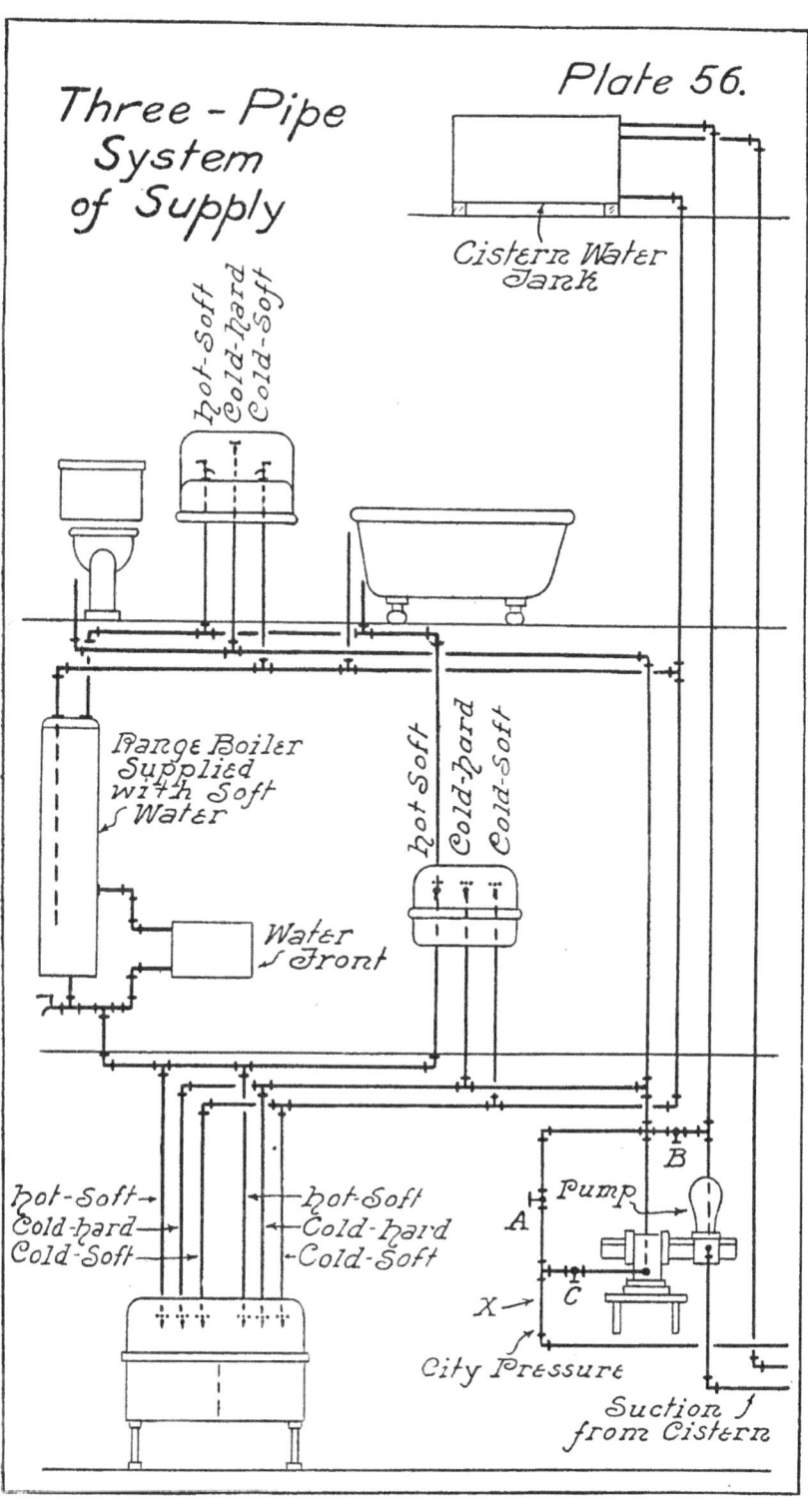

THE THREE-PIPE SYSTEM OF SUPPLY

In many sections of the country, owing to the nature of the soil through which the water supply flows, water supplied for domestic purposes is exceedingly hard, and therefore naturally presents a most difficult problem for the community to solve. It does not concern the supply for drinking purposes, for the flushing of water closets, and for certain other uses, but hard water is entirely unsatisfactory for toilet use, for washing clothes, the washing of dishes, etc. Furthermore, while hot water that is hard would be objectionable for many uses, the heating of hard water is also attended by a very great annoyance in the rapid filling of the water front and range connections with a deposit of lime, making their frequent renewal a matter of much expense and inconvenience.

Under these conditions, a system of hot and cold water supply known as the three-pipe system, may be used to very great advantage. The general features of this system may be observed in Plate 56.

In the installation of the three-pipe system, three lines of supply are provided to such fixtures as sinks, lavatories and wash trays, where hard cold water may be required for drinking or rinsing purposes. From the three bibbs at these fixtures may be drawn soft cold water, hard cold water, and soft hot water. At baths hot and cold soft water may be drawn, and of course water closets are provided with hard cold water only.

It will be understood that in places where the natural supply is hard, any supply of soft water that may be obtained must be used as economically as possible.

The system is simple in construction, and not expensive to install, although costing somewhat more than the common system. The street supply is piped direct to the pump, and from the pump direct to the fixtures which are to be provided with hard water. When hard water is drawn at any of these fixtures, the street supply passes through the pump, serving also to operate the pump, thereby causing the latter to draw soft water from the cistern and deliver it to the attic tank.

From the soft-water tank in the attic, a supply of soft water is piped down to those fixtures requiring this kind of water, and a branch taken to supply the range boiler. Thus nothing but soft water passes through the boiler, water front and connections. From the boiler, hot water is delivered to fixtures in the ordinary manner.

It is necessary to provide for a supply of hot hard water, in the event that the supply of cistern water fails. This is done by means of the connections and valves at the pump. When there is a supply of soft water available, valves A and B are closed, and valve C open. When the soft-water supply gives out, and hard water must of necessity be used for all purposes, all that is required is to open valve B, which will allow city water to fill the entire system, including the boiler.

When the cistern is empty, and it is required to use only hard cold water, valve B should remain closed, also valve C, and valve A opened. This will allow city water to enter the cold-water piping, without passing through the pump.

The attic tank should have an overflow pipe, and if economy in the use of soft cistern water is to be observed, the pipe should lead back to the cistern, in order that the overflow water may not be lost. Instead of running as shown in our illustration, the overflow may discharge onto the roof, and from this point flow back to the cistern.

If a supply for sprinkling or other such purpose is to be provided, connection should be made on the street side of the connection to the pump, as at X, so that sprinkling may not keep the pump operating.

Plate LVII

THE SOFTENING OF HARD WATER FOR DOMESTIC PURPOSES

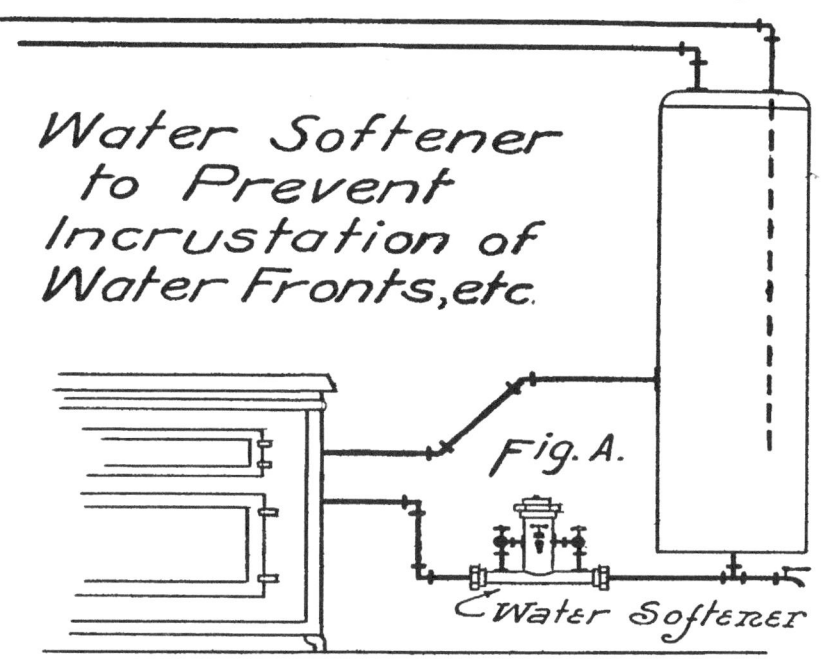
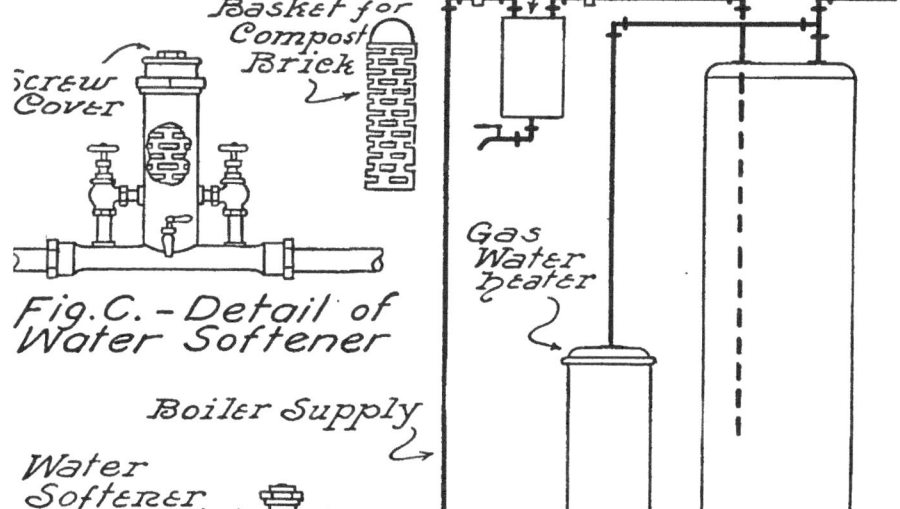

THE SOFTENING OF HARD WATER FOR DOMESTIC PURPOSES

In the consideration of the three-pipe system, under Plate 56, a method was described for overcoming the incrustation of water fronts and range connections, incident to the use of hard water, by means of a separate storage of soft water, which would generally be rain water collected in cisterns.

For various reasons, such as an insufficient supply of rain water, this method may not always be satisfactory, and we believe that the following method will often be found preferable. We allude to the use of a water-softening device, several of which have been introduced, designed for use in connection with domestic water supplies.

The construction of a water-softening device of this type, and its application, are shown in Plate 57. In Fig. A the device is shown connected to the return pipe of the range connection, which is the ordinary practice, although, as shown in Fig. B, it may be connected to the boiler supply. If desirable in any case to soften hot water, it may be connected to the hot water piping with equally good results.

The softening is accomplished in a very simple manner, by passing the hard water over a "Kompost" brick, a water-softening composition which converts the sulphates or carbonates in the water into phosphates. As shown in Fig. C, the cylindrical "Kompost" brick is contained in a basket, and this is placed in the feed cylinder of the device. As the water flows about this brick, after a time it wears away, and may be easily replaced with a new brick. Following are instructions for using the water softener:

After it has been connected, and water turned on, hot water faucets should be opened to allow all grease to be drawn out of the system. The two valves should then be turned off, the drain cock opened, the screw cover removed, and the basket with its brick, dropped into the chamber. The cover is then replaced, and the valves opened not more than one-quarter turn, the water softener then being ready for use.

As long as any of the softening composition remains in the chamber, all water passing through it will be thoroughly softened, and turbid water clarified. The composition used is of a mineral nature, containing nothing that is in any way harmful to health or to fabrics.

As the water is thoroughly neutralized before it reaches the water front, it is clear that incrustation of the water front with lime cannot occur in the use of this water-softening device. The deposit of lime takes place chiefly in the heating of the water, so that the water front and hot-water flow-pipe between range and boiler suffer mostly.

A feature that deserves special attention is that while the deposit of lime fills the water front and connections, thereby reducing the effective size of piping, this coating also acts as an insulation, which makes the heating of the water much more difficult, and in the use of instantaneous heaters and gas water-heaters especially, greatly increases the amount of gas used, and therefore the cost for gas.

In Fig. B the device is shown connected to the supply to the boiler, with a special tank in use for the collection of sediment, which may be removed from time to time through the sediment cock. The coating of the coils of instantaneous heaters with lime takes place in a comparatively short space of time, and the employment of soft water will be found of special advantage in their use.

The water-softening device which has been described may also be used to very great advantage in the case of heating-boilers. As the water is softened before entering the boiler, there is no possibility of the formation of scale, and if such a device be applied to a boiler already affected by scale, this will gradually disappear, as the soft water disintegrates the lime.

The water softener has a valuable application also for automobile garages. Considerable difficulty is occasioned in using hard water in automobiles, which soft water would entirely overcome. An excellent plan for garages, where only cold water is required, consists in the use of a range boiler without boiler tube, the boiler being supplied through a top opening with soft water. The supply of soft water may be piped from one of the top openings to points of delivery.

It may be stated that generally the attempt to clear water fronts of lime deposit by the use of acids is not very successful. A plan which seems to work successfully, however, is to make use of two water fronts. When one becomes useless, owing to lime deposit, it may be removed and replaced with the other water front. By the time the second water front is in bad condition, the lime in the first one will have become disintegrated by the action of the air.

Plate LVIII

SPECIAL PROBLEMS AND DEVICES IN HOT-WATER SUPPLY

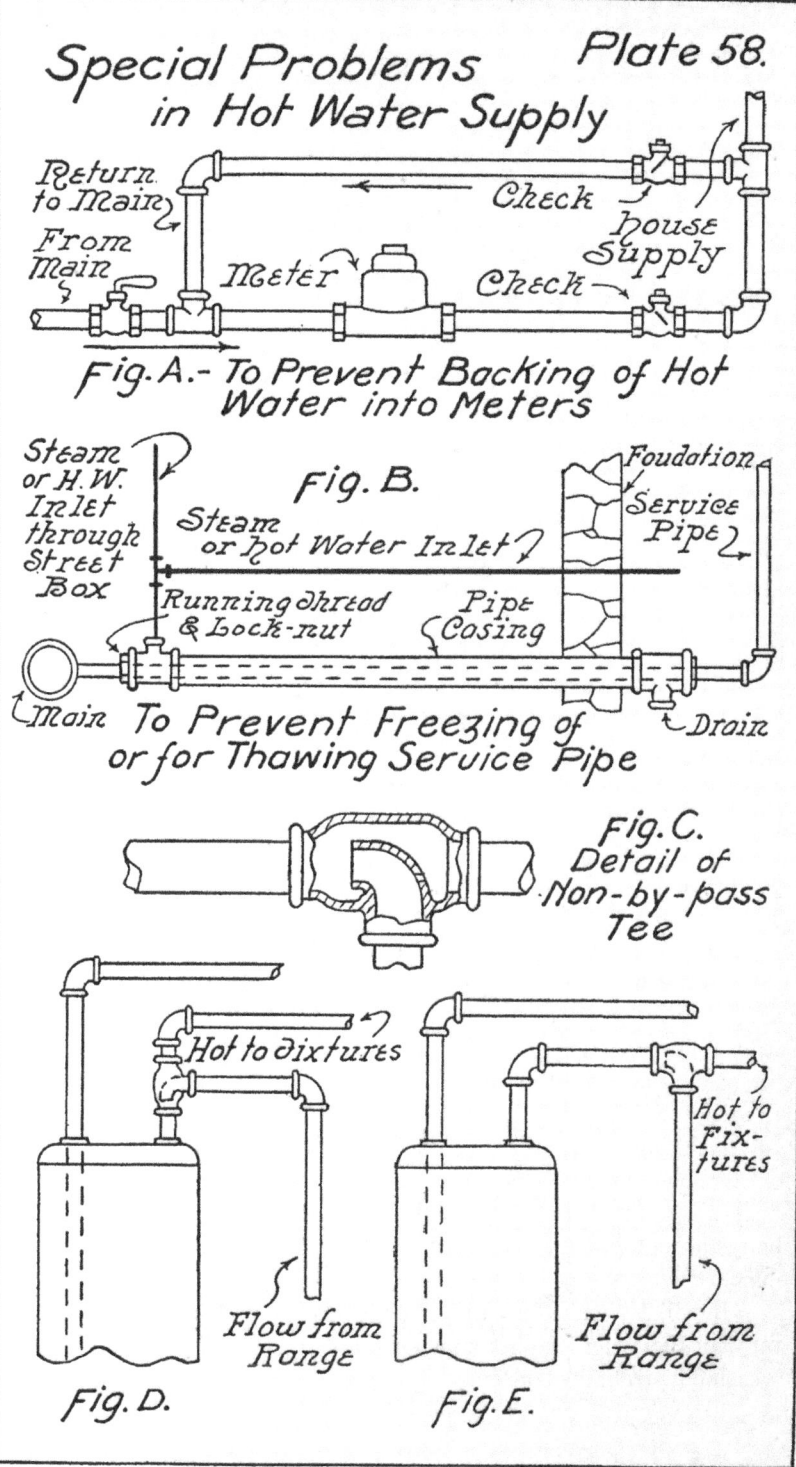

SPECIAL PROBLEMS AND DEVICES IN HOT-WATER SUPPLY

PROBABLY there is no branch of the plumbing industry which constantly presents more difficult situations than hot-water supply and circulation, and the consideration of some of these problems, with the methods applied in their solution, should prove of interest and value.

The matter of expansion for range boilers introduces problems which are sometimes difficult to solve. Under some conditions, for instance, hot water from the boiler will back into the cold-water pipe supplying the boiler, in which event there is great danger of damage to the meter. In overcoming this trouble, recourse has often been made to the use of a check valve on the supply pipe, the action of which would be to prevent expansion of the boiler in this direction. Expansion back into the water mains is the natural and necessary outlet for excessive pressure in direct pressure boilers, and if such a path is not provided, a water front explosion is the common result. The use of check valves in this way is by no means uncommon among careless or ignorant workmen, and the results are often disastrous both to life and to property.

If such a course is to be followed, it becomes necessary to use a safety valve in connection with the check valve, although this does not absolutely insure against bad results, as the safety valve may be defective, or may stick and refuse to operate. Under these conditions, the method presented in Fig. A, Plate 58, will be found very useful. It consists in the use of a by-pass around the meter, with two check valves closing in opposite directions, one on the by-pass and the other on the house supply. The latter serves to prevent expansion into the meter, and the check valve on the by-pass prevents any flow to the house through it, but allows expansion to take place back into the water main.

It will be seen that this arrangement allows all water to pass through the meter, while removing the danger to it of damage from a back flow from the boiler.

In the case of boilers supplied from an attic tank, there is no chance of this damage to meters, because of the different nature of the supply connections.

In Fig. B, Plate 58, is shown a method that will be found very effective in thawing frozen service pipes, and also in preventing freezing. As shown, the plan is to encase the service pipe in a second pipe, closing the opening of each end of the casing by a lock-nut working on a running thread, and closing against a packing.

At either end of the casing a tee is used. Into the outer tee a pipe of small size is connected, one branch rising through the street box, and another passing into the cellar through the foundation. By means of steam or hot water, entering through either branch, the pipe may be thawed whenever it freezes, or it may be kept from freezing. The casing is drained through the inner tee, just inside the foundation, and should point downward.

Another problem concerns the trouble experienced in the by-passing under certain conditions, of gas-water-heater connections made into the top of the boiler. In this by-passing, which is not due to the heater itself, cold water draws in and mixes with the hot water at the point where the ordinary tee connection is made. This trouble is overcome by the use of a fitting known as a non-by-pass tee, which is illustrated in cross section by Fig. C, Plate 58. Fig. D shows the fitting connected to a rising line of hot water, and Fig. E to a horizontal line.

Mixing of cold water with hot water may also occur from other causes. For instance, it sometimes happens that the boiler tube is carelessly omitted, or has become so corroded that it breaks off. Either of these things will allow cold water to enter the top of the boiler, and cause either cold or lukewarm water to be drawn at the fixtures.

Another subject not generally well understood is the matter of air-lock on hot-water piping.

Air-lock often prevents flow of hot water to fixtures, and it will generally be found that when such a state exists, it is in connection with a system which has a very low pressure.

If the air pressure is greater than the water pressure, air-lock results, but if the water pressure is the greater, the air-lock will be overcome. The trouble seldom occurs in the case of direct pressure supplies, owing to the fact that they generally are under sufficient pressure to overcome the air. The pressure required to do this amounts to about one pound for each two feet of vertical air-lock, and if there

SPECIAL PROBLEMS IN HOT-WATER SUPPLY

is a back pressure, the amount of it would have to be added. It is a common practice to turn down from the top of the boiler with the hot-water pipe, and it is at the point where the turn is made that air-lock occurs. This can be overcome in the case of the tank-supply system, by taking an expansion pipe from this point, up to and over the tank.

It may also be done by taking a branch supply to some fixture above, from this high point.

Under certain conditions it may sometimes be very convenient to reduce the size of a range boiler without making a change in boilers. This may be done effectively by taking the cold-water connection to the water front out of the side opening of the boiler, instead of from the bottom, and connecting the range flow-pipe at the top. This method has the effect of reducing the size of the boiler to that part of it which is above the side opening. Such a reduction in size might often be of advantage during the warm months, when only the gas water-heater is in use, and economy in the use of gas becomes a matter of importance.

The cold-water connection to the water front, from the side opening of the boiler, as mentioned above, is a good one for another reason. It is preferable to the common connection from the bottom of the boiler, for the reason that when the water is taken from this part of the boiler, it is free of rust and sediment, and in the use of gas water-heaters, this is of special importance, as the presence of sediment will, after a time, fill the coils and destroy the effectiveness of the heater.

SUGGESTIONS FOR ESTIMATING PLUMBING CONSTRUCTION

SUGGESTIONS FOR ESTIMATING PLUMBING CONSTRUCTION

It is the belief of the author that a special chapter devoted to the subject of the estimating of plumbing work will add to the value of this work in the eyes of many of its readers.

The plumbing fraternity at large are just as careless in their estimating of labor and material as those who are connected with other lines of construction. The plumber who keeps a close account of these things, and knows, when the work is completed, just how much he has made or lost, is the exception. It is a fact, indeed, that many do not seem to wish to know when a contract has been finished at a loss, and it is also a fact that the author has met those who have frankly refused to figure into their estimate such incidentals as gasoline, screws, putty, freight, cartage, etc., for fear of losing the contract. This would appear to be a strange thing in a business man, for these items represent an expense which must be met just as certainly as such items as traps, ferrules, etc.

On the other hand, many of the successful plumbing firms follow a very exact system of estimating, and keep a close account of all stock and labor used on each contract, thus being able to figure exactly the amount of profit or loss on any completed piece of work. Many firms, however, while estimating accurately and safely on stock and labor items, do not figure any percentage into their contracts to cover inside expenses, that is, rent, office expenses, telephone, etc. This is a matter of great importance, and consideration or nonconsideration of it often means the success or failure of the firm. Any firm doing a construction business must, along certain lines, be guided by past experience in estimating certain items. The expense of conducting business, which includes the items named above and many others, is a matter which must be figured largely by looking into those expenses of the past, and from the comparison of this amount with the gross amount of business done, the percentage that must be allowed for the conducting of business may be arrived at. Thus, if it costs a firm $500 to carry on a yearly business of $10,000, the percentage that must be allowed for this item of expense is 5%. This is a matter which varies greatly with different firms, some being able to conduct business at much less expense than others.

It is claimed by many firms doing a moderate amount of business that 15% is not too large an allowance for business expenses. Instead of giving this as the proper percentage to be added, however, it is the opinion of the author that each firm should approximate the amount in the manner above mentioned.

Another important matter is the amount of profit which may fairly be charged on contract work. It is a well-known fact to many of the readers of this work that at the present time many contracts are taken at as low a percentage of profit as 5%.

When it is considered that, in its anxiety to obtain a contract, a firm is willing to take it at this low figure, generally without adding any percentage for the expense of conducting business or for extras that may be overlooked in estimating, it is clear that the greater the number of such contracts taken by the firm, the sooner they must go into bankruptcy. There are many plumbing concerns, it may safely be said, who would be better off if they never took contract work, for the losses that must be sustained in this branch of their business must be offset by the profits derived from their jobbing or repair work, or bankruptcy is their only end. A profit of 25% on contract work, according to the author's opinion, is by no means too great. It may be said, however, that on large work a safe profit of a less amount may be satisfactory.

It is well understood by the author that these matters must be regulated by each individual concern, and it is equally well understood that if a firm is to carry on a successful and honest business, living profits must be secured, and that to secure them no legitimate business expense can be shirked in making estimates of cost.

The first essential in estimate work is a complete and reliable form of estimate, the use of which is very necessary, as it is not within the power of any man to remember at all times the scores of items that should enter a plumbing estimate. The low bidder on contract work is often low because he has forgotten to figure on some important item. The writer recalls a firm which secured a certain contract and found, when the work was under way, that all the water closets—six in number—had been omitted, which meant the completion of the work at a loss. The use of a correct estimate

SUGGESTIONS FOR ESTIMATING

sheet avoids these troubles. In connection with this subject there is shown an estimate sheet which is very satisfactory. In this connection, however, it must be stated that it is a difficult matter to construct an estimate sheet that will please everyone, and that an estimate sheet entirely satisfactory for one part of the country may not answer the purpose of some other section, owing to the great differences that may exist in the methods and materials employed. If unable to secure a satisfactory published form of estimate, one arranged to suit individual tastes may be printed at small cost.

PLUMBING ESTIMATE

Made by....................... Date............................

Soil Pipe

EX. HEAVY		STANDARD	
ft.	2″	ft.	2″
ft.	3″	ft.	3″
ft.	4″	ft.	4″
ft.	5″	ft.	5″
ft.	6″	ft.	6″
ft.	8″	ft.	8″

Fittings

Traps	2″	3″	4″	5″
Ys	2″	3″	4″	5″
Tees	2″	3″	4″	5″
TYs	2″	3″	4″	5″
Bends	2″	3″	4″	5″
Hubs	2″	3″	4″	5″
Dbl Hubs	2″	3″	4″	5″
Vent Ts	2″	3″	4″	5″
Vent Caps	2″	3″	4″	5″
Increasers	2″	3″	4″	5″
Reducers	2″	3″	4″	5″
Offsets	2″	3″	4″	5″
Dbl Ys or Ts	2″	3″	4″	5″

Cl'nouts, I. B. or Br.		2″	3″	4″		5″
Misc. Fittings						
Hooks		Hangers		Clamps		
Caulking Lead			lbs.			
Oakum	lbs.		Gasoline		gals.	
Roof Flanges		3″	4″	5″		6″

Galvanized Pipe

ft. ½"   ft. ¾"   ft. 1"   ft. 1¼"
ft. 1½"   ft. 2"   ft. 2½"   ft. 3"

Galvanized Fittings

Galv. Fittings, Water
Galv. Fittings, Vent   1¼"   1½"   2"

Brass Work

Br. Ferrules   2"   4"
S & W Cocks   ½"   ¾"   1"   1¼"
Valves   ½"   ¾"   1"   1¼"
Sill Cocks
Solder Nipples   ½"   ¾"   1"
Solder Nipples   1¼"   1½"   2"
Solder Unions

Brass Pipe

½"   ¾"   1"   1¼"
Fittings

Brass Tubing

⅝"   ¾"   ⅞"   1"
1¼"   1½"   2"
Fittings

Lead Pipe

lbs. ⅜"   lbs. ½"   lbs. ⅝"   lbs. ¾"
lbs. 1"   lbs. 1¼"   lbs. 1½"   lbs. 2"
Total Lead Pipe   lbs.   Sheet Lead   lbs.
Solder   lbs.   prs. Lead Tacks

Gas Piping,   Outlets
Meter Connections

Water   Gas   Range

Sinks, Iron

Soapstone or Slate   Enamel or Porcelain
Brackets   Bibbs
Traps   Ferrules   Gaskets

Wash Trays

Legs   Covers   Bibbs
Plugs   Chain   Traps   Ferrules

SUGGESTIONS FOR ESTIMATING

H. W. Boilers

Copper	Galv.	
Boiler Stands	Tubes	Valves
Sed. Cocks	House Tank	Ball Cock and Valve

Pantry Sinks

Pantry Cocks	Plugs, Chain, Stays
Traps	Ferrules

Water Closets

....
....

Tanks	Tank Boards	Seats
Brackets	Chain & Pull	Lead Bends
N. P. Flush & Supply Pipes		N. P. Flanges
Ball Cock & Valve		Ferrules
Clamps Bolts	Floor Flanges	Floor Slabs
Local Vent & Fittings	2″	3″

Bath Tubs

....

Bath Cocks	Plug & Chain	N. P. Supplies
Waste & Overflow	N. P. Valves	N. P. Flanges
Traps	Ferrules	

Lavatories

....
....

Bowls	Cocks	Brackets	Plugs
Chain & Stays	Clamps	Traps	Ferrules
Gaskets	N. P. Supplies	N. P. Wastes	
N. P. Traps	N. P. Flanges	N. P. Valves	Marble

Urinals

N. P. Flush Pipes	Valves	Tanks	Cocks
Traps	Ferrules	Marble	Slate

Slop Sinks

Tanks	Cocks	Traps	Ferrules

Miscellaneous

Pumps	Air Chambers	Valves
Screws	Putty	Plaster Paris
Tile Pipe & F't'gs	Carpenter	Excavating
Carfare	Board	Fr't & Cartage
Labor	Days, Plumber	Helper
	Total	
	Add for Expense	%
	" " Profit	%
	Total Estimate	

There are several features connected with estimate sheets that are worth mentioning.

In the estimate sheet shown, for instance, such items as traps, ferrules, bibbs, etc., are to be found under each fixture. Some may prefer to have such items lumped, rather than scattered, but in presenting in connection with each fixture the items that are needed in the installation of that fixture there is possibly less danger of omissions.

Under brass work, however, such items as brass ferrules and valves are given, although appearing under the different fixtures. This is necessary, as such material as ferrules and valves may be used for purposes not identified with any particular fixture. Such an item as lead pipe is more conveniently and accurately figured, and with less labor, in the lump than under respective fixtures.

Before being able to figure material accurately and intelligently, it is necessary to have a slight understanding at least of architects' plans.

The term "plan" is used in general to designate all architects' drawings. Technically, however, a plan is a view looking down onto an object, and an elevation is a view looking at the object from the front or the side.

In the case of the floor plans, they show locations of fixtures and pipes, and cellar plans show horizontal measurements of soil piping, water piping, etc.

The front or side elevation of the building, on the other hand, shows the distances between floors, from which can be estimated the heights of the vertical lines of pipe.

Architects' plans are never drawn full size, but always at some

SUGGESTIONS FOR ESTIMATING

standard scale, usually ¼ in. to the foot for small buildings and ⅛ in. to the foot for large buildings.

In order to measure piping from such a drawing, it is necessary to understand how to use a scale. In the work of an architect or engineer, where the object of which drawings are made, is very large, it is necessary to show the object on a smaller scale. If the scale is ¼ in. to the foot, a quarter inch measured on any of the drawings represents one foot in the actual work itself, and if the scale is ⅛ in. to the foot, any measurement of ⅛ in. represents one foot in the actual work.

The general custom in estimating material is to estimate the soil piping first, and by this is meant the house drain and all its connections, the stacks and their main vent lines.

The cellar plan (see Plate 31) is first referred to, and the lengths of the several sizes of horizontal piping measured at the proper scale.

If Plate 31 is drawn at a scale of ⅛ in. to the foot, the straight run from outside the cellar wall to the cleanout at the end will be found to be 5⅝ in., representing 45 ft. of 4-in. pipe.

In the same way the branches, fresh-air inlet, etc., are estimated, the measurements in ordinary work being made without reference to the space taken up by fittings; that is, measurements for straight pipe are taken without deducting anything for fittings.

The excess measurement thus obtained will make a due allowance for loss in cutting lengths of pipe. If, however, fittings are very close together, as in the use of a number of branch fittings for a line of water closets, this method of measuring may be modified. Attention is next directed to the elevation of the building being figured, in order to estimate the lengths of straight pipe in the vertical main lines. The points to be considered may be observed from Plate 33, which shows an elevation of a plumbing system.

The vertical lengths may be found by measuring on the elevation the distance from the cellar bottom to a point usually 2 ft. above the roof.

If the roof is flat, these lengths will be the same, but in the case of pitched roofs, reference to either the front or side elevation will show at what point the stack passes through, thus enabling the estimator to find its length.

The main vertical vent lines, vertical rain-leader connections, the vertical part of the fresh-air inlet, and other vertical lines should next be measured, and the total lengths of each size of pipe inserted in the estimate.

It is a very good plan to divide each amount of soil pipe, if of cast iron, between single- and double-hub pipe, as the latter will be found very convenient in many places.

The next thing in order is the estimating of soil-pipe fittings, including main-vent fittings.

The fittings needed in the cellar on horizontal lines will be evident from reference to the cellar plan, which should always show a plan of the horizontal cellar work. A rough sketch of the vertical lines, both soil, waste, and vent, with their fittings and connections into the horizontal lines, will be found very helpful in estimating the fittings to be used. The pipes shown in such a sketch may be represented by single lines instead of double lines, as in Plate 33.

Unless designated in such a sketch, the estimating of fittings must generally depend upon the picture of the work, at different points, which the estimator holds in his mind. While this method often results in the omission of fittings, the practical estimator can generally, if careful, figure very close to the fittings needed. At the same time, very few plumbing systems are estimated which do not call for a considerably greater number of fittings when the work is actually constructed than was estimated. These extra fittings are largely bends and offsets used in getting around obstructions which did not appear from the plans or were unnoticed by the estimator. Allowance should be made for extra fittings and extra material of other kinds. Many practical men claim that the extra stock demanded, over and above that figured in the estimate, will average about 5%.

The fittings should be arranged according to size and character, as seen in the estimate form shown. Before leaving this part of the work, other materials, such as cleanouts, hangers, clamps, roof flanges, oakum, caulking lead, and gasoline should be estimated.

The estimating of caulking lead is an approximation, but experience will enable the estimator to come very close to the true amount. This item is very generally estimated offhand, which often comes wide of the mark.

On large work, especially, a definite estimate should be made, the following being a reliable method. It is clearly seen that no

SUGGESTIONS FOR ESTIMATING

caulked joint will be called for excepting where there is a hub. Therefore, estimate one hub for each length of pipe, the number of lengths being found by dividing the total lengths of soil pipe by 5. In the case of fittings, such as bends, count one hub, tees and Ys two hubs, and double fittings three or more hubs, as the case may be.

In the case of a 4 × 2 Y, one hub would be 4 in. and the other 2 in. The number of hubs of each size should be added, and the amounts multiplied by the weight of lead for the respective size of joint.

The amount of lead used for the several sizes of caulked joints is not a definite amount, as different workmen will naturally use different amounts. The following table shows weights of lead joints:

Size	Joint	Weight
2-in.	lead joint	1½ lbs.
3-in.	" "	2¼ "
4-in.	" "	3 "
5-in.	" "	3¾ "
6-in.	" "	4½ "
7-in.	" "	5¼ "
8-in.	" "	6 "
10-in.	" "	7½ "

These weights represent ¾ lb. for each inch in size of the pipe. Many will claim that 1 lb. to the inch is not too much to figure on.

The weights of lead found necessary for the different sizes of pipe, added together, will give the total amount of caulking lead required.

Oakum is generally estimated offhand. The following table will give an idea, however, of the amount of oakum necessary for joints of different sizes:

2-in.	lead joint	3 ft. oakum
3-in.	" "	4½ " "
4-in.	" "	5 " "
5-in.	" "	6½ " "
6-in.	" "	7½ " "
7-in.	" "	8½ " "
8-in.	" "	9½ " "
10-in.	" "	12 " "

Such fittings as cleanouts, plugs, and ferrules do not have to be taken into account in estimating caulking lead and oakum, for the hubs into which these fittings are caulked have already been counted.

In the estimating of lead waste and vent pipe it is simply a matter of figuring mentally the amount of each size needed; and knowing the number of pounds per foot of the various sizes, the total weight may be found. It is necessary to know the total weight of both waste, vent, and supply pipe if of lead, as this material is sold by the pound and not by the foot. In filling out the estimate sheet, however, the estimator should be careful to fill out against each size the amount of that size necessary, as when it comes to ordering stock the number of feet of each size will need to be known.

A table of weights of lead pipe is necessary to figure this item from. The following is a table of safe weights for ordinary work:

Diameter of Lead Supply Pipe	Weight per foot
3/8 in.	1½ lbs.
½ "	2 "
5/8 "	2½ "
¾ "	3 "
1 "	4 "

Diameter of Lead Waste Pipe	Weight per foot
1 in.	2 lbs.
1¼ "	2½ "
1½ "	3½ "
2 "	4 "
4 "	6 "

In connection with lead pipe, wiping solder should also be figured. The number of joints of each size may be quickly estimated, and knowing the amount of solder necessary for a joint of each size, the total weight of solder may easily be found. It is very customary for plumbers to estimate solder according to fixtures—so much for a sink, so much for a water closet, etc. In figuring many plumbing systems this would be safe if the estimator has a correct idea of the amount necessary for each fixture. In work which is out of the ordinary run, however, it might not be safe to estimate in this way.

In getting at the full amount of solder, lead supply-pipe joints and connections, flush and supply-pipe joints for water closets, for urinals, slop sinks, etc., must be taken into account.

SUGGESTIONS FOR ESTIMATING

The amount of solder used per joint of the different sizes is a variable quantity, as some workmen make much heavier joints than others. It is customary among some estimators to allow one pound of solder per joint, regardless of size, including the small supply-pipe joints, as well as the large-size waste and vent-pipe joints. This might possibly have averaged safely in the days of lead supply work, but as work is now generally constructed, a better way would seem to be to find by practice the weights of joints of the several sizes, and thus make the estimate a close and accurate one. The following table may be used as a guide, though undoubtedly varying widely from the custom of many workmen:

Diameter of Pipe...	½ in.	⅝ in.	¾ in.	1 in.	1¼ in.	1½ in.	2 in.	4 in.
Solder per Joint...	¾ lb.	1 lb.	1 lb.	1¼ lbs.	1½ lbs.	1¾ lbs.	2–2½ lbs.	3–4 lbs.

In the matter of galvanized piping, the number of feet of each size should be estimated.

To find the amount of galvanized supply pipe, brass or lead, as the case may be, reference must be made to the cellar and floor plans mostly in figuring out horizontal runs, and the elevation referred to, to give vertical measurements. The matter of fittings on supply work is a difficult matter to estimate in detail, as they are numerous, and it is hardly possible to figure on just what fittings and the respective amounts of each that are going to be required. On such items as these the estimator of experience will often cast up the amount in his own mind after a little study of the plans, and he may usually come very close to the amount of cost represented in the item.

The preservation of old estimates and complete lists of stock used will often allow the estimator to refer to them and get a line on work of similar nature which he may be figuring. Galvanized vent fittings should be estimated in detail as far as possible, just as soil-pipe fittings are estimated.

Stop cocks, valves, sill cocks, solder nipples, and unions should also be estimated as nearly in detail as possible, as an offhand estimate of material that represents so much cost as these items is not a safe thing.

Gas piping often enters into the plumbing contract. It is sometimes safe on new work to approximate the cost of the gas piping at so much per outlet. If this can be done it saves considerable labor in figuring out the cost of different sizes to be used, fittings, and labor.

Reference to previous work of similar nature is of much help in this connection. Estimating at so much per outlet is not a safe method on old work, that is, where gas piping is to be installed in an old house. Many plumbers are inclined to estimate old work in this way, however, and often suffer loss thereby.

Water, gas, and range connections are not generally considered a part of the general plumbing contract in many sections, but in other sections must be included.

There is little to be said on the matter of estimating fixtures and their trimmings. Sizes and list prices may be found in the catalogues of jobbers and manufacturers, and knowing the prevailing discount, the net cost may be easily arrived at. Many fixtures, water closets, for instance, are often figured complete, that is, instead of having to figure the crockery, tank, brackets, chain and pull, etc., in detail, a cost price of the entire outfit may be obtained. This is true of other fixtures also—lavatories, urinals, etc.

When so figured, however, the estimator must be careful to note any items required in the specifications which are not included in the combination price.

The estimating of marble and slate may often be made very easy by the use of the table of contents of marble slabs shown under Plate 2. The area found from this table, multiplied by the cost per square foot, will give the cost of the marble required.

Much loss may be sustained if miscellaneous items are not given due consideration, items such as carfare, board, cartage, etc. In some sections of the country the excavating for pipe trenches, etc., and the laying of tile pipe is included in the mason's contract, rather than in the plumber's.

Of much importance to the person who is just entering upon the work of estimating, and desirous of general information, is the method of carrying out costs against the different items in the estimate. Nearly all plumbing goods are sold and billed at a discount from a list price, and in carrying costs in an estimate on plumbing work it is necessary to have not only these list prices, but also the prevailing discounts on the different lines of material. It would systematize the work of estimating and make it far easier if the estimator would bring all these lists together in a book of proper size,

SUGGESTIONS FOR ESTIMATING

so that when it comes to figuring costs, the list price and discount on any material whatever may be referred to without having to refer to numerous catalogues and lists that may require considerable searching for before they can be located. The matter of list prices and discounts on such materials as cast- and wrought-iron pipe, brass goods, etc., has been systematized to a considerable extent during recent years, and is handled more easily therefore. For instance, the lists of standard and extra-heavy cast-iron pipe are so arranged now that one discount applies to both grades, whereas formerly there was one discount on standard and another on extra-heavy pipe.

In order to show how the cost of material may be carried out on an estimate, it will be pertinent to the subject to show the cost figured on a list of soil pipe and a list of soil-pipe fittings.

In the following list, after the style of pipe or fitting is named, is given the list price per foot of soil pipe or the list price per single fitting, then the total number of feet of pipe or total number of fittings reckoned at this list:

	List		Net
20 ft. 2 in. X. H. C. I. Pipe	$0.35	$7.00	
50 " 3 " " " "	.65	32.50	
60 " 4 " " " "	.80	48.00	
25 " 4 " Standard C. I. Pipe	.40	10.00	
		$97.50	
Disc. 25%	....	.....	$73.13
8 2 in. X. H. Bends	$0.50	$4.00	
6 3 " " "	.95	5.70	
4 4 " " "	1.15	4.60	
2 4 " Standard Bends	.80	1.60	
6 2 " " Ys	.90	5.40	
2 3 " " "	1.50	3.00	
1 3 " x 2 in. Standard Ys	1.40	1.40	
3 4 " Standard Ys	1.90	5.70	
6 4 " x 2 in. Standard Ys	1.70	10.20	
2 4 " X. H. T-Y	1.90	3.80	
1 4 " x 2 in. X. H. Ys	2.70	2.70	
2 4 " X. H. Running Traps	2.75	5.50	
3 2 " " Inverted Ys	1.25	3.75	
		$57.35	
Disc. 30—5—5%	....	.....	$36.13

As seen from the above, the discount on pipe is taken on the total pipe footing, and the discount on fittings is taken on the total fittings footing. This is a much less laborious undertaking than the taking of the discount on each pipe or fitting, and there is less opportunity of error.

The discounts that are given on certain lines of plumbing material are often very complex, such a discount as 25—10—5% being very common. It will be of interest to beginners in the work of estimating to understand the manner in which such discounts are figured out. In the first place, if the above-mentioned discount can be estimated on $1, the net amount remaining after taking the discount may be used as a multiplier for that particular discount.

Thus, when the discount mentioned is deducted from $1 it leaves .6413. Now, if a discount of 25—10—5% is to be applied to any amount, $50.35, for instance, the net amount derived can be found by multiplying by the multiplier .6413. Thus, $50.35 × .6413 = $32.29 net. Let us see how the net multiplier .6413 was obtained. It is not meant that the three separate discounts, 25, 10, and 5% are to be added together. If this were so, the full amount, 40%, could be given.

The meaning of the discount 25—10—5% is that 25% is to be deducted from the list price, and from the remainder 10% deducted, and from this second remainder 5% deducted.

This would be a tedious method to apply, and instead of following this practice, the use of a table of net multipliers will be of very great value in the saving of time and labor: 1.00 × .75 = .75, .75 × .90 = .675, .675 × .95 = .6413. This series of operations gives the multiplier desired, the net amount each time being multiplied by 1.00 minus the next discount, the multipliers thus being 1.00 — .25 = .75, 1.00 — .10 = .90, 1.00 — .05 = .95.

If a published table of discounts cannot be procured, the estimator may make one to include whatever range of discounts may be desired. There are very handy tables published, which show discounts from 10% up to 85%. These tables are arranged in the following manner, which may be followed or modified by the estimator in working out his own table of discounts:

SUGGESTIONS FOR ESTIMATING

Discount—Per Cent	Decimal Equivalent	Net Amount or Multiplier
25—	.25	.75
25—2½	.2688	.7313
25—2½—2½	.2870	.7130
25—2½—5	.3053	.6947
25—2½—7½	.3236	.6764
25—2½—10	.3419	.6581
25—5	.2875	.7125
25—5—2½	.3053	.6947
25—5—5	.3231	.6769
25—5—7½	.3409	.6591
25—5—10	.3588	.6413
25—7½	.3063	.6938
25—7½—2½	.3236	.6764
25—7½—5	.3409	.6591
25—7½—7½	.3583	.6417
25—7½—10	.3756	.6244
25—10	.3250	.6750
25—10—2½	.3419	.6581
25—10—5	.3588	.6413
25—10—7½	.3756	.6244
25—10—10	.3925	.6075
25—10—10—5	.4229	.5771
27½	.275	.725
27½—2½	.2931	.7069
27½—2½—2½	.3108	.6892

he amounts in the column of decimal equivalents simply show
lue of the different discounts when reduced to decimals. A
rison of decimal equivalents will show that in some cases dif-
discounts really mean the same thing.
hus the discount 25—2½—7½ is of just the same value as
;count 25—7½—2½.
 connection with the subject of estimating, no attempt will be
to give instructions concerning the estimating of labor. The
 appreciates the fact that this information will be sought fully
:h as any that has been given, but an attempt at advising the
g of certain amounts of time for certain amounts of work
 misleading, and no doubt, if followed, might lead to trouble,
ılly among new estimators of insufficient experience to allow

for various different conditions. For instance, the methods of construction and the choice of material varies considerably in different parts of the country, and, furthermore, much depends upon the workmen themselves, some doing a far greater amount of work per day than others. Labor is certainly the most difficult item to estimate, so many conditions entering into the matter. In many towns and cities certain classes of building construction are very general. For instance, in certain cities three-flat houses may be universally used, while in another two-flat and six-flat houses may be the rule. The plumber who has much of such work to do soon learns from experience the amount of labor necessary to figure, almost to an hour, and, in fact, is often able to give a very close offhand estimate of the entire work on such a house after a glance at the plans and specifications has assured him of the nature and number of fixtures. The estimator that is wise, however, is not usually ready to make a *bona fide* estimate on any system of plumbing without first going over the work very carefully, for it needs only a small difference here and there to make a considerable total difference. The practice of giving offhand final estimates is always to be condemned, as they may often lead to trouble later. Moreover, such estimates are unlikely to take into account any change in prices of material.

As already intimated, however, much benefit may be derived from reference to lists of stock and labor used on previous work of similar style and character to that which is to be estimated. This is especially true of such work as is to be found in the regulation line of dwellings, flats, and like buildings. The comparisons should not be made, by the way, without making due allowance for any change in prices that may have come about in the meantime.

Many plumbing systems, however, cannot be expected to be of a similar nature to other work previously constructed by the firm, in which case there is little benefit to be derived from a general comparison. Here experience and good judgment must be called into service.

The employer or estimator who is properly posted in his business will know how many feet of soil pipe of different sizes his workmen will be able to run in a day, how long he must allow for the roughing-in of each fixture under the methods followed by his men and under the ordinances of his city, and how long it will take to do the finishing work on each fixture. By thus figuring the work in

SUGGESTIONS FOR ESTIMATING

detail the total should be arrived at with a sufficient amount of exactness.

In the matter of estimating labor, especially, there is no one who can do it so successfully as the man who is working at the trade and is fully acquainted with modern methods of construction.

If a systematic account is to be kept of all labor and material used on work, it is necessary to use some form of time card, from which an exact account of all labor and stock items may be obtained. Such a form is shown, in connection with this subject, below.

This form is very convenient, although some employers may prefer a different style.

The item of labor is given in detail on the front of the card, and stock used in connection with that particular job, No. 73, may be noted on the reverse side. The main part of the card is to be handed to the workman, while the stub is torn off at the perforated line and retained in the office until the card is turned in.

WM. GREENE & CO.

Given to ....
....
..............190
No. 73....

....

WM. GREENE & CO.   STOCK USED.

No. 73....
Ordered by..........................
Ordered for..........................
Street and No........................
Wants ....
....
....
....
....

WORK COMMENCED.

Date .... Hour........

COMPLETED.

Date................. Hour ....
.... Hour work ....
.... "   " ....
.... "   " ....
.... "   " ....
.... Hours contract ....
.... "   " ....
.... "   " ....
.... "   " ....
Made out by ....
Charged by...........................

Front Side.   Reverse Side.

TIME AND STOCK CARD.

SUGGESTIONS FOR ESTIMATING

As previously stated, if the estimator is to perform his work easily and intelligently, he must keep thoroughly posted on the current prices of material. In order that this may be done systematically many firms now keep run of quotations by means of a card system, such a card being seen below, and being placed in the S section of the file. All soil-pipe data should appear on this card, from which will be known the latest and most favorable discount on that material. In carrying out such quotations it is well to use a private system of characters to represent figures. A similar card should be used for each class of material, as lead pipe, traps, etc.

```
              SOIL PIPE.
The J. B. S. Co.—N. Y. City—Jan. 1.........    25-10
M. & B. Co.—Boston—Feb. 2...............          30
The J. B. S. Co.—N. Y. City—Mar. 3........    25-10-5
R. M. & C. Co.—Phila.—Mar. 15 ...........      25-10
```

Another much more valuable and comprehensive cost card is shown on page 386. This card can be made to tell the complete story of each item of material used. It is equally valuable in keeping costs, for use in ordering, in checking invoices, in recording freight allowances, and for billing purposes.

In conclusion it may be said that for many reasons, and because of many varying conditions, the subject of estimating is one of the most difficult subjects connected with the plumbing trade upon which to give instruction.

To a certain extent, definite information, data, and advice may safely be given, but beyond that, success in accurate and intelligent estimating must result chiefly from a knowledge gained by experience, from the application of good judgment, and from systematic methods, the latter being of as much importance as any other factor.

Stop and Waste Cocks

Firm	Size and No.	Quantity	List	Discount	Net	Freight Allowed	Selling Price	
							Large Quantity	Small Quantity
A. B. C. Brass Works	#2–½"	Doz.	21.60	80-10-5-5	3.51	125 lbs.	$4.58 doz.	50c. each

INDEX

INDEX

A

Adjustable slop-sink trap, 49.
Air admitted to trap seal, 75.
Air chambers, use of, 212.
Air, circulation of, in sewers, 102.
    through vent system, 90.
Air, lifeless, in bath rooms, 144.
Air-lock caused by double trapping, 78.
    on siphon supply systems, 317.
    on hot-water supply systems, 362.
    prevented by fresh-air inlet, 104.
Air pressure for smoke test, 171.
Air pump to relieve water siphon, 317.
Air supply for plumbing system, 84.
Air test, 167, 170.
    objections to, 170.
    pressure for, 170.
Air valve on hydraulic ram, 312.
Alum for sand filtration, 220.
Animal charcoal for filters, 219.
Apartment buildings, hot-water supply for, 211.
    plumbing for, 211, 217.
Architects' plans reading and use of, 358.
Architects' scale, use of, 373.
Areas, drainage of, 109.
Artificial draft for local vents, 125.
Asphaltum, pipes coated with, 87.
Atmospheric pressure, amount of, 314.
Attic storage tank, 287.
    supply for, 287.
Attic tank, 238.
Automatic cellar drainer, 112.
Automatic control of hot-water tanks, 349.
Automatic flushing, 245.
    of range water closets, 44.
    of urinals, 257.
Automatic flush tank, action of, 245.
    construction, location of, etc., 246.
Automatic flush tanks for public toilet rooms, 234.

Automatic sewage ejector, 277, 278.
    action of, 278.
    advantages of, 280.
    for large work, 280.
    for marine work, 282.
Automatic sewage ejector, for public sewage, 281.
    proper size of, 281.
Automatic sewage lift, 277, 278.
    action of, 278.
    advantages of, 280.
    for large work, 280.
    for marine work, 282.
    for public sewage, 281.
    proper size of, 281.
    venting of, 279.
Automatic sewage siphons, 305.
    action of, 306.
    use of, 305.
Automatic siphon for range water closets, 44.
Automatic sump tank, 280.
    action of, 280.
Automatic tank regulators, 211.
Automatically flushed urinals and slop sinks, 246.

B

Back pressure on trap seals, 74.
Back pressure, relief of, 84.
Backs for urinals, 50.
Back-water valve, use of, 111.
Bacteria, action of, in filtration, 219.
    action of, in septic tank, 299.
    action of, on sewage, 304.
    in soil, 294.
Ball-cock floats, 40.
Ball-cocks, 39.
    requirements of, 40.
Bar sinks, connection of, 66.
Basins for lavatories, sizes of, 24.
Baskets, wire, for roof pipes, 91.
Bath establishments, construction of floors and walls of, 237.
    plumbing for, 237.

INDEX

Bath-room connections, 131, 137, 138, 143, 149.
Bath-room fixtures, 139, 150.
Bath rooms, 131, 137, 143, 149.
    cleanliness of, 131.
Bath rooms, lighting of, 144.
    tiling of, 139.
    ventilation of, 144.
Bath traps, 77.
    cleanouts for, 31, 138.
Bath tub, 31.
    connections for, 31.
    construction of, 31.
    drum trap for, 31, 81, 149.
    sizes of, 31.
    to enamel, 31.
    trimmings for, 32.
Bedfordshire lip urinal, 50.
Bending brass pipe, 202.
Bends in fresh-air inlet, 104.
Bends, quarter, for circuit vents, 188.
    for deep-seal traps, 109.
    use of, 89.
Bidet, 51.
    connections for, 51.
    mixer for, 51.
    supplies for, 51.
Bi-transit waste, 32.
Blind vent, 157.
Blow-off from boilers, 66.
Boilers, double, 337.
    connections for, 338.
    construction of, 337.
    cut-offs for, 338.
    drainage of, 338.
    expansion pipes on, 337.
    purpose of, 337.
    supply for, 337.
    where used, 337.
Boilers, large horizontal, supporting of, 343.
Boilers, large horizontal, use of, 343.
Boilers, heating, soft water for, 358.
Boilers hot-water, automatic control of, 349.
    capacities of, 344.
    heating of, by steam, 343.
    proper size of, 213, 343.
    steam coils for, 344.
Boilers, range, for residences, 211.
    heating of, 328.
    materials for, 192, 211.
    size of, 211.
    to reduce effective size of, 363.

Boiler tube, breaking-off of, 362.
Bone-black for filtering purposes, 219.
Bowls for lavatories, sizes of, 24.
    patent overflow, 24.
Branch vents, 84.
    running of, 184.
Brass and cast-iron pipe connections, 88.
Brass and wrought-iron pipe connections, 88.
Brass cleanouts, 162.
Brass drainage fittings, 202.
Brass ferrules, use of, 88.
    use of, on Durham system, 272.
    weights and sizes of, 272.
Brass flap valve, use of, 62.
Brass floor flange, use of, 119.
Brass for drainage purposes, 274.
Brass pipe, joints on, 202.
    to bend, 202.
    use of, 92, 192.
    use of, on waste and vent work, 201.
    weights of, 202.
Brass pipe vises, use of, 202.
Brass pipe wrenches, use of, 202.
Brass soldering nipples, weights and sizes of, 272.
Brass work, estimating of, 377.
    of poor quality, 158.
Brewery drainage, 62.
Brick piers to support piping, 95.
By-pass, 77, 157.
    for water meter, 361.
By-passing in gas water heaters, 362.

C

Capillary action on trap seals, 74.
Caps for roof pipes, 91.
Cast iron, action of electrolysis on, 267.
    for drainage purposes, 274.
Cast-iron and brass pipe connections, 88.
Cast-iron and lead pipe connections, 88.
Cast-iron and wrought-iron pipe connections, 88.
Cast-iron pipe, 87.
    coating of, 87, 162.
    connections of wrought-iron pipe into, 262.
    for house sewer, 197.
    for wastes, 137.
    joints on, 87.

INDEX

Cast-iron pipe, life of, 264, 265.
    supporting of, 95.
    underground, 162.
    use of, 92.
    weights of, 87.
Cast-iron sinks, sizes of, 17, 18.
Catch basin, cellar trap for, 111.
    construction of, 241.
    for cellar drain, 111.
    for kitchen waste, 56, 57.
    for rain water, 327.
    for refrigerator rooms, etc., 62
    for stable waste, 241.
    for subsoil drainage, 111.
Caulked joints, 87.
    weights of, 88, 361.
Caulking lead, estimating of, 374.
Cellar bottom, grading of, 111.
    gutters in, 111.
Cellar drain, 110.
    catch basin for, 111.
    into house drain, 196.
    trap for, 111.
Cellar drainage, disposal of, 112.
Cellar drainer, 112.
    action of, 112.
    amount of water raised by, 112.
    height to which it will raise, 112.
    location of, 112.
    supply pipes for, 112.
    water pressure for, 112.
Cements for marble, 24.
    for slate and soapstone, 19.
Centralizing of plumbing, 143.
Centrifugal pump for raising sewage, 277.
Cesspools, 293.
    banking and turfing of, 295.
    combination tight and leeching, 293, 295.
    connected to sewers, 293.
    displaced by septic tanks, 299.
    forms of, 293.
    fresh-air inlet of, 294.
    leeching, 293, 294.
    location of, 289, 294.
    manner of entering drains into, 296.
    prohibited for tenement houses, etc., 208.
    rain water into, 295.
    supporting vents from, 96.
    tight, 293, 294.
    trapping of, 294.

Cesspools, use of, in cities, 296.
    venting of, 285, 294.
Change in direction of pipes, cleanouts at, 164.
Charcoal, animal, for filters, 219.
Check valves, use of, 361.
Child's bath, 32.
    connections of, 32.
Chilling of main trap seal, 104.
Chimney connections of local vents, 127, 156.
Circuit vents, 187.
    construction of, 187.
    for line of water closets, 242.
    for public toilet rooms, 187, 234.
    quarter bends on, 188.
Circulation of air in sewers, 102.
    through vent system, 90.
Circulation of hot water, 328.
Circulation work, advantages of, 213.
Cistern filters, 325.
    action of, 326, 327.
    catch basin for, 327.
    construction of, 326, 327.
Cisterns for storing rain water, 288.
    size of, 289.
Cleanout cover, trap vent through, 82.
Cleanout joints, 163.
Cleanout screws, material of, 162.
Cleanouts, 162.
    brass, 162.
    depending on putty joints, 156.
    end, 162, 163.
    for traps, 77.
    gaskets for, 163.
    ground joint, 163.
    iron body, 162.
    on bath traps, 31, 77, 138.
    on drainage pipes, 89.
    on drum traps, 164.
    on horse stall connections, 69.
    on house drain, 162.
    on local vent flue connection, 127.
    on main trap, 104, 105, 162, 163.
    on rain leaders, 163.
    on refrigerator wastes, 65.
    on sink waste, 55.
    on slop sinks, 49.
    on. traps, location of, 164.
    on traps under floors, 77.
    on vents, 76, 164.
    size of, 163.
    submerged, 82, 83, 164.
    threads for, 163.

INDEX

Coating of cast-iron pipe, 87.
Coils, steam, for hot-water boilers, 344.
Cold-air box, distance of fresh-air inlet from, 104.
Combination cocks, 33.
Combination sink and wash tray, 19.
Comfort stations, ventilation of, 127.
Compressed air for sewage ejectors, 278.
Compression system, 220.
Compression work, 33.
    advantages of, 212.
Concealed piping, testing of, 167.
Condensation in vent pipes, 84, 184.
    care of, 89.
    drainage of, 90.
Condensing tank, use of, 66.
Contact filter beds, 302, 305.
Contagion carried by local vents, 125.
Continuous venting, 76, 175.
Continuous venting, advantages of, 175, 180.
    economy of, 180, 183.
    for apartment houses, 179.
    for groups of fixtures, 176.
    for lines of lavatories, 233.
    for two-floor work, 179.
    for two lines of fixtures, 183.
    from special fittings, 201.
    of lavatories, 23, 176.
    of lines of fixtures, 271.
    of lines of urinals, 256.
    of S trap, 81, 83.
    of water closets, 187.
Corrosion of drainage pipes, 264.
    vent pipes, 264.
Cost of estimating of, 378.
Cost card, 386.
Cottage house, plumbing for, 191.
Country house, water supply for, 325.
    hot-water supply for, 328.
Country plumbing, 285.
Courts, etc., of tenement houses, drainage of, 208.
Courtyards, drainage of, 109.
Cowls for roof pipes, 91.
Crazing of water closets, 119.
Cup joints, 88.
Cut-offs for double boilers, 338.

D

Dead end, 155.
Deep-seal trap, use of, 109.
    for rain leaders, 207.

Deflector for grease trap, 56.
Direct-pressure ball-cocks, 40.
Discharge chamber of the septic tank, 301.
Discounts on plumbing goods, 378.
    table of, 381.
Domestic filter, construction of, 218.
Double-acting force pump, 315.
Double-acting hydraulic ram, 314, 325.
Double apartment buildings, plumbing for, 217.
    continuous venting for, 179.
Double boilers, 337.
    connections for, 338.
    construction of, 337.
    cut-offs for, 338.
    drainage of, 338.
    expansion pipes on, 337.
    purpose of, 337.
    supply for, 337.
    where used, 337.
Double fittings, venting from, 223.
Double hubs, use of, 89.
Double-hub pipe, use of, 89.
Double testing plug, 169.
Double trapping, 78, 111, 156.
Double T-Y, use of, 89.
Draft for local vents, 125.
Drain tile inside cellar, 156.
    for subsoil drains, 111.
Drainage system, separate, for each house, 103.
Drainer cellar, 112.
Draw-offs, drainage from, 66.
Drinking fountains, 228.
    in toilet rooms, 228.
Drip pan for attic storage tank, 288.
    for refrigerator, 61.
Drip sink for refrigerator, 61.
Drips from boilers, 66.
Driven wells, remarks on, 316.
    system of, 315.
Drum trap, 81.
    cleanouts on, 164.
    connections for, 81.
    for bath tub, 31, 81, 149.
    for country plumbing, 285.
    for laundry tubs, 19, 82.
    for refrigerator, 61.
    obstructions in, 82, 83.
    serving two or more fixtures, 82.
    siphonage of, 81.
    stoppage of, 82.
    unvented, 81.

INDEX 393

Drum trap, vent of, through cleanout cover, 82.
Durham system, 261.
    advantage of, 97, 262.
    compared with common system, 261.
    defects of, 262, 263, 264, 265.
    fittings for, 261, 262.
    floor flange for, 120.
    for greenhouses, 263.
    joints on, 261, 262.
    urinals on, 257.
    use of soldering nipples and brass ferrules on, 272.
    used in high buildings, 263.
    water-closet floor connections for, 271, 272.
    work of, 271.

E

Earthenware pipe for drains, 110.
    for house sewer, 197.
    inside cellar, 156.
    joints on, 197.
    prohibition of, 196.
Ejector, automatic sewage, 277, 278.
    action of, 278.
    advantages of, 280.
    for large work, 280.
    for marine work, 282.
    for public sewage, 281.
    proper size of, 281
    venting of, 279.
Electricity, thawing of pipes by, 331.
Electrolysis, action of, 266.
    cause of, 266.
    destruction of pipes by, 265.
    general remarks on, 268.
    of cast iron, 267.
    remedy for, 267.
Elevators, hydraulic, drainage from, 66.
Enamelled lavatories, 23.
Enamelling for bath tub, 31.
End cleanouts, 162, 163.
Engine house, plumbing for, 241.
    floor drains for, 241.
Estimate sheet, form of, 369.
    remarks on, 372.
Estimating of brass work, 377.
    caulking lead, 374.
    cost, 378.
    fixtures and trimmings, 364.
    gas piping, 377.

Estimating of labor, 381.
    lead pipe, 376.
    marble and slate, 378.
    miscellaneous items, 378.
    pipe and fittings, 373.
    plumbing construction, 367.
    supply pipe, 377.
    wiping solder, 376.
Evaporation decreased by continuous venting, 176.
    of rain leader trap seals, 207.
    of trap seals, 74, 77, 110.
Excavations, drainage of, 112.
Exhaust steam for heating hot-water tanks, 343.
Exhausts, drainage connections of, 66.
Expansion pipes on double boilers, 337.
Exposed surfaces of water closets, 115.
Exterior lighting desirable, 144.
Extra heavy soil pipe, 87.

F

Factories, automatic flushing for, 245.
    regulation of plumbing in, 208.
    waste and soil lines for, 242.
Factory lavatories, 247.
    plumbing, 241.
    toilet rooms, 241.
    toilet rooms, floors for, 242.
    toilet rooms, lighting of, 242.
    toilet rooms, ventilation of, 241, 242.
    wash sinks, 242, 247.
Fans, ventilation by use of, 128, 227.
Ferrule connections included in roughing, 161.
Ferrules, brass, use of, 88.
    weights and sizes of, 272.
Filter beds, contact, 302, 305.
    primary, 302, 305.
Filtered water supply, 217.
    for swimming pool, 238.
    open gravity tank for, 220.
    overhead tank for, 220.
    pressure tank for, 220.
    storage of, 220.
Filtering materials, 219.
Filters, animal charcoal for, 219.
    care of, 218.
    cleansing of, 219.
    for hotels, restaurants, hospitals, etc., 218.
    for rain water, 289.

394 INDEX

Filters, gravity, use of, 218.
    pressure, construction of, 219.
    pressure, use of, 218.
Filters, cistern, 325.
    action of, 326, 327.
    construction of, 326, 327.
Filtration of water, 217.
    for commercial purposes, 217.
    of sewage, 304.
    through the soil, 294.
    two forms of, 217.
Final test, the, 167.
First test, the, 167.
Fittings, brass drainage, 202.
    estimating of, 373.
    extra, allowance of, 374.
    for Durham system, 261.
    special, for underground sewage purification systems, 304.
Fittings, special waste and vent, 38, 143, 201.
    venting from, 223.
Fixture vents, requirements of, 84, 184.
Fixture wastes, long, 162.
Fixtures, estimating of, 378.
    for bath rooms, 139, 150.
    groups of, continuous vents for, 176.
    in cellar, 201.
Fixtures, porcelain, use of, 139.
Flanges, roof, 91.
Flap valve, use of, 62, 65.
Flat buildings, refrigerator drainage for, 205.
Flexible wooden sink mat, 18.
Floats for ball-cocks, 40.
Floor connections for Durham system, 271, 272.
    for water closets, 37, 119.
    putty, 119.
Floor drains for bath establishments, 237.
    for engine house, 241.
    for ice houses, refrigerator rooms, etc., 62.
    for laundries, etc., 62.
    for public toilet rooms, 227.
    for stables, 241.
    flushing of, 109.
    flushing rim, 237.
    into house drain, 196.
    into surface sewer, 110.
    size of, 109.

Floor drains, trappings of, 110.
    traps for, 109.
Floor flange, brass, use of, 119.
    for Durham system, 120.
Floor slabs for urinals, 256.
    setting of, 33.
Floor timbers, cutting of, 133.
Floors for factory toilet rooms, 242.
    public toilet rooms, 227.
Flues, local vent connections into, 127.
Flush pipe for water closet, 37.
Flush tank, automatic action of, 245.
    size construction, location, etc., 246.
Flush tanks, concealing of, 234.
    for slop sink, 50.
    for water closet, 37.
    for water closets of public toilet rooms, 234.
Flushing, automatic, 245.
Flushing of floor drains, 109.
    of range water closets, 44.
    of water closets, 115.
Flushing-rim floor drains, 109, 237.
    slop sinks, 49.
    type of fixtures for public toilet rooms, 234.
    urinals, 50, 256.
    water closets, etc., 119.
Flushing valves, 37.
    concealed, 234.
    for slop sinks, 43, 251.
    for urinals, 43, 251, 252, 257.
    for water closets, 43, 251.
    necessary pressure for, 251.
    operation of, 251.
    sizes of connections for, 251.
    storage tanks for, 251, 252.
    under direct pressure, 251.
    under tank pressure, 251.
    use of, 251.
Foot bath, 32.
    connections of, 32.
Force pump, use of the, 287.
    double-acting, 315.
Foul-air ducts for public toilet rooms, 227.
Freezing of main trap seal, 104.
    protection of pipes against, 321.
Fresh-air ducts for public toilet rooms, 227.

INDEX

Fresh-air inlet, 84, 104.
  bends in, 104.
  carried underground, 105.
  connection of, 104.
  distance from windows, etc., 104.
  errors in, 157.
  for cesspool trap, 294.
  for sewage tank, 278.
  not for drainage, 104.
  of underground trap, 106.
  opening of, 104.
  protection of end of, 104.
  purpose of, 104.
  should not be omitted, 155.
  size of, 105.
  through foundation, 105.
Frost in roof pipes, 91.
Frost-proof water closets, 70.
Frozen water pipes thawed by electricity, 331.
  by steam and hot water, 362.
Fuller work, 33, 212.

G

Gaskets for cleanouts, 163.
Gas mains destroyed by electrolysis, 265.
Gas piping, estimating of, 377.
Gas sewer, in plumbing system, 101.
Gas water heaters, by-passing in, 362.
Glass floats, 40.
Grading of cellar bottom, 111.
  of pipes, 88.
Gravity filters, construction of, 218.
  use of, 218.
Gravity water supply, 286.
Grease, collection of, in pipes, 57.
  collection of, in main trap, 104.
  entering sinks, 55.
  in sewage, 55.
  traps, 55.
  deflector for, 56.
  material for, 56.
  underground, 56.
  water jacket for, 56.
Greenhouses, Durham system for, 263.
Grit chamber of septic tank, 299.
Ground-joint cleanouts, 163.
Groups of fixtures, continuous vents for, 176.
Gutter for shower bath, construction of, 237.
  for urinals, 256.
  in cellar bottom, 111.

H

Hair-felt to protect pipes from freezing, 321.
Hangers, sizes of, 96.
Hard water, effect of, 353.
  softening of, 357.
Headers, construction of, 339.
  use of, on supply work, 214, 339.
  use of, 95.
Heated air, action of, 123, 126.
Heater, the P. P., 343.
Heating boilers, soft water for, 358.
Heating systems, drainage from, 66.
Hoar frost in roof pipes, 91.
Hooks, use of, 95.
Hoppers, long, use of, 70.
Horizontal boilers, large, supporting of, 343.
  use of, 343.
Horizontal piping, cleanouts on, 163.
Horse stall, plumbing of, 69.
Horse trough, connections for, 70.
  construction of, 70.
Hotel sink, 55.
Hot water, circulation of, 328.
  backing of, into meters, 361.
Hot-water boilers, automatic control of, 349.
  capacities of, 344.
  proper size of, 343.
  steam coils for, 344.
Hot-water heating systems, drainage of, 66.
Hot-water supply for apartment buildings, 211.
  country house, 287, 328.
  large buildings, 343, 344.
  office buildings, 211.
Hot-water tanks, automatic control of, 349.
  size of, 213.
House drain, 195.
  cleanouts on, 162.
  connections into, 106, 196.
  main stack at end of, 191.
  material for, 196.
  overhead, 112.
  running of, 195, 201.
  size of pipe for, 201.
House sewer, 195.
  cast-iron pipe for, 197.
  connections into public sewer, 198.

House sewer, extent of, 197.
    material for, 197.
    size of pipe for, 201.
House tank, use of, 213.
House trap, 101.
    advantages of, 103, 110.
    cleanouts on, 104, 105, 162, 163.
    connection at, 196.
    for tenement houses, 103.
    freezing of, 104.
    in large cities, 103.
    object of, 101.
    objections to, 102.
    on country systems, 286.
    outside of foundation, 106.
    setting of, 105.
    stoppage of, 104.
Hubs, double, use of, 89.
Hydraulic elevators, drainage from, 66.
Hydraulic engines, action of, 313.
    waste of water by, 313.
    work done by, 313.
Hydraulic ram, double-acting, 314, 325.
Hydraulic rams, 311.
    air valve on, 312.
    connections for, 311.
    drive pipe of, 313.
    force pipe from, 313.
    head of supply to, 312, 313.
    operation of, 311.
    source of supply for, 311.
    use of, 287.
    waste of water by, 313.
    waste valve of, 312.
    work done by, 313.

I

Ice boxes, connections for, 62.
Ice houses, drainage of, 62.
Increase of pipes through roof, 90, 155.
Increasers, forms of, 90.
    use of, 91.
Indirect-pressure ball-cocks, 40.
Infection through untrapped plumbing system, 103.
Inspection of the plumbing system, 172.
Internal partitions in traps, 74.
Iron-body cleanouts, 162.

J

Jacket, water, for grease trap, 56.
Joints, caulked, weights of, 88.

Joints, caulked, cup, 88.
    on cast-iron pipe, 87.
    on local vent pipes, 126.
    overcast, 88.
    rust, 88.

K

Keyboard, use of, 214.
Kitchen sinks, 17.
    connections for, 17.
    construction of, 17, 18.
    for hotels, etc., 17.
    hot-water supply for, 17.
    setting of, 17, 18.
    sizes of, 17.
    waste for, 161.
Kitchen waste, catch basin for, 56.

L

Labor, estimating of, 381.
Laundry drainage, 62.
Laundry tubs, 18.
    connections for, 19.
    construction of, 18.
    drum trap for, 19, 82.
    in cellars, 205.
Lavatories, 23.
    connections for, 23.
    connections for group of, 271.
    construction of, 23.
    continuous venting of, 23, 176.
    double batteries of, 229, 233.
    for factories, 247.
    lines of, continuous venting for, 233.
    marble slabs for, 24.
    shower for, 32.
    S trap for, 133.
    trimmings for, 32.
Lavatory bowls, setting of, 24.
    sizes of, 24.
Lead and cast-iron pipe connections, 88.
Lead bend, connections into, 131, 156.
    connection of, 37.
Lead, connections without use of, 149.
    caulking, estimating of, 374.
    plumbing without use of, 271.
    sheet, weights of, 192.
    when not to be used as waste, 137.
Lead joints, caulked, 87.
    extra, allowance for, 88.
    weights of, 375.

INDEX

Lead pipe, decrease in use of, 184.
    estimating of, 376.
    light weights of used, 158.
    objections to, 137.
    sags in, 162.
    supporting of, 162.
    use of, 92.
    use of, on small work, 191.
    weights of, 192, 376.
Lead supply pipe, weights of, 192.
Lead waste pipes, advantages of, 273.
    objections to, 273.
    weights of, 192.
Lead work, displacing of, 137.
    light material used on, 192.
Leader pipes, cleanouts on, 163.
    connections of, 196.
    outside of house, 106.
    size of, 198.
Lift-force pump, action and construction of, 315.
Lift pump, action and construction of, 315.
Lifts, automatic sewage, 277, 278.
    action of, 278.
    advantages of, 280.
    for large work, 280.
    for marine work, 282.
    for public sewage, 281.
    proper size of, 281.
    venting of, 279.
Lifts, water, drainage from, 66.
Lighting, exterior, desirable, 144.
    of bath room, 144.
    of factory toilet rooms, 242.
    of toilet rooms, 228.
Lip urinal, 50, 256.
    flushing rim for, 119.
Live steam for heating hot-water tanks, 343.
Local vents, 83, 123.
    action of, 123, 124.
    chimney connections of, 127.
    connections of, with flues, 127.
    contagion carried by, 125.
    draft for, 125.
    for bath rooms, 144.
    for range water closets, 45.
    for slop sinks, 49.
    for urinals, 255.
    grading of, 155.
    joints on, 126.
    material for, 126.
    pitch of, 126.

Local vents, poor work on, 156, 157.
    purpose of, 123.
    required in unlighted and unventilated toilet rooms, 124.
    running of, 126.
    sizes of, 125.
    special, on water closet, 234.
    two systems of, 125.
    use of, in public toilet rooms, 246.
Local vents, main area of, 127.
    sizes of, 126.
Lodging houses, regulation of plumbing in, 207.
Long hoppers, use of, 70.
Loop vents, 188.
    for lines of water closets, 242.
    sizes of, 188.
Low-down tank, 43.
Low-down water closet, 43.
    siphon form for, 118.
Low-pressure steam-heating systems, drainage from, 66.

M

Main local vents, area of, 127.
Main soil pipe, vent connection into, 90.
Main stack at end of house drain, 191.
Main traps, 101.
    advantages of, 103, 110.
    cleanouts on, 104, 105, 162, 163.
    connection at, 196.
    for tenement houses, 103.
    freezing of, 104.
    in large cities, 103.
    object of, 101.
    objections to, 102.
    on country systems, 286.
    outside of foundation, 106.
    setting of, 105.
    stoppage of, 104.
    use of two, 197.
Main vents, 84.
    connections of, 90, 184.
    in high buildings, 223.
    into stack, 155.
    not required, 138.
    undesirable connection of, 91.
Main waste pipe, vent connection into, 90.
Manholes, purpose of, 102.
Manure to protect pipes from freezing, 321.

INDEX

Marble cements, 24.
Marble, cleaning of, 145.
    decrease in use of, 139.
    estimating of, 378.
    for lavatories, 24.
Marble floor slabs, setting of, 33.
Marble slabs for lavatories, 24.
    table of contents of, 25.
Mechanical devices in water closets, 115.
    for vents, 175.
Mechanical seals in traps, 74.
Mechanical ventilation, 127.
Mixer for bidet, 51.
Momentum affects trap seal, 74.

N

Nickel-plated supplies, 33.
Non-by-pass tees, use of, 362.
Non-siphonable traps, 73.
    use of, 149.

O

Oakum, amount of, for caulked joints, 375.
    estimating of, 375.
Obstructions in drum traps, 82, 83.
Odors in toilet rooms, 24.
Office buildings, hot water supply for, 211.
    plumbing for, 223.
Offset water closets, use of, 118.
Offsets in stacks, 89.
Oil of peppermint for testing, 171.
Open gravity tank, 220.
Open plumbing, advantages of, 119, 131.
Overcast joints, 88.
Overflows, cleaning of, 145.
    connection of, 77.
    for swimming pools, 238.
    from attic tanks, 287.
    from tanks, 62.
Overhead house drain, 112.
    piping, support of, 95.
    tank, use of, 220.

P

Painting of soil pipe, 145.
Pan water closet, objections to, 115.
Pantry sink, 25.
    connections for, 25.
    construction of, 25.
    setting of, 25.

Partitions for stalls in toilet rooms, 228.
    for toilet rooms, construction of, 208.
    for urinals, 50.
Patent overflow bowl, 24.
Paved courts, drainage of, 109.
Pedestal urinal, 257.
Peppermint, mixture of, for testing, 171.
    test, 167.
    objections to, 171.
Pipe connections, various, 88.
Pipe-supporting fittings, 95.
Pipes, pitch of drainage and vent, 88.
    supported by piers, 95.
    thawing of, by electricity, 331.
    to protect against frost, 321.
Piston pumps for raising sewage, 278.
Pitch of pipes, 88.
Plans, architects', reading and use of, 372.
Plugs, double-testing, 169.
    testing, 168.
Plumbing, inspection of, 172.
    testing of, 167.
Plunge bath, change of water in, 237.
    connections for, 237.
    construction of, 237.
    filtered water for, 238.
Plunger water closets, objections to, 115.
Pneumatic water supply, 309.
    advantages of, 310.
    applications of, 309, 310.
    operation of, 309.
    pressure from, 310.
    tanks for, 309, 310.
Poor practices in plumbing, 155.
Porcelain, cleaning of, 145.
    fixtures, use of, 139, 150.
    for filtering purposes, 219.
    lavatories, 23.
    urinals, 256.
Practices, poor, in plumbing, 155.
Pressure filters, construction of, 219.
    use of, 218.
Pressure for air test, 170.
    for smoke test, 171.
    for water test, 169.
Pressure supply system, 213.
Pressures, water, table of, 169.
Prices of plumbing material, 385.
Primary filter beds, 302, 305.
Profit on plumbing construction, 368.

INDEX 399

Provisions, drainage of rooms for storage of, 62.
Public toilet rooms, automatic flushing for, 245.
    circuit vents for, 187, 234.
    concealed work in, 233.
    drinking fountains in, 228.
    floor drains for, 227.
    floors of, 227.
    flush tanks in, 234.
    flushing-rim type of fixtures for, 234.
    lavatories for, 229.
    lighting of, 228.
    local vent in, 246.
    partitions in, 228.
    plumbing for, 227, 233.
    range water closets in, 228.
    urinals for, 255.
    ventilation of, 127, 227.
    water closets for, 234.
Pumping by windmill, 318.
Pumps, 314.
    centrifugal, for raising sewage, 277, 278.
    double-acting force, 315.
    for lifting sewage, 277.
    lift, action and construction of, 315.
    lift-force, action and construction of, 315.
    operated by windmills, 318.
    piston, for raising sewage, 278.
    suction, action of, 314.
Putty floor connections, 119.

Q

Quarter bends for deep-seal traps, 109.
    on circuit vents, 188.
    use of, 89.
Quick-closing work, disadvantages of, 212.

R

Rain leaders, 205.
    cleanouts on, 163.
    connected to house drain, advantages of, 207.
    connections for, 196.
    leep-seal traps for, 207.
    evaporation of traps on, 207.
    exposed, 206.
    how run, 206.

Rain leaders, inside, 206.
    into street gutters, 206.
    into surface house drain, 206.
    into surface sewer, 110.
    material for, 206.
    outside of house, 106.
    size of, 198, 205, 206.
    two or more connected together, 206.
    use of traps on, 205.
Rain water, catch basin for, 327.
    filtering of, 289.
    impurities in, 325.
    into cesspools, 295.
    purification of, 326.
    storage of, 288, 325, 327.
    storage tanks for, 328.
Rain-water filters, action of, 326, 327.
    construction of, 326, 327.
Rain-water separators, 289.
Ram pit, waste from, 313.
Rams, hydraulic, 311.
    air valve on, 312.
    connections for, 311.
    double-acting, 314, 325.
    drive pipe of, 313.
    force pipe from, 313.
    head of supply to, 312, 313.
    operation of, 311.
    source of supply for, 311.
    use of, 287.
    waste of water by, 313.
    waste valve of, 312.
    work done by, 313.
Range boilers for residences, 211.
    heating of, 328.
    material for, 192, 211.
    size of, 211.
    to reduce effective size of, 363.
Range water closets, 44.
    in public toilet rooms, 228.
    objections to, 44.
Reaming of ends of wrought-iron pipe, 261.
Recessed drainage fittings, 261.
Refrigerator drainage for flat buildings, 205.
Refrigerator drip sink, 61.
Refrigerator lines, 65.
    connections into, 65.
Refrigerator rooms, drainage of, 62.
Refrigerator traps, 65.
Refrigerators, 61.
    connections for, 65.

Refrigerators, drip pan for, 61.
    errors in connections of, 157.
Regulating cylinder for windmill, 311.
Regulators for tanks, 211.
Residences, plumbing for, 201.
    range boilers for, 211.
Restaurant sink, 55.
Roof connections, 91.
Roof flanges, 91.
Roof, fresh-air inlet through, 105.
    overflow onto, 62.
    size of pipes through, 155.
Roof pipes, escape of gases through, 101.
    frost in, 91.
    requirements of, 91.
    support of, 96.
    use of caps and cowls on, 91.
Roof vents, 84.
Roughing-in, 161.
Roughing test, 167.
    preparations for, 168.
Roughing, work included in, 161.
Running of soil pipe, 95.
Rust in vent system, 90, 91.
Rust joints, 88.

S

S traps, 73, 75.
    cleanouts for bath, 138.
    continuous vents for, 81.
    for country plumbing, 285.
    for lavatories, 133.
    forms of, 76.
    use of, 175.
Safe for attic storage tank, 288.
Safe wastes, connection of, 62.
Sand for filtering purposes, 219.
Sawdust to protect pipes from freezing, 321.
Scale, architects', use of, 373.
Scale in vent system, 90, 91.
Schools, automatic flushing for, 245.
Scouring action of Straps, 76.
Seal of traps, 73, 74.
    causes affecting, 74.
    evaporation of, 110, 176.
Seat vent, 123.
Self-cleansing factory sink, 247.
Separate drainage system for each house, 103.
Separate waste entrances for fixtures, 131, 132, 137, 138.
Separators, rain-water, 289.
Septic tank, 299.

Septic tank, action of, 299.
    action of bacteria in, 299.
    construction of, 299.
    discharge chamber of, 301.
    displaces cesspools, 299.
    disposal of contents of, 301.
    final disposal from, 302.
    light, air, and warmth of, 299.
    size of, 299.
    use of, 299.
    venting of, 285.
Service pipes destroyed by electrolysis, 265.
    frozen, thawed by electricity, 331.
    thawing of, by steam or hot water, 362.
Setting of lavatory bowls, 24.
    marble floor slabs, 33.
Settling chamber of septic tank, 299.
Sewage below sewer level, disposal of, 277.
    filtration of, through soil, 302.
    lifting of, 277.
    pressure necessary to raise, 279.
    underground, disposal of, 302.
Sewage ejector, automatic, 277, 278.
    action of, 278.
    advantages of, 280.
    for large work, 280.
    for marine work, 282.
    for public sewage, 281.
    proper size of, 281.
    venting of, 279.
Sewage lifts, automatic, 277, 278.
    action of, 278.
    advantages of, 280.
    for large work, 280.
    for marine work, 282.
    for public sewage, 281.
    proper size of, 281.
    venting of, 279.
Sewage pumps, use of, 277.
Sewage siphons, automatic, 305.
    action of, 306.
    use of, 305.
Sewage system, surface, rain leaders into, 206.
Sewer gas in plumbing system, 101.
Sewer level, disposal of sewage below, 277.
Sewers, circulation of air in, 102.
    cesspools connected to, 293.
    house sewer connections into, 198.

INDEX

Sewers, ventilation of, 102.
Sheet lead, weights of, 192.
Shellac for painting pipes, 145.
Shower bath, 32.
    connections for, 32.
    construction of, 32.
    waste from, 237.
Shower for lavatory, 32.
Sink, bar, connection of, 66.
Sink, cast-iron, sizes of, 17.
Sink, drip, for refrigerator, 61.
Sink for discharge of cellar drainer, 112.
Sink, hotel or restaurant, 55.
Sink, kitchen, 17.
    connections for, 17.
    construction of, 17, 18.
    for hotels, etc., 17.
    hot-water supply for, 17.
    setting of, 17, 18.
    waste for, 161.
Sink mat, flexible wooden, 18.
Sink, pantry, 25.
    connections for, 25.
    construction of, 25.
    setting of, 25.
Sink, slop, 49.
    automatic flushing of, 247.
    connections for, 49.
    flush tank for, 50.
Sink, soda fountain, connection of, 66.
Sink, stall, 69, 241.
Sink, vegetable wash, 18.
    construction of, 18.
Sinks, wash, for factories, 242, 247.
Siphon, action of, 75.
    automatic, for range water closets, 44.
    for automatic urinal, 247.
    water raised by, 316.
Siphonage applied to the water closet, 117.
    in unvented plumbing systems, 229.
    of drum traps, 81, 83.
    of traps, 74, 138.
    of traps, prevention of, 176.
    of unvented traps, 149.
    of water-closet traps, 38.
    prevented by venting, 75.
    water supply by, 316.
Siphonic influences on traps, 39.
Siphonic water supply, 286, 316.
Siphon-jet urinal, 257.

Siphon-jet water closet, 115.
Siphon water closet, 43, 115.
    for low-down style, 118.
Siphons, automatic sewage, 305.
    action of, 306.
    use of, 305.
Sitz bath, 32.
    connections for, 32.
Slabs, floor, setting of, 33.
Slabs, marble, for lavatories, 24.
    table of contents of, 25.
Slate, cement for mending, 19.
    estimating of, 378.
    for urinals, 50.
Slate factory sink, 247.
Slate urinals, 256.
    flushing of, 256.
Slop hopper, waste-preventive, 50.
Slop sink, 49.
    automatic flushing of, 247.
    connections for, 49.
    flush tank for, 50.
    flushing rim for, 119.
    flushing valves for, 251.
    local venting of, 123, 124.
    operated by flush valves, 43.
Smoke, materials to produce, 171.
Smoke machine, 171.
Smoke test, 167.
Smoke test, advantages of, 172.
    air pressure for, 171.
    connections for, 171.
Soapstone, cement for mending, 19.
Soda fountain sinks, connection of, 66.
Softening of hard water, 357.
Soft water, supply of, 353.
    for garages, 358.
    for heating boilers, 358.
Soil pipe, 87.
    changes in direction of, 89.
    connections for, 87.
    definition of, 87.
    extra heavy, 87.
    for factories, 242.
    measuring of, 373.
    painting of, 145.
    running of, 95.
    size of, 90.
    standard, 87.
    supported on tiled floors, 234.
    supporting of, 95.
Soil pipe stacks in high buildings, size of, 223.
Soil pipe stoppers, 168.

Soil vents, 84.
    definition of, 138.
Solder, wiping, amount for different joints, 377.
    estimating of, 362.
Soldering nipples, weights and sizes of, 272.
    use of, on Durham system, 272.
Special waste fittings, 38.
Stable drains, 110.
Stable waste into catch basin, 241.
Stables, floor drains for, 241.
    plumbing for, 69, 70, 241.
Stacks, alignment of, 89.
    in high buildings, size of, 223.
    main, at end of house drain, 191.
    offsets in, 89.
    running of, 133.
    sizes of, 90.
    testing of, 169.
    through roof, 89.
Stall sink for stables, 69, 241.
Standard soil pipe, 87.
Standards for soil pipe, 234.
Standing overflow for horse trough, 70.
Steam coils for hot-water boilers, 211, 343, 344.
Steam for automatic sewage lifts, 280.
    heating of boilers by, 343.
Steam-heating systems, drainage from, 66.
Steel and iron, differences between, 264.
Steel pipe, life of, 263, 264, 265.
Stone for filtering purposes, 219.
Stoppers, soil pipe, 168.
Storage tanks, 238.
    attic, 287.
    construction of, 238.
    covered, 238.
    for flushing valves, 251, 252.
    for rain water, 328.
    supply for, 238.
    supporting of, 238.
Submerged cleanouts, 82, 83, 164.
Subsoil drainage, 111.
    catch basin for, 111.
    disposal of, 112.
Subsoil drains, construction of, 111.
    drain tile for, 111.
    grading of, 111.
    into surface sewer, 110.
Suction of sewage pump, 278.
Suction pipes, lead used for, 273.

Suction pump, action of, 314.
Sump tank, automatic, 280.
Supplies, nickel-plated, 33.
Supply for double boiler, 337.
    hot water, for large buildings, 343.
Supply pipe, estimating of, 377.
    for cellar drainer, 112.
    large hot water, 344.
    material for, 192.
Supply systems, headers for, 214.
    street pressure, 213.
    tank pressure, 213.
    three-pipe, 353.
Supply tanks, 238.
Supporting of roof pipes, 91, 96.
    soil pipe, 95.
Surface sewage system, rain leaders into, 206.
Surface sewers, 110.
Surface venting, 123.
Swimming pool, change of water in, 237.
    connections for, 237.
    construction of, 237.
    filtered water for, 238.

T

Tank overflow, 62.
Tank-pressure system of supply, 213.
Tank regulators, 211.
Tanks, attic storage, 287.
    automatic flush, action of, 245.
    automatic sump, 280.
    condensing, use of, 66.
    flush, concealing of, 234.
    hot water, automatic control of, 349.
    low-down, 43.
    open gravity, use of, 220.
    overhead, use of, 220.
    septic, 299.
    size of, 213.
    storage, for flushing valves, 251, 252.
    venting of, 285.
Tanks, capacity of, to find, 319.
    for double boiler, 337.
    for pneumatic water supply, 309, 310.
    for storage and supply, 238.
    for storing rain water, 328.
Tapped fittings, use of, 90.
Tar, pipes coated with, 87.

INDEX

Tees, use of, on drainage system, 89.
    wrong use of, 155.
Tell-tale, use of, 287.
Tenement houses, drainage of yards, courts, and areas of, 208.
    main trap used in, 103.
    regulation of plumbing in, 207.
    ventilation of toilet rooms of, 208.
Testing of concealed piping, 167.
    high stacks, 169.
    old work, 167.
    plumbing system, 167.
    plumbing system in sections, 169.
Testing plugs, 168.
    double, 169.
Tests, air, 167.
    advantages of, 170.
    objections to, 170.
    pressure for, 170.
    final, 167.
    first, 167.
    forms of, 167.
    peppermint, 167, 171.
    peppermint, objections to, 171.
    purpose of, 167.
    roughing, 167.
    roughing, preparations for, 168.
    smoke, 167, 171.
    smoke, advantages of, 172.
    smoke, connections for, 171.
    water, 167.
    water, by whom made, 168.
    water, pressure of, 169.
    water, when applied, 161.
Thawing pipes by electricity, 331.
    by steam and hot water, 362.
Three-pipe system of supply, 353.
Tiling of bath rooms, 139.
Timbers, cutting of, 133.
Time card, 383, 384.
Toilet apartments of tenement houses, ventilation of, 208.
Toilet rooms, lighting of, 228.
    for factories, floors for, 242.
    for factories, lighting of, 242.
    for factories, ventilation of, 242.
    for factories, 242.
    odors in, 24.
    public, automatic flushing for, 245.
    public, circuit vents for, 187.
    public, concealed work in, 233.
    public, floor drains for, 227.

Toilet rooms, public, floors of, 227.
    public, partitions in, 208, 228.
    public, plumbing for, 227, 233.
    public, urinals for, 255.
    public, use of lavatories in, 229.
    public, use of local vent in, 246.
    public, use of range water closets in, 228.
    water closets, underground, disposal of waste from, 277.
    water closets, ventilation of, 123, 124, 127, 227.
Toilet soaps, odors from use of, 144.
Trap, definition of, 73.
    for line of shower baths, 237.
    serving two fixtures, 82, 131, 132.
Traps, adjustable for slop sink, 49.
    cleanouts for, 77.
    deep-seal, for rain leaders, 207.
    deep-seal, use of, 109.
    drum, cleanouts on, 164.
    drum, connections for, 81.
    drum, for bath tub, 81, 149.
    drum, for country plumbing, 285.
    drum, for laundry tubs, 82.
    drum, for refrigerators, 61.
    drum, obstructions in, 82, 83.
    drum, siphonage of, 81, 83.
    drum, stoppage of, 82.
    drum, unvented, 81.
    fixture, cleaning of, 145.
    for bath tubs, 31, 77.
    for cellar drain, 111.
    for floor and yard drains, 109.
    for refrigerators, 65.
    for various fixtures, sizes of, 77.
    formed by sags in lead pipe, 162.
    grease, 55.
    half-S, venting of, 175.
    house, 101.
    house, advantages of, 103, 110.
    house, cleanouts on, 104, 105, 162, 163.
    house, for tenement houses, 103.
    house, freezing of, 104.
    house, in large cities, 103.
    house, object of, 101.
    house, objections to, 102.
    house, outside of foundation, 106.
    house, setting of, 105.
    house, stoppage of, 104.
    how set, 77.

Traps, internal partitions in, 74.
　location of cleanouts on, 164.
　main, 101.
　main, advantages of, 103, 110.
　main, connection at, 196.
　main, for tenement houses, 103.
　main, in large cities, 103.
　main, object of, 101.
　main, objections to, 102.
　main, on country systems, 286.
　main, outside of foundation, 106
　main, setting of, 105.
　main, stoppage of, 104.
　mechanical seals in, 74.
　non-siphonable, 73.
　non-siphonable, use of, 149.
　objections to venting of, 175.
　prevention of siphonage of, 176
　rain leader, cleanouts on, 163.
　requirements of, 73.
　S, 73.
　S, cleanout for, 138.
　S, for country plumbing, 285.
　S, for lavatories, 133.
　S, siphonage of, 138.
　S, siphonic influences on, 39.
　S, stoppage of vents of, 175.
　S, under floors, 77.
　underground, cleanouts on, 163.
　unvented, siphonage of, 149.
　use of, on rain leaders, 205.
　use of S, 175.
　the water-closet, 115.
Trapping of fixtures, errors in, 156.
　floor and yard drains, 110.
　rain leaders, 106.
Trap cleanouts submerged, 82, 83.
Trap seals, causes affecting, 74.
　definition of, 73.
　evaporation of, 74, 77, 110.
　evaporation of decreased, by continuous venting, 176.
　of rain leader traps, evaporation of, 207.
　of water closet, 115.
Trap vents, requirements of, 84, 184.
Trench work, 198.
Trimmings for baths, 32.
　for lavatories, 32.
　fixture, estimating of, 378.
Trough, horse, 70.
Trough urinal, 257.
Tubs, laundry, 18.
Two-flat house, plumbing for, 205.

Two-floor work, continuous venting for, 179.
T-Ys, use of, 89, 155.

U

Underground cast-iron pipe, 162.
　disposal of contents of septic tank, 302.
　drain pipe, how run, 198.
　grease traps, 56.
　piping destroyed by electrolysis, 265.
　plumbing systems, subsoil drainage of, 277, 280.
　purification of sewage, 302.
　toilet rooms, disposal of waste from, 277.
　traps, cleanouts on, 163.
　wrought-iron pipe, 162.
Unvented plumbing systems, siphonage in, 229.
Urinals, 50.
　automatic flushing of, 257.
　automatically flushed, 246, 256.
　connections for, 50.
　connections for group of, 271.
　continuous venting of, 256.
　floor slabs for, 256.
　flushing rim, 256.
　flushing valves for, 251, 252, 257.
　for public toilet rooms, 255.
　gutters for, 256.
　lip, 256.
　lip, flushing rim for, 119.
　local venting of, 123, 124, 255.
　materials for connections of, 273.
　on Durham system, 257.
　operated by flush valves, 43.
　partitions and backs for, 50.
　pedestal, 257.
　porcelain, 256.
　setting of, 50.
　siphon-jet, 257.
　slate, 256.
　slate for, 50.
　trough, 257.
　waste-preventive, 50.

V

Vacuum formed in cellar drainer, 112.
Valve waste, connections for, 214.

INDEX

Valve water closets, objections to, 115.
Vegetable wash sink, 18.
   construction of, 18.
Vent, main lines of, in high buildings, 223.
Vent not required for water closet, 138.
Vent through cleanout cover, 82.
Vent system, corrosion of piping of, 264.
   rust, scale, and condensation in, 90, 91.
Vents, blind, 157.
   branch, 84.
   branch, running of, 184.
   circuit and loop for lines of water closets, 242.
   circuit, construction of, 187.
   circuit, for public toilet rooms, 187.
   circuit, quarter bends on, 188.
   cleanouts on, 76, 164.
   for Durham system, 261.
   loop, 188.
   sizes of, 188.
   main, 84.
   main, connection of, 90, 184.
   main, not required, 138.
   main, materials for, 92, 184.
   mechanical devices for, 175.
   pitch of, 184.
   soil and waste, definitions of, 138.
   stoppage of, 175.
   trap, requirements of, 84.
   various forms of, 83.
Ventilation by use of fans, 128.
   mechanical, 127.
   of bath room, 144.
   of comfort stations, 127.
   of factory toilet rooms, 242.
   of public toilet rooms, 127, 227.
   of sewers, 102.
   of tenement-house toilet rooms, 208.
   of toilet rooms, 123.
   requirements for, 124.
Venting, 73.
   circuit, 187.
   circuit, in public toilet rooms, 234.
   continuous, 175.

Venting, continuous, advantages of, 175, 180.
   continuous, economy of, 180, 183.
   continuous, for apartment houses, 179.
   continuous, for groups of fixtures, 176.
   continuous, for lavatories, 176.
   continuous, for line of fixtures, 271.
   continuous, for lines of lavatories, 233.
   continuous, for lines of urinals, 256.
   continuous, for S trap, 81, 83.
   continuous, for two-floor work, 179.
   continuous, for two lines of fixtures, 183.
   continuous, for water closets, 187.
   continuous, from double fittings, 223.
   continuous, objections to, 175.
   of cesspools, 285, 294.
   of condensing tank, 66.
   of fixtures at distance from main vent, 184.
   fixtures at distance from stack, 137.
   of half S trap, 175.
   of lines of water closets, 187, 188, 242.
   of S traps, 76.
   of septic tanks, 285.
   of sewage ejectors, 279.
   of slop sink, 49.
   of water closets, 38, 223.
   of water closet from crockery, 155.
   of water-closet trap, 143.
   poor practices in, 156.
   practical requirements, of, 83, 184.
   prevents siphonage, 75.
Vertical pipes, running of, 133.
   support of, 96.
Vertical stacks, running of, 89.
Vises for brass pipe, use of, 202.
Vitreous chinaware for water closets, 118.
Vitrified earthen pipe for drains, 110.

W

Wash-down water closet, 115, 116.
Wash-down siphon water closet, 117.
Washout water closet, 115, 116, 117.
Wash sinks for factories, 242.
Wash trays, 18.
    connections for, 19.
    construction of, 18.
    drum trap for, 19, 82.
    in cellars, 205.
Waste and vent fittings, special, 201.
Waste connections, cleaning of, 145.
    separate entrance of, into stack, 131, 132, 137, 138.
Waste fittings, special, 143.
Waste pipe, definitions of, 87.
    main, measuring of, 373.
    size of, 90.
Waste-preventive slop hopper, 50.
    urinal, 50.
Waste valve of hydraulic ram, operation of, 312.
Waste vents, 84, 138.
Water, natural purification of, 290.
    plumbing system filled with, 169.
    wasted by the hydraulic ram, 313.
Water closets, 115.
    automatic flush for, 245.
    circuit and loop vents for, 242.
    connections for, 37.
    continuous venting of, 187.
    exposed surface in, 115.
    floor connections for, 37, 119.
    floor connections for Durham system, 271, 272.
    crazing of, 119.
    flush pipe to, 37.
    flush tank for, 37.
    flush valve for, 37, 43.
    flushing of, 115.
    flushing rim for, 119.
    flushing valves for, 251.
    for public toilet rooms, 234.
    frost-proof, 70.
    in factories, number of, 207.
    in public toilet rooms, flush tanks for, 234.
    in tenement houses, etc., number of, 207.
    local vent a part of, 234.
    local venting of, 123.
    location of, 119.
Water closets, low-down, 43.
    material for, 118.
    modern, advantages of, 115.
    no mechanical devices in, 115.
    offset, use of, 118.
    pan, valve, and plunger, 115.
    principal forms of, 115.
    range, 44.
    requirements of, 115.
    siphon, 115, 118.
    siphonage applied to, 117.
    siphonage of, 38.
    siphon-jet, 115.
    trap seal of, 115.
    vented from crockery, 38, 155.
    vented from lead bend, 38.
    vented from T-Y fitting, 38.
    ventilation of, 119.
    venting of, 38, 143, 223.
    venting of lines of, 187, 188, 242.
    venting of, unnecessary, 138.
    wash-down, 115.
    wash-down siphon, 117.
    washout, 115, 116.
    waste from, 37.
    water jet applied to, 117.
    when unnecessary to vent, 205.
Water jacket for grease trap, 56.
Water jet applied to water closet, 117.
Water lifts, drainage from, 66.
Water mains, destroyed by electrolysis, 265.
    frozen, thawed by electricity, 331.
Water meters, backing of hot water into, 361.
    by-pass for, 361.
Water pipe, estimating of, 377.
Water pressures, table of, 169.
Water-softening device, 357.
Water supply by siphonage, 286, 316.
    for attic storage tanks, 287.
    for country systems, 286, 325.
    for double boilers, 337.
    gravity, 286.
    pipes, material for, 192.
    pneumatic, 309.
Water test, 167.
    by whom made, 168.
    pressure of, 169.
    when applied, 161.
Weight of piping of plumbing system, 96.

INDEX

Wells, driven, 315, 316.
   for windmill pumping, 319.
   forms of, 290.
   location of, 289.
Wheel pits, drainage of, 112.
Windmills, regulating cylinder for, 311.
   pumping by, 318.
   wells for, 319.
Windmill pumps, 318.
Windows, distance of fresh-air inlet from, 104.
Wiping solder, amount for different joints, 377.
   estimating of, 376.
Wire baskets for roof pipes, 91.
Wooden laundry tubs, 19.
   sinks, 19.
   sink mat, 18.
Wrenches for brass pipe, use of, 202.
Wrought-iron and brass pipe connections, 88.
Wrought-iron and cast-iron pipe connections, 88.
Wrought-iron drainage pipe, weights of, 261.
Wrought-iron pipes, advantage of, 97.
   connection of into cast-iron pipe, 262.
   cutting and reaming of, 261.
   for refrigerator work, 65.
   life of, 263, 264, 265.
   underground, 162.
   use of, 92.

Y

Y branch, use of, 89, 155.
Yard drains, 109.
   into surface sewers, 110.
   size of, 109.
   trapping of, 109, 110.
Yards, drainage of, 109, 208.

JUST PUBLISHED

STANDARD PRACTICAL PLUMBING

By R. M. STARBUCK
Author of "Modern Plumbing Illustrated," Etc., Etc.

450 PAGES   347 SPECIALLY MADE ILLUSTRATIONS

PRICE $3.00

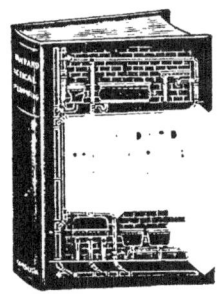

"**STANDARD PRACTICAL PLUMBING**" is indispensable to the Master Plumber, the Journeyman Plumber, and the Apprentice Plumber. As the book is Specially Strong in its Exhaustive Treatment of the SKILLED WORK OF THE PLUMBER, it commends itself at once to Every One Working in Any Branch of the Plumbing Trade.

Of the three hundred and forty-seven illustrations contained in the book, One Hundred of them are full page illustrations. The illustrations all being drawn expressly for this work Show the Most Modern and Best Practice in Plumbing Construction.

Plumbing in all its branches is treated within the pages of this book, and a large amount of space is devoted to a very complete and practical treatment of the subject of Hot Water Supply and Circulation and Range Boiler Work.

Another valuable feature is the special chapter on Drawing for the Plumber.

IT CONTAINS THE FOLLOWING ILLUSTRATED CHAPTERS

I. The Plumber's Tools.	XVII. Improved Plumbing Connections.
II. Wiping Solder, Composition and Use.	XVIII. Residence Plumbing.
III. Joint Wiping.	XIX. Plumbing for Hotels, Schools, Factories, Stables, Etc.
IV. Lead Work.	XX. Modern Country Plumbing.
V. Traps.	XXI. Filtration of Sewage and Water Supply.
VI. Siphonage of Traps.	XXII. Hot and Cold Supply.
VII. Venting.	XXIII. Range Boilers; Circulation.
VIII. Continuous Venting.	XXIV. Circulating Pipes.
IX. House Sewer and Sewer Connections.	XXV. Range Boiler Problems.
X. House Drain.	XXVI. Hot Water for Large Buildings.
XI. Soil Piping, Roughing.	XXVII. Water Lift and Its Use.
XII. Main Trap and Fresh Air Inlet.	XXVIII. Multiple Connections for Hot Water Boilers; Heating of Radiation by Supply System.
XIII. Floor, Yard, Cellar Drains, Rain Leaders, Etc.	
XIV. Fixture Wastes.	
XV. Water Closets.	XXIX. Theory for the Plumber.
XVI. Ventilation.	XXX. Drawing for the Plumber.

THE NORMAN W. HENLEY PUBLISHING CO.,
132 NASSAU STREET,   -   NEW YORK.

JUST PUBLISHED

Modern Plumbing Illustrated

By R. M. STARBUCK

Author of "Questions and Answers on the Practice and Theory of Sanitary Plumbing"

400 Large Quarto Pages. Fully Illustrated by Fifty-five full pages of detailed engravings, which have been made specially for this book

PRICE, $4.00

The Only Thorough and Practical Work Issued on the Modern and Most Approved Methods of Plumbing Construction. Illustrating and Describing the Drainage and Ventilation of Dwellings, Apartments and Public Buildings, etc. The Standard Work for Plumbers, Architects, Builders, Property Owners, and for Boards of Health and Plumbing Examiners.

THE author of this book, Mr. R. M. Starbuck, is one of the leading authorities on plumbing in the United States. The book represents the highest standard of plumbing work. It has been adopted and used as a reference book by the United States Government, in its sanitary work in Cuba, Porto Rico and the Philippines, and by the principal Boards of Health of the United States and Canada.

It gives Connections, Sizes and Working Data for All Fixtures and Groups of Fixtures. It is helpful to the Master Plumber in Demonstrating to His Customers and in Figuring of Work. It gives the Mechanic and Student quick and easy Access to the Best Modern Plumbing Practice. Suggestions for Estimating Plumbing Construction are contained in its pages. This book represents, in a word, the latest and best up-to-date practice, and should be in the hands of every architect, sanitary engineer and plumber who wishes to keep himself up to the minute on this important feature of construction.

CONTAINS FOLLOWING CHAPTERS, EACH ILLUSTRATED WITH A FULL-PAGE PLATE

1 Kitchen Sink, Laundry Tubs, Vegetable Wash Sink
2 Lavatories—Pantry Sinks, Contents of Marble Slabs
3 Bath Tub—Foot and Sitz Bath, Shower Bath
4 Water Closets—Venting of Water Closets
5 Low-Down Water Closets—Water Closets Operated by Flush Valves—Water Closet Range
6 Slop Sink—Urinals—The Bidet
7 Hotel or Restaurant Sink—Grease Trap
8 Refrigerators—Safe Wastes—Laundry Waste
9 Lines of Refrigerators, Bar Sinks—Soda Fountain Sinks
10 Horse Stall, Frost-Proof Water Closets
11 Connections for S Traps, Venting
12 Connections for Drum Traps
13 Soil Pipe Connections
14 Supporting of Soil Pipe
15 Main Trap and Fresh Air Inlet
16 Floor Drains and Cellar Drains—Subsoil Drainage
17 Water Closets and Floor Connections
18 Local Venting
19 Connections for Bath Rooms
20 Connections for Bath Rooms, Continued
21 Connections for Bath Rooms, Continued
22 Connections for Bath Rooms, Continued
23 Examples of Poor Practice
24 Roughing-Work Ready for Test
25 Testing of Plumbing System
26 Method of Continuous Venting
27 Continuous Venting for Two-Floor Work
28 Continuous Venting for Two Lines of Fixtures on Three or More Floors
29 Continuous Venting of Water Closets
30 Plumbing for Cottage House
31 Construction for Cellar Piping
32 Plumbing for Residence—Use of Special Fittings
33 Plumbing for Two-Flat House
34 Plumbing for Apartment Building
35 Plumbing for Double Apartment Building
36 Plumbing for Office Building
37 Plumbing for Public Toilet Rooms
38 Plumbing for Public Toilet Rooms, Continued
39 Plumbing for Bath Establishment
40 Plumbing for Engine House—Factory Plumbing
41 Automatic Flushing for Schools, Factories, etc.
42 Use of Flushing Valves
43 Urinals for Public Toilet Rooms
44 The Durham System—The Destruction of Pipes by Electrolysis
45 Construction of Work Without Use of Lead
46 Automatic Sewage Lift—Automatic Sump Tank
47 Country Plumbing
48 Construction of Cesspools
49 Septic Tank and Automatic Sewage Siphon
50 Country Plumbing
51 Water Supply for Country House
52 Thawing of Water Mains and Service by Electricity
53 Double Boilers
54 Hot Water Supply of Large Buildings
55 Automatic Control of Hot Water Tank
Suggestions for Estimating Plumbing Construction

WHAT IS SAID OF THIS BOOK

"This volume is the most complete general statement of American plumbing methods as executed by the best workmen at the present time."—*Engineering Record.*

"A plumbers Hand Book including the most practical up-to-date handling of the questions of drainage, sewerage, and water supply."—*Engineering News.*

THE NORMAN W. HENLEY PUBLISHING CO.
132 NASSAU STREET, - NEW YORK.

JUST PUBLISHED

Practical
STEAM AND HOT=WATER HEATING
and Ventilation

By ALFRED G. KING

Octavo. 367 Pages. Containing over 300 detailed illustrations. The larger part of them, having been made from original diagrams, specially drawn for the book

PRICE $3.00

The Most Elaborate and Complete Work That Has Ever Been Published for the Use of Heating Contractors, Journeymen Steam Fitters, Steam Fitters' Apprentices, Architects and Builders

THIS book is the standard and latest work published on the subject and has been prepared for the use of all engaged in the business of steam, hot-water heating and ventilation. It is an original and exhaustive work. Tells how to get heating contracts, how to install heating and ventilating apparatus, the best business methods to be used, with "Tricks of the Trade" for shop use. Rules and data for estimating radiation and cost and such tables and information as makes it an indispensable work for everyone interested in steam, hot-water heating and ventilation. It describes all the principal systems of steam, hot-water, vacuum, vapor and vacuum-vapor heating, together with the new accelerated systems of hot-water circulation, including chapters on up-to-date methods of ventilation and the fan or blower system of heating and ventilation.

You should secure a copy of this book, as each chapter contains a mine of practical information.

CONTAINING CHAPTERS ON

I Introduction. II. Heat. III. Evolution of Artificial Heating Apparatus. IV. Boiler Surface and Settings. V. The Chimney Flue. VI. Pipe and Fittings. VII. Valves, Various Kinds. VIII. Forms of Radiating Surfaces. IX. Locating of Radiating Surfaces. X. Estimating Radiation. XI. Steam-Heating Apparatus. XII. Exhaust-Steam Heating. XIII. Hot-Water Heating. XIV. Pressure Systems of Hot-Water Work. XV. Hot-Water Appliances. XVI. Greenhouse Heating. XVII. Vacuum Vapor and Vacuum Exhaust Heating. XVIII. Miscellaneous Heating. XIX. Radiator and Pipe Connections. XX. Ventilation. XXI. Mechanical Ventilation and Hot-Blast Heating. XXII. Steam Appliances. XXIII. District Heating. XXIV. Pipe and Boiler Covering. XXV. Temperature Regulation and Heat Control. XXVI. Business Methods. XXVII. Miscellaneous. XXVIII. Rules, Tables and Useful Information.

Valuable Data and Tables Used for Estimating, Installing and Testing of Steam and Hot-Water and Ventilating Apparatus Are Given.

THE NORMAN W. HENLEY PUBLISHING CO.,
132 NASSAU STREET, - NEW YORK.

JUST PUBLISHED

MECHANICAL DRAWING FOR PLUMBERS

By R. M. STARBUCK

Author of "Standard Practical Plumbing," "Modern Plumbing Illustrated," Etc., Etc.

132 Pages   Illustrated with 150 Specially-made Engravings

PRICE $1.50

A Concise, Comprehensive and Practical Treatise on the Subject of Mechanical Drawing, in Its Various Modern Applications to the Work of All who are in Any Way Connected with the Plumbing Trade

NOTHING will so help the plumber in estimating and in explaining work to customers and workmen as a knowledge of drawing, and to the workman it is of inestimable value if he is to rise above his position to positions of greater responsibility.

This book gives ample instruction, presenting a complete course in drafting plumbing installation and fixtures, including many good ideas in neat and simple sketching.

AMONG THE CHAPTERS CONTAINED ARE:

1. Value to Plumber of Knowledge of Drawing—Tools Required and Their Use—Common Views Needed in Mechanical Drawing. 2. Perspective versus Mechanical Drawing in Showing Plumbing Construction. 3. Correct and Incorrect Methods in Plumbing Drawing—Plan and Elevation Explained. 4. Floor and Cellar Plans and Elevation—Scale Drawings—Use of Triangles. 5. Use of Triangles—Drawing of Fittings, Traps, Etc. 6. Drawing Plumbing Elevations and Fittings. 7. Instructions in Drawing Plumbing Elevations. 8. The Drawing of Plumbing Fixtures—Scale Drawings. 9. Drawing of Fixtures and Fittings. 10. Inking of Drawings. 11. Shading of Drawings. 12. Shading of Drawings. 13. Sectional Drawings—Drawing of Threads. 14. Plumbing Elevations from Architect's Plan. 15. Elevations of Separate Parts of the Plumbing System. 16. Elevations from Architect's Plans. 17. Drawing of Detail Plumbing Connections. 18. Architect's Plans and Plumbing Elevations of Residence. 19. Plumbing Elevations of Residence (continued)—Plumbing Plans for Cottage. 20. Plumbing Elevations—Roof Connections. 21. Plans and Plumbing Elevations for Six-flat Building. 22. Drawing of Various Parts of the Plumbing System—Use of Scales. 23. Use of Architect's Scales. 24. Special Features in the Illustrations of Country Plumbing. 25. Drawing of Wrought Iron Piping, Valves, Radiators, Coils, Etc. 26. Drawing of Piping to Illustrate Heating Systems.

This work is concise, comprehensive and practical, dealing simply and clearly with the subject of drawing such as the plumber needs in his work.

WHAT IS SAID OF THIS BOOK

"This book will be found of value for the information on design, indirectly conveyed by the illustrations, as well as for the instruction in drafting."—*Engineering News*.

"This book supplies a want, long felt by the practical plumber."—*Scientific American*.

THE NORMAN W. HENLEY PUBLISHING CO.,
132 NASSAU STREET,   -   NEW YORK.

JUST PUBLISHED!   AN INDISPENSABLE WORK!

500 PLAIN ANSWERS TO DIRECT QUESTIONS

ON

STEAM, HOT-WATER, VAPOR AND VACUUM HEATING

By ALFRED G. KING

Author of "Practical Steam, Hot Water Heating and Ventilation" and "Practical Heating Illustrated," Etc., Etc.

214 Pages.   **PRICE $1.50.**   127 Illustrations.

AN UP-TO-DATE AND THOROUGHLY PRACTICAL BOOK ON HEATING WITHOUT AN EQUAL

This practical treatise consists of twenty-four chapters, covering with 500 questions and their answers—Steam, Hot Water, Vapor and Vacuum Heating. The subject matter is absolutely correct and explained in simple language. If you can't answer all of the following questions you need this book. The answers to these and 500 more are to be found within the pages.

Why should a chimney be built round or square? How are cast iron boilers rated? What are the cooling surfaces of a building? What is meant by exhaust heating? For what purposes is an equalizing pipe employed? What is accelerated hot water heating? Describe the principle of vacuum heating? What is the thermostatic principle? What is a non-mechanical system of vacuum heating? What type of radiators is employed for vapor heating? Describe atmospheric pressure. How is the capacity of a round or rectangular tank determined? What method is employed to determine the safe working pressure of a tubular boiler? Etc., Etc.

This book tells "HOW" and also tells "WHY". No work of its kind has ever been published. It answers all the questions regarding each method or system that would be asked by the steam fitter or heating contractor, and may be used as a text or reference book, and for examination questions by TRADE SCHOOLS OR STEAM FITTERS' ASSOCIATIONS.

Rules, data, tables and descriptive methods are given together with much other detailed information of daily practical use to those engaged in or interested in the various methods of heating.

Valuable to those preparing for examinations. Answers every question asked relating to modern Steam, Hot-Water, Vapor and Vacuum Heating.

AMONG THE CONTENTS ARE

The Theory and Laws of Heat.
Methods of Heating.
Chimneys and Flues.
Boilers for Heating.
Boiler Trimmings and Settings.
Radiation.
Steam Heating.
Boiler, Radiator and Pipe Connections for Steam Heating.
Hot Water Heating.
The Two-Pipe Gravity System of Hot Water Heating.
The Circuit System of Hot Water Heating.
The Overhead System of Hot Water Heating.

Boiler, Radiator and Pipe Connections for Gravity Systems of Hot Water Heating.
Accelerated Hot Water Heating.
Expansion Tank Connections.
Domestic Hot Water Heating.
Valves and Air Valves.
Vacuum, Vapor and Vacuo-Vapor Heating.
Mechanical Systems of Vacuum Heating.
Non-Mechanical Vacuum Systems.
Vapor Systems.
Atmospheric and Modulating Systems.
Heating Greenhouses.
Information, Rules and Tables.

The Norman W. Henley Publishing Company,

132 NASSAU STREET, NEW YORK, U. S. A.

The Most Valuable Techno-Chemical Receipt Book Published
Henley's Twentieth Century Book of
RECIPES
FORMULAS
AND PROCESSES

Edited by GARDNER D. HISCOX, M.E.

Price $3.00 Cloth Binding $4.00 Half Morocco Binding
800 Large Octavo (6 x 9½) Pages

Contains over 10,000 Selected Scientific, Chemical, Technological and Practical Recipes and Processes, including hundreds of so-called Trade Secrets for every business

To present here even a limited number of the subjects which find a place in this valuable work would be difficult. Suffice it to say that in its pages will be found matter of intense interest and immeasurable practical value to the scientific amateur and to him who wishes to obtain a knowledge of the many processes used in the arts, trades and manufactures, a knowledge which will render his pursuits more instructive and remunerative. Serving as a reference book to the small and large manufacturer and supplying intelligent seekers with the information necessary to conduct a process, the work will be found of inestimable worth to the Metallurgist, the Photographer, the Perfumer, the Painter, the Manufacturer of Glues, Pastes, Cements, and Mucilages, the Compounder of Alloys, the Cook, the Physician, the Druggist, the Electrician, the Brewer, the Engineer, the Foundryman, the Machinist, the Potter, the Tanner, the Confectioner, the Chiropodist, the Manicure, the Manufacturer of Chemical Novelties and Toilet Preparations, the Dyer, the Electroplater, the Enameler, the Engraver, the Provisioner, the Glass Worker, the Goldbeater, the Watchmaker and Jeweler, the Hat Maker, the Ink Manufacturer, the Optician, the Farmer, the Dairyman, the Paper Maker, the Wood and Metal Worker, the Chandler and Soap Maker, the Veterinary Surgeon, and the Technologist in general.

Among the Recipes given are:

Bleaching Recipes	Soap Making	Household Formulas
Etching and Engraving Recipes	Leather and Its Preparation	Waterproofing Recipes
Recipes for Glass Making	Recipes for Alloys	Fireproofing Recipes
Paper Making Recipes	Recipes for Solders	Recipes for Cements, Glues, Mucilages
Recipes for Ointments	Photographic Formulas	Fireworks Recipes
Mirror-Making Formulas	Shoe Dressing Recipes	Recipes for Eradicators
Paint Making Formulas	Stove Blacking Recipes	Alcohol and its Uses
Gilding Recipes	Rust Preventive Recipes	Recipes for Essences and Extracts
Galvanizing Recipes	Recipes for Lubricants	Dentifrice Recipes
Bronzing Recipes	Recipes for Oils	Cosmetic Recipes
Tinning Recipes	Recipes for Dyes, Colors, and Pigments	Perfume Recipes
Silvering Recipes	Recipes for Dryers	Tanning Recipes
Recipes for Adhesives	Ink Recipes	Metallurgical Formulas
Recipes for Plating and Enameling	Recipes for Artificial Gem Making	Hair Restorers
Cleaning Processes	Jewelers' and Watchmakers' Recipes	Depilatories

And many thousands more — Equally Important in the Arts and Manufactures

The Norman W. Henley Publishing Company,
132 NASSAU STREET, NEW YORK, U. S. A.

PRACTICAL SCIENTIFIC TECHNICAL

EACH BOOK IN THIS CATALOGUE IS WRITTEN BY AN EXPERT AND IS WRITTEN SO YOU CAN UNDERSTAND IT

THE NORMAN W. HENLEY PUBLISHING COMPANY
Publishers of Scientific and Practical Books
132 Nassau Street   New York, U. S. A.

Any book in this Catalogue sent prepaid on receipt of price.

SUBJECT INDEX

	PAGE
Accidents	20
Air Brakes	18, 21
Arithmetics	10, 21
Automobiles	1, 2, 3
Automobile Charts	3
Bevel Gears	16
Boilers	19
Brazing	4
Cams	16
Car Charts	5
Change Gear	16
Charts	3, 4, 5
Compressed Air	6
Concrete	6, 7, 8
Cycle-Cars	2
Dictionaries	8
Dies	9
Drawing	9, 10
Drop-Forging	9
Dynamo	11
Electricity	10, 11, 12
Factory Management	13
Ford Automobile	1
Fuel	14
Gas Engines	14, 15, 16
Gears	16
Horse-Power Chart	6
Hot-Water Heating	29
Hydraulics	16
India Rubber	27
Interchangeable Manufacturing	21
Inventions	16
Knots	17
Lathe Work	17
Link Motion	19
Liquid Air	18
Locomotive Boilers	19
Locomotive Engineering	18, 19, 20, 21

	PAGE
Machinists' Books	21, 22, 23
Manual Training	23
Marine Engines	23
Mechanical Movements	22
Motor-Cycles	2, 4
Oil Engines	15
Patents	16
Pattern Making	23
Perfumery	24
Plumbing	24, 25, 26
Producer Gas	15
Punches	9
Railroad Accidents	20
Receipt Book	26
Rope Work	17
Rubber Stamps	27
Saws	27
Sheet-Metal Working	9
Shop Construction	21
Shop Management	21
Shop Tools	22
Sketching Paper	10
Soldering	4
Splices	17
Steam Engineering	27, 28, 29
Steam Heating	29
Steel	30
Switchboards	11, 13
Tapers	18
Telephone	13
Threads	23
Tools	21, 22
Valve Gear	20
Valve Setting	19
Ventilation	29
Walschaert Valve Gear	20
Wireless Telephones and Telegraphy	13
Wiring	11, 12

☞ ANY OF THESE BOOKS PROMPTLY SENT PREPAID TO ANY ADDRESS IN THE WORLD ON RECEIPT OF PRICE.

☞ *How to Remit.*—By Postal Money Order, Express Money Order, Bank Draft or Registered Letter.

CATALOGUE OF GOOD, PRACTICAL BOOKS

AUTOMOBILES AND MOTORCYCLES

THE MODERN GASOLINE AUTOMOBILE—ITS DESIGN, CONSTRUCTION, MAINTENANCE AND REPAIR. By Victor W. Pagé, M.E.

The latest and most complete treatise on the Gasoline Automobile ever issued. Written in simple language by a recognized authority, familiar with every branch of the automobile industry. Free from technical terms. Everything is explained so simply that anyone of average intelligence may gain a comprehensive knowledge of the gasoline automobile. The information is up-to-date and includes, in addition to an exposition of principles of construction and description of all types of automobiles and their components, valuable money-saving hints on the care and operation of motor-cars propelled by internal combustion engines. Among some of the subjects treated might be mentioned: Torpedo and other symmetrical body forms designed to reduce air resistance; sleeve valve, rotary valve and other types of silent motors; increasing tendency to favor worm-gear power-transmission; universal application of magneto ignition; development of automobile electric-lighting systems; block motors; underslung chassis; application of practical self-starters; long stroke and offset cylinder motors; latest automatic lubrication systems; silent chains for valve operation and, change-speed gearing; the use of front wheel brakes and many other detail refinements. By a careful study of the pages of this book one can gain practical knowledge of automobile construction that will save time, money and worry. The book tells you just what to do, how and when to do it. Nothing has been omitted, no detail has been slighted. Every part of the automobile, its equipment, accessories, tools, supplies, spare parts necessary, etc., have been discussed comprehensively. If you are or intend to become a motorist, or are in any way interested in the modern Gasoline Automobile, this is a book you cannot afford to be without. Over 800 6x9 pages—and more than 500 new and specially made detail illustrations, as well as many full-page and double-page plates, showing all parts of the automobile. Including 11 large folding plates. Price $2.50

WHAT IS SAID OF THIS BOOK:

"It is the best book on the Automobile seen up to date."—J. H. Pile, Associate Editor *Automobile Trade Journal.*

"Every Automobile Owner has use for a book of this character."—*The Tradesman.*

"This book is superior to any treatise heretofore published on the subject."—*The Inventive Age.*

"We know of no other volume that is so complete in all its departments, and in which the wide field of automobile construction with its mechanical intricacies is so plainly handled, both in the text and in the matter of illustrations."—*The Motorist.*

"The book is very thorough, a careful examination failing to disclose any point in connection with the automobile, its care and repair, to have been overlooked."—*Iron Age.*

"Mr. Pagé has done a great work, and benefit to the Automobile Field."—W. C. Hasford, Mgr. Y. M. C. A. Automobile School, Boston, Mass.

"It is just the kind of a book a motorist needs if he wants to understand his car."—*American Thresherman.*

THE MODEL T FORD CAR, ITS CONSTRUCTION, OPERATION AND REPAIR. By Victor W. Pagé, M.E.

This is a complete instruction book. All parts of the Ford Model T Car are described and illustrated; the construction is fully described and operating principles made clear to everyone. Every Ford owner needs this practical book. You don't have to guess about the construction or where the trouble is, as it shows how to take all parts apart and how to locate and fix all faults. The writer, Mr. Pagé, has operated a Ford car for four years and writes from actual knowledge. Among the contents are: 1. The Ford Car. Its Parts and Their Functions. 2. The Engine and Auxiliary Groups. How the Engine Works—The Fuel Supply System—The Carburetor—Making the Ignition Spark—Cooling and Lubrication. 3. Details of Chassis. Change Speed Gear—Power Transmission—Differential Gear Action—Steering Gear—Front Axle—Frame and Springs—Brakes. 4. How to Drive and Care for the Ford. The Control System Explained—Starting the Motor—Driving the Car—Locating Roadside Troubles—Tire Repairs—Oiling the Chassis—Winter Care of Car. 5. Systematic Location of Troubles and Remedies. Faults in Engine—Faults in Carburetor—Ignition Troubles—Cooling and Lubrication System Defects—Adjustment of Transmission Gear—General Chassis Repairs. 95 illustrations. 300 pages. Two large folding plates. Price $1.00

CATALOGUE OF GOOD, PRACTICAL BOOKS

QUESTIONS AND ANSWERS RELATING TO MODERN AUTOMOBILE CONSTRUCTION, DRIVING AND REPAIR. By VICTOR W. PAGÉ, M.E.

A practical self-instructor for students, mechanics and motorists, consisting of thirty-six lessons in the form of questions and answers, written with special reference to the requirements of the non-technical reader desiring easily understood, explanatory matter relating to all branches of automobiling. The subject-matter is absolutely correct and explained in simple language. If you can't answer all of the following questions, you need this work. The answers to these and nearly 2000 more are to be found in its pages. Give the name of all important parts of an automobile and describe their functions? Describe action of latest types of kerosene carburetors? What is the difference between a "Double" ignition system and a "dual" ignition system? Name parts of an induction coil? How are valves timed? What is an electric motor starter and how does it work? What are advantages of worm drive gearing? Name all important types of ball and roller bearings? What is a "Three-quarter" floating axle? What is a two-speed axle? What is the Vulcan electric gear shift? Name the causes of lost power in automobiles? Describe all noises due to deranged mechanism and give causes? How can you adjust a carburetor by the color of the exhaust gases? What causes "popping" in the carburetor? What tools and supplies are needed to equip a car? How do you drive various makes of cars? What is a differential lock and where is it used? Name different systems of wire wheel construction, etc., etc.? A popular work at a popular price. 5¼ x 7½. Cloth. 622 pages, 392 illustrations, 3 folding plates. Price $1.50

WHAT IS SAID OF THIS BOOK:

"If you own a car—get this book."—*The Glassworker.*
"Mr. Pagé has the faculty of making difficult subjects plain and understandable."—*Bristol Press.*
"We can name no writer better qualified to prepare a book of instruction on automobiles than Mr. Victor W. Pagé."—*Scientific American.*
"The best automobile catechism that has appeared."—*Automobile Topics.*
"There are few men, even with long experience, who will not find this book useful. Great pains have been taken to make it accurate. Special recommendation must be given to the illustrations, which have been made specially for the work. Such excellent books as this greatly assist in fully understanding your automobile."—*Engineering News.*
"Here is a book that should be in the cycle repairer's kit."—*American Blacksmith.*
"The best way for any rider to thoroughly understand his machine, is to get a copy of this book; it is worth many times its price."—*Pacific Motorcyclist.*

MOTORCYCLES, SIDE CARS AND CYCLECARS, THEIR CONSTRUCTION, MANAGEMENT AND REPAIR. By VICTOR W. PAGÉ, M.E.

The only complete work published for the motorcyclist and cyclecarist. Describes fully all leading types of machines, their design, construction, maintenance, operation and repair. This treatise outlines fully the operation of two- and four-cycle power plants and all ignition, carburetion and lubrication systems in detail. Describes all representative types of free engine clutches, variable speed gears and power transmission systems. Gives complete instructions for operating and repairing all types. Considers fully electric self-starting and lighting systems, all types of spring frames and springs forks and shows leading control methods. For those desiring technical information a complete series of tables and many formulæ to assist in designing are included. The work tells how to figure power needed to climb grades, overcome air resistance and attain high speeds. It shows how to select gear ratios for various weights and powers, how to figure braking efficiency required, gives sizes of belts and chains to transmit power safely, and shows how to design sprockets, belt pulleys, etc. This work also includes complete formulæ for figuring horse-power, shows how dynamometer tests are made, defines relative efficiency of air- and water-cooled engines, plain and anti-friction bearings and many other data of a practical, helpful, engineering nature. Remember that you get this information in addition to the practical description and instructions which alone are worth several times the price of the book. 550 pages. 350 specially made illustrations, 5 folding plates. Cloth. Price . $1.50

CATALOGUE OF GOOD, PRACTICAL BOOKS

AUTOMOBILE AND MOTORCYCLE CHARTS

CHART. GASOLINE ENGINE TROUBLES MADE EASY—A CHART SHOWING SECTIONAL VIEW OF GASOLINE ENGINE. Compiled by VICTOR W. PAGÉ, M.E.

It shows clearly all parts of a typical four-cylinder gasoline engine of the four-cycle type. It outlines distinctly all parts liable to give trouble and also details the derangements apt to interfere with smooth engine operation.
Valuable to students, motorists, mechanics, repairmen, garagemen, automobile salesmen, chauffeurs, motorboat owners, motor-truck and tractor drivers, aviators, motorcyclists, and all others who have to do with gasoline power plants.
It simplifies location of all engine troubles, and while it will prove invaluable to the novice, it can be used to advantage by the more expert. It should be on the walls of every public and private garage, automobile repair shop, club house or school. It can be carried in the automobile or pocket with ease, and will insure against loss of time when engine trouble manifests itself.
This sectional view of engine is a complete review of all motor troubles. It is prepared by a practical motorist for all who motor. More information for the money than ever before offered. No details omitted. Size 25x38 inches. Securely mailed on receipt of . . . . **25 cents**

CHART. LOCATION OF FORD ENGINE TROUBLES MADE EASY. Compiled by VICTOR W. PAGÉ, M.E.

This shows clear sectional views depicting all portions of the Ford power plant and auxiliary groups. It outlines clearly all parts of the engine, fuel supply system, ignition group and cooling system, that are apt to give trouble, detailing all derangements that are liable to make an engine lose power, start hard or work irregularly. This chart is valuable to students, owners, and drivers, as it simplifies location of all engine faults. Of great advantage as an instructor for the novice, it can be used equally well by the more expert as a work of reference and review. It can be carried in the tool-box or pocket with ease and will save its cost in labor eliminated the first time engine trouble manifests itself. Prepared with special reference to the average man's needs and is a practical review of all motor troubles because it is based on the actual experience of an automobile engineer-mechanic with the mechanism the chart describes. It enables the non-technical owner or operator of a Ford car to locate engine derangements by systematic search, guided by easily recognized symptoms instead of by guesswork. It makes the average owner independent of the roadside repair shop when touring. Must be seen to be appreciated. Size 25x38 inches. Printed on heavy bond paper. Price . . . . **25 cents**

CHART. LUBRICATION OF THE MOTOR CAR CHASSIS. Compiled by VICTOR W. PAGÉ, M.E.

This chart presents the plan view of a typical six-cylinder chassis of standard design and all parts are clearly indicated that demand oil, also the frequency with which they must be lubricated and the kind of oil to use. A practical chart for all interested in motor-car maintenance. Size 24x38 inches. Price . . . . **25 cents**

CHART. LOCATION OF CARBURETION TROUBLES MADE EASY. Compiled by VICTOR W. PAGÉ, M.E.

This chart shows all parts of a typical pressure feed fuel supply system and gives causes of trouble, how to locate defects and means of remedying them. Size 24x38 inches. Price . . . . **25 cents**

CHART. LOCATION OF IGNITION SYSTEM TROUBLES MADE EASY. Compiled by VICTOR W. PAGÉ, M.E.

In this diagram all parts of a typical double ignition system using battery and magneto current are shown, and suggestions are given for readily finding ignition troubles and eliminating them when found. Size 24x38 inches. Price . . . . . **25 cents**

CATALOGUE OF GOOD, PRACTICAL BOOKS

CHART. LOCATION OF COOLING AND LUBRICATION SYSTEM FAULTS. Compiled by VICTOR W. PAGÉ, M.E.

This composite diagram shows a typical automobile power plant using pump circulated water-cooling system and the most popular lubrication method. Gives suggestions for curing all overheating and loss of power faults due to faulty action of the oiling or cooling group. Size 24x38 inches. Price . . . . **25 cents**

CHART. MOTORCYCLE TROUBLES MADE EASY. Compiled by VICTOR W. PAGÉ, M.E.

A chart showing sectional view of a single-cylinder gasoline engine. This chart simplifies location of all power-plant troubles. A single-cylinder motor is shown for simplicity. It outlines distinctly all parts liable to give trouble and also details the derangements apt to interfere with smooth engine operation. This chart will prove of value to all who have to do with the operation, repair or sale of motorcycles. No details omitted. Size 30x20 inches. Price . . . . **25 cents**

BRAZING AND SOLDERING

BRAZING AND SOLDERING. By JAMES F. HOBART.

The only book that shows you just how to handle any job of brazing or soldering that comes along; it tells you what mixture to use, how to make a furnace if you need one. Full of valuable kinks. The fifth edition of this book has just been published, and to it much new matter and a large number of tested formulæ for all kinds of solders and fluxes have been added. Illustrated. . . . . **25 cents**

CHARTS

GASOLINE ENGINE TROUBLES MADE EASY—A CHART SHOWING SECTIONAL VIEW OF GASOLINE ENGINE. Compiled by VICTOR W. PAGÉ.

It shows clearly all parts of a typical four-cylinder gasoline engine of the four-cycle type. It outlines distinctly all parts liable to give trouble and also details the derangements apt to interfere with smooth engine operation.
Valuable to students, motorists, mechanics, repairmen, garagemen, automobile salesmen, chauffeurs, motor-boat owners, motor-truck and tractor drivers, aviators, motorcyclists, and all others who have to do with gasoline power plants.
It simplifies location of all engine troubles, and while it will prove invaluable to the novice, it can be used to advantage by the more expert. It should be on the walls of every public and private garage, automobile repair shop, club house or school. It can be carried in the automobile or pocket with ease and will insure against loss of time when engine trouble manifests itself.
This sectional view of engine is a complete review of all motor troubles. It is prepared by a practical motorist for all who motor. No details omitted. Size 25x38 inches. . . . . **25 cents**

LUBRICATION OF THE MOTOR CAR CHASSIS.

This chart presents the plan view of a typical six-cylinder chassis of standard design and all parts are clearly indicated that demand oil, also the frequency with which they must be lubricated and the kind of oil to use. A practical chart for all interested in motor-car maintenance. Size 24x38 inches. Price . . . . **25 cents**

LOCATION OF CARBURETION TROUBLES MADE EASY.

This chart shows all parts of a typical pressure feed fuel supply system and gives causes of trouble, how to locate defects and means of remedying them. Size 24x38 inches Price . . . . **25 cents**

LOCATION OF IGNITION SYSTEM TROUBLES MADE EASY.

In this chart all parts of a typical double ignition system using battery and magneto current are shown and suggestions are given for readily finding ignition troubles and eliminating them when found. Size 24x38 inches. Price . . . . . **25 cents**

CATALOGUE OF GOOD, PRACTICAL BOOKS

LOCATION OF COOLING AND LUBRICATION SYSTEM FAULTS.
  This composite chart shows a typical automobile power plant using pump circulated water-cooling system and the most popular lubrication method. Gives suggestions for curing all overheating and loss of power faults due to faulty action of the oiling or cooling group. Size 24x38 inches. Price . . . . **25 cents**

MOTORCYCLE TROUBLES MADE EASY—A CHART SHOWING SECTIONAL VIEW OF SINGLE-CYLINDER GASOLINE ENGINE. Compiled by VICTOR W. PAGÉ.
  This chart simplifies location of all power-plant troubles, and will prove invaluable to all who have to do with the operation, repair or sale of motorcycles. No details omitted. Size 25x38 inches. Price . . . . **25 cents**

LOCATION OF FORD ENGINE TROUBLES MADE EASY. Compiled by VICTOR W. PAGÉ, M.E.
  This shows clear sectional views depicting all portions of the Ford power plant and auxiliary groups. It outlines clearly all parts of the engine, fuel supply system, ignition group and cooling system, that are apt to give trouble, detailing all derangements that are liable to make an engine lose power, start hard or work irregularly. This chart is valuable to students, owners, and drivers, as it simplifies location of all engine faults. Of great advantage as an instructor for the novice, it can be used equally well by the more expert as a work of reference and review. It can be carried in the toolbox or pocket with ease and will save its cost in labor eliminated the first time engine trouble manifests itself. Prepared with special reference to the average man's needs and is a practical review of all motor troubles because it is based on the actual experience of an automobile engineer-mechanic with the mechanism the chart describes. It enables the non-technical owner or operator of a Ford car to locate engine derangements by systematic search, guided by easily recognized symptoms instead of by guesswork. It makes the average owner independent of the roadside repair shop when touring. Must be seen to be appreciated. Size 25x38 inches. Printed on heavy bond paper. Price, ... **25 cents**

MODERN SUBMARINE CHART — WITH 200 PARTS NUMBERED AND NAMED.
  A cross-section view, showing clearly and distinctly all the interior of a Submarine of the latest type. You get more information from this chart, about the construction and operation of a Submarine, than in any other way. No details omitted—everything is accurate and to scale. It is absolutely correct in every detail, having been approved by Naval Engineers. All the machinery and devices fitted in a modern Submarine Boat are shown, and to make the engraving more readily understood, all the features are shown in operative form, with Officers and Men in the act of performing the duties assigned to them in service conditions. This CHART IS REALLY AN ENCYCLOPEDIA OF A SUBMARINE. . . . . **25 cents**

BOX CAR CHART.
  A chart showing the anatomy of a box car, having every part of the car numbered and its proper name given in a reference list. . . . . **25 cents**

GONDOLA CAR CHART.
  A chart showing the anatomy of a gondola car, having every part of the car numbered and its proper reference name given in a reference list. . . . . **25 cents**

PASSENGER-CAR CHART.
  A chart showing the anatomy of a passenger-car, having every part of the car numbered and its proper name given in a reference list. . . . . **25 cents**

STEEL HOPPER BOTTOM COAL CAR.
  A chart showing the anatomy of a steel Hopper Bottom Coal Car, having every part of the car numbered and its proper name given in a reference list. . . . . **25 cents**

CATALOGUE OF GOOD, PRACTICAL BOOKS

TRACTIVE POWER CHART.
A chart whereby you can find the tractive power or drawbar pull of any locomotive without making a figure. Shows what cylinders are equal, how driving wheels and steam pressure affect the power. What sized engine you need to exert a given drawbar pull or anything you desire in this line. . . . . **50 cents**

HORSE-POWER CHART
Shows the horse-power of any stationary engine without calculation. No matter what the cylinder diameter of stroke, the steam pressure of cut-off, the revolutions, or whether condensing or non-condensing, it's all there. Easy to use, accurate, and saves time and calculations. Especially useful to engineers and designers. **50 cents**

BOILER ROOM CHART. By GEO. L. FOWLER.
A chart—size 14x28 inches—showing in isometric perspective the mechanisms belonging in a modern boiler room. The various parts are shown broken or removed, so that the internal construction is fully illustrated. Each part is given a reference number, and these, with the corresponding name, are given in a glossary printed at the sides. This chart is really a dictionary of the boiler room—the names of more than 200 parts being given. . . . . **25 cents**

COMPRESSED AIR

COMPRESSED AIR IN ALL ITS APPLICATIONS. By GARDNER D. HISCOX.
This is the most complete book on the subject of Air that has ever been issued, and its thirty-five chapters include about every phase of the subject one can think of. It may be called an encyclopedia of compressed air. It is written by an expert, who, in its 665 pages, has dealt with the subject in a comprehensive manner, no phase of it being omitted. Includes the physical properties of air from a vacuum to its highest pressure, its thermodynamics, compression, transmission and uses as a motive power, in the Operation of Stationary and Portable Machinery, in Mining, Air Tools, Air Lifts, Pumping of Water, Acids, and Oils; the Air Blast for Cleaning and Painting, the Sand Blast and its Work, and the Numerous Appliances in which Compressed Air is a Most Convenient and Economical Transmitter of Power for Mechanical Work. Railway Propulsion, Refrigeration, and the Various Uses to which Compressed Air has been applied. Includes forty-four tables of the physical properties of air, its compression, expansion, and volumes required for various kinds of work, and a list of patents on compressed air from 1875 to date. Over 500 illustrations, 5th Edition, revised and enlarged. Cloth bound, $5.00. Half Morocco, price **$6.50**

CONCRETE

JUST PUBLISHED—CONCRETE WORKERS' REFERENCE BOOKS. A SERIES OF TWELVE POPULAR HANDBOOKS FOR CONCRETE USERS. Prepared by A. A. HOUGHTON. . . . . Each 50c.
The author, in preparing this Series, has not only treated on the usual types of construction, but explains and illustrates molds and systems that are not patented, but which are equal in value and often superior to those restricted by patents. These molds are very easily and cheaply constructed and embody simplicity, rapidity of operation, and the most successful results in the molded concrete. Each of these Twelve books is fully illustrated, and the subjects are exhaustively treated in plain English.

CONCRETE WALL FORMS. By A. A. HOUGHTON.
A new automatic wall clamp is illustrated with working drawings. Other types of wall forms, clamps, separators, etc., are also illustrated and explained. (No. 1 of Series) . . . . **50 cents**

CONCRETE FLOORS AND SIDEWALKS. By A. A. HOUGHTON.
The molds for molding squares, hexagonal and many other styles of mosaic floor and sidewalk blocks are fully illustrated and explained. (No. 2 of Series) . . **50 cents**

PRACTICAL CONCRETE SILO CONSTRUCTION. By A. A. HOUGHTON.
Complete working drawings and specifications are given for several styles of concrete silos, with illustrations of molds for monolithic and block silos. The tables, data, and information presented in this book are of the utmost value in planning and constructing all forms of concrete silos. (No. 3 of Series) . . . . **50 cents**

CATALOGUE OF GOOD, PRACTICAL BOOKS

MOLDING CONCRETE CHIMNEYS, SLATE AND ROOF TILES. By A. A. HOUGHTON.
The manufacture of all types of concrete slate and roof tile is fully treated. Valuable data on all forms of reinforced concrete roofs are contained within its pages. The construction of concrete chimneys by block and monolithic systems is fully illustrated and described. A number of ornamental designs of chimney construction with molds are shown in this valuable treatise. (No. 4 of Series.) . . . . **50 cents**

MOLDING AND CURING ORNAMENTAL CONCRETE. By A. A. HOUGHTON.
The proper proportions of cement and aggregates for various finishes, also the method of thoroughly mixing and placing in the molds, are fully treated. An exhaustive treatise on this subject that every concrete worker will find of daily use and value (No. 5 of Series.) . . . . **50 cents**

CONCRETE MONUMENTS, MAUSOLEUMS AND BURIAL VAULTS. By A. A. HOUGHTON.
The molding of concrete monuments to imitate the most expensive cut stone is explained in this treatise, with working drawings of easily built molds. Cutting inscriptions and designs is also fully treated. (No. 6 of Series.) . . . . **50 cents**

MOLDING CONCRETE BATHTUBS, AQUARIUMS AND NATATORIUMS. By A. A. HOUGHTON.
Simple molds and instruction are given for molding many styles of concrete bathtubs, swimming-pools, etc. These molds are easily built and permit rapid and successful work. (No. 7 of Series.) . . . . **50 cents**

CONCRETE BRIDGES, CULVERTS AND SEWERS. By A. A. HOUGHTON.
A number of ornamental concrete bridges with illustrations of molds are given. A collapsible center or core for bridges, culverts and sewers is fully illustrated with detailed instructions for building. (No. 8 of Series.) . . . . **50 cents**

CONSTRUCTING CONCRETE PORCHES. By A. A. HOUGHTON.
A number of designs with working drawings of molds are fully explained so any one can easily construct different styles of ornamental concrete porches without the purchase of expensive molds. (No. 9 of Series.) . . . . **50 cents**

MOLDING CONCRETE FLOWER-POTS, BOXES, JARDINIERES, ETC. By A. A. HOUGHTON.
The molds for producing many original designs of flower-pots, urns, flower-boxes, jardinieres, etc., are fully illustrated and explained, so the worker can easily construct and operate same. (No. 10 of Series.) . . . . **50 cents**

MOLDING CONCRETE FOUNTAINS AND LAWN ORNAMENTS. By A. A. HOUGHTON.
The molding of a number of designs of lawn seats, curbing, hitching posts, pergolas, sun dials and other forms of ornamental concrete for the ornamentation of lawns and gardens, is fully illustrated and described. (No. 11 of Series) . . . . . . **50 cents**

CONCRETE FROM SAND MOLDS. By A. A. HOUGHTON.
A Practical Work treating on a process which has heretofore been held as a trade secret by the few who possessed it, and which will successfully mold every and any class of ornamental concrete work. The process of molding concrete with sand molds is of the utmost practical value, possessing the manifold advantages of a low cost of molds, the ease and rapidity of operation, perfect details to all ornamental designs, density and increased strength of the concrete, perfect curing of the work without attention and the easy removal of the molds regardless of any undercutting the design may have. 192 pages. Fully illustrated. Price **$2.00**

ORNAMENTAL CONCRETE WITHOUT MOLDS. By A. A. HOUGHTON.
The process for making ornamental concrete without molds has long been held as a secret, and now, for the first time, this process is given to the public. The book reveals the secret and is the only book published which explains a simple, practical

CATALOGUE OF GOOD, PRACTICAL BOOKS

method whereby the concrete worker is enabled, by employing wood and metal templates of different designs, to mold or model in concrete any Cornice, Archivolt, Column, Pedestal, Base Cap, Urn or Pier in a monolithic form—right upon the job. These may be molded in units or blocks, and then built up to suit the specifications demanded. This work is fully illustrated, with detailed engravings. Price . $2.00

POPULAR HANDBOOK FOR CEMENT AND CONCRETE USERS. By MYRON H. LEWIS.

This is a concise treatise of the principles and methods employed in the manufacture and use of cement in all classes of modern works. The author has brought together in this work all the salient matter of interest to the user of concrete and its many diversified products. The matter is presented in logical and systematic order, clearly written, fully illustrated and free from involved mathematics. Everything of value to the concrete user is given, including kinds of cement employed in construction, concrete architecture, inspection and testing, waterproofing, coloring and painting, rules, tables, working and cost data. The book comprises thirty-three chapters, as follows: Introductory. Kinds of Cements and How They are Made. Properties. Testing and Requirements of Hydraulic Cement. Concrete and its Properties. Sand, Broken Stone and Gravel for Concrete. How to Proportion the Materials. How to Mix and Place Concrete. Forms of Concrete Construction. The Architectural and Artistic Possibilities of Concrete. Concrete Residences. Mortars, Plasters and Stucco, and How to Use them. The Artistic Treatment of Concrete Surfaces. Concrete Building Blocks. The Making of Ornamental Concrete. Concrete Pipes, Fences, Posts, etc. Essential Features and Advantages of Reenforced Concrete. How to Design Reenforced Concrete Beams, Slabs and Columns. Explanations of the Methods and Principles in Designing Reenforced Concrete Beams and Slabs. Systems of Reenforcement Employed. Reenforced Concrete in Factory and General Building Construction. Concrete in Foundation Work. Concrete Retaining Walls, Abutments and Bulkheads. Concrete Arches and Arch Bridges. Concrete Beam and Girder Bridges. Concrete in Sewerage and Drainage Works. Concrete Tanks, Dams and Reservoirs. Concrete Sidewalks, Curbs and Pavements. Concrete in Railroad Constructions. The Utility of Concrete on the Farm. The Waterproofing of Concrete Structure. Grout of Liquid Concrete and Its Use. Inspection of Concrete Work. Cost of Concrete Work. Some of the special features of the book are: 1. The Attention Paid to the Artistic and Architectural Side of Concrete Work. 2. The Authoritative Treatment of the Problem of Waterproofing Concrete. 3. An Excellent Summary of the Rules to be Followed in Concrete Construction. 4. The Valuable Cost Data and Useful Tables given. A valuable Addition to the Library of Every Cement and Concrete User. Price $2.50

WHAT IS SAID OF THIS BOOK:

"The field of Concrete Construction is well covered and the matter contained is well within the understanding of any person."—*Engineering-Contracting.*
"Should be on the bookshelves of every contractor, engineer, and architect in the land."—*National Builder.*

WATERPROOFING CONCRETE. By MYRON H. LEWIS.

Modern Methods of Waterproofing Concrete and Other Structures. A condensed statement of the Principles, Rules, and Precautions to be Observed in Waterproofing and Dampproofing Structures and Structural Materials. Paper binding. Illustrated. Price . . . . 50 cents

DICTIONARIES

STANDARD ELECTRICAL DICTIONARY. By T. O'CONOR SLOANE.

An indispensable work to all interested in electrical science. Suitable alike for the student and professional. A practical handbook of reference containing definitions of about 5000 distinct words, terms and phrases. The definitions are terse and concise and include every term used in electrical science. Recently issued. An entirely new edition. Should be in the possession of all who desire to keep abreast with the progress of this branch of science. Complete, concise and convenient. 682 pages. 393 illustrations. Price $3.00

CATALOGUE OF GOOD, PRACTICAL BOOKS

DIES—METAL WORK

DIES: THEIR CONSTRUCTION AND USE FOR THE MODERN WORKING OF SHEET METALS. By J. V. Woodworth.
A most useful book, and one which should be in the hands of all engaged in the press working of metals; treating on the Designing, Constructing, and Use of Tools, Fixtures and Devices, together with the manner in which they should be used in the Power Press, for the cheap and rapid production of the great variety of sheet-metal articles now in use. It is designed as a guide to the production of sheet-metal parts at the minimum of cost with the maximum of output. The hardening and tempering of Press tools and the classes of work which may be produced to the best advantage by the use of dies in the power press are fully treated. Its 505 illustrations show dies, press fixtures and sheet-metal working devices, the descriptions of which are so clear and practical that all metal-working mechanics will be able to understand how to design, construct and use them. Many of the dies and press fixtures treated were either constructed by the author or under his supervision. Others were built by skilful mechanics and are in use in large sheet-metal establishments and machine shops. 5th Edition. Price $3.00

PUNCHES, DIES AND TOOLS FOR MANUFACTURING IN PRESSES. By J. V. Woodworth.
This work is a companion volume to the author's elementary work entitled "Dies, Their Construction and Use." It does not go into the details of die-making to the extent of the author's previous book, but gives a comprehensive review of the field of operations carried on by presses. A large part of the information given has been drawn from the author's personal experience. It might well be termed an Encyclopedia of Die-Making, Punch-Making, Die-Sinking, Sheet-Metal Working, and Making of Special Tools, Sub-presses, Devices and Mechanical Combinations for Punching, Cutting, Bending, Forming, Piercing, Drawing, Compressing and Assembling Sheet-Metal Parts, and also Articles of other Materials in Machine Tools. 2d Edition. Price $4.00

DROP FORGING, DIE-SINKING AND MACHINE-FORMING OF STEEL. By J. V. Woodworth.
This is a practical treatise on Modern Shop Practice, Processes, Methods, Machine Tools, and Details treating on the Hot and Cold Machine-Forming of Steel and Iron into Finished Shapes; together with Tools, Dies, and Machinery involved in the manufacture of Duplicate Forgings and Interchangeable Hot and Cold Pressed Parts from Bar and Sheet Metal. This Book fills a demand of long standing for information regarding drop-forgings, die-sinking and machine-forming of steel and the shop practice involved, as it actually exists in the modern drop-forging shop. The processes of die-sinking and force-making, which are thoroughly described and illustrated in this admirable work, are rarely to be found explained in such a clear and concise manner as is here set forth. The process of die-sinking relates to the engraving or sinking of the female or lower dies, such as are used for drop-forgings, hot and cold machine forging, swedging and the press working of metals. The process of force-making relates to the engraving or raising of the male or upper dies used in producing the lower dies for the press-forming and machine-forming of duplicate parts of metal. In addition to the arts above mentioned the book contains explicit information regarding the drop-forging and hardening plants, designs, conditions, equipment, drop hammers, forging machines, etc., machine forging, hydraulic forging, autogenous welding and shop practice. The book contains eleven chapters, and the information contained in these chapters is just what will prove most valuable to the forged-metal worker. All operations described in the work are thoroughly illustrated by means of perspective half-tones and outline sketches of the machinery employed. 300 detailed illustrations. Price. $2.50

DRAWING—SKETCHING PAPER

PRACTICAL PERSPECTIVE. By Richards and Colvin.
Shows just how to make all kinds of mechanical drawings in the only practical perspective isometric. Makes everything plain so that any mechanic can understand a sketch or drawing in this way. Saves time in the drawing room, and mistakes in the shops. Contains practical examples of various classes of work. 3d Edition. **50 cents**

CATALOGUE OF GOOD, PRACTICAL BOOKS

LINEAR PERSPECTIVE SELF-TAUGHT. By HERMAN T. C. KRAUS.

This work gives the theory and practice of linear perspective, as used in architectural, engineering and mechanical drawings. Persons taking up the study of the subject by themselves will be able, by the use of the instruction given, to readily grasp the subject, and by reasonable practice become good perspective draftsmen. The arrangement of the book is good; the plate is on the left-hand, while the descriptive text follows on the opposite page, so as to be readily referred to. The drawings are on sufficiently large scale to show the work clearly and are plainly figured. There is included a self-explanatory chart which gives all information necessary for the thorough understanding of perspective. This chart alone is worth many times over the price of the book. 2d Revised and enlarged Edition. $2.50

SELF-TAUGHT MECHANICAL DRAWING AND ELEMENTARY MACHINE DESIGN. By F. L. SYLVESTER, M.E., Draftsman, with additions by ERIK OBERG, associate editor of "Machinery."

This is a practical treatise on Mechanical Drawing, and Machine Design, comprising the first principles of geometric and mechanical drawing, workshop mathematics, mechanics, strength of materials and the calculations and design of machine details. The author's aim has been to adapt this treatise to the requirements of the practical mechanic and young draftsman and to present the matter in as clear and concise a manner as possible. To meet the demands of this class of students, practically all the important elements of machine design have been dealt with, and in addition algebraic formulas have been explained, and the elements of trigonometry treated in the manner best suited to the needs of the practical man. The book is divided into 20 chapters, and in arranging the material, mechanical drawing, pure and simple, has been taken up first, as a thorough understanding of the principles of representing objects facilitates the further study of mechanical subjects. This is followed by the mathematics necessary for the solution of the problems in machine design which are presented later, and a practical introduction to theoretical mechanics and the strength of materials. The various elements entering into machine design, such as cams, gears, sprocket-wheels, cone pulleys, bolts, screws, couplings, clutches, shafting and fly-wheels, have been treated in such a way as to make possible the use of the work as a text-book for a continuous course of study. It is easily comprehended and assimilated even by students of limited previous training. 330 pages, 215 engravings. Price . . $2.00

A NEW SKETCHING PAPER.

A new specially ruled paper to enable you to make sketches or drawings in isometric perspective without any figuring or fussing. It is being used for shop details as well as for assembly drawings, as it makes one sketch do the work of three, and no workman can help seeing just what is wanted. Pads of 40 sheets, 6x9 inches, **25 cents.** Pads of 40 sheets, 9x12 inches, **50 cents**; 40 sheets, 12x18, Price $1.00

ELECTRICITY

ARITHMETIC OF ELECTRICITY. By Prof. T. O'CONOR SLOANE.

A practical treatise on electrical calculations of all kinds reduced to a series of rules, all of the simplest forms, and involving only ordinary arithmetic; each rule illustrated by one or more practical problems, with detailed solution of each one. This book is classed among the most useful works published on the science of electricity, covering as it does the mathematics of electricity in a manner that will attract the attention of those who are not familiar with algebraical formulas. 20th Edition. 160 pages. Price $1.00

COMMUTATOR CONSTRUCTION. By WM. BAXTER, JR.

The business end of any dynamo or motor of the direct current type is the commutator. This book goes into the designing, building, and maintenance of commutators, shows how to locate troubles and how to remedy them; everyone who fusses with dynamos needs this. 4th Edition . . . . 25 cents

CATALOGUE OF GOOD, PRACTICAL BOOKS

DYNAMO BUILDING FOR AMATEURS, OR HOW TO CONSTRUCT A FIFTY-WATT DYNAMO. By ARTHUR J. WEED, Member of N. Y. Electrical Society.

A practical treatise showing in detail the construction of a small dynamo or motor, the entire machine work of which can be done on a small foot lathe. Dimensioned working drawings are given for each piece of machine work, and each operation is clearly described. This machine, when used as a dynamo, has an output of fifty watts; when used as a motor it will drive a small drill press or lathe. It can be used to drive a sewing machine on any and all ordinary work. The book is illustrated with more than sixty original engravings showing the actual construction of the different parts. Among the contents are chapters on: 1. Fifty-Watt Dynamo. 2. Side Bearing Rods. 3. Field Punching. 4. Bearings. 5. Commutator. 6. Pulley. 7. Brush Holders. 8. Connection Board. 9. Armature Shaft. 10. Armature. 11. Armature Winding. 12. Field Winding. 13. Connecting and Starting. Price, paper, 50 cents. Cloth **$1.00**

ELECTRIC WIRING, DIAGRAMS AND SWITCHBOARDS. By NEWTON HARRISON.

A thoroughly practical treatise covering the subject of Electric Wiring in all its branches, including explanations and diagrams which are thoroughly explicit and greatly simplify the subject. Practical, every-day problems in wiring are presented and the method of obtaining intelligent results clearly shown. Only arithmetic is used. Ohm's law is given a simple explanation with reference to wiring for direct and alternating currents. The fundamental principle of drop of potential in circuits is shown with its various applications. The simple circuit is developed with the position of mains, feeders and branches; their treatment as a part of a wiring plan and their employment in house wiring clearly illustrated. Some simple facts about testing are included in connection with the wiring. Molding and conduit work are given careful consideration; and switchboards are systematically treated, built up and illustrated, showing the purpose they serve, for connection with the circuits, and to shunt and compound wound machines. The simple principles of switchboard construction, the development of the switchboard, the connections of the various instruments, including the lightning arrester, are also plainly set forth.

Alternating current wiring is treated, with explanations of the power factor, conditions calling for various sizes of wire, and a simple way of obtaining the sizes for single-phase, two-phase and three-phase circuits. This is the only complete work issued showing and telling you what you should know about direct and alternating current wiring. It is a ready reference. The work is free from advanced technicalities and mathematics, arithmetic being used throughout. It is in every respect a handy, well-written, instructive, comprehensive volume on wiring for the wireman, foreman, contractor, or electrician. 272 pages; 105 illustrations. Price **$1.50**

ELECTRIC TOY MAKING, DYNAMO BUILDING, AND ELECTRIC MOTOR CONSTRUCTION. By Prof. T. O'CONOR SLOANE.

This work treats of the making at home of electrical toys, electrical apparatus, motors, dynamos and instruments in general, and is designed to bring within the reach of young and old the manufacture of genuine and useful electrical appliances. The work is especially designed for amateurs and young folks.

Thousands of our young people are daily experimenting, and busily engaged in making electrical toys and apparatus of various kinds. The present work is just what is wanted to give the much needed information in a plain, practical manner, with illustrations to make easy the carrying out of the work. 20th Edition. Price **$1.00**

PRACTICAL ELECTRICITY. By Prof. T. O'CONOR SLOANE.

This work of 768 pages was previously known as Sloane's Electricians' Hand Book, and is intended for the practical electrician who has to make things go. The entire field of electricity is covered within its pages. Among some of the subjects treated are: The Theory of the Electric Current and Circuit, Electro-Chemistry, Primary Batteries, Storage Batteries, Generation and Utilization of Electric Powers, Alternating Current, Armature Winding, Dynamos and Motors, Motor Generators, Operation of the Central Station Switchboards, Safety Appliances, Distribution of Electric Light and Power, Street Mains, Transformers, Arc and Incandescent Lighting, Electric Measurements, Photometry, Electric Railways, Telephony, Bell-Wiring, Electric-Plating, Electric Heating, Wireless Telegraphy, etc. It contains no useless theory; everything is to the point. It teaches you just what you want to know about electricity. It is the standard work published on the subject. Forty-one chapters, 556 engravings. Price **$2.50**

II

CATALOGUE OF GOOD, PRACTICAL BOOKS

ELECTRICITY SIMPLIFIED. By Prof. T. O'Conor Sloane.

The object of "Electricity Simplified" is to make the subject as plain as possible and to show what the modern conception of electricity is; to show how two plates of different metal, immersed in acid, can send a message around the globe; to explain how a bundle of copper wire rotated by a steam engine can be the agent in lighting our streets, to tell what the volt, ohm and ampere are, and what high and low tension mean; and to answer the questions that perpetually arise in the mind in this age of electricity. 13th Edition. 172 pages. Illustrated. Price $1.00

HOUSE WIRING. By Thomas W. Poppe.

This work describes and illustrates the actual installation of Electric Light Wiring, the manner in which the work should be done, and the method of doing it. The book can be conveniently carried in the pocket. It is intended for the Electrician, Helper and Apprentice. It solves all Wiring Problems and contains nothing that conflicts with the rulings of the National Board of Fire Underwriters. It gives just the information essential to the Successful Wiring of a Building. Among the subjects treated are: Locating the Meter. Panel Boards. Switches. Plug Receptacles. Brackets. Ceiling Fixtures. The Meter Connections. The Feed Wires. The Steel Armored Cable System. The Flexible Steel Conduit System. The Ridig Conduit System. A digest of the National Board of Fire Underwriters' rules relating to metallic wiring systems. Various switching arrangements explained and diagrammed. The easiest method of testing the Three- and Four-way circuits explained. The grounding of all metallic wiring systems and the reason for doing so shown and explained. The insulation of the metal parts of lamp fixtures and the reason for the same described and illustrated. 125 pages. Fully illustrated. Flexible cloth. Price . . . . 50 cents

WHAT IS SAID OF THIS BOOK:

"The information given is exact and exhaustive without being too technical or overladen with details."—*Druggists' Circular.*

HOW TO BECOME A SUCCESSFUL ELECTRICIAN. By Prof. T. O'Conor Sloane.

Every young man who wishes to become a successful electrician should read this book. It tells in simple language the surest and easiest way to become a successful electrician. The studies to be followed, methods of work, field of operation and the requirements of the successful electrician are pointed out and fully explained. Every young engineer will find this an excellent stepping stone to more advanced works on electricity which he must master before success can be attained. Many young men become discouraged at the very outstart by attempting to read and study books that are far beyond their comprehension. This book serves as the connecting link between the rudiments taught in the public schools and the real study of electricity. It is interesting from cover to cover. Eighteenth Revised Edition, just issued. 205 pages. Illustrated. Price $1.00

STANDARD ELECTRICAL DICTIONARY. By T. O'Conor Sloane.

An indispensable work to all interested in electrical science. Suitable alike for the student and professional. A practical handbook of reference containing definitions of about 5,000 distinct words, terms and phrases. The definitions are terse and concise and include every term used in electrical science. Recently issued. An entirely new edition. Should be in the possession of all who desire to keep abreast with the progress of this branch of science. In its arrangement and typography the book is very convenient. The word or term defined is printed in black-faced type which readily catches the eye, while the body of the page is in smaller but distinct type. The definitions are well worded, and so as to be understood by the non-technical reader. The general plan seems to be to give an exact, concise definition, and then amplify and explain in a more popular way. Synonyms are also given, and references to other words and phrases are made. A very complete and accurate index of fifty pages is at the end of the volume; and as this index contains all synonyms, and as all phrases are indexed in every reasonable combination of words, reference to the proper place in the body of the book is readily made. It is difficult to decide how far a book of this character is to keep the dictionary form, and to what extent it may assume the encyclopedia form. For some purposes, concise, exactly worded definitions are needed; for other purposes, more extended descriptions are required. This book seeks to satisfy both demands, and does it with considerable success. Complete, concise and convenient. 682 pages. 393 illustrations. Twelfth Edition. Price $3.00

CATALOGUE OF GOOD, PRACTICAL BOOKS

SWITCHBOARDS. By WILLIAM BAXTER, JR.

This book appeals to every engineer and electrician who wants to know the practical side of things. It takes up all sorts and conditions of dynamos, connections and circuits, and shows by diagram and illustration just how the switchboard should be connected. Includes direct and alternating current boards, also those for arc lighting, incandescent and power circuits. Special treatment on high voltage boards for power transmission. 2d Edition. 190 pages. Illustrated. Price $1.50

TELEPHONE CONSTRUCTION, INSTALLATION, WIRING, OPERATION AND MAINTENANCE. By W. H. RADCLIFFE and H. C. CUSHING.

This book is intended for the amateur, the wireman, or the engineer who desires to establish a means of telephonic communication between the rooms of his home, office, or shop. It deals only with such things as may be of use to him rather than with theories.

Gives the principles of construction and operation of both the Bell and Independent instruments; approved methods of installing and wiring them; the means of protecting them from lightning and abnormal currents; their connection together for operation as series or bridging stations; and rules for their inspection and maintenance. Line wiring and the wiring and operation of special telephone systems are also treated.

Intricate mathematics are avoided, and all apparatus, circuits and systems are thoroughly described. The appendix contains definitions of units and terms used in the text. Selected wiring tables, which are very helpful, are also included. Among the subjects treated are Construction, Operation, and Installation of Telephone Instruments; Inspection and Maintenance of Telephone Instruments; Telephone Line Wiring; Testing Telephone Line Wires and Cables; Wiring and Operation of Special Telephone Systems, etc. 100 pages. 125 illustrations $1.00

WIRELESS TELEGRAPHY AND TELEPHONY SIMPLY EXPLAINED. By ALFRED P. MORGAN.

This is undoubtedly one of the most complete and comprehensible treatises on the subject ever published, and a close study of its pages will enable one to master all the details of the wireless transmission of messages. The author has filled a long-felt want and has succeeded in furnishing a lucid, comprehensible explanation in simple language of the theory and practice of wireless telegraphy and telephony.

Among the contents are: Introductory; Wireless Transmission and Reception—The Aerial System, Earth Connections—The Transmitting Apparatus, Spark Coils and Transformers, Condensers, Helixes, Spark Gaps, Anchor Gaps, Aerial Switches—The Receiving Apparatus, Detectors, etc.—Tuning and Coupling, Tuning Coils, Loose Couplers, Variable Condensers, Directive Wave Systems—Miscellaneous Apparatus, Telephone Receivers, Range of Stations, Static Interference—Wireless Telephones, Sound and Sound Waves, The Vocal Cords and Ear—Wireless Telephone, How Sounds Are Changed into Electric Waves—Wireless Telephones, The Apparatus—Summary. 154 pages. 156 engravings. Price $1.00

WHAT IS SAID OF THIS BOOK:

"This book should be in both the home and school library."—*The Youths' Instructor.*

WIRING A HOUSE. By HERBERT PRATT.

Shows a house already built; tells just how to start about wiring it; where to begin; what wire to use; how to run it according to Insurance Rules; in fact, just the information you need. Directions apply equally to a shop. Fourth edition . . **25 cents**

FACTORY MANAGEMENT, ETC.

MODERN MACHINE SHOP CONSTRUCTION, EQUIPMENT AND MANAGEMENT. By O. E. PERRIGO, M.E.

The only work published that describes the modern machine shop or manufacturing plant from the time the grass is growing on the site intended for it until the finished product is shipped. By a careful study of its thirty-two chapters the practical man may economically build, efficiently equip, and successfully manage the modern machine shop or manufacturing establishment. Just the book needed by those contemplating

CATALOGUE OF GOOD, PRACTICAL BOOKS

the erection of modern shop buildings, the rebuilding and reorganization of old ones, or the introduction of modern shop methods, time amd cost systems. It is a book written and illustrated by a practical shop man for practical shop men who are too busy to read *theories* and want *facts*. It is the most complete all-around book of its kind ever published. It is a practical book for practical men, from the apprentice in the shop to the president in the office. It minutely describes and illustrates the most simple and yet the most efficient time and cost system yet devised. Price . $5.00

FUEL

COMBUSTION OF COAL AND THE PREVENTION OF SMOKE. By WM. M. BARR.

This book has been prepared with special reference to the generation of heat by the combustion of the common fuels found in the United States, and deals particularly with the conditions necessary to the economic and smokeless combustion of bituminous coals in Stationary and Locomotive Steam Boilers.

The presentation of this important subject is systematic and progressive. The arrangement of the book is in a series of practical questions to which are appended accurate answers, which describe in language, free from technicalities, the several processes involved in the furnace combustion of American fuels; it clearly states the essential requisites for perfect combustion, and points out the best methods for furnace construction for obtaining the greatest quantity of heat from any given quality of coal. Nearly 350 pages, fully illustrated. Price $1.00

GAS ENGINES AND GAS

THE GASOLINE ENGINE ON THE FARM: ITS OPERATION, REPAIR AND USES. By XENO W. PUTNAM.

This is a practical treatise on the Gasoline and Kerosene Engine intended for the man who wants to know just how to manage his engine and how to apply it to all kinds of farm work to the best advantage.

This book abounds with hints and helps for the farm and suggestions for the home and housewife. There is so much of value in this book that it is impossible to adequately describe it in such small space. Suffice to say that it is the kind of a book every farmer will appreciate and every farm home ought to have. Includes selecting the most suitable engine for farm work, its most convenient and efficient installation, with chapters on troubles, their remedies, and how to avoid them. The care and management of the farm tractor in plowing, harrowing, harvesting and road grading are fully covered; also plain directions are given for handling the tractor on the road. Special attention is given to relieving farm life of its drudgery by applying power to the disagreeable small tasks which must otherwise be done by hand. Many home-made contrivances for cutting wood, supplying kitchen, garden, and barn with water, loading, hauling and unloading hay, delivering grain to the bins or the feed trough are included; also full directions for making the engine milk the cows, churn, wash, sweep the house and clean the windows, etc. Very fully illustrated with drawings of working parts and cuts showing Stationary, Portable and Tractor Engines doing all kinds of farm work. All money-making farms utilize power. Learn how to utilize power by reading the pages of this book. It is an aid to the result getter, invaluable to the up-to-date farmer, student, blacksmith, implement dealer and, in fact, all who can apply practical knowledge of stationary gasoline engines or gas tractors to advantage. 530 pages. Nearly 180 engravings. Price $2.00

WHAT IS SAID OF THIS BOOK:

"Am much pleased with the book and find it to be very complete and up-to-date. I will heartily recommend it to students and farmers whom I think would stand in need of such a work, as I think it is an exceptionally good one."—*N. S. Gardiner*, Prof. in Charge, Clemson Agr. College of S. C.; Dept. of Agri. and Agri. Exp. Station, Clemson College, S. C.

"I feel that Mr. Putnam's book covers the main points which a farmer should know." —*R. T. Burdick*, Instructor in Agronomy, University of Vermont, Burlington, Vt.

"It will be a valuable addition to our library upon Farm Machinery."—*James A. Farra*, Inst. in Agri. Engineering, State University of Ky., Lexington, Ky.

CATALOGUE OF GOOD, PRACTICAL BOOKS

GASOLINE ENGINES: THEIR OPERATION, USE AND CARE. By A. HYATT VERRILL.

The simplest, latest and most comprehensive popular work published on Gasoline Engines, describing what the Gasoline Engine is; its construction and operation; how to install it; how to select it; how to use it and how to remedy troubles encountered. Intended for Owners, Operators and Users of Gasoline Motors of all kinds. This work fully describes and illustrates the various types of Gasoline Engines used in Motor Boats, Motor Vehicles and Stationary Work. The parts, accessories and appliances are described, with chapters on ignition, fuel, lubrication, operation and engine troubles. Special attention is given to the care, operation and repair of motors, with useful hints and suggestions on emergency repairs and makeshifts. A complete glossary of technical terms and an alphabetically arranged table of troubles and their symptoms form most valuable and unique features of this manual. Nearly every illustration in the book is original, having been made by the author. Every page is full of interest and value. A book which you cannot afford to be without. 275 pages. 152 specially made engravings. Price $1.50

GAS, GASOLINE, AND OIL ENGINES. By GARDNER D. HISCOX.

Just issued, 1915 revised and enlarged edition. Every user of a gas engine needs this book. Simple, instructive, and right up-to-date. The only complete work on the subject. Tells all about the running and management of gas, gasoline and oil engines, as designed and manufactured in the United States. Explosive motors for stationary marine and vehicle power are fully treated, together with illustrations of their parts and tabulated sizes, also their care and running are included. Electric ignition by induction coil and jump spark are fully explained and illustrated, including valuable information on the testing for economy and power and the erection of power plants.

The rules and regulations of the Board of Fire Underwriters in regard to the installation and management of gasoline motors is given in full, suggesting the safe installation of explosive motor power. A list of United States Patents issued on gas, gasoline, and oil engines and their adjuncts from 1875 to date is included. 484 pages. 410 engravings. Price $2.50

GAS ENGINE CONSTRUCTION, OR HOW TO BUILD A HALF-HORSE-POWER GAS ENGINE. By PARSELL and WEED.

A practical treatise of 300 pages describing the theory and principles of the action of Gas Engines of various types and the design and construction of a half-horse-power Gas Engine, with illustrations of the work in actual progress, together with the dimensioned working drawings, giving clearly the sizes of the various details; for the student, the scientific investigator, and the amateur mechanic. This book treats of the subject more from the standpoint of practice than that of theory. The principles of operation of Gas Engines are clearly and simply described, and then the actual construction of a half-horse-power engine is taken up, step by step, showing in detail the making of the Gas Engine. 3d Edition. 300 pages. Price $2.50

HOW TO RUN AND INSTALL GASOLINE ENGINES. By C. VON CULIN.

1915 revised and enlarged edition just issued. The object of this little book is to furnish a pocket instructor for the beginner, the busy man who uses an engine for pleasure or profit, but who does not have the time or inclination for a technical book, but simply to thoroughly understand how to properly operate, install and care for his own engine. The index refers to each trouble, remedy, and subject alphabetically. Being a quick reference to find the cause, remedy and prevention for troubles, and to become an expert with his own engine. Pocket size. Paper binding. Price . . 25 cents

MODERN GAS ENGINES AND PRODUCER GAS PLANTS. By R. E. MATHOT.

A guide for the gas engine designer, user, and engineer in the construction, selection, purchase, installation, operation, and maintenance of gas engines. More than one book on gas engines has been written, but not one has thus far even encroached on the field covered by this book. Above all Mr. Mathot's work is a practical guide. Recognizing the need of a volume that would assist the gas engine user in understanding thoroughly the motor upon which he depends for power, the author has discussed his subject without the help of any mathematics and without elaborate theoretical explanations. Every part of the gas engine is described in detail, tersely, clearly, with a thorough understanding of the requirements of the mechanic. Helpful suggestions as to the purchase of an engine, its installation, care, and operation, form a most valuable feature of the work. 320 pages. 175 detailed illustrations. Price . $2.50

CATALOGUE OF GOOD, PRACTICAL BOOKS

THE MODERN GAS TRACTOR. By VICTOR W. PAGÉ.

A complete treatise describing all types and sizes of gasoline, kerosene and oil tractors. Considers design and construction exhaustively, gives complete instructions for care, operation and repair, outlines all practical applications on the road and in the field. The best and latest work on farm tractors and tractor power plants. A work needed by farmers, students, blacksmiths, mechanics, salesmen, implement dealers, designers and engineers. 500 pages. Nearly 300 illustrations and folding plates. Price **$2.00**

GEARING AND CAMS

BEVEL GEAR TABLES. By D. AG. ENGSTROM.

A book that will at once commend itself to mechanics and draftsmen. Does away with all the trigonometry and fancy figuring on bevel gears, and makes it easy for anyone to lay them out or make them just right. There are 36 full-page tables that show every necessary dimension for all sizes or combinations you're apt to need. No puzzling, figuring or guessing. Gives placing distance, all the angles (including cutting angles), and the correct cutter to use. A copy of this prepares you for anything in the bevel-gear line. 3d Edition. 66 pages. **$1.00**

CHANGE GEAR DEVICES. By OSCAR E. PERRIGO.

A practical book for every designer, draftsman, and mechanic interested in the invention and development of the devices for feed changes on the different machines requiring such mechanism. All the necessary information on this subject is taken up, analyzed, classified, sifted, and concentrated for the use of busy men who have not the time to go through the masses of irrelevant matter with which such a subject is usually encumbered and select such information as will be useful to them.
It shows just what has been done, how it has been done, when it was done, and who did it. It saves time in hunting up patent records and re-inventing old ideas. 88 pages. **$1.00**

DRAFTING OF CAMS. By LOUIS ROUILLION.

The laying out of cams is a serious problem unless you know how to go at it right. This puts you on the right road for practically any kind of cam you are likely to run up against. 3d Edition. . . . . **25 cents**

HYDRAULICS

HYDRAULIC ENGINEERING. By GARDNER D. HISCOX.

A treatise on the properties, power, and resources of water for all purposes. Including the measurement of streams, the flow of water in pipes or conduits; the horse-power of falling water, turbine and impact water-wheels, wave motors, centrifugal, reciprocating and air-lift pumps. With 300 figures and diagrams and 36 practical tables. All who are interested in water-works development will find this book a useful one, because it is an entirely practical treatise upon a subject of present importance, and cannot fail in having a far-reaching influence, and for this reason should have a place in the working library of every engineer. Among the subjects treated are: Historical Hydraulics, Properties of Water, Measurement of the Flow of Streams; Flow from Sub-surface Orifices and Nozzles; Flow of Water in Pipes; Siphons of Various Kinds; Dams and Great Storage Reservoirs; City and Town Water Supply; Wells and Their Reinforcement; Air Lift Methods of Raising Water; Artesian Wells; Irrigation of Arid Districts; Water Power; Water Wheels; Pumps and Pumping Machinery; Reciprocating Pumps; Hydraulic Power Transmission; Hydraulic Mining; Canals; Ditches; Conduits and Pipe Lines; Marine Hydraulics; Tidal and Sea Wave Power, etc. 320 pages. Price **$4.00**

INVENTIONS—PATENTS

INVENTORS' MANUAL, HOW TO MAKE A PATENT PAY.

This is a book designed as a guide to inventors in perfecting their inventions, taking out their patents and disposing of them. It is not in any sense a Patent Solicitor's

CATALOGUE OF GOOD, PRACTICAL BOOKS

Circular nor a Patent Broker's Advertisement. No advertisements of any description appear in the work. It is a book containing a quarter of a century's experience of a successful inventor, together with notes based upon the experience of many other inventors.

Among the subjects treated in this work are: How to Invent. How to Secure a Good Patent. Value of Good Invention. How to Exhibit an Invention. How to Interest Capital. How to Estimate the Value of a Patent. Value of Design Patents. Value of Foreign Patents. Value of Small Inventions. Advice on Selling Patents. Advice on the Formation of Stock Companies. Advice on the Formation of Limited Liability Companies. Advice on Disposing of Old Patents. Advice as to Patent Attorneys. Advice as to Selling Agents. Forms of Assignments. License and Contracts. State Laws Concerning Patent Rights. 1900 Census of the United States by Counts of Over 10,000 Population. Revised edition. 120 pages. Price . . **$1.00**

KNOTS

KNOTS, SPLICES AND ROPE WORK. By A. HYATT VERRILL.

This is a practical book giving complete and simple directions for making all the most useful and ornamental knots in common use, with chapters on Splicing, Pointing, Seizing, Serving, etc. This book is fully illustrated with one hundred and fifty original engravings, which show how each knot, tie or splice is formed, and its appearance when finished. The book will be found of the greatest value to Campers, Yachtsmen, Travelers, Boy Scouts, in fact, to anyone having occasion to use or handle rope or knots for any purpose. The book is thoroughly reliable and practical, and is not only a guide, but a teacher. It is the standard work on the subject. Among the contents are: 1. Cordage, Kinds of Rope. Construction of Rope, Parts of Rope Cable and Bolt Rope. Strength of Rope, Weight of Rope. 2. Simple Knots and Bends. Terms Used in Handling Rope. Seizing Rope. 3. Ties and Hitches. 4. Noose, Loops and Mooring Knots. 5. Shortenings, Grommets and Salvages. 6. Lashings, Seizings and Splices. 7. Fancy Knots and Rope Work. 128 pages. 150 original engravings. Price . . . . **60 cents**

LATHE WORK

LATHE DESIGN, CONSTRUCTION, AND OPERATION, WITH PRACTICAL EXAMPLES OF LATHE WORK. By OSCAR E. PERRIGO.

A new revised edition, and the only complete American work on the subject, written by a man who knows not only how work ought to be done, but who also knows how to do it, and how to convey this knowledge to others. It is strictly up-to-date in its descriptions and illustrations. Lathe history and the relations of the lathe to manufacturing are given; also a description of the various devices for feeds and thread cutting mechanisms from early efforts in this direction to the present time. Lathe design is thoroughly discussed, including back gearing, driving cones, thread-cutting gears, and all the essential elements of the modern lathe. The classification of lathes is taken up, giving the essential differences of the several types of lathes including, as is usually understood, engine lathes, bench lathes, speed lathes, forge lathes, gap lathes, pulley lathes, forming lathes, multiple-spindle lathes, rapid-reduction lathes, precision lathes, turret lathes, special lathes, electrically-driven lathes, etc. In addition to the complete exposition on construction and design, much practical matter on lathe installation, care and operation has been incorporated in the enlarged 1915 edition. All kinds of lathe attachments for drilling, milling, etc., are described and complete instructions are given to enable the novice machinist to grasp the art of lathe operation as well as the principles involved in design. A number of difficult machining operations are described at length and illustrated. The new edition has nearly 500 pages and 350 illustrations. Price **$2.50**

WHAT IS SAID OF THIS BOOK:

"This is a lathe book from beginning to end, and is just the kind of a book which one delights to consult,—a masterly treatment of the subject in hand."—*Engineering News*.

"This work will be of exceptional interest to anyone who is interested in lathe practice, as one very seldom sees such a complete treatise on a subject as this is on the lathe."—*Canadian Machinery*.

CATALOGUE OF GOOD, PRACTICAL BOOKS

TURNING AND BORING TAPERS. By Fred H. Colvin.

There are two ways to turn tapers; the right way and one other. This treatise has to do with the right way; it tells you how to start the work properly, how to set the lathe, what tools to use and how to use them, and forty and one other little things that you should know. Fourth edition . . . . **25 cents**

LIQUID AIR

LIQUID AIR AND THE LIQUEFACTION OF GASES. By T. O'Conor Sloane.

This book gives the history of the theory, discovery, and manufacture of Liquid Air, and contains an illustrated description of all the experiments that have excited the wonder of audiences all over the country. It shows how liquid air, like water, is carried hundreds of miles and is handled in open buckets. It tells what may be expected from it in the near future.

A book that renders simple one of the most perplexing chemical problems of the century. Startling developments illustrated by actual experiments.

It is not only a work of scientific interest and authority, but is intended for the general reader, being written in a popular style—easily understood by every one. Second edition. 365 pages. Price **$2.00**

LOCOMOTIVE ENGINEERING

AIR-BRAKE CATECHISM. By Robert H. Blackall.

This book is a standard text book. It covers the Westinghouse Air-Brake Equipment, including the No. 5 and the No. 6 E. T. Locomotive Brake Equipment; the K (Quick, Service) Triple Valve for Freight Service; and the Cross-Compound Pump. The operation of all parts of the apparatus is explained in detail, and a practical way of finding their peculiarities and defects, with a proper remedy, is given. It contains 2,000 questions with their answers, which will enable any railroad man to pass any examination on the subject of Air Brakes. Endorsed and used by air-brake instructors and examiners on nearly every railroad in the United States. 26th Edition. 411 pages, fully illustrated with colored plates and diagrams. **$2.00**

AMERICAN COMPOUND LOCOMOTIVES. By Fred H. Colvin.

The only book on compounds for the engineman or shopman that shows in a plain practical way the various features of compound locomotives in use. Shows how they are made, what to do when they break down or balk. Contains sections as follows:—A Bit of History. Theory of Compounding Steam Cylinders. Baldwin Two-Cylinder Compound. Pittsburg Two-Cylinder Compound. Rhode Island Compound. Richmond Compound. Rogers Compound. Schenectady Two-Cylinder Compound. Vauclain Compound. Tandem Compounds. Baldwin Tandem. The Colvin-Wightman Tandem. Schenectady Tandem. Balanced Locomotives. Baldwin Balanced Compound. Plans for Balancing. Locating Blows. Breakdowns. Reducing Valves. Drifting. Valve Motion. Disconnecting. Power of Compound Locomotives. Practical Notes.

Fully illustrated and containing ten special "Duotone" inserts on heavy Plate Paper, showing different types of Compounds. 142 pages. Price **$1.00**

COMBUSTION OF COAL AND THE PREVENTION OF SMOKE. By Wm. M. Barr.

This book has been prepared with special reference to the generation of heat by the combustion of the common fuels found in the United States and deals particularly with the conditions necessary to the economic and smokeless combustion of bituminous coal in Stationary and Locomotive Steam Boilers.

Presentation of this important subject is systematic and progressive. The arrangement of the book is in a series of practical questions to which are appended accurate answers, which describe in language free from technicalities the several processes involved in the furnace combustion of American fuels; it clearly states the essential requisites for perfect combustion, and points out the best methods of furnace construction for obtaining the greatest quantity of heat from any given quality of coal. Nearly 350 pages, fully illustrated. Price **$1.00**

CATALOGUE OF GOOD, PRACTICAL BOOKS

DIARY OF A ROUND-HOUSE FOREMAN. By T. S. Reilly.
This is the greatest book of railroad experiences ever published. Containing a fund of information and suggestions along the line of handling men, organizing, etc., that one cannot afford to miss. 176 pages. Price $1.00

LINK MOTIONS, VALVES AND VALVE SETTING. By Fred H. Colvin, Associate Editor of *American Machinist*.
A handy book for the engineer or machinist that clears up the mysteries of valve setting. Shows the different valve gears in use, how they work, and why. Piston and slide valves of different types are illustrated and explained. A book that every railroad man in the motive power department ought to have. Contains chapters on Locomotive Link Motion, Valve Movements, Setting Slide Valves, Analysis by Diagrams, Modern Practice, Slip of Block, Slice Valves, Piston Valves, Setting Piston Valves, Joy-Allen Valve Gear, Walschaert Valve Gear, Gooch Valve Gear, Alfree-Hubbell Valve Gear, etc., etc. Fully illustrated. Price . . . . 50 cents

LOCOMOTIVE BOILER CONSTRUCTION. By Frank A. Kleinhans.
The construction of boilers in general is treated, and, following this, the locomotive boiler is taken up in the order in which its various parts go through the shop. Shows all types of boilers used; gives details of construction; practical facts, such as life of riveting, punches and dies; work done per day, allowance for bending and flanging sheets, and other data. Including the recent Locomotive Boiler Inspection Laws and Examination Questions with their answers for Government Inspectors. Contains chapters on Laying Out Work; Flanging and Forging; Punching; Shearing; Plate Planing; General Tables; Finishing Parts; Bending; Machinery Parts; Riveting; Boiler Details; Smoke Box Details; Assembling and Calking; Boiler Shop Machinery, etc., etc.
There isn't a man who has anything to do with boiler work, either new or repair work, who doesn't need this book. The manufacturer, superintendent, foreman, and boiler worker—all need it. No matter what the type of boiler, you'll find a mint of information that you wouldn't be without. Over 400 pages, five large folding plates. Price $3.00

LOCOMOTIVE BREAKDOWNS AND THEIR REMEDIES. By Geo. L. Fowler. Revised by Wm. W. Wood, Air-Brake Instructor. Just issued. Revised pocket edition.
It is out of the question to try and tell you about every subject that is covered in this pocket edition of Locomotive Breakdowns. Just imagine all the common troubles that an engineer may expect to happen some time, and then add all of the unexpected ones, troubles that could occur, but that you have never thought about, and you will find that they are all treated with the very best methods of repair. Walschaert Locomotive Valve Gear Troubles, Electric Headlight Troubles, as well as Questions and Answers on the Air Brake are all included. 294 pages. 7th Revised Edition. Fully illustrated. $1.00

LOCOMOTIVE CATECHISM. By Robert Grimshaw.
The revised edition of "Locomotive Catechism," by Robert Grimshaw, is a New Book from Cover to Cover. It contains twice as many pages and double the number of illustrations of previous editions. Includes the greatest amount of practical information ever published on the construction and management of modern locomotives. Specially Prepared Chapters on the Walschaert Locomotive Valve Gear, the Air-Brake Equipment and the Electric Head Light are given.
It commends itself at once to every Engineer and Fireman, and to all who are going in for examination or promotion. In plain language, with full, complete answers, not only all the questions asked by the examining engineer are given, but those which the young and less experienced would ask the veteran, and which old hands ask as "stickers." It is a veritable Encyclopedia of the Locomotive, is entirely free from mathematics, easily understood and thoroughly up-to-date. Contains over 4,000 Examination Questions with their Answers. 825 pages, 437 illustrations and three folding plates. 28th Revised Edition. $2.50

PRACTICAL INSTRUCTOR AND REFERENCE BOOK FOR LOCOMOTIVE FIREMEN AND ENGINEERS. By Chas. F. Lockhart.
An entirely new book on the Locomotive. It appeals to every railroad man, as it tells him how things are done and the right way to do them. Written by a man who

CATALOGUE OF GOOD, PRACTICAL BOOKS

has had years of practical experience in locomotive shops and on the road firing and running. The information given in this book cannot be found in any other similar treatise. Eight hundred and fifty-one questions with their answers are included, which will prove specially helpful to those preparing for examination. Practical information on: The Construction and Operation of Locomotives; Breakdowns and their Remedies; Air Brakes and Valve Gears. Rules and Signals are handled in a thorough manner. As a book of reference it cannot be excelled. The book is divided into six parts, as follows: 1. The Fireman's Duties. 2. General Description of the Locomotive. 3. Breakdowns and their Remedies. 4. Air Brakes. 5. Extracts from Standard Rules. 6. Questions for Examination. The 851 questions have been carefully selected and arranged. These cover the examinations required by the different railroads. 368 pages. 88 illustrations. Price $1.50

PREVENTION OF RAILROAD ACCIDENTS, OR SAFETY IN RAILROADING.
By GEORGE BRADSHAW.

This book is a heart-to-heart talk with Railroad Employees, dealing with facts, not theories, and showing the men in the ranks, from every-day experience, how accidents occur and how they may be avoided. The book is illustrated with seventy original photographs and drawings showing the safe and unsafe methods of work. No visionary schemes, no ideal pictures. Just plain facts and Practical Suggestions are given. Every railroad employee who reads the book is a better and safer man to have in railroad service. It gives just the information which will be the means of preventing many injuries and deaths. All railroad employees should procure a copy; read it, and do your part in preventing accidents. 169 pages. Pocket size. Fully illustrated. Price . . . . 50 cents

TRAIN RULE EXAMINATIONS MADE EASY. By G. E. COLLINGWOOD.

This is the only practical work on train rules in print. Every detail is covered, and puzzling points are explained in simple, comprehensive language, making it a practical treatise for the Train Dispatcher, Engineman, Trainman, and all others who have to do with the movements of trains. Contains complete and reliable information of the Standard Code of Train Rules for single track. Shows Signals in Colors, as used on the different roads. Explains fully the practical application of train orders, giving a clear and definite understanding of all orders which may be used. The meaning and necessity for certain rules are explained in such a manner that the student may know beyond a doubt the rights conferred under any orders he may receive or the action required by certain rules. As nearly all roads require trainmen to pass regular examinations, a complete set of examination questions, with their answers, are included. These will enable the student to pass the required examinations with credit to himself and the road for which he works. 256 pages. Fully illustrated with Train Signals in Colors. Price $1.25

THE WALSCHAERT AND OTHER MODERN RADIAL VALVE GEARS FOR LOCOMOTIVES. By WM. W. WOOD.

If you would thoroughly understand the Walschaert Valve Gear you should possess a copy of this book, as the author takes the plainest form of a steam engine—a stationary engine in the rough, that will only turn its crank in one direction—and from it builds up—with the reader's help—a modern locomotive equipped with the Walschaert Valve Gear, complete. The points discussed are clearly illustrated; two large folding plates that show the positions of the valves of both inside or outside admission type, as well as the links and other parts of the gear when the crank is at nine different points in its revolution, are especially valuable in making the movement clear. These employ sliding cardboard models which are contained in a pocket in the cover.

The book is divided into five general divisions, as follows: 1. Analysis of the gear. 2. Designing and erecting the gear. 3. Advantages of the gear. 4. Questions and answers relating to the Walschaert Valve Gear. 5. Setting valves with the Walschaert Valve Gear; the three primary types of locomotive valve motion; modern radial valve gears other than the Walschaert: the Hobart All-free Valve and Valve Gear, with questions and answers on breakdowns; the Baker-Pilliod Valve Gear; the Improved Baker-Pilliod Valve Gear, with questions and answers on breakdowns.

The questions with full answers given will be especially valuable to firemen and engineers in preparing for an examination for promotion. 245 pages. Third Revised Edition. Price $1.50

CATALOGUE OF GOOD, PRACTICAL BOOKS

WESTINGHOUSE E-T AIR-BRAKE INSTRUCTION POCKET BOOK. By WM. W. WOOD, Air-Brake Instructor.

Here is a book for the railroad man, and the man who aims to be one. It is without doubt the only complete work published on the Westinghouse E-T Locomotive Brake Equipment. Written by an Air-Brake Instructor who knows just what is needed. It covers the subject thoroughly. Everything about the New Westinghouse Engine and Tender Brake Equipment, including the standard No. 5 and the Perfected No. 6 style of brake, is treated in detail. Written in plain English and profusely illustrated with Colored Plates, which enable one to trace the flow of pressures throughout the entire equipment. The best book ever published on the Air Brake. Equally good for the beginner and the advanced engineer. Will pass any one through any examination. It informs and enlightens you on every point. Indispensable to every engineman and trainman.

Contains examination questions and answers on the E-T equipment. Covering what the E-T Brake is. How it should be operated. What to do when defective. Not a question can be asked of the engineman up for promotion, on either the No. 5 or the No. 6 E-T equipment, that is not asked and answered in the book. If you want to thoroughly understand the E-T equipment get a copy of this book. It covers every detail. Makes Air-Brake troubles and examinations easy. Price $1.50

MACHINE-SHOP PRACTICE

AMERICAN TOOL MAKING AND INTERCHANGEABLE MANUFACTURING. By J. V. WOODWORTH.

A "shoppy" book, containing no theorizing, no problematical or experimental devices, there are no badly proportioned and impossible diagrams, no catalogue cuts, but a valuable collection of drawings and descriptions of devices, the rich fruits of the author's own experience. In its 500-odd pages the one subject only, Tool Making, and whatever relates thereto, is dealt with. The work stands without a rival. It is a complete practical treatise on the art of American Tool Making and system of interchangeable manufacturing as carried on to-day in the United States. In it are described and illustrated all of the different types and classes of small tools, fixtures, devices, and special appliances which are in general use in all machine-manufacturing and metalworking establishments where economy, capacity, and interchangeability in the production of machined metal parts are imperative. The science of jig making is exhaustively discussed, and particular attention is paid to drill jigs, boring, profiling and milling fixtures and other devices in which the parts to be machined are located and fastened within the contrivances. All of the tools, fixtures, and devices illustrated and described have been or are used for the actual production of work, such as parts of drill presses, lathes, patented machinery, typewriters, electrical apparatus, mechanical appliances, brass goods, composition parts, mould products, sheet metal articles, dropforgings, jewelry, watches, medals, coins, etc. 531 pages. Price $4.00

MACHINE-SHOP ARITHMETIC. By COLVIN-CHENEY.

This is an arithmetic of the things you have to do with daily. It tells you plainly about: how to find areas in figures; how to find surface or volume of balls or spheres; handy ways for calculating; about compound gearing; cutting screw threads on any lathe; drilling for taps; speeds of drills; taps, emery wheels, grindstones, milling cutters, etc.; all about the Metric system with conversion tables; properties of metals; strength of bolts and nuts; decimal equivalent of an inch. All sorts of machine-shop figuring and 1,001 other things, any one of which ought to be worth more than the price of this book to you, and it saves you the trouble of bothering the boss. 6th edition. 131 pages. Price . . . . 50 cents

MODERN MACHINE-SHOP CONSTRUCTION, EQUIPMENT AND MANAGEMENT. By OSCAR E. PERRIGO.

The only work published that describes the Modern Shop or Manufacturing Plant from the time the grass is growing on the site intended for it until the finished product is shipped. Just the book needed by those contemplating the erection of modern shop buildings, the rebuilding and reorganization of old ones, or the introduction of Modern Shop Methods, time and cost systems. It is a book written and illustrated by a practical shop man for practical shop men who are too busy to read theories and want facts. It is the most complete all-round book of its kind ever published. 400 large quarto pages. 225 original and specially-made illustrations. 2d Revised and Enlarged Edition. Price $5.00

21

CATALOGUE OF GOOD, PRACTICAL BOOKS

THE WHOLE FIELD OF MECHANICAL MOVEMENTS COVERED BY MR. HISCOX'S TWO BOOKS

We publish two books by Gardner D. Hiscox that will keep you from "inventing" things that have been done before, and suggest ways of doing things that you have not thought of before. Many a man spends time and money, pondering over some mechanical problem, only to learn, after he has solved the problem, that the same thing has been accomplished and put in practice by others long before. Time and money spent in an effort to accomplish what has already been accomplished are time and money LOST. The whole field of mechanics, every known mechanical movement, and practically every device is covered by these two books. If the thing you want has been invented, it is illustrated in them. If it hasn't been invented, then you'll find in them the nearest things to what you want, some movements or devices that will apply in your case, perhaps; or which will give you a key from which to work. No book or set of books ever published is of more real value to the Inventor, Draftsman, or practical Mechanic than the two volumes described below.

MECHANICAL MOVEMENTS, POWERS, AND DEVICES. By GARDNER D. HISCOX.

This is a collection of 1,890 engravings of different mechanical motions and appliances, accompanied by appropriate text, making it a book of great value to the inventor, the draftsman, and to all readers with mechanical tastes. The book is divided into eighteen sections or chapters, in which the subject-matter is classified under the following heads: Mechanical Powers; Transmission of Power; Measurement of Power; Steam Power; Air Power Appliances; Electric Power and Construction; Navigation and Roads; Gearing; Motion and Devices; Controlling Motion; Horological; Mining; Mill and Factory Appliances; Construction and Devices; Drafting Devices; Miscellaneous Devices, etc.   12th edition.   400 octavo pages.   Price . . . **$2.50**

MECHANICAL APPLIANCES, MECHANICAL MOVEMENTS AND NOVELTIES OF CONSTRUCTION. By GARDNER D. HISCOX.

This is a supplementary volume to the one upon mechanical movements. Unlike the first volume, which is more elementary in character, this volume contains illustrations and descriptions of many combinations of motions and of mechanical devices and appliances found in different lines of machinery, each device being shown by a line drawing with a description showing its working parts and the method of operation. From the multitude of devices described and illustrated might be mentioned, in passing, such items as conveyors and elevators, Prony brakes, thermometers, various types of boilers, solar engines, oil-fuel burners, condensers, evaporators, Corliss and other valve gears, governors, gas engines, water motors of various descriptions, air ships, motors and dynamos, automobile and motor bicycles, railway lock signals, car couplers, link and gear motions, ball bearings, breech block mechanism for heavy guns, and a large accumulation of others of equal importance.   1,000 specially made engravings.   396 octavo pages.   2d Edition.   Price **$2.50**

MACHINE-SHOP TOOLS AND SHOP PRACTICE. By W. H. VANDERVOORT.

A work of 555 pages and 673 illustrations, describing in every detail the construction, operation, and manipulation of both hand and machine tools. Includes chapters on filing, fitting, and scraping surfaces; on drills, reamers, taps, and dies; the lathe and its tools; planers, shapers, and their tools; milling machines and cutters; gear cutters and gear cutting; drilling machines and drill work; grinding machines and their work; hardening and tempering; gearing, belting, and transmission machinery; useful data and tables.   6th edition.   Price **$3.00**

THE MODERN MACHINIST. By JOHN T. USHER.

This is a book showing, by plain description and by profuse engravings made expressly for the work, all that is best, most advanced, and of the highest efficiency in modern machine-shop practice, tools, and implements, showing the way by which and through which, as Mr. Maxim says, "American machinists have become and are the finest mechanics in the world." Indicating as it does, in every line, the familiarity of the author with every detail of daily experience in the shop, it cannot fail to be of service to any man practically connected with the shaping or finishing of metals.

There is nothing experimental or visionary about the book, all devices being in actual use and giving good results. It might be called a compendium of shop methods, showing a variety of special tools and appliances which will give new ideas to many

CATALOGUE OF GOOD, PRACTICAL BOOKS

mechanics, from the superintendent down to the man at the bench. It will be found a valuable edition to any machinist's library, and should be consulted whenever a new or difficult job is to be done, whether it is boring, milling, turning, or planing, as they are all treated in a practical manner. Fifth edition. 320 pages. 250 illustrations. Price $2.50

"SHOP KINKS." By Robert Grimshaw.

A book of 400 pages and 222 illustrations, being entirely different from any other book on machine-shop practice. Departing from conventional style, the author avoids universal or common shop usage and limits his work to showing special ways of doing things better, more cheaply and more rapidly than usual. As a result the advanced methods of representative establishments of the world are placed at the disposal of the reader. This book shows the proprietor where large savings are possible, and how products may be improved. To the employee it holds out suggestions that, properly applied, will hasten his advancement. No shop can afford to be without it. It bristles with valuable wrinkles and helpful suggestions. It will benefit all, from apprentice to proprietor. Every machinist, at any age, should study its pages. Fifth edition. Price $2.50

THREADS AND THREAD CUTTING. By Colvin and Stabel.

This clears up many of the mysteries of thread-cutting, such as double and triple threads, internal threads, catching threads, use of hobs, etc. Contains a lot of useful hints and several tables. Third edition. Price . . . . 25 cents

MANUAL TRAINING

ECONOMICS OF MANUAL TRAINING. By Louis Rouillion.

The only book published that gives just the information needed by all interested in Manual Training, regarding Buildings, Equipment, and Supplies. Shows exactly what is needed for all grades of the work from the Kindergarten to the High and Normal School. Gives itemized lists of everything used in Manual Training Work and tells just what it ought to cost. Also shows where to buy supplies, etc. Contains 174 pages, and is fully illustrated. 2d edition. Price $1.50

MARINE ENGINEERING

MODERN SUBMARINE CHART.

A cross-section view, showing clearly and distinctly all the interior of a Submarine of the latest type. You get more information from this chart about the construction and operation of a submarine than in any other way. No details omitted—everything is accurate and to scale. It is absolutely correct in every detail, having been approved by naval engineers. All the machinery and devices fitted in a modern Submarine Boat are shown, and to make the engraving more readily understood all the features are shown in operative form, with Officers and Men in the act of performing the duties assigned to them in service conditions. THIS CHART IS REALLY AN ENCYCLOPEDIA OF A SUBMARINE. It is educational and worth many times its cost. Mailed in a tube for . . . . 25 cents

PATTERN MAKING

PRACTICAL PATTERN MAKING. By F. W. Barrows.

This book, now in its second edition, is a comprehensive and entirely practical treatise on the subject of pattern making, illustrating pattern work in both wood and metal, and with definite instructions on the use of plaster of paris in the trade. It gives specific and detailed descriptions of the materials used by pattern makers and describes the tools, both those for the bench and the more interesting machine tools; having complete chapters on the Lathe, the Circular Saw, and the Band Saw. It gives many examples of pattern work, each one fully illustrated and explained with much detail. These examples, in their great variety, offer much that will be found of interest to all pattern makers, and especially to the younger ones, who are seeking information on the more advanced branches of their trade.

In this second edition of the work will be found much that is new, even to those who have long practised this exacting trade. In the description of patterns as adapted to the Moulding Machine many difficulties which have long prevented the rapid and

CATALOGUE OF GOOD, PRACTICAL BOOKS

economical production of castings are overcome; and this great, new branch of the trade is given much space. Stripping plate and stool plate work and the less expensive vibrator, or rapping plate work, are all explained in detail.

Plain, everyday rules for lessening the cost of patterns, with a complete system of cost keeping, a detailed method of marking, applicable to all branches of the trade, with complete information showing what the pattern is, its specific title, its cost, date of production, material of which it is made, the number of pieces and coreboxes, and its location in the pattern safe, all condensed into a most complete card record, with cross index.

The book closes with an original and practical method for the inventory and valuation of patterns. Containing nearly 350 pages and 170 illustrations. Price . $2.00

PERFUMERY

PERFUMES AND COSMETICS, THEIR PREPARATION AND MANUFACTURE. By G. W. Askinson, Perfumer.

A comprehensive treatise, in which there has been nothing omitted that could be of value to the perfumer or manufacturer of toilet preparations. Complete directions for making handkerchief perfumes, smelling-salts, sachets, fumigating pastilles; preparations for the care of the skin, the mouth, the hair, cosmetics, hair dyes and other toilet articles are given, also a detailed description of aromatic substances; their nature, tests of purity, and wholesale manufacture, including a chapter on synthetic products, with formulas for their use. A book of general, as well as professional interest, meeting the wants not only of the druggist and perfume manufacturer, but also of the general public. Among the contents are: 1. The History of Perfumery. 2. About Aromatic Substances in General. 3. Odors from the Vegetable Kingdom. 4. The Aromatic Vegetable Substances Employed in Perfumery. 5. The Animal Substances Used in Perfumery. 6. The Chemical Products Used in Perfumery. 7. The Extraction of Odors. 8. The Special Characteristics of Aromatic Substances. 9. The Adulteration of Essential Oils and Their Recognition. 10. Synthetic Products. 11. Table of Physical Properties of Aromatic Chemicals. 12. The Essences or Extracts Employed in Perfumery. 13. Directions for Making the Most Important Essences and Extracts. 14. The Division of Perfumery. 15. The Manufacture of Handkerchief Perfumes. 16. Formulas for Handkerchief Perfumes. 17. Ammoniacal and Acid Perfumes. 18. Dry Perfumes. 19. Formulas for Dry Perfumes. 20. The Perfumes Used for Fumigation. 21. Antiseptic and Therapeutic Value of Perfumes. 22. Classification of Odors. 23. Some Special Perfumery Products. 24. Hygiene and Cosmetic Perfumery. 25. Preparations for the Care of the Skin. 26. Manufacture of Casein. 27. Formulas for Emulsions. 28. Formulas for Cream. 29. Formulas for Meals, Pastes and Vegetable Milk. 30. Preparations Used for the Hair. 31. Formulas for Hair Tonics and Restorers. 32. Pomades and Hair Oils. 33. Formulas for the Manufacture of Pomades and Hair Oils. 34. Hair Dyes and Depilatories. 35. Wax Pomades, Bandolines and Brilliantines. 36. Skin Cosmetics and Face Lotions. 37. Preparations for the Nails. 38. Water Softeners and Bath Salts. 39. Preparations for the Care of the Mouth. 40. The Colors Used in Perfumery. 41. The Utensils Used in the Toilet. Fourth edition much enlarged and brought up-to-date. Nearly 400 pages, illustrated. Price $5.00

WHAT IS SAID OF THIS BOOK:

" The most satisfactory work on the subject of Perfumery that we have ever seen.

" We feel safe in saying that here is a book on Perfumery that will not disappoint you, for it has practical and excellent formulæ that are within your ability to prepare readily.

" We recommend the volume as worthy of confidence, and say that no purchaser will be disappointed in securing from its pages good value for its cost, and a large dividend on the same, even if he should use but one per cent of its working formulæ. There is money in it for every user of its information."—*Pharmaceutical Record.*

PLUMBING

MECHANICAL DRAWING FOR PLUMBERS. By R. M. Starbuck.

A concise, comprehensive and practical treatise on the subject of mechanical drawing in its various modern applications to the work of all who are in any way connected with the plumbing trade. Nothing will so help the plumber in estimating and in

CATALOGUE OF GOOD, PRACTICAL BOOKS

explaining work to customers and workmen as a knowledge of drawing, and to the workman it is of inestimable value if he is to rise above his position to positions of greater responsibility. Among the chapters contained are: 1. Value to plumber of knowledge of drawing; tools required and their use; common views needed in mechanical drawing. 2. Perspective versus mechanical drawing in showing plumbing construction. 3. Correct and incorrect methods in plumbing drawing; plan and elevation explained. 4. Floor and cellar plans and elevation; scale drawings; use of triangles. 5. Use of triangles; drawing of fittings, traps, etc. 6. Drawing plumbing elevations and fittings. 7. Instructions in drawing plumbing elevations. 8. The drawing of plumbing fixtures; scale drawings. 9. Drawings of fixtures and fittings. 10. Inking of drawings. 11. Shading of drawings. 12. Shading of drawings. 13. Sectional drawings; drawing of threads. 14. Plumbing elevations from architect's plan. 15. Elevations of separate parts of the plumbing system. 16. Elevations from the architect's plans. 17. Drawings of detail plumbing connections. 18. Architect's plans and plumbing elevations of residence. 19. Plumbing elevations of residence (continued); plumbing plans for cottage. 20. Plumbing elevations; roof connections. 21. Plans and plumbing elevations for six-flat building. 22. Drawing of various parts of the plumbing system; use of scales. 23. Use of architect's scales. 24. Special features in the illustrations of country plumbing. 25. Drawing of wrought-iron piping, valves, radiators, coils, etc. 26. Drawing of piping to illustrate heating systems. 150 illustrations. Price $1.50

MODERN PLUMBING ILLUSTRATED. By R. M. STARBUCK.

This book represents the highest standard of plumbing work. It has been adopted and used as a reference book by the United States Government, in its sanitary work in Cuba, Porto Rico, and the Philippines, and by the principal Boards of Health of the United States and Canada.

It gives connections, sizes and working data for all fixtures and groups of fixtures. It is helpful to the master plumber in demonstrating to his customers and in figuring work. It gives the mechanic and student quick and easy access to the best modern plumbing practice. Suggestions for estimating plumbing construction are contained in its pages. This book represents, in a word, the latest and best up-to-date practice and should be in the hands of every architect, sanitary engineer and plumber who wishes to keep himself up to the minute on this important feature of construction. Contains following chapters, each illustrated with a full-page plate: Kitchen sink, laundry tubs, vegetable wash sink; lavatories, pantry sinks, contents of marble slabs; bath tub, foot and sitz bath, shower bath; water closets, venting of water closets; low-down water closets, water closets operated by flush valves, water closet range; slop sink, urinals, the bidet; hotel and restaurant sink, grease trap; refrigerators, safe wastes, laundry waste, lines of refrigerators, bar sinks, soda fountain sinks; horse stall, frost-proof water closets; connections for S traps, venting; connections for drum traps; soil pipe connections; supporting of soil pipe; main trap and fresh air inlet; floor drains and cellar drains, subsoil drainage; water closets and floor connections; local venting; connections for bath rooms; connections for bath rooms, continued; connections for bath rooms, continued; connections for bath rooms, continued; examples of poor practice; roughing work ready for test; testing of plumbing system; method of continuous venting; continuous venting for two-floor work; continuous venting for two lines of fixtures on three or more floors; continuous venting of water closets; plumbing for cottage house; construction for cellar piping; plumbing for residence, use of special fittings; plumbing for two-flat house; plumbing for apartment building, plumbing for double apartment building; plumbing for office building; plumbing for public toilet rooms; plumbing for public toilet rooms, continued; plumbing for bath establishment; plumbing for engine house, factory plumbing; automatic flushing for schools, factories, etc.; use of flushing valves; urinals for public toilet rooms; the Durham system, the destruction of pipes by electrolysis; construction of work without use of lead; automatic sewage lift; automatic sump tank; country plumbing; construction of cesspools; septic tank and automatic sewage siphon; country plumbing; water supply for country house; thawing of water mains and service by electricity; double boilers; hot water supply of large buildings; automatic control of hot water tank; suggestion for estimating plumbing construction. 400 octavo pages, fully illustrated by 58 full-page engravings. New, revised and enlarged edition just issued. Price . $4.00

STANDARD PRACTICAL PLUMBING. By R. M. STARBUCK.

A complete practical treatise of 450 pages covering the subject of Modern Plumbing in all its branches, a large amount of space being devoted to a very complete and practical treatment of the subject of Hot Water Supply and Circulation and Range Boiler Work. Its thirty chapters include about every phase of the subject one can think of, making it an indispensable work to the master plumber, the journeyman plumber, and the apprentice plumber, containing chapters on: the plumber's tools;

CATALOGUE OF GOOD, PRACTICAL BOOKS

wiping solder; composition and use; joint wiping; lead work; traps; siphonage of traps; venting; continuous venting; house sewer and sewer connections; house drain; soil piping, roughing; main trap and fresh air inlet; floor, yard, cellar drains, rain leaders, etc.; fixture wastes; water closets; ventilation; improved plumbing connections; residence plumbing; plumbing for hotels, schools, factories, stables, etc.; modern country plumbing; filtration of sewage and water supply; hot and cold supply; range boilers; circulation; circulating pipes; range boiler problems; hot water for large buildings; water lift and its use; multiple connections for hot water boilers; heating of radiation by supply system; theory for the plumber; drawing for the plumber. Fully illustrated by 347 engravings. Price $3.00

RECIPE BOOK

HENLEY'S TWENTIETH CENTURY BOOK OF RECIPES, FORMULAS AND PROCESSES. Edited by GARDNER D. HISCOX.

The most valuable Techno-chemical Formula Book published, including over 10,000 selected scientific, chemical, technological, and practical recipes and processes.

This is the most complete Book of Formulas ever published, giving thousands of recipes for the manufacture of valuable articles for everyday use. Hints, Helps, Practical Ideas, and Secret Processes are revealed within its pages. It covers every branch of the useful arts and tells thousands of ways of making money, and is just the book everyone should have at his command.

Modern in its treatment of every subject that properly falls within its scope, the book may truthfully be said to present the very latest formulas to be found in the arts and industries, and to retain those processes which long experience has proven worthy of a permanent record. To present here even a limited number of the subjects which find a place in this valuable work would be difficult. Suffice to say that in its pages will be found matter of intense interest and immeasurably practical value to the scientific amateur and to him who wishes to obtain a knowledge of the many processes used in the arts, trades and manufacture, a knowledge which will render his pursuits more instructive and remunerative. Serving as a reference book to the small and large manufacturer and supplying intelligent seekers with the information necessary to conduct a process, the work will be found of inestimable worth to the Metallurgist, the Photographer, the Perfumer, the Painter, the Manufacturer of Glues, Pastes, Cements, and Mucilages, the Compounder of Alloys, the Cook, the Physician, the Druggist, the Electrician, the Brewer, the Engineer, the Foundryman, the Machinist, the Potter, the Tanner, the Confectioner, the Chiropodist, the Manicure, the Manufacturer of Chemical Novelties and Toilet Preparations, the Dyer, the Electroplater, the Enameler, the Engraver, the Provisioner, the Glass Worker, the Goldbeater, the Watchmaker, the Jeweler, the Hat Maker, the Ink Manufacturer, the Optician, the Farmer, the Dairyman, the Paper Maker, the Wood and Metal Worker, the Chandler and Soap Maker, the Veterinary Surgeon, and the Technologist in general.

A mine of information, and up-to-date in every respect. A book which will prove of value to EVERYONE, as it covers every branch of the Useful Arts. Every home needs this book; every office, every factory, every store, every public and private enterprise—EVERYWHERE—should have a copy. 800 pages. Price . . . $3.00

WHAT IS SAID OF THIS BOOK:

"Your Twentieth Century Book of Recipes, Formulas, and Processes duly received. I am glad to have a copy of it, and if I could not replace it, money couldn't buy it. It is the best thing of the sort I ever saw." (Signed) M. E. TRUX, Sparta, Wis.

"There are few persons who would not be able to find in the book some single formula that would repay several times the cost of the book."—*Merchants' Record and Show Window.*

"I purchased your book 'Henley's Twentieth Century Book of Recipes, Formulas and Processes' about a year ago and it is worth its weight in *gold*."—WM. H. MURRAY, Bennington, Vt.

"THE BOOK WORTH THREE HUNDRED DOLLARS"

"On close examination of your 'Twentieth Century Receipt Book,' I find it to be a very valuable and useful book with the very best of practical information obtainable. The price of the book, $3.00, is very small in comparison to the benefits which one can obtain from it. I consider the book worth fully three hundred dollars to anyone."—DR. A. C. SPETTS, New York.

CATALOGUE OF GOOD, PRACTICAL BOOKS

"ONE OF THE WORLD'S MOST USEFUL BOOKS"
"Some time ago, I got one of your 'Twentieth Century Books of Formulas' and have made my living from it ever since. I am alone since my husband's death with two small children to care for and am trying so hard to support them. I have customers who take from me Toilet Articles I put up, following directions given in the book, and I have found everyone of them to be fine."—MRS. J. H. MCMAKEN, West Toledo, Ohio.

RUBBER

RUBBER HAND STAMPS AND THE MANIPULATION OF INDIA RUBBER. By T. O'CONOR SLOANE.

This book gives full details on all points, treating in a concise and simple manner the elements of nearly everything it is necessary to understand for a commencement in any branch of the India Rubber Manufacture. The making of all kinds of Rubber Hand Stamps, Small Articles of India Rubber, U. S. Government Composition, Dating Hand Stamps, the Manipulation of Sheet Rubber, Toy Balloons, India Rubber Solutions, Cements, Blackings, Renovating Varnish, and Treatment for India Rubber Shoes, etc.; the Hektograph Stamp Inks, and Miscellaneous Notes, with a Short Account of the Discovery, Collection and Manufacture of India Rubber, are set forth in a manner designed to be readily understood, the explanations being plain and simple. Including a chapter on Rubber Tire Making and Vulcanizing; also a chapter on the uses of rubber in Surgery and Dentistry. Third revised and enlarged edition. 175 pages. Illustrated $1.00

SAWS

SAW FILINGS AND MANAGEMENT OF SAWS. By ROBERT GRIMSHAW.

A practical hand-book on filing, gumming, swaging, hammering, and the brazing of band saws, the speed, work, and power to run circular saws, etc. A handy book for those who have charge of saws, or for those mechanics who do their own filing, as it deals with the proper shape and pitches of saw teeth of all kinds and gives many useful hints for gumming, setting, and filing, and is a practical aid to those who use saws for any purpose. Complete tables of proper shape, pitch, and saw teeth as well as sizes and number of teeth of various saws are included. Third edition, revised and enlarged. Illustrated. Price $1.00

STEAM ENGINEERING

AMERICAN STATIONARY ENGINEERING. By W. E. CRANE.

This book begins at the boiler room and takes in the whole power plant. A plain talk on every-day work about engines, boilers, and their accessories. It is not intended to be scientific or mathematical. All formulas are in simple form so that any one understanding plain arithmetic can readily understand any of them. The author has made this the most practical book in print; has given the results of his years of experience, and has included about all that has to do with an engine room or a power plant. You are not left to guess at a single point. You are shown clearly what to expect under the various conditions; how to secure the best results; ways of preventing "shut downs" and repairs; in short, all that goes to make up the requirements of a good engineer, capable of taking charge of a plant. It's plain enough for practical men and yet of value to those high in the profession.

A partial list of contents is: The boiler room, cleaning boilers, firing, feeding; pumps, inspection and repair; chimneys, sizes and cost; piping; mason work; foundations; testing cement; pile driving; engines, slow and high speed; valves; valve setting; Corliss engines, setting valves, single and double eccentric; air pumps and condensers; different types of condensers; water needed; lining up; pounds; pins not square in crosshead or crank; engineers' tools; pistons and piston rings; bearing metal; hardened copper; drip pipes from cylinder jackets; belts, how made, care of; oils; greases; testing lubricants; rules and tables, including steam tables; areas of segments;

CATALOGUE OF GOOD, PRACTICAL BOOKS

squares and square roots; cubes and cube root; areas and circumferences of circles. Notes on: Brick work; explosions; pumps; pump valves; heaters, economizers; safety valves; lap, lead, and clearance. Has a complete examination for a license etc., etc. Second edition. 285 pages. Illustrated. Price $2.00

EMINENT ENGINEERS. By DWIGHT GODDARD.

Everyone who appreciates the effect of such great inventions as the Steam Engine, Steamboat, Locomotive, Sewing Machine, Steel Working, and other fundamental discoveries, is interested in knowing a little about the men who made them and their achievements.

Mr. Goddard has selected thirty-two of the world's engineers who have contributed most largely to the advancement of our civilization by mechanical means, giving only such facts as are of general interest and in a way which appeals to all, whether mechanics or not. 280 pages. 35 illustrations. Price $1.50

ENGINE RUNNER'S CATECHISM. By ROBERT GRIMSHAW.

A practical treatise for the stationary engineer, telling how to erect, adjust, and run the principal steam engines in use in the United States. Describing the principal features of various special and well-known makes of engines: Temper Cut-off, Shipping and Receiving Foundations, Erecting and Starting, Valve Setting, Care and Use, Emergencies, Erecting and Adjusting Special Engines.

The questions asked throughout the catechism are plain and to the point, and the answers are given in such simple language as to be readily understood by anyone. All the instructions given are complete and up-to-date; and they are written in a popular style, without any technicalities or mathematical formulæ. The work is of a handy size for the pocket, clearly and well printed, nicely bound, and profusely illustrated.

To young engineers this catechism will be of great value, especially to those who may be preparing to go forward to be examined for certificates of competency; and to engineers generally it will be of no little service, as they will find in this volume more really practical and useful information than is to be found anywhere else within a like compass. 387 pages. Seventh edition. Price $2.00

HORSEPOWER CHART.

Shows the horsepower of any stationary engine without calculation. No matter what the cylinder diameter of stroke, the steam pressure of cut-off, the revolutions, or whether condensing or non-condensing, it's all there. Easy to use, accurate, and saves time and calculations. Especially useful to engineers and designers. **50 cents**

MODERN STEAM ENGINEERING IN THEORY AND PRACTICE. By GARDNER D. HISCOX.

This is a complete and practical work issued for Stationary Engineers and Firemen, dealing with the care and management of boilers, engines, pumps, superheated steam, refrigerating machinery, dynamos, motors, elevators, air compressors, and all other branches with which the modern engineer must be familiar. Nearly 200 questions with their answers on steam and electrical engineering, likely to be asked by the Examining Board, are included.

Among the chapters are: Historical; steam and its properties; appliances for the generation of steam; types of boilers; chimney and its work; heat economy of the feed water; steam pumps and their work; incrustation and its work; steam above atmospheric pressure; flow of steam from nozzles; superheated steam and its work; adiabatic expansion of steam; indicator and its work; steam engine proportions; slide valve engines and valve motion; Corliss engine and its valve gear; compound engine and its theory; triple and multiple expansion engine; steam turbine; refrigeration; elevators and their management; cost of power; steam engine troubles; electric power and electric plants. 487 pages. 405 engravings. 3d Edition. . . . $3.00

STEAM ENGINE CATECHISM. By ROBERT GRIMSHAW.

This unique volume of 413 pages is not only a catechism on the question and answer principle, but it contains formulas and worked-out answers for all the Steam problems that appertain to the operation and management of the Steam Engine. Illustrations of various valves and valve gear with their principles of operation are given. Thirty-four Tables that are indispensable to every engineer and fireman that wishes to be progressive and is ambitious to become master of his calling are within its pages. It is a most valuable instructor in the service of Steam Engineering. Leading engineers have recommended it as a valuable educator for the beginner as well as a reference book

CATALOGUE OF GOOD, PRACTICAL BOOKS

for the engineer. It is thoroughly indexed for every detail. Every essential question on the Steam Engine with its answer is contained in this valuable work. Sixteenth edition. Price $2.00

STEAM ENGINEER'S ARITHMETIC. By COLVIN-CHENEY.
A practical pocket-book for the steam engineer. Shows how to work the problems of the engine room and shows "why." Tells how to figure horsepower of engines and boilers; area of boilers; has tables of areas and circumferences; steam tables; has a dictionary of engineering terms. Puts you on to all of the little kinks in figuring whatever there is to figure around a power plant. Tells you about the heat unit; absolute zero; adiabatic expansion; duty of engines; factor of safety; and a thousand and one other things; and everything is plain and simple—not the hardest way to figure, but the easiest. Second Edition. . . . . 50 cents

STEAM HEATING AND VENTILATION

PRACTICAL STEAM, HOT-WATER HEATING AND VENTILATION. By A. G. KING.
This book is the standard and latest work published on the subject and has been prepared for the use of all engaged in the business of steam, hot-water heating, and ventilation. It is an original and exhaustive work. Tells how to get heating contracts, how to install heating and ventilating apparatus, the best business methods to be used, with "Tricks of the Trade" for shop use. Rules and data for estimating radiation and cost and such tables and information as make it an indispensable work for every one interested in steam, hot-water heating, and ventilation. It describes all the principal systems of steam, hot-water, vacuum, vapor, and vacuum-vapor heating, together with the new accelerated systems of hot-water circulation, including chapters on up-to-date methods of ventilation and the fan or blower system of heating and ventilation. Containing chapters on: I. Introduction. II. Heat. III. Evolution of artificial heating apparatus. IV. Boiler surface and settings. V. The chimney flue. VI. Pipe and fittings. VII. Valves, various kinds. VIII. Forms of radiating surfaces. IX. Locating of radiating surfaces. X. Estimating radiation. XI. Steamheating apparatus. XII. Exhaust-steam heating. XIII. Hot-water heating. XVI. Pressure systems of hot-water work. XV. Hot-water appliances. XVI. Greenhouse heating. XVII. Vacuum vapor and vacuum exhaust heating. XVIII. Miscellaneous heating. XIX. Radiator and pipe connections. XX. Ventilation. XXI. Mechanical ventilation and hot-blast heating. XXII. Steam appliances. XXIII. District heating. XXIV. Pipe and boiler covering. XXV. Temperature regulation and heat control. XXVI. Business methods. XXVII. Miscellaneous. XXVIII. Rules, tables, and useful information. 367 pages. 300 detailed engravings. Second Edition—Revised. Price $3.00

500 PLAIN ANSWERS TO DIRECT QUESTIONS ON STEAM, HOT-WATER, VAPOR AND VACUUM HEATING PRACTICE. By ALFRED G. KING.
This work, just off the press, is arranged in question and answer form; it is intended as a guide and text-book for the younger, inexperienced fitter and as a reference book for all fitters. This book tells "how" and also tells "why." No work of its kind has ever been published. It answers all the questions regarding each method or system that would be asked by the steam fitter or heating contractor, and may be used as a text or reference book, and for examination questions by Trade Schools or Steam Fitters' Associations. Rules, data, tables and descriptive methods are given together with much other detailed information of daily practical use to those engaged in or interested in the various methods of heating. Valuable to those preparing for examinations. Answers every question asked relating to modern Steam, Hot-Water, Vapor and Vacuum Heating. Among the contents are: The Theory and Laws of Heat. Methods of Heating. Chimneys and Flues. Boilers for Heating. Boiler Trimmings and Settings. Radiation. Steam Heating. Boiler, Radiator and Pipe Connections for Steam Heating. Hot Water Heating. The Two-Pipe Gravity System of Hot Water Heating. The Circuit System of Hot Water Heating. The Overhead System of Hot Water Heating. Boiler, Radiator and Pipe Connections for Gravity Systems of Hot Water Heating. Accelerated Hot Water Heating. Expansion Tank Connections. Domestic Hot Water Heating. Valves and Air Valves. Vacuum Vapor and Vacuo-Vapor Heating. Mechanical Systems of Vacuum Heating. Non-Mechanical Vacuum Systems. Vapor Systems. Atmospheric and Modulating Systems. Heating Greenhouses. Information, Rules and Tables. 200 pages. 127 illustrations. Octavo. Cloth. Price $1.50

CATALOGUE OF GOOD, PRACTICAL BOOKS

STEEL

STEEL: ITS SELECTION, ANNEALING, HARDENING, AND TEMPERING. By E. R. MARKHAM.

This work was formerly known as "The American Steel Worker," but on the publication of the new, revised edition, the publishers deemed it advisable to change its title to a more suitable one. It is the standard work on Hardening, Tempering, and Annealing Steel of all kinds.

This book tells how to select, and how to work, temper, harden, and anneal steel for everything on earth. It doesn't tell how to temper one class of tools and then leave the treatment of another kind of tool to your imagination and judgment, but it gives careful instructions for every detail of every tool, whether it be a tap, a reamer or just a screw-driver. It tells about the tempering of small watch springs, the hardening of cutlery, and the annealing of dies. In fact, there isn't a thing that a steel worker would want to know that isn't included. It is the standard book on selecting, hardening, and tempering all grades of steel. Among the chapter headings might be mentioned the following subjects: Introduction; the workman; steel; methods of heating; heating tool steel; forging; annealing; hardening baths; baths for hardening; hardening steel; drawing the temper after hardening; examples of hardening; pack hardening; case hardening; spring tempering; making tools of machine steel; special steels; steel for various tools; causes of trouble; high speed steels, etc. 400 pages. Very fully illustrated. Fourth Edition. Price $2.50

HARDENING, TEMPERING, ANNEALING, AND FORGING OF STEEL. By J. V. WOODWORTH.

A new work treating in a clear, concise manner all modern processes for the heating annealing, forging, welding, hardening, and tempering of steel, making it a book of great practical value to the metal-working mechanic in general, with special directions for the successful hardening and tempering of all steel tools used in the arts, including milling cutters, taps, thread dies, reamers, both solid and shell, hollow mills, punches and dies, and all kinds of sheet metal working tools, shear blades, saws, fine cutlery, and metal cutting tools of all description, as well as for all implements of steel both large and small. In this work the simplest and most satisfactory hardening and tempering processes are given.

The uses to which the leading brands of steel may be adapted are concisely presented, and their treatment for working under different conditions explained, also the special methods for the hardening and tempering of special brands.

A chapter devoted to the different processes for Case-hardening is also included, and special reference made to the adaptation of machinery steel for tools of various kinds. Fourth Edition. 288 pages. 201 illustrations. Price $2.50

TRACTORS

THE MODERN GAS TRACTOR. By VICTOR W. PAGÉ.

A complete treatise describing all types and sizes of gasoline, kerosene, and oil tractors. Considers design and construction exhaustively, gives complete instructions for care, operation and repair, outlines all practical applications on the road and in the field. The best and latest work on farm tractors and tractor power plants. A work needed by farmers, students, blacksmiths, mechanics, salesmen, implement dealers, designers, and engineers. 500 pages. Nearly 300 illustrations and folding plates. Price $2.00

THE HOME-MADE TRACTOR. By XENO W. PUTNAM.

A practical treatise on the construction of small and special purpose tractors in the home workshop from the odds and ends of cast-off machinery available on nearly every farm. This work shows the farmer how, at small expense, to make his gasoline engine conveniently portable by making it self-moving. It guides him in the construction of a practical farm tractor that is capable of hauling, harvesting, plowing and doing all the ordinary farm work in which the propulsion of other machinery is required. Twenty-four chapters are contained in this book and it is illustrated with over 153 working engravings showing many successfully built and tested home-made tractors. Bound in cloth, 12mo. Price $2.00

ImTheStory.com

Personalized Classic Books in many genre's

Unique gift for kids, partners, friends, colleagues

Customize:

- Character Names
- Upload your own front/back cover images (optional)
- Inscribe a personal message/dedication on the inside page (optional)

Customize many titles Including
- Alice in Wonderland
- Romeo and Juliet
- The Wizard of Oz
- A Christmas Carol
- Dracula
- Dr. Jekyll & Mr. Hyde
- And more...